The Ex Post Facto Clause

The Ex Post Facto Clause

Its History and Role in a Punitive Society

Wayne A. Logan

Steven M. Goldstein Professor
Florida State University College of Law

OXFORD
UNIVERSITY PRESS

OXFORD
UNIVERSITY PRESS

Oxford University Press is a department of the University of Oxford. It furthers
the University's objective of excellence in research, scholarship, and education
by publishing worldwide. Oxford is a registered trade mark of Oxford University
Press in the UK and certain other countries.

Published in the United States of America by Oxford University Press
198 Madison Avenue, New York, NY 10016, United States of America.

Library of Congress Cataloging-in-Publication Data
Names: Logan, Wayne A., 1960- author.
Title: The ex post facto clause : its history and role in a punitive
society / Wayne A. Logan, Steven M. Goldstein Professor, Florida State
University College of Law.
Description: New York : Oxford University Press, [2023] |
Series: Studies crime amd public policy series |
Includes bibliographical references and index. |
Identifiers: LCCN 2022002098 (print) | LCCN 2022002099 (ebook) |
ISBN 9780190053505 (hardback) | ISBN 9780190053529 (epub)
Subjects: LCSH: Ex post facto laws—United States.
Classification: LCC KF9247 .L64 2022 (print) | LCC KF9247 (ebook) |
DDC 345.73/04—dc23/eng/20220203
LC record available at https://lccn.loc.gov/2022002098
LC ebook record available at https://lccn.loc.gov/2022002099

DOI: 10.1093/oso/9780190053505.001.0001

1 3 5 7 9 8 6 4 2

Printed by Sheridan Books, Inc., United States of America

Contents

Acknowledgments

I owe special thanks to many for their assistance with this book. Most notably, I thank my wonderful research assistants, Alexander Lenk, Genevieve Lemley, Samuel Forte, and Bradley Fehrenbach, who provided top-notch help in tracking down legal and historical sources. I am immensely grateful for their consistent good cheer, dogged persistence, and attention to detail. I also thank the FSU Law Research Center librarians who provided much-needed help in countless instances, especially Kat Klepfer and Margaret Clark. Finally, I thank FSU Law for its support during the several-year duration of the project.

Introduction

When accounts of the preceding fifty years of American history are written, one of the most important developments noted will certainly be the nation's sustained embrace of draconian penal policies. In an era when being "tough on crime" was seen as a political necessity, politicians competed to out-tough one another.[1] Although the laws they enacted were most commonly future oriented, for instance, increasing prison terms and imposing mandatory minimum sentences, many assumed a retroactive cast, targeting individuals previously convicted of crimes, a more readily identifiable yet equally disdained group.

That the political process would operate in such a way is not surprising.[2] What is surprising, and disappointing, however, is that it would do so largely unhindered by a critically important, but to date little studied, constitutional provision: the Ex Post Facto Clause of the US Constitution. This book chronicles this history and makes the case for the clause playing a much more robust role in constraining what has been called the "penal populism"[3] of American legislatures.

The decision by the framers of the Constitution to prohibit ex post facto laws—in Latin, literally meaning "law after fact"[4]—in the body of the Constitution was no accident. Nor was their decision to actually impose two such limits: in Article I, section 9, restricting Congress, and Article I, section 10, restricting state legislatures,[5] in a document otherwise primarily dedicated to defining the structure and operation of the federal government. Although scholarly debate has long existed over the meaning and purpose of various provisions of the Constitution, there is no questioning that the ex post facto prohibitions were motivated by the framers' acute concern over the recognized propensity of legislatures to enact burdensome retroactive laws targeting politically unpopular individuals.[6] Alexander Hamilton spoke to this concern in the *Federalist Papers* when he singled out the clause as a prime reason for state ratification of the constitution, writing that ex post facto laws "have been, in all ages, the favorite and most formidable instruments of tyranny."[7] To Hamilton, the "[p]rohibition of ex post facto laws" was among the greatest "securities to liberty and republicanism [the Constitution] contains."[8]

The Ex Post Facto Clause. Wayne A. Logan, Oxford University Press. © Oxford University Press 2023.
DOI: 10.1093/oso/9780190053505.003.0001

Fellow *Federalist Papers* contributor James Madison described ex post facto laws as "contrary to the first principles of the social compact, and to every principle of sound legislation,"[9] and regarded the clause as an integral part of the Constitution's "bulwark in favor of personal security and private rights," which redeemed the absence of a Bill of Rights.[10]

Early members of the Supreme Court were equally aware of the need to constrain legislatures. Justice Samuel Chase, in *Calder v. Bull* (1798),[11] one of the court's first decisions, wrote that "the advocates of [ex post facto] laws were stimulated by ambition, or personal resentment, and vindictive malice. To prevent such, and similar, acts of violence and injustice . . . the Federal and State Legislatures were prohibited from passing any . . . Ex Post Facto Law."[12] A few years later, in *Fletcher v. Peck* (1810),[13] Chief Justice John Marshall echoed this view, recognizing that "the framers of the constitution viewed, with some apprehension, the violent acts which might grow out of the feelings of the moment" and that adoption of the Ex Post Facto Clause reflected among Americans "a determination to shield themselves . . . from the effects of those sudden and strong passions to which men are exposed."[14]

Over time, a veritable "who's who" of disfavored Americans has invoked the Ex Post Facto Clause as a basis for protection: including, in the late 1860s, Confederate sympathizers; at the turn of the twentieth century, immigrants and prostitutes; in the 1950s, former members of the Communist Party; and, since the 1990s, convicted sex offenders. In one of the two Confederate sympathizer cases, *Cummings v. Missouri* (1867),[15] the Supreme Court invalidated on ex post facto grounds the conviction of a Roman Catholic priest who preached without satisfying the state's required "loyalty oath." Although the law on its face targeted professional association, the court found that in actuality it retroactively punished the petitioner, and was a product of "the excited action of the State[] . . . that the Framers of the Federal Constitution intended to guard."[16] The Ex Post Facto Clause, the court stated, "was intended to secure the liberty of the citizen" and "cannot be evaded by the form in which the power of the State is exerted."[17]

The Supreme Court, however, has since been far less zealous in enforcing the clause, repeatedly rejecting ex post facto challenges to laws retroactively imposing onerous burdens on individuals previously convicted of crimes. Today, the Ex Post Facto Clause exists as a constitutional palimpsest, written over repeatedly by the court, its intended purpose and function significantly obscured yet still recoverable. This volume, which provides the first book-length, modern-era examination of the Ex Post Facto Clause, undertakes the important task of historical recovery, with the goal of reinvigorating the clause to serve its intended role as a constitutional check on legislative excess, so needed in today's unforgiving and harshly punitive society.

The book proceeds as follows. The initial chapters, 1 to 5, survey the Framing Era history of the Ex Post Facto Clause and the Supreme Court's decisions over the years construing and applying it. As will be evident, the decisions have resulted in a vastly less robust limit on legislative authority than that envisioned by Hamilton, Madison, and others during the 1787 Convention in Philadelphia, and the state ratifying conventions thereafter.

Chapters 6 and 7 advance proposals to remedy several of the major shortcomings identified. Chapter 6 offers a new test for what will be called the "punishment question," which determines whether a retroactive law is punitive in nature, a threshold requirement for any successful ex post facto challenge. The deferential, highly formalistic, historically static test employed by the court over the past several decades is both inconsistent with the framers' obvious disdain for burdensome retroactive laws and the court's far more critical early ex post facto decisions. The test is especially problematic today, given the frequently indulged tendency of legislatures to impose burdensome retroactive laws of a "quasi-criminal" nature that defy ready classification.[18] These include non-carceral collateral consequences of conviction (e.g., subjecting individuals previously convicted of crimes to registration and community notification by means of government-run internet websites) that the framers could not have imagined.

Chapter 7 offers several other provocative proposals concerning the coverage of the clause: that coverage should extend beyond the four categories identified by the court in *Calder v. Bull*; that there should be a rethinking of what qualifies as a "law" within the prohibition of the clause; that coverage of the clause should extend beyond criminal laws, also contrary to *Calder*; and a rethinking of the modern court's refusal to include "procedural" laws within the scope of the clause.

Of the proposals, removing the criminal-centric limit would have most practical significance because it would significantly expand the reach of the clause. A large body of historical evidence, however, supports the view that during the Framing Era ex post facto laws were understood to encompass both civil and criminal laws. Furthermore, disavowing the requirement would have several significant benefits. First, it would obviate the need for modern legislatures to camouflage burdensome retroactive laws with misleading labels and "civil" window dressing, and eliminate the need for courts to answer the long-vexing "punishment question." Removing the criminal-centric focus would also align with calls by "originalists" to interpret and apply the Constitution in a way that is consistent with its original understanding, and

find favor among constitutional "textualists," given the absence of any language in the clause limiting its coverage to penal laws. If such a broadening
comes to pass, ironically, originalism and textualism—significantly shaped
by conservatives in response to perceived liberal judicial activism resulting
in expanded personal rights—could be the impetus for a broader, pro-civil
liberties use of the Ex Post Facto Clause as a limit on the exercise of legislative authority. Much as the Supreme Court has insisted with regard to the
Fourth Amendment, in the Bill of Rights, such a broadened understanding is
warranted because it will ensure that the clause "provide[s] *at a minimum* the
degree of protection it afforded when it was adopted."[19]

The case for reinvigorated, more robust coverage, however, does not rest
upon Framing Era history alone. As important, change is needed because of
the many major developments since 1787 in the nation's social, political, and
institutional landscape, which have at once validated the framers' concerns
and amplified the need for the changes urged. One shift concerns a marked
transformation in the national zeitgeist, as crime, criminals, crime control,
and crime victims have come to figure centrally in the lawmaking process,
driving it toward unprecedented punitiveness. Contemporaneous with this
shift, institutionally, the legislative branch has grown more powerful, and
the executive branch has emerged as a major player in formulating, not only
implementing, criminal justice policy. Meanwhile, the judiciary has experienced a relative diminution in its role. Today, judges (and juries) play only a
modest part in a system dominated by plea bargains, and courts have become
less engaged in critically scrutinizing criminal laws, and more dedicated to
being "faithful agents" of legislatures, which has had the effect of facilitating,
rather than curbing, the punitive impulses of legislatures.

The book's closing chapter shifts perspective from the domestic to the
global realm. It first details how ex post facto laws gained foremost international attention after World War II in the trials of Nazi and Japanese authorities for their wartime atrocities. As a moral matter, holding the defendants
to account understandably enjoyed widespread support. However, concern
arose that the legal charges lodged—including "crimes against humanity"—
violated ex post facto principles because they did not formally exist when the
prosecuted conduct occurred. In significant part due to this controversy, the
ex post facto prohibition, and the associated principle of legality, grew in international stature, thereafter becoming a specified right in international
declarations and national constitutions, including the Universal Declaration
of Human Rights (adopted by the United Nations in 1948). The chapter
examines how the prohibition has since become a mainstay in constitutions
throughout the world and in the charters of modern-day war tribunals. The

chapter concludes with discussion of yet another international human rights value emerging after the war, human dignity, and how it aligns with, and can inform, the understanding and enforcement of the Ex Post Facto Clause in the US Constitution.

Taken together, the chapters are intended to serve as a resource for understanding the evolution and content of modern ex post facto doctrine and provide the basis for its reinvigoration in the nation's constitutional order. There always have been, and there always will be, disdained individuals to serve as attractive subjects of burdensome retroactive laws. The potential political gain is simply too great, and the political risk too small, for events to be otherwise. The challenge lies in ensuring that the Ex Post Facto Clause, one of the select few civil liberty protections found in the body of the US Constitution, is allowed to serve as the "bulwark" envisioned by James Madison and his Framing Era colleagues. If this occurs, we can better guarantee, in Supreme Court Justice Hugo Black's words, that the government complies with the fundamental command that it "should turn square corners in dealing with the people,"[20] no matter how worthy of disdain they may be.

1

Background and Early History

Concern over laws imposing retroactive harms dates back to at least Roman times. "What the law permits in the past, it bans for the future," proclaimed an early third-century Roman maxim.[1] The antipathy was later evidenced in the thinking of English jurists and legal commentators, themselves admirers of Roman legal thought. Lord Bracton, in 1250, for instance, declared that "time is to be taken into account, since every new constitution ought to impose a form upon future matters, and not upon things past."[2] Later, in the mid-eighteenth century, William Blackstone wrote that "[a]ll laws should be . . . made to commence in futuro, and [individuals should] be notified before their commencement."[3] One also sees the sentiment in the famous Latin maxim, believed to be coined by an early nineteenth-century German jurist, but reflecting a view dating back centuries, "nullum crimen sine lege, nulla poena sine lege," which roughly translated means "no crime nor punishment without law."[4]

Americans, fresh from victory over the British in the Revolutionary War (1775–1783), imported much of their vanquished foe's legal perspectives. Among these was the disdain for ex post facto laws, which an American periodical of the time referred to as "poison to free constitutions, and pregnant with calamity to the community."[5] This chapter first surveys the history of American constitutional efforts designed to prohibit such laws, starting with those adopted early on by states, followed by prohibitions contained in the proposed US Constitution, later ratified by the states in their respective conventions.

Early State Constitutional Provisions

In May 1776, the Second Continental Congress advised the colonies to devise new governments.[6] Although by then a small handful of colonies had already taken action, others commenced efforts to prescribe in writing the structure and powers of government and the limits under which it would be expected to operate. As one modern commentator put it, "[t]he framers of

The Ex Post Facto Clause. Wayne A. Logan, Oxford University Press. © Oxford University Press 2023.
DOI: 10.1093/oso/9780190053505.003.0002

early state constitutions hoped that reducing the principal terms of the social compact to clear and ringing language would prevent violations of the
agreement and would clearly expose any violations that did occur."[7] Unlike
the English, who for centuries were governed by an unwritten constitution,
Americans sought to specify the powers and limits of government, in the hope
of better protecting their rights.[8] In doing so, as Professor Gordon Wood recognized, "[t]he American revolutionaries virtually established the modern
idea of a written constitution."[9]

By summer 1787, all states (other than Connecticut and Rhode Island) had
ratified new constitutions.[10] For the most part, the early state constitutions focused on broad issues of governmental structure, operation and power, rather
than individual rights.[11] One exception concerned recent laws imposed,
first by the British and later colonial legislatures, that retroactively imposed
harms on individuals. One form of law, ex post facto, will be addressed at
length here. Another, bill of attainder, is "a legislative act which inflicts punishment without a judicial trial."[12] In his *Commentaries on the Constitution
of the United States*, published in 1833, celebrated legal scholar and Supreme
Court Justice Joseph Story wrote that during the Revolutionary War, "bills of
attainder, and ex post facto acts of confiscation, were permitted to a wide extent...."[13]

Concern over such laws manifested in specific form in five of the eleven
early state constitutions.[14] The Maryland Constitution, adopted in late
November 1776, is thought to entail the first American constitutional use of
the Latin phrase "ex post facto."[15] Its Declaration of Rights provided that "retrospective laws, punishing facts committed before the existence of such laws,
and by them only declared criminal, are oppressive, unjust, and incompatible with liberty; wherefore no ex post facto law ought to be made."[16] North
Carolina adopted a provision identical to that of Maryland.[17] Massachusetts's
provision, contained in its Declaration of Rights, read "Laws made to punish
for actions done before the existence of such laws, and which have not been
declared crimes by preceding laws, are unjust, oppressive, and inconsistent
with the fundamental principles of a free government."[18] Delaware's provision,
adopted in September 1776 and placed in its Declaration of Rights, provided
"That retrospective Laws, punishing Offenses committed before the Existence
of such Laws, are oppressive and unjust, and ought not to be made."[19] In New
Hampshire, in 1784 the state replaced its initial constitution of 1776, including
in its bill of rights a provision stating that "[r]etrospective laws are highly injurious, oppressive, and unjust. No such laws, therefore, should be made, either
for the decision of civil causes, or the punishment of offenses."[20]

The Federal Constitutional Convention
(Philadelphia, May 14–September 17, 1787)

In response to the failed effort at maintaining an effective national government, based on the Articles of Confederation (taking effect in early 1781), fifty-five delegates (actually, technically referred to as "deputies") from twelve of the thirteen states convened in Philadelphia in Summer 1787 to draft a federal constitution (Rhode Island did not attend).[21] Testament to the political delicacy of the enterprise, the proceedings were not open to the public and delegates agreed to a vow of secrecy,[22] to enhance the prospect of full and frank discussion without fear of external rebuke or reprisal.[23]

The actual testamentary record of the proceedings is rather sparse, principally made up of two original source documents. The first is the *Official Journal* of the Convention, kept by the convention's secretary, William Jackson (who was not a delegate). The *Journal*, which was published in 1819 under the supervision of Secretary of State John Quincy Adams, contains no discussion of the floor debates and only a sporadic record of votes and procedural developments.[24] James Madison, delegate of Virginia, also kept a record, which he revised and edited until his death in 1836. Madison's last will and testament directed that his *Notes* not be published until after his death, and they were eventually sold to the federal government by his wife Dolly Madison and published in 1840.[25] Madison's *Notes of the Debates in the Federal Convention* contain extensive accounts of the proceedings and are regarded as a major reference source.[26] They are, however, regarded by scholars as incomplete and at times unreliable,[27] reflecting, as some have contended, Madison's evolving personal and political biases.[28]

A principal secondary source was published in 1911. In that year, Max Farrand, a history professor at Yale University, published the first three volumes of what became a four-volume history of the convention. The compilation, published as *Records of the Federal Constitution of 1787*, has been updated over the years as new sources became available (volume IV was published by historian James Hutson in 1937). It today remains the go-to secondary historical source of the constitutional convention. Farrand organized the materials in chronological order, and provided editorial comments noting inconsistencies among sources. Farrand mainly relied on the *Official Journal* and Madison's *Notes* but also consulted other sources (e.g., sporadic notes of delegates such as Rufus King (Massachusetts)).

The convention convened in late May 1787, and for weeks the delegates heatedly debated momentous questions, including the structure of the federal government, its powers, and how the citizens of the respective states would be represented in what became the US Congress.[29] It was not until relatively late in the gathering, August 22, that the prohibition of ex post facto laws was discussed. Madison in his *Notes* relates that on that date amid discussion of the limits to be imposed on Congress, Eldridge Gerry (Massachusetts) and James McHenry (Maryland) "moved to insert after the 2d sect. art: 7, the clause following, to wit, 'The Legislature shall pass no bill of attainder nor (any) ex post facto law.' "[30] Gerry "urged the nessity [sic] of this prohibition, which he said was greater in the national than the State Legislatur[e], because the number of members in the former being fewer, they were on that account the more to be feared."[31] Delegates thereafter unanimously endorsed the proposed ban on bills of attainder, but several argued against inclusion of the ex post facto law prohibition.[32]

Debate records highlight that the reluctance was motivated by reasons other than any measure of favor for ex post facto laws, believing them contrary to natural law, and therefore inherently and self-evidently improper.[33] Gouverneur Morris (New Jersey) "thought the precaution as to ex post facto laws unnecessary."[34] Oliver Ellsworth (Connecticut), who later served as chief justice of the US Supreme Court, contended that "there was no lawyer, no civilian who would not say that ex post facto laws were void of themselves. It cannot then be necessary to prohibit them."[35] James Wilson (Pennsylvania), also a future Supreme Court justice and one of the most learned legal minds at the convention, worried that including an ex post facto prohibition would cast negative light on the new nation, manifesting an ignorance of natural law. Wilson stated that including the prohibition would "bring reflexions on the Constitution—and proclaim that we are ignorant of the first principles of Legislation, or are constituting a Government which will be so."[36]

Proponents of including an ex post facto prohibition did not disagree,[37] but consistent with historian Forrest McDonald's characterization of the Framers as a "hard-headed, practical band of men,"[38] insisted on the real-world reasons for adoption.[39] Daniel Carroll (Maryland) maintained that "[e]xperience overruled all other calculations," and that "in whatever light [ex post facto laws] might be viewed by civilians or others, the State Legislatures had passed them, and they had taken effect."[40] Hugh Williamson (North Carolina) averred that "[s]uch a prohibitory clause is in the Constitution of North Carolina, and though it has been violated, it has done good there & may do good here, because the Judges can take hold of it."[41] Dr. William Samuel Johnson (Connecticut), however, thought including the prohibition unnecessary and problematic for "implying improper suspicion of the National Legislature."[42]

On August 22, the delegates approved the provision, which eventually was contained in Article I, section 9 of the Constitution: seven states voted yes,[43] three no,[44] and one (North Carolina) "divided."[45] (As for the balance of the thirteen states, Rhode Island, as noted, did not send delegates to the Convention; and New York was not eligible to vote because two of its three delegates were absent.)[46]

Six days later, on August 28, an ex post prohibition regarding states was considered. By this point in the proceedings, delegates had specified state prohibitions on coining money, granting letters of marque, entering into treaties, and other prohibitions eventually contained in Article I, section 10 of the Constitution, but had not prohibited bills of attainder, ex post facto laws, or laws impairing obligations of contracts.[47]

On August 28, Rufus King (Massachusetts) moved for inclusion of a provision prohibiting states from interfering in "private contracts."[48] King's motion reflected prevalent concern over state laws retroactively relieving debtors of their payment obligations to creditors,[49] a practice outlawed in the Northwest Ordinance, which had recently been adopted by the Continental Congress.[50] The motion prompted objections from several delegates, including George Mason (Virginia) who argued that some retroactive laws might be "proper, & essential,"[51] offering as an example a law shortening the statute of limitations (the period in which one can sue) for a civil suit on an "open account" (a series of transactions between a buyer and seller with an expectation of future transactions).[52] James Wilson, in response to opponents' arguments, offered that the "answer to these objections is that *retrospective* interferences only are to be prohibited."[53] James Madison then asked "[i]s not that already done by the prohibition of ex post facto laws, which will oblige the Judges to declare such interferences null & void[?]"[54]

Madison's *Notes* reflect that John Rutledge (South Carolina) then advanced a substitute motion, relative to that of King: to insert—"nor pass bills of attainder, nor retrospective* laws,"[55] with the asterisk denoting that the *Official Journal* used "ex post facto," not "retrospective." Farrand later editorialized that the *Journal* was correct in stating "nor pass any bill of attainder or ex post facto law," based on comparison to other sources.[56] Ultimately, the Rutledge motion to prohibit states from passing bills of attainder and ex post facto laws passed, with delegates approving by the same margin as they did a few days earlier regarding Congress, by a vote of 7-3.[57]

The *Official Journal* contains no entry for August 29 regarding ex post facto matters. However, Madison's *Notes* report without elaboration that on that day John Dickinson (Delaware) "mentioned to the House that on examining

Blackstone's *Commentaries*, he found that the terms 'ex post facto' related to criminal cases only; that they would not consequently restrain the States from retrospective laws in civil cases, and that some further provision for this purpose would be requisite."[58]

On September 8, the delegates created a Committee of Style and Arrangement to "revise the style of and arrange the articles which had been agreed to by the House."[59] The committee consisted of five delegates elected for the job: William Johnson (Connecticut), Alexander Hamilton (New York), Gouverneur Morris (Pennsylvania), James Madison (Virginia), and Rufus King (Massachusetts), with Morris assuming primary drafting responsibility.[60] On September 12 the committee delivered a draft of the Constitution and copies were prepared for convention delegates, who in the following days reviewed the document.

On September 14, Elbridge Gerry (Massachusetts) argued with regard to the impairment of contracts that "Congress ought to be laid under like prohibitions," and made a motion to that effect. No second materialized, however, and the motion was not acted upon by the convention.[61]

Also on September 14, George Mason (Virginia) moved to strike the ex post facto prohibition regarding Congress, expressing concern that the prohibition was overbroad.[62] Mason stated that he "thought it not sufficiently clear that the prohibition meant by this phrase was limited to cases of a criminal nature—and no Legislature ever did or can altogether avoid them in Civil cases."[63] Thereafter, Madison's *Notes* relate, "Mr. Gerry 2ded. the motion but (with a view) to extend the prohibition to 'Civil cases,' which he thought ought to be done."[64] The motion was unanimously rejected.[65] On the next day, September 15, Mason expressed his opposition to the state and federal ex post facto bans, stating

> Both the general legislature and the State legislature are expressly prohibited making ex post facto laws; though there never was nor can be a legislature but must and will make such laws, when necessity and the public safety require them; which will hereafter be a breach of all the constitutions in the Union, and afford precedents for other innovations.[66]

Ultimately, on September 17, 1787, the convention approved the Constitution "by the Unanimous Consent of the States present" (as noted, Rhode Island did not attend and New York did not vote due to a paucity of delegates present), and it was submitted to the states for consideration.[67] The draft contained seven articles, reduced and restyled from the twenty-three referred to the Committee on Style and Arrangement.[68]

The language approved by the convention was substantially similar to that ultimately codified in the Constitution, but for the sake of completeness warrants brief discussion. The verbiage referred to the Committee on Style and Arrangement regarding states (what became Article I, section 10) read: "No State shall . . . pass any bill of attainder or ex post facto laws . . .,"[69] which appears in almost verbatim form in the Committee's final version ("No state shall . . . pass any bill of attainder, nor ex post facto laws. . . .").[70] The provision regarding Congress (what became Article I, section 9), however, experienced a transformation. In particular, the text submitted to the committee used active voice ("[t]he Legislature shall pass no bill of attainder nor any ex post facto laws")[71] yet, without explanation, the version that the committee presented used passive voice ("[n]o bill of attainder shall be passed, nor any ex post facto law").[72] Unlike other provisions, as to which scholars have maintained the committee made substantive—not only stylistic—alterations,[73] the variations regarding the ex post facto prohibitions do not reflect any significant substantive change.[74]

Ultimately, the provisions concerning the ex post facto prohibitions, which exist to this today, read as follows (emphasis added):

 Article I, section 9, clause 3: "No Bill of Attainder or **ex post facto Law** shall be passed."

 Article I, section 10, clause 1: "No State shall enter into any Treaty, Alliance, or Confederation; grant Letters of Marque and Reprisal; coin Money; emit Bills of Credit; make any Thing but gold and silver Coin a Tender in Payment of Debts; pass any Bill of Attainder, **ex post facto Law**, or Law impairing the Obligation of Contracts, or grant any Title of Nobility."

As is evident from a comparison of the final text of Article I, states are subject to a much longer list of prohibitions. Congress and states are both prohibited from enacting ex post facto laws and bills of attainder,[75] yet states—not Congress—are also prohibited from enacting laws "impairing the Obligation of Contracts" and engaging in a variety of other behaviors (e.g., coining money and emitting bills of credit). Although the asymmetry cannot be explained with certainty, one reason might lie in the chronology of the approvals of the respective provisions. Prohibitions concerning Congress were considered and approved on August 22, 1787;[76] state prohibitions were debated and approved a week later.[77] According to one late nineteenth-century commentator, the presence of a contract impairment provision in the state-focused provision, but not the federal, was the result of James Dickinson, who on the day after approval of the state ex post facto prohibition, reported to his colleagues that

Blackstone deemed only criminal laws as coming within the scope of the prohibition:

> Consequently, the famous clause prohibiting a state from impairing the obligation of a contract was adopted; and no such restraint was placed upon congress, because the convention seven days previously, supposed that the term ex post facto covered only criminal but civil matters, and in that ignorance, adopted the clause prohibiting congress passing bills of attainder or *ex post facto* laws.[78]

This assessment, even if correct on timing, however, does not explain the absence of a contracts prohibition in Article I, section 9, regarding Congress. Indeed, the Committee of Style and Arrangement, history now shows, took the liberty of inserting the contracts impairment provision in the list of state prohibitions after efforts by delegate Rufus King to add a contracts prohibition stalled on August 28. Precisely why the Committee did not also include a contract-related prohibition regarding Congress remains unclear but there is reason to conclude that delegates were most concerned about the expansive power of state legislatures,[79] not Congress, which the Constitution subjected to greater enumerated checks and balances on its authority.[80] The more expansive list of state prohibitions, historian Forrest McDonald argued, also reflected greater concern over the demonstrated state legislative propensity to violate property rights,[81] especially those of Loyalists in the wake of the Revolution.[82]

James Madison, at the time of the convention,[83] was especially concerned about the parochial tendencies of state legislatures in particular, and worried about the "fluctuating policy" and "sudden changes" frequently besetting them.[84] As Madison told his colleagues in the First Congress, the limits on state power in Article I, section 10, were "wise and proper restrictions in the Constitution. I think there is more danger of those powers being abused by the State Governments than by the Government of the United States."[85] Madison's fellow delegates were well aware of state legislative abuses under the Articles of Confederation. Such laws included those targeting Loyalists for recriminations of various kinds, passage of protectionist commercial laws and debtor relief laws, and issuance of paper money that inevitably depreciated in value.[86] Framing Era records, in short, make clear the delegates' significant concern over the tendency of state legislatures to enact laws infringing liberty and threatening economic instability and private property,[87] the latter often motivated by desires to unfairly dissolve the debts of their constituents.[88]

Madison's concern was such that he proposed that Congress have the power to "negative" any state law believed unwise or contrary to interests of the union.[89] The effort was voted down on July 17,[90] five weeks before debates on the limits on state legislative authority (contained in Article I, section 10) took place. As one commentator has noted, "[o]nly when that effort had narrowly failed did the delegates turn to the more precisely tailored protections against the most common excesses of democracy in the states."[91]

Despite this undisguised concern regarding the abusive legislative behavior of states, Article VII of the draft Constitution required that ratifying conventions be held in the states, with at least nine of the thirteen needed to ratify the document, and have it take effect in the new nation.[92]

State Ratifying Conventions

The campaign to encourage state adoption of the draft Constitution involved one of the most famous political theory tracts of all time: the *Federalist Papers*. Composed by Alexander Hamilton and James Madison, and to a considerably lesser extent John Jay (who was ailing at the time), the *Federalist Papers* consisted of eighty-five essays directed to residents of New York (a major state, then an epicenter of Anti-Federalists, who resisted ratification). The essays, written anonymously under the pen name Publius, appeared October 1787–May 1788 in New York newspapers, and were republished in newspapers elsewhere and in book form.[93]

In addition to containing expansive arguments defending the Constitution's approach to tripartite governance and other structural concerns, the tracts contained several particularly fervid passages backing the prohibition of ex post facto laws. Madison, in Number 44, proclaimed that the ex post facto provisions in Article I prevented abusive laws that were "contrary to the first principles of the social compact, and to every principle of sound legislation."[94] Prohibiting ex post facto laws, along with bills of attainder and those impairing the obligation of contracts, provided a

> bulwark in favor of personal security and private rights . . . The sober people of America are weary of the fluctuating policy which has directed the public councils. They have seen with regret and indignation that sudden changes and legislative interferences, in cases affecting personal rights, become jobs in the hands of enterprising and influential speculators, and snares to the more industrious and less informed part of the community. They have seen, too, that one legislative interference is but the first link of a long chain of repetitions, every subsequent interference being naturally produced by the effects of the preceding.[95]

Madison, aware that several state constitutions had similar prohibitions, regarded the federal constitutional prohibition as necessary further protection, reasoning that "additional fences against these dangers ought not to be omitted."[96]

The draft Constitution received a positive response in several states—Delaware, the first to ratify, followed by Pennsylvania, New Jersey, and Georgia—but faced serious, sometimes volatile opposition in several others, the populous and influential states of Massachusetts, Virginia, and New York in particular.[97] A major basis for opposition was the lack of a declaration or bill of rights, extending to citizens specific rights and protections, as provided in many state constitutions of the time.[98] Anti-Federalists worried that the Constitution afforded the national government too much power, along with a corresponding loss of power among states and their citizens. An additional, separate bill of rights would "serve as a barrier between the general government and the respective states and their citizens."[99] They argued that inclusion in the draft of specified prohibitions, such as regarding ex post facto laws and bills of attainder, created the possibility that the federal government would violate other, unspecified rights.[100]

Federalists, James Madison and Alexander Hamilton chief among them, thought specification of particular rights against federal intrusion unnecessary.[101] To their minds, not only did every right not specified remain reserved to the people,[102] but specification of particular rights might imply a federal power to rescind rights that went un-enumerated.[103] They also believed that the prescribed limited nature of the federal government envisioned made federal abuse unlikely and that state constitutions protected citizens' rights.[104] Hamilton, in *Federalist* Number 84, made the prohibitions contained in Article I a keystone in his position that no bill of rights was necessary, emphasizing that the draft Constitution established "the writ of *habeas corpus*, the prohibition of *ex post facto* laws, and TITLES OF NOBILITY . . . [which] are perhaps greater securities to liberty and republicanism than any it contains. . . . [Ex post facto laws] have been, in all ages, the favorite and most formidable instruments of tyranny."[105]

As with the federal convention in Philadelphia, the records of the state ratifying conventions are incomplete and at times unreliable.[106] No records exist of five conventions—Delaware, New Jersey, Georgia, North Carolina, and Rhode Island (the last of the thirteen states to ratify), and only fragmentary records exist of debates in four states—Connecticut, Maryland, South Carolina, and New Hampshire. The most extensive records concern the conventions of Pennsylvania, Massachusetts, Virginia and New York,[107] which involved the participation of one or more delegates who also attended the federal constitutional convention in summer 1787.

The primary historical source for the state ratifying conventions is what is known as *Elliot's Debates*, a five-volume collection first published between 1827–1830 by journalist Jonathan Elliot.[108] In Pennsylvania, the second state to ratify the Constitution, on December 12, 1787, by a vote of 46-23,[109] the ex post facto prohibitions were mentioned only in passing. James Wilson, a very active participant in the federal convention, singled out the ex post facto limit on state laws as among "the restraints placed on the state governments" that "[i]f only [they] were inserted in this Constitution, I think it would be worth our adoption," and averred that "[f]atal experience has taught us, dearly taught us, the value of these restraints."[110] Thomas McKean backed the prohibition so that "men will not be exposed to have their actions construed into crimes."[111]

Massachusetts was the sixth state to ratify, on February 6, 1788, by a vote of 187-168.[112] Ex post facto laws were mentioned only once and even then not in the context of a debate. Delegate Theodore Sedwick, in response to delegate William Wedgery's comment "whether a man in a deferent [sic] State holding securities against other States Cant [sic] Sue at this Court," offered that such a scenario "will come under the ex post facto law."[113] Also, a newspaper item of the time in the *Massachusetts Centinel* singled out the draft Constitution's ex post facto prohibition as a main selling point for ratification. In particular, the perceived broader reach of the federal prohibition, encompassing both civil and criminal laws, filled a gap left by the provision in the Massachusetts Constitution, which prohibited only criminal laws:

> [O]ur state bill of rights is silent as to any ex post facto laws which relate to property, and civil prosecutions; though it must be confessed that such laws are as much against the nature of government as those relating to crime. *The federal constitution has accordingly guarded against such laws*, and clearly, because some states, of which our own is one, have not observed such a restriction.[114]

Records from Virginia, New York and North Carolina, the tenth, eleventh, and twelfth states to ratify, although not technically needed for ratification (as noted, only nine states were needed), provide the fullest discussion of the ex post facto prohibition. The Virginia Convention, which ratified on June 25, 1788, by a vote of 89-79, was an especially star-studded affair, with framers James Madison, George Mason, and Edmund Randolph playing major roles in the often heated debates.[115] Patrick Henry, a fiery and accomplished orator, who passed on an opportunity to attend the federal convention, also figured centrally.

A major issue looming over the Virginia debates, as well as other states, was whether the ex post facto prohibition would affect the value of paper money issued by states and the Continental Congress. The value of the paper money in circulation had depreciated rapidly and significantly as a result of its massive infusion into the economy during the Revolutionary War, a situation worsened by very effective British counterfeiting. States desired a scaling law that would make the paper money reflect its actual market—not face—value. Concern existed, however, that such a retroactive law would be deemed ex post facto, because it would devalue the paper money, a concern raised by Patrick Henry and George Mason.[116] Henry vigorously argued that the lack of a retroactive scaling law would impose staggering costs, requiring "shilling for shilling" (i.e., face value) payment of Virginia's share of the national debt with undervalued paper money. This would redound to the benefit of speculators (often in the north) and to the detriment of the public: "If no ex post facto laws be made, what is to become of the old Continental paper dollars? Will not this country be forced to pay in gold in silver, shilling for shilling? . . . [This] is an all-important question, because the property of this country is not commensurate to the enormous demand."[117]

Madison, in a voice so weak that it "could not be heard" by the reporter,[118] and had to be repeated by fellow delegate Edmund Randolph, related that at the Philadelphia Convention "ex post facto laws" had been "interpreted" as relating only to criminal cases.[119] Randolph, Federalist governor of Virginia and a holder of paper money,[120] stated that "Ex post facto laws, if taken technically, relate[d] solely to criminal cases."[121] Randolph elaborated:

> What greater security can we have against arbitrary proceedings in criminal jurisprudence than this? In addition to the interpretation of the Convention, let me show [] still greater authority. The same clause provides that no bill of attainder shall be passed. It shows that the attention of the Convention was drawn to criminal matters alone. Shall it be complained, against this government, that it prohibits the passing of a law annexing a punishment to an act which was lawful at the time of committing it? With regard to retrospective laws, there is no restraint.[122]

Mason was unmoved, and expressed concern, as he had in Philadelphia, that the prohibition would ban useful retroactive civil statutes,[123] especially laws of Congress reducing the postwar national debt, chargeable to states, that was held by money speculators.[124] Mason argued that whatever "technical definition[]"ex post facto might have, common understanding was not limited to criminal laws: "Whatever it may be at the bar, or in a professional line," Mason stated, "I conceive that, according to the common acceptation of the words, *ex post facto* laws and retrospective laws are synonymous terms."[125] Would Virginia be wise "to trust business of this sort to technical definition?"[126] No, Mason argued, an express provision should be included to avoid such a broad interpretation. Again, the concern manifested regarding the fiscal impact of requiring states to bear the cost of paying for inflated paper money:

> [W]e must pay it shilling for shilling . . . The amount will surpass the value of the property of the United States. Neither the state legislatures nor Congress can make an ex post facto law. The nominal value must therefore be paid. Where is the power in the new government to settle this money so as to prevent the country from being ruined? When they prohibit the making ex post facto laws, they will have no authority to prevent our being ruined by paying that money at its nominal value.[127]

Patrick Henry also persisted. He again argued that the ex post facto prohibitions barred states and Congress from enacting laws allowing for the scaling of money to account for its depreciated value.[128] Henry also expressed a more limited view of the prohibitory scope of retroactive criminal laws, stating that "[t]hose who declare war against the human race may be struck out of existence as soon as they are apprehended . . . A pirate, an outlaw, or a common enemy to all mankind, may be put to death at any time. It is justified by the laws of nature and nations."[129]

The North Carolina Convention ratification debates also focused on the ex post facto prohibition. Delegates there actually met twice, the first time adjourning without ratification. However, only records exist of the first meeting (the second meeting, where ratification actually occurred, by a vote of 195-77, on November 21, 1789, lacks records).[130] In North Carolina, concern over the relation between the ex post facto prohibition and the value of depreciated paper money also figured prominently. However, paper money (especially issued by the state) was relatively popular, prompting Federalists to argue that the prohibition protected the value of existing paper money.[131] Anti-Federalist Timothy Bloodworth expressed concern over whether a law could be enacted that would in effect penalize holders of paper money, asking, "Will it be an ex post facto law to compel the payment of money now due in silver coin? If suit be brought in the federal court against one of our citizens, for a sum of money, will paper money be received to satisfy the judgment? I inquire for information; my mind is not yet satisfied."[132] Federalist James Iredell, a future US Supreme Court justice, responded to Bloodworth:

Mr. Chairman, with respect to this clause, it cannot have the operation contended for. There is nothing in the Constitution which affects our present paper money. It prohibits, for the future, the emitting of any, but it does not interfere with the paper money now actually in circulation in several states. There is an express clause which protects it. It provides that there shall be no ex post facto law. This would be ex post facto, if the construction contended for were right.[133]

In a January 1788 pamphlet responding to George Mason's objections to the Constitution more generally, Iredell (writing under the name "Marcus") made clear his disdain for ex post facto laws, and the need for the Constitution to expressly prohibit them:

[I]n my opinion this very prohibition is one of the most valuable parts of the new constitution. . . . Sure I am, they have been the instrument of some of the grossest acts of tyranny that were ever exercised, and have this never failing consequence, to put the minority in the power of a passionate and unprincipled majority . . . This very clause, I think, is worth ten thousand declarations of rights, if this, the most essential right of all, was omitted in them. A man may feel some pride in his security, when he knows that what he does innocently and safely today in accordance with the laws of his country, cannot be tortured into guilt and danger tomorrow.[134]

Records from the New York ratifying convention reflect only modest discussion of the ex post facto prohibition. There, Thomas Tredwell proposed an amendment specifically confining the ex post facto prohibition to criminal laws, so that it "shall not be construed to prevent calling public defaulters to account."[135] The proposed amendment failed and the convention narrowly (30-27) backed the Constitution on July 26, 1788, proffering in additional good measure a raft of documents including proposed amendments and declarations, among them that "the prohibition contained in the said Constitution, against ex post facto laws, extends only to laws concerning crimes."[136]

* * *

In short, based on the available historical record, the ex post facto prohibition was the subject of some discussion in the states. No objections appear to have been made to the prohibition regarding criminal statutes; rather, delegates expressed concern that the ban extended to retroactive laws of a civil nature, especially those affecting debts and the value of currency. Anti-Federalists voiced similar concerns outside the convention, in newspapers and other mass communication methods of the day.[137]

Ultimately, despite persistent concern among opponents over the lack of a bill of rights, on June 21, 1788 the Constitution received the necessary approval of a ninth state, when New Hampshire ratified the document.[138] A few days later, Virginia ratified, as did New York in late July 1788.[139] Remarkably, George Washington, the nation's first president, took the oath of office in late April 1789 when only eleven states comprised the national union.[140]

Wishing to bring laggard states North Carolina and Rhode Island[141] into the national fold,[142] and allay lingering Anti-Federalist sentiment within states more generally,[143] the First Congress, with US Representative James Madison (Virginia) in the lead,[144] drafted a Bill of Rights and sent it to the states for approval in late September 1789.[145] Thereafter, North Carolina and Rhode Island ratified and joined the union in late 1789 and 1790, respectively.[146] What became the Bill of Rights, the first ten amendments to the US Constitution, in mid-December 1791 ultimately received the two-thirds state support needed and became the law of the land.[147]

Summary

Although delegates to the Philadelphia Convention got around to discussing ex post facto laws relatively late in the convention, there is no mistaking their determination to ban their enactment. Indeed, the US Constitution contains not one, but two, unequivocal prohibitions: directed to the "National Legislature" (i.e., Congress), in Article I, section 9, and state legislatures, in Article I, section 10. This was done even though ex post facto laws were considered "void of themselves," so obviously wrong that the blanket prohibitions in Article I would cause international embarrassment. But "experience overruled all other calculations," especially regarding state legislatures, which federal constitutional law otherwise left largely free to act as they wished, so long as they had a republican form of government (Art. IV, sec. 4).

The ex post facto prohibitions, along with the other limits imposed on state legislatures and Congress in sections 9 and 10 of Article I, reflected the framers' acute concern over what Chief Justice John Marshall would later call the "feelings of the moment," the "sudden and strong passions" that can drive legislative excess.[148] By the mid-1780s, initial satisfaction over increasing the democratic representativeness and power of state legislatures in particular[149] had given way to concern over their excesses,[150] what historian Gordon Wood termed their "democratic despotism."[151] As Alexander Hamilton wrote in the *Federalist Papers*, "how easy it is for men . . . to be zealous advocates for the rights of the citizens when they are invaded by others, and as soon as they have it in their power, to become the invaders themselves."[152] Hamilton, mindful that the draft Constitution lacked a bill or declaration of rights, emphasized that the ex post facto prohibitions numbered among the "great[est] securities to liberty and republicanism" contained in the Constitution.[153] Fellow *Federalist Papers* contributor James Madison considered the prohibitions part of a constitutional "bulwark in favor of personal security and private rights."[154]

To the framers of the Constitution, the need to impose such a double-walled bulwark, limiting Congress and state legislatures, was immediate and necessary. As the Supreme Judicial Court of Maine would recognize over two centuries later, "[t]he framers' decision to include the ex post facto clause in the body of the Constitution adopted in 1787, and not to defer consideration to the amendment process that would follow, is evidence that the framers viewed the federal ban on ex post facto laws as fundamental to the protection of individual liberty."[155]

2

The Supreme Court Weighs In:
Calder v. Bull (1798)

As Chapter 1 made clear, the framers were very concerned about the propensity of legislatures to engage in arbitrary and vindictive retroactive lawmaking and included in Article I of the Constitution express prohibitions of the practice. This chapter picks up where Chapter 1 left off, examining how the early Supreme Court interpreted the meaning and scope of the Ex Post Facto Clause. The court first did so in *Calder v. Bull* (1798), roughly a decade after the Constitution took effect. Despite its importance, *Calder*, which today remains the court's seminal Ex Post Facto Clause decision, has been criticized on several grounds, but mainly for its principle conclusion: that the clause prohibits only retroactive criminal (not also civil) laws.

The chapter begins with discussion of a foundational question: whether the Supreme Court had the institutional authority it exercised in *Calder*, in particular the power of a judicial tribunal to entertain a challenge to the work of a coordinate branch (in *Calder*, a legislature). Attention then turns to *Calder* itself, which provided a lengthy exposition of what the court saw as the historical provenance of the criminal-centric view it adopted. Thereafter, the discussion focuses on the mass of historical evidence contradicting the court's limited view of coverage, some of which was touched upon in Chapter 1. Taken together, the historical record backs the view that both the technical or professional and general public understanding of ex post facto laws during the Framing Era was inclusive of civil and criminal laws. The chapter concludes with a survey of the several provocative theories advanced by modern scholars explaining why the court adopted a criminal-centric view in *Calder*, despite the abundant historical evidence to the contrary.

Judicial Review

The framers of the US Constitution created a federal system that divides power among three coequal branches of government, enjoying separate and

The Ex Post Facto Clause. Wayne A. Logan, Oxford University Press. © Oxford University Press 2023.
DOI: 10.1093/oso/9780190053505.003.0003

independent powers. The legislative branch, consisting of Congress, is responsible for enacting laws (Article I); the executive branch, consisting of the president and vice president (and later executive branch agencies), is to enforce laws (Article II); and the judicial branch, consisting of "one supreme Court, and in such inferior Courts as the Congress may from time to time ordain and establish," is to interpret laws (Article III). By design, the three branches are intended to prevent the concentration of power and allow the respective branches to serve as checks and balances on one another.

In *Federalist* Number 78, Alexander Hamilton, a framer of the Constitution and an eminent lawyer of his day,[1] wrote at length on the essential role of courts as independent legal arbiters, characterizing them as "peculiarly essential in a limited Constitution."[2] Hamilton understood a "limited Constitution" as one containing "certain specified exceptions to the legislative authority . . . for instance, [] that it shall pass no bills of attainder, no *ex post facto* laws, and the like."[3] Ultimately, he stated, the responsibility for checking legislative overreach fell to the judicial branch, reasoning that

> [l]imitations of this kind can be preserved in practice no other way than through the medium of courts of justice, whose duty it must be to declare all acts contrary to the manifest tenor of the Constitution void. Without this, all the reservations of particular rights of privileges would amount to nothing.[4]

Hamilton rejected the notion that legislative branch actors should serve as "constitutional judges of their own powers." It was "far more rational to suppose that the courts were designed to be an intermediate body" to guard against legislative overreach and protect constitutional rights.[5] The legislative branch enacted laws but interpretation and review of the constitutionality of those laws was the job of courts:

> The interpretation of the laws is the proper and peculiar province of the courts. A constitution is, in fact, and must be regarded by the judges as, a fundamental law. It therefore belongs to them to ascertain its meaning as well as the meaning of any particular act proceeding from the legislative body.[6]

James Wilson, another leading legal theoretician of his time, and future Supreme Court justice, fresh from his work at the Philadelphia Convention, similarly recognized the need for judicial review when urging adoption of the Constitution at the Pennsylvania ratifying convention:

> Controversies may certainly arise under this constitution and the laws of the
> United States, and is it not proper that there should be judges to decide them?...If
> a law should be made inconsistent with those powers vested by this instrument
> in Congress, the judges, as a consequence of their independence, and the partic-
> ular powers of government being defined, will declare such law to be null and void.
> For the power of the constitution predominates. Anything therefore, that shall be
> enacted by Congress contrary thereto, will not have the force of law.[7]

James Madison likewise viewed the judiciary as key to protecting rights.
When introducing the proposed Bill of Rights to the First Congress in June
1789, Madison proclaimed that courts would ensure that the "paper barriers"
protecting individual rights become "an impenetrable bulwark."[8]

Calder v. Bull

In 1798, in one of its first decisions construing the Constitution,[9] before Chief
Justice Marshall's famous recognition in *Marbury v. Madison* (1803) that it is
"the province and duty of the Judicial Department to say what the law is,"[10] the
Supreme Court got its chance to fulfill its role as constitutional expositor.[11]
It did so in a case requiring interpretation of Article I's prohibition of ex post
facto laws (that in section 10, in particular, concerning state enactments). The
case, *Calder v. Bull*,[12] had rather unusual facts for what turned out to be a decision of major importance regarding the constitutional prohibition of ex post
facto laws.[13]

In *Calder*, a Connecticut probate court issued a decree disapproving
of and refusing to record a will from which Bull stood to inherit land. The
Connecticut General Court, at that point also sitting as the Connecticut legislature,[14] subsequently passed "a resolution or law" vacating the judgment and
granting a new hearing in the dispute over the will.[15] Bull and her husband
prevailed at the new hearing, and Calder and her husband, who previously
benefited when the will was deemed invalid, argued that "the awarding of a
new trial, was the effect of a legislative act, and that it is unconstitutional, because an ex post facto law."[16]

After two continuances, for reasons that remain unclear,[17] the matter was
argued before the US Supreme Court in February 1798, and on August 1 the
court issued its opinion, unanimously rejecting Calder's ex post facto argument. Although at the time there were six justices on the court, only four issued opinions—Justices Samuel Chase, James Iredell, William Paterson, and
William Cushing.[18] They wrote separately, *seriatim*, consistent with English

judicial practice.[19] Therefore, there was no opinion "for the Court," unlike modern-day practice.

Three justices—Paterson, Iredell, and Cushing—expressed concern that the challenged act was an exercise of judicial, not legislative authority, meaning that it was not a "law" within the ex post facto prohibition.[20] Iredell in particular wrote that the power of the legislature to "superintend the Courts of Justice . . . is judicial in nature; and whenever it is exercised, as in the present instance, it is an exercise of judicial, not legislative, authority."[21] Another combination of three justices—Chase, Iredell, and Paterson—offered what turned out to be the key ruling in the case: that the ex post facto prohibition covered only criminal laws, not civil (such as the challenged probate action).[22] Justice Cushing authored a brief two-sentence opinion, omitting any discussion of whether the Ex Post Facto Clause prohibited only criminal laws, simply stating that the legal act challenged was "not touched by the Federal Constitution."[23]

Today, Justice Chase's comparatively lengthy opinion is considered the primary exposition of the ex post facto claim in *Calder*. After expressing what he saw as the constraining effect of natural law on legislative enactments, Chase noted that the ban on ex post facto laws "very probably arose from the knowledge, that the Parliament of Great Britain claimed and exercised a power to pass such laws," citing examples involving the Earl of Strafford (1641), Sir John Fenwick (1696), Lord Clarendon (1669), and the Bishop of Atterbury (1723).[24] "With very few exceptions," Chase wrote, "the advocates of such laws were stimulated by ambition, or personal resentment, and vindictive malice. To prevent such, and similar, acts of violence and injustice, I believe, the Federal and State Legislatures, were prohibited from passing any bill of attainder; or any ex post facto law."[25] Furthermore, ex post facto laws violated the social compact underlying the Constitution, intended "to establish justice, to promote the general welfare, to secure the blessings of liberty; and to protect their persons and property from violence."[26] Chase continued:

> [t]here are certain vital principles in our free Republican governments, which will determine and over-rule an apparent and flagrant abuse of legislative power; as to authorize manifest injustice by positive law; or to take away that security for personal liberty, or private property, for the protection whereof of the government was established. An ACT of the Legislature (for I cannot call it a law) contrary to the great first principles of the social compact, cannot be considered a rightful exercise of legislative authority.[27]

Chase thereafter explained that he felt obliged to define the meaning and parameters of the ex post facto prohibition, reasoning that it "necessarily requires some explanation; for, naked and without explanation, it is unintelligible, and means nothing. Literally, it is only, that a law shall not be passed concerning, and after the fact, or thing done, or action committed. I would ask, what fact; of what nature, or kind; and by whom done?"[28] Chase then zeroed in on what he saw as the "plain and obvious meaning and intention of the prohibition":

> that the Legislatures of the several states, shall not pass laws, after a fact done by a subject, or citizen, which shall have relation to such fact, and shall punish him for having done it. The prohibition considered in this light, is an additional bulwark in favour of the personal security of the subject, to protect his person from punishment by legislative acts, having a retrospective operation.[29]

On the question of what the clause covered, Chase wrote that it was not "inserted to secure the citizen in his private rights, of either property, or contracts. . . ."[30] Such civil matters were regulated by other prohibitions in Article I, section 10 (such as concerning the impairment of contracts). The ex post facto prohibition only concerns retroactive criminal—not civil—laws because a broader reading would render these other prohibitions superfluous. The ex post facto prohibition was intended to

> secure the person of the subject from injury, or punishment, in consequence of such law. If the prohibition against making ex post facto laws was intended to secure personal rights from being affected, or injured, by such laws, and the prohibition is sufficiently extensive for that object, the other restraints, I have enumerated, were unnecessary, and therefore improper; for both of them are retrospective.[31]

In defense of his view that the ex post facto prohibition encompassed only criminal laws, Chase noted that "[t]he expressions 'ex post facto laws,' are technical, they had been in use long before the Revolution, and had acquired an appropriate meaning, by Legislators, Lawyers, and Authors."[32] The "technical" meaning was reflected in the work of hallowed legal commentators William Blackstone and Richard Wooddeson (Blackstone's successor at Oxford), and "the author of the *Federalist* [presumably Madison in Number 44], who I esteem superior to both, for his extensive and accurate knowledge of the true principles of Government."[33] In additional support, Chase pointed to the criminal-centric definitions of ex post facto laws in the declaration of rights in several state constitutions.[34] Justice Paterson wrote that the words ex post facto "must be taken in their technical, which is also their common and general, application, and are to be understood in their literal sense," which was that they are of a criminal (not civil) nature.[35] Justice Iredell wrote that

> the true construction of the prohibition extends to criminal, not to civil, cases. It is only in criminal cases, indeed, in which the danger to be guarded against, is greatly to be apprehended . . . The temptation to such abuses of power is unfortunately too alluring for human virtue; and, therefore, the framers of the American Constitutions have wisely denied to the respective Legislatures, Federal as well as State, the possession of the power itself. . . . The policy, the reason and humanity, of the prohibition, do not, I repeat, extend to civil cases, to cases that merely affect the private property of citizens.[36]

As noted, Justice Cushing did not opine on the specific issue.[37]

Consistent with his view of the criminal-centric prohibition of the clause, Chase also provided the other key takeaway from *Calder*—the categories of laws that come "within the words and the intent of the prohibition":

> 1st. Every law that makes an action, done before the passing of the law, and which was innocent when done, criminal; and punishes such action. 2nd. Every law that aggravates a crime, or makes it greater than it was, when committed. 3rd. Every law that changes the punishment, and inflicts a greater punishment, than the law annexed to the crime, when committed. 4th. Every law that alters the legal rules of evidence, and receives less, or different, testimony, than the law required at the time of the commission of the offence, in order to convict the offender.[38]

At the end of the foregoing list Chase suggested that the four categories identified were perhaps not exclusive, stating that "[a]ll these, and similar laws, are manifestly unjust and oppressive."[39]

Three of the four justices writing opinions (Chase, Paterson, and Iredell) were at pains to condemn ex post facto laws and the tendency of governments to enact them. Chase wrote:

> All the restrictions contained in the Constitution of the United States on the power of the State Legislatures, were provided in favour of the authority of the Federal Government. The prohibition against their making any ex post facto laws was introduced for greater caution, and very probably arose from the knowledge, that the Parliament of Great Britain claimed and exercised a power to pass such laws . . . The ground for the exercise of such legislative power was this, that the safety of the kingdom depended on the death, or other punishment, of the offender: as if traitors, when discovered, could be so formidable, or the government

so insecure! With very few exceptions, the advocates of such laws were stimulated by ambition, or personal resentment, and vindictive malice. To prevent such, and similar, acts of violence and injustice, I believe, the Federal and State Legislatures, were prohibited from passing any bill of attainder; or any ex post facto law.[40]

Paterson said of ex post facto laws: "The historic page abundantly evinces, that the power of passing such laws should be withheld from legislators; as it is a dangerous instrument in the hands of bold, unprincipled, aspiring, and party men, and has been two often used to effect the most detestable purposes."[41] And Iredell:

The history of every country in Europe will furnish flagrant instances of tyranny exercised under the pretext of penal dispensations. Rival factions, in their efforts to crush each other, have superseded all the forms, and suppressed all the sentiments, of justice; while attainders, on the principle of retaliation and proscription, have marked all the vicissitudes of party triumph. The temptation to such abuses of power is unfortunately too alluring for human virtue; and, therefore, the framers of the American Constitutions have wisely denied to the respective Legislatures, Federal as well as State, the possession of the power itself: They shall not pass any ex post facto law; or, in other words, they shall not inflict a punishment for any act, which was innocent at the time it was committed; nor increase the degree of punishment previously denounced for any specific offence.[42]

Questioning *Calder:* Early Judicial Doubts

Today, over two centuries after being decided, *Calder* remains the authoritative decision on the meaning and scope of the Ex Post Facto Clause. It is now accepted that the clause only prohibits retroactive criminal laws that concern one or more of the four categories identified by Justice Chase in his *Calder* opinion (despite the caveat of seeming nonexclusivity he provided, noted earlier).

Although it remains in the pantheon of Supreme Court decisions, *Calder* is subject to a number of very basic critiques. First, at a fundamental level, much of Justice Chase's opinion, and for that matter the opinions of Justices Iredell and Paterson (less so Justice Cushing, with his brief vague two-sentence opinion) is what lawyers refer to as *obiter dictum*—literally, "something said in passing," a statement incidental to the basis on which a case is resolved, and therefore not binding authority. This is because, as the justices themselves noted, the behavior challenged was judicial not legislative in nature: the

Connecticut legislature, as was rather common at the time, was acting in a judicial capacity, not passing a "law" as required by Article I.[43] Only this conclusion was necessary to the court's decision. Other conclusions, most importantly that the clause only prohibits retroactive criminal laws and its coverage is limited to the four categories specified by Justice Chase,[44] were also unnecessary and therefore also non-binding dictum.

Even more fundamentally, the *Calder* Court's crucial holding that only criminal laws come within the ex post facto prohibition has long been questioned. In *Satterlee v. Matthewson* (1829),[45] Justice William Johnson, who was not on the Supreme Court when *Calder* was decided, provided the first explicit critique of *Calder*'s criminal-centric view. In *Satterlee*, the court addressed a challenge against a Pennsylvania statute that effectively made a once void land deed valid, which petitioners alleged violated the Contracts Clause in Article I, section 10 ("No State shall . . . pass any Bill of Attainder, ex post facto Law, or Law impairing the Obligation of Contracts . . ."). The majority opinion in *Satterlee*, authored by Justice Bushrod Washington (nephew of George Washington), resolved the question on procedural grounds, avoiding the Contracts Clause issue, and Justice Johnson concurred with the result. In a highly unusual "note" appended to his concurrence, Johnson, who two years before in another case (*Ogden v. Saunders*, 1827),[46] intimated the same view, took the opportunity to address the "the unhappy idea, that the phrase 'ex post facto' in the constitution of the United States, was confined to criminal cases exclusively; a decision which leaves a large class of arbitrary legislative acts without the prohibitions of the constitution."[47]

Thereafter, Justice Johnson, in addition to emphasizing that the criminal-centric holding in *Calder* was dictum,[48] provided an expansive point-by-point refutation of the evidence advanced by Justice Chase in *Calder* in support of criminal law centrism.[49] With respect to the inference that the text regarding state prohibitions in Article I, section 10 favored a criminal limit, Justice Johnson reasoned that "by placing 'ex post facto' laws between bills of attainder, which are exclusively criminal, and laws violating the obligation of contracts, which are exclusively civil, it would rather seem that *ex post facto laws* partook of both characters, was common to both purposes."[50] Justice Chase's reliance on Wooddeson and Blackstone was misplaced, Johnson wrote, because the passages cited stood only for the proposition that retroactive criminal laws are especially problematic, not that they are the only kind of prohibited ex post facto law.[51] Furthermore, Chase's invocation of an unnamed contributor to the *Papers*, which Johnson presumed to be James Madison, was poor authority, because the writer has made no attempt at giving a distinct exposition of the phrase, as used in the constitution. Bills of attainder, ex post facto laws, and laws impairing the obligation of contracts, are all considered together; and regarded, as they really are, as forming together "a bulwark, in favor of personal security and private rights;" but on the separate office of each, in the work of defence, he makes no remark, and attempts no definition or distribution.[52]

Johnson also contended that Justice Chase misstated the existence of the criminal law limit in state constitutions. The Massachusetts and Delaware constitutions Chase invoked did not contain the phrase "ex post facto," and only North Carolina and Maryland "would seem to have applied the phrase in the restricted sense."[53] Of Maryland, which was "copied" by North Carolina, Johnson wrote that the restrictive view of Chase was likely influenced by the fact that he was a delegate to the Maryland constitutional convention.[54]

Finally, Johnson elaborated on what he saw as the "great reason which influenced" *Calder*'s narrow construction of the Clause, namely that the justices "considered its application to civil cases as unnecessary, and fully supplied by the prohibition to pass laws impairing the obligation of contracts."[55] The belief, Johnson maintained (and which later chapters demonstrate), resulted from a misunderstanding of the many retroactive laws that can adversely affect individuals, beyond contracts:

the learned judges could not then have foreseen the great variety of forms in which the violations of private right have since been presented to this court . . . This court has had more than once to toil up hill, in order to bring within the restriction on the states to pass laws violating the obligation of contracts, the most obvious cases to which the constitution was intended, to extend its protection; a difficulty, which it is obvious, might often be avoided, by giving to the phrase ex post facto its original and natural application.[56]

Although not mentioned by Justice Johnson, Justice Iredell, who concurred in *Calder*, previously viewed the ex post facto prohibition as covering both retroactive civil and criminal laws. At the state ratifying conventions, especially in Virginia and North Carolina, a major question was whether paper money issued by states and the Continental Congress could be devalued retroactively. In this regard, Iredell, a staunch Federalist, when a delegate in the North Carolina convention in the summer of 1788, vigorously resisted Anti-Federalist arguments that the clause in Article I, section 10, restraining states from issuing paper money would discredit state paper currency then in circulation. The limit in Article I, section 10 prohibited *future* paper money circulation, and the Ex Post Facto Clause would protect money already in circulation, making clear his view of its civil application.[57]

Furthermore, in conjunction with the North Carolina ratifying debates, Iredell penned an essay ("Marcus I") published in 1788 evidencing his broader understanding, stating: "The people are expressly secured . . . against ex post facto laws, so that the tenure of any property at any time held under the principles of the common law, cannot be altered by any act of the future general legislature."[58] In his responses to the objections lodged by Anti-Federalist George Mason in the Virginia Ratifying Convention, Iredell wrote that "[t]he people are expressly secured (contrary to Mr. Mason's wishes) against ex post facto laws; so that the tenure of any property at any time held under the principles of the common law, cannot be altered by any future act of the general legislature."[59]

Justice Johnson's note in *Satterlee* also failed to discuss the role played by Justice William Paterson in *Calder*. Of the four justices writing in *Calder* (Chase, Iredell, Paterson, Cushing), only Paterson attended the Philadelphia Framing Convention in 1787 (doing so as a New Jersey delegate), but he had departed Philadelphia when the discussions and votes regarding the clause occurred in late August and September 14, returning only to sign the Constitution on September 17.[60] Paterson concurred with Justice Chase's opinion in *Calder*, but only three years earlier, when "riding circuit" as justices did at the time,[61] he adopted a broader view of the ex post facto prohibition in a Pennsylvania case, *Van Horne's Lessee v. Dorrance* (1795).[62] *Dorrance* concerned an ongoing land dispute between Pennsylvania and Connecticut and a law passed by the Pennsylvania legislature affecting the rights of Connecticut settlers in northeastern Pennsylvania. In rejecting both constitutional claims based on impairment of contract and ex post facto, Paterson, in reference to the ex post facto claim, made no reference whatsoever to a limit on its coverage to criminal cases.[63]

Other early era prominent jurists also expressed doubt over the soundness of the *Calder* criminal law limit. Although not citing *Calder*, one of the earliest and most important Supreme Court decisions under the leadership of Chief Justice John Marshall, *Fletcher v. Peck* (1810),[64] is one such example. *Fletcher* concerned a law enacted by the Georgia legislature that retroactively revoked land grants to purchasers without notice, which was challenged on contract clause grounds. The court, with Marshall writing, backed the challenge, marking the first time the court invalidated a state law on constitutional grounds. In the course of his opinion, Marshall signaled his broad understanding of the ex post facto prohibition, stating that "[a]n ex post facto law is one which renders an act punishable in a manner in which it was not punishable when it was committed. *Such a law may inflict penalties on the person, or it may inflict pecuniary penalties which may swell the public treasury.*"[65]

Joseph Story, both a Supreme Court justice and a highly respected constitutional scholar of his time, wrote in his *Commentaries on the Constitution* (1833) that "ex post facto laws, in a comprehensive sense, embrace all retrospective laws, whether they are of a civil or criminal nature."[66] Story wrote that if the question of the applicable scope of the clause were assessed in a case of first impression, before *Calder*, Justice Johnson's analysis and conclusions in *Satterlee* "would be entitled to grave consideration."[67] Earlier, in 1814 when riding circuit, Story stated in an opinion that "[o]n principle, every statute which takes away or impairs vested rights acquired under existing laws, or creates a new obligation, imposes a new duty, or attaches a new liability in respect to transactions or considerations already past, may be deemed retrospective."[68] Thomas Jefferson, while not directly involved in drafting the Constitution or its approval (in Virginia, his home state), but nonetheless a key player in the nation's early history, took a similarly expansive view.[69]

The other limitation recognized by Justice Chase in *Calder*—concerning the four categories of law identified—is also open to question. As noted, the categories are dictum, given the facts of the case, and their scope, contrary to the modern view regarding them as finite and exclusive, is nothing of the kind (recall Justice Chase's use of the phrase "[a]ll these, and similar laws"). Moreover, researchers have cast doubt on the historical provenance of the limited categories themselves.[70]

Finally, Justice Chase's inference that civil application of the clause is contrary to the text of Article I, section 10, because of the inclusion of explicit civil prohibitions (concerning laws relating to contracts and issuance of legal tender), is problematic for the reasons identified by Justice Johnson in *Satterlee*, as well as the fact that Article I, section 9 contains no parallel limits on Congress. As one commentator recently noted, "this logic gives us the strange result that states can pass civil ex post facto laws (because of the existence of the contract and legal tender clauses) while Congress cannot pass civil ex post facto laws (because the prohibition on ex post facto laws with respect to Congress [in section 9] is not accompanied by the contracts and legal tender clauses)."[71]

Questioning *Calder:* More Recent Scholarly Doubts

Most scholars, dating back to at least 1900,[72] are of the view that during the Framing Era ex post facto laws were understood by both the lay public and those using a "technical" or "professional" understanding to encompass both retroactive civil and criminal laws.[73] In 1922, for instance, Professor Oliver Field noted that James Madison, a key participant at the Philadelphia Convention, and a main chronicler of events there, believed that the ex post facto prohibition encompassed civil and criminal laws. Field points to Madison's question on August 28 at the convention, in response to a motion to include a provision barring state interference with contracts, "Is not that already done by the prohibition of ex post facto laws, which will oblige the Judgers to declare them null & void?"[74] Of this, Field reasons that Madison was

> evidently of the impression that *ex post facto* applies to civil as well as to criminal matters. It is odd that no member of the Convention took the trouble to inform him that he was laboring under a serious misapprehension. It is hardly credible that such a slip should be permitted without some member calling it to his attention. Madison does not record any answer given to his query.[75]

Furthermore, Field asserted that the use of "ex post facto" in the *Official Journal*, the other principal original historical source chronicling the proceedings, and Madison's corresponding use of the term "retrospective" in his *Notes*, shows that the terms "were used synonymously. It is improbable that Madison alone understood the terms to have the meaning he attaches to them . . . During the entire debate recorded in this connection there is a notable absence of anything pertaining to criminal affairs."[76] Also, later, at the Virginia ratifying convention, where ex post facto laws received perhaps their most sustained attention, Patrick Henry, George Nicolas, and George Mason quite clearly regarded the prohibition to encompass civil and criminal matters.[77]

More recently, Professor John Mikhail wrote in 2019 that "[t]here is, in fact, a mountain of evidence that ex post facto laws were commonly understood at the founding to include both civil and criminal laws—and that [in *Calder*] Chase, Iredell, and Paterson were aware of this fact."[78] In addition to citing numerous historical sources such as found in newspapers and broadsides in support of a broader view, Mikhail notes that "[a]ll told . . . there appear to be approximately three dozen founding era cases which contradict the claim made by Justices Chase, Iredell, and Patterson in *Calder v. Bull* that the phrase 'ex post facto law' was understood at the time to be a technical term limited to retroactive criminal laws."[79] Professor Evan Zoldan, in a 2015 article analyzing an even more extensive array of historical sources, convincingly shows that not only did the technical/professional understanding of ex post facto encompass civil and criminal laws, but the general public/lay understanding did as well.[80]

Finally, when considering the accuracy of the understanding advanced in *Calder*, it is important to note that the case was decided in 1798. As a consequence, the justices wrote without the benefit of any record of the discussions and debates taking place at the Philadelphia Convention. The proceedings were held in secret and none of the justices were present. Even the skeletal record provided in the *Official Journal* was not available until 1819, and Madison's *Notes* were published even later, in 1840. Nor did the justices in *Calder* have access to records from the state ratifying conventions, which were not available until 1827 with the publication of *Elliot's Debates*.

In the face of this convincing evidence, what explains the unanimous contrary view of the *Calder* Court?

One admittedly cynical view was advanced by Professor William Crosskey, of the University of Chicago School of Law. In a widely cited 1947 article, Crosskey at length argued that *Calder* was wrong to limit the prohibition to criminal cases.[81] Later, in his treatise on the history and interpretation of the Constitution, first published in 1953,[82] and in a 1968 article, published posthumously, Crosskey accused James Madison of deliberate misstatements in his notes regarding the supposed criminal-centric prohibition.[83] In particular, Crosskey maintained that Madison fabricated his report that John Dickinson on August 29, 1787, informed his fellow delegates that Blackstone regarded the ex post facto prohibition to only extend to criminal laws.[84] The Supreme Court[85] and commentators[86] have since erroneously relied on this account, which Crosskey maintained was the result of Madison's "editorial ingenuity," designed to align with his broader view of the retrospective scope of the Contracts Clause and more limited view of the power to regulate interstate commerce, a view emerging later in his life (when the *Notes* were published).[87]

This revisionist view is echoed by Professor Mikhail, who in his 2019 article contended that Madison's account in his *Notes* was colored by a desire to jibe with his several post-convention public statements suggesting espousal of a criminal-centric view of coverage.[88]

Although today scholars generally agree that Madison's *Notes* in general often raise reliability concerns,[89] and those from August 22 to September 17 in particular (when the ex post facto provisions were debated and voted upon) are especially problematic,[90] they usually have been less cynical in their assessment of why this is so.[91] Moreover, no concrete evidence has materialized supporting Madison's purported fabrication regarding Dickinson.[92]

Crosskey also advanced another account for *Calder's* criminal-centric focus. In his 1947 law review article, noted earlier, he suggested that the justices' view was motivated by their personal concern for one of their brethren, Justice James Wilson. Wilson, an esteemed lawyer from Pennsylvania and signer of both the Declaration of Independence and the Constitution, who sat on the court at the time of *Calder*, was heavily indebted as the result land speculation and the financial panic of 1796 to 1797. Indeed, by the time *Calder* was argued in February 1798, Wilson had fled Philadelphia, where the court was then sitting, to avoid creditors and potential jail. Wilson's fellow justices had arranged for him to ride circuit in North Carolina where, falling ill in part due to the strain, he took refuge at the home of his friend Justice James Iredell in Edenton, North Carolina.[93] Crosskey speculated that the opinions in *Calder* were designed to aid Wilson, who would benefit from the retroactive application of a federal bankruptcy law, decidedly civil in nature, then being considered by Congress. Crosskey argued that limiting the ex post facto prohibition to criminal laws would aid Wilson, who died by a "violent nervous fever" not long after *Calder* was decided. To help their friend and colleague, Crosskey maintained, the justices needed to rely on "flimsy grounds."[94]

In his 2019 article, Professor Mikhail agreed with Crosskey's view of the broader original meaning of the ex post facto prohibition,[95] and also doubted the accuracy of Madison's account of convention deliberations.[96] However, Mikhail argued that the *Calder* justices had a different motivation for their criminal-centric focus, albeit also relating to their colleague James Wilson.[97] In particular, he attributes the narrow view of the *Calder* Court to the justices' concern over the rampant land speculation occurring at the time, in which major land holding companies urged a broad application of the ex post facto prohibition because it would protect their financial position. Wilson played a major part in the ventures—as a landowner and attorney for a large real estate entity (of which he was president and a shareholder). Wilson, for instance, in 1797, a year before *Calder*, wrote members of Congress a letter on behalf of the entity, quoting extensively from Justice Paterson's opinion in *Dorrance* (noted above) adopting a broad view of ex post facto coverage, which would bar Virginia and other states from voiding prior land titles.[98] In short, rather than seeking to benefit Wilson personally, Mikhail reasons that his fellow justices were affected by Wilson's "heavy-handed appeal to judicial authority and conspicuous conflict of interest," which were "probably a source of embarrassment."[99] According to Professor Mikhail:

> Because of its heavy-handedness, Wilson's letter was probably a major source of embarrassment to his fellow Justices, who by this time were keenly aware of how the ex post facto clauses were being used as a weapon by various land companies in thorny disputes over western lands. If this is correct, then these facts may help to explain the path that Chase, Iredell, and Paterson elected to take in *Calder v. Bull*, construing the clauses narrowly and limiting them to retroactive criminal laws.[100]

Mikhail concludes that this embarrassment "may have influenced the justices' opinions in *Calder v. Bull*, a matter that calls for further investigation."[101]

Summary and Conclusion

As discussed, *Calder*, despite its landmark status, has long been criticized. Regarding the criminal law limit especially, strong reason exists to doubt Chase's assertion that he was "under a necessity to give a construction, or explanation of the words 'ex post facto laws,' because they have not any certain meaning attached to them."[102] On the contrary, it seems that when the Constitution originated, both the "technical" and ordinary lay understanding of the ex post facto prohibition covered both civil and criminal laws, not only criminal.[103] Whether Professor William Crosskey was correct in his accusation that Madison intentionally doctored his notes, or was merely mistaken, is really of no practical significance. This is because Delegate James Dickinson's purported revelation about criminal-centric focus, if it indeed occurred, was actually voiced the day after the vote on the prohibition of state ex post facto laws.[104]

From the Framing Era to today there never has been disagreement over the unconstitutionality of retroactive criminal laws, a domain where late eighteenth-century jurist and scholar Richard Wooddeson wrote, "justice wears her sternest aspect."[105] The controversy has been whether the ex post facto prohibition also covers retroactive civil laws, a position that today has very substantial historical support. This broader understanding will perhaps soon have considerable practical, not only theoretical academic, importance. This is because we live in a time when "originalist" interpretations of the Constitution have gained considerable currency among judges and justices, a matter addressed in Chapter 7. Moreover, for reasons noted, sound basis exists to doubt the exclusivity of the four categories of prohibited laws identified by Justice Chase in *Calder*, both due to lack of historical provenance, and Chase's own statement that the four categories "*and similar laws*, are manifestly unjust and oppressive."[106] Further still, as a technical matter, both apparent bedrock holdings can be categorized as dictum, and therefore unworthy of judicial deference.

As the following chapters confirm, however, *Calder*'s limited application to criminal laws, along with the four categories it identified, remain in effect, albeit with some judicial deviations along the way.

3

Formative Nineteenth-Century Developments

Although critically important, the Supreme Court's decision in *Calder v. Bull* in 1798 was only the first of the court's many decisions over the years interpreting and applying the Constitution's ex post facto prohibitions. This chapter examines the decisions from the nineteenth century, when the court addressed multiple challenges, producing a body of decisional law that resonates to this day. Indeed, the nineteenth century can be viewed as a halcyon era, highlighting the court's dedication to invoking the protective cloak of the clause, amid major social, political, and economic developments in the nation, including a bloody civil war.

Antebellum Era

The Supreme Court, under the leadership of Chief Justice John Marshall, entertained its first post-*Calder* case mentioning the clause twelve years later in *Fletcher v. Peck* (1810).[1] In *Fletcher*, the court addressed a challenge to a Georgia statute enacted in 1796 that rescinded a thirty-five million acre land grant the legislature had fraudulently extended to private land speculators (at very low prices) one year earlier.[2] The rescission law was enacted when it was learned that bribes were provided for the generous deal, prompting a group of newly elected legislators to later rescind the fraudulent grant.[3] In 1800, Peck purchased a parcel of the land in question, and subsequently sold it to Fletcher, who later sued Peck for breach of contract, alleging that the rescission of the initial grant had invalidated Peck's title to the land.[4] If the Georgia legislature possessed the authority to rescind the 1795 land grant, Fletcher was entitled to recover the money he paid. However, if the legislature lacked such authority, its 1796 law was invalid and Peck's original title to the land was valid.

In a unanimous decision authored by Chief Justice Marshall (with a separate concurring opinion by Justice William Johnson),[5] the court first deemed the rescission law invalid based on the "impairment of contracts" clause,

The Ex Post Facto Clause. Wayne A. Logan, Oxford University Press. © Oxford University Press 2023.
DOI: 10.1093/oso/9780190053505.003.0004

contained in Article I, section 10 of the Constitution.[6] Although acknowledging that the fraud underlying the initial land grant was "deplorable," the court held that the clause prohibited state interference with contracts between private parties and between private parties and the state itself (as in the case), meaning that the contract was binding even though it was illegally secured.[7] In so doing, the court made clear its awareness of the potential for legislative populist excesses among states, such as swept the Georgia legislature, noting:

> Whatever respect might have been felt for the state sovereignties, it is not to be disguised that the framers of the constitution viewed, with some apprehension, the violent acts which might grow out of the feelings of the moment; and that the people of the United States, in adopting that instrument, have manifested a determination to shield themselves and their property from the effects of those sudden and strong passions to which men are exposed. The restrictions on the legislative power of the states are obviously founded in this sentiment; and the constitution of the United States contains what may be deemed a bill of rights for the people of each state.[8]

The court also characterized the rescission law as an ex post facto law,[9] which it defined as "one which renders an act punishable in a manner in which it was not punishable when it was committed. Such a law may inflict penalties on the person, or may inflict pecuniary penalties which swell the public treasury."[10] Then, without any reference to *Calder*, the court articulated a considerably broader conception of the ex post facto prohibition, arguably encompassing civil (not only criminal) laws burdening individuals, stating that it precludes a legislature from "passing a law by which a man's estate, or any part of it, shall be seized for a crime which was not declared, by some previous law, to render him liable to that punishment."[11]

Under this definition, the Georgia legislature's law rescinding the land contract was punitive. To conclude otherwise, Marshall wrote, would do "violence . . . to the natural meaning of [the] words [ex post facto]. . . ."[12] The Georgia law "had the effect of an ex post facto law," in that it seized property based on conduct later deemed fraudulent.[13] Either under "general principles which are common to our free institutions, or by the particular provisions of the constitution of the United States," the legislature impermissibly passed a law that retroactively deprived Fletcher of his vested property interest in the land he acquired, which "had the effect of a [prohibited] ex post facto law."[14]

Fletcher today remains a landmark decision of the Marshall Court, the first time the Supreme Court declared a state law unconstitutional.[15] In the opinion, moreover, Chief Justice Marshall made clear the court's view of the structural role played by the ex post facto prohibition as limiting the power of legislatures to retroactively annul vested contract and property rights.

With respect to ex post facto jurisprudence, however, the precedential force of *Fletcher* remains uncertain. This is so for two reasons. First, although Marshall's opinion in *Fletcher* plainly voices a broader applicable scope of the ex post facto prohibition, compared to the narrow view articulated in *Calder*, the opinion failed to cite *Calder*, making it difficult to say that the latter decision's narrower view was formally renounced. Second, in a technical sense, much like *Calder*, the language in *Fletcher* concerning the Ex Post Facto Clause is arguably dictum, as the case was decided on the basis of the Contracts Clause (also contained in Article I, section 10, of the Constitution).[16] The Georgia law challenged had "the effect of an ex post facto law," but perhaps technically was not an ex post facto law in itself; however, Marshall clearly espoused an equivalence regarding the indisputably civil coverage of the Contracts Clause and the Ex Post Facto Clause.

The court's next discussion of ex post facto came in 1827, in *Ogden v. Saunders*,[17] a case where the outcome was also determined by the Contracts Clause. Much like *Fletcher*, however, the decision illuminated the justices' view regarding the scope of the ex post facto prohibition.[18]

Ogden addressed the constitutionality of a New York State bankruptcy law that discharged a party from a debt resulting from a contract entered into after the bankruptcy law was enacted. Justice Bushrod Washington authored the main opinion of the 4-3 majority, which held that the Contracts Clause was not implicated because the effect of the New York law was prospective, and therefore did not "impair[]" an "obligation of contract."[19] As in *Fletcher v. Peck*, no reference to *Calder* appears, yet the opinion, while averring that the ex post facto prohibition pertains only to punitive laws, expressed a broad view of what qualifies as a penal sanction, stating: "The States are forbidden to pass any bill of attainder or ex post facto law, by which a man shall be punished criminally or penally, by loss of life, of his liberty, property, or reputation, for an act which, at the time of its commission, violated no existing law of the land."[20]

Justice Washington, much like Chief Justice Marshall had in *Fletcher v. Peck*, zeroed in on what he saw as the structural constitutional purpose of the ex post facto prohibition:

Why did the authors of the constitution turn their attention to this subject, which, at the first blush, would appear to be peculiarly fit to be left to the discretion of those who have the police and good government of the State under their management

and control? The only answer to be given is, because laws of this character are oppressive, unjust, and tyrannical; and, as such, are condemned by the universal sentence of civilized man. The injustice and tyranny which characterizes ex post facto
laws, consists altogether in their retrospective operation, which applies with equal
force, although not exclusively, to bills of attainder.[21]

Concurring in the result, Justice William Johnson also noted that the ex
post facto prohibition reflected the framers' concern over state legislative
excesses: "By classing bills of attainder, ex post facto laws, and laws impairing
the obligation of contracts together, the general intent becomes very apparent; it is a general provision against arbitrary and tyrannical legislation
over existing rights, whether of person or property."[22] Significantly, moreover, Johnson also took the opportunity to voice his disagreement with the
Calder Court's narrow criminal-centric focus, with *Calder* yet again going
unmentioned:

> It is true, that some confusion has arisen from an opinion, which seems early, and
> without due examination, to have found its way into this Court; that the phrase
> 'ex post facto,' was confined to laws affecting criminal acts alone. The fact, upon
> examination, will be found otherwise; for neither in its signification or uses is it
> thus restricted. It applies to civil as well as to criminal acts, and with this enlarged
> signification attached to that phrase, the purport of the clause would be, "*that
> the States shall pass no law, attaching to the acts of individuals other effects or
> consequences than those attached to them by the laws existing at their date; and all
> contracts thus construed, shall be enforced according to their just and reasonable
> purport.*"[23]

As it turned out, Justice Johnson's rejection of the criminal-centric scope
of *Calder* was only his opening salvo. As noted in Chapter 2, *Satterlee
v. Matthewson* (1829),[24] decided two years after *Ogden*, contained an extended
critique of the *Calder* view. Johnson, who was not sitting on the court when
Calder was decided some thirty years before, lodged his criticism in a "note"
appended to his concurrence in *Satterlee*, yet another Contracts Clause case,
this time a challenge against a state law that effectively validated a once-void
land deed. The majority opinion in *Satterlee*, authored by Justice Bushrod
Washington, ultimately resolved the case on procedural grounds, avoiding
the Contracts Clause issue.

In his concurring opinion, Johnson provided a thorough critique of what
he termed "the unhappy idea, that the phrase 'ex post facto' in the constitution
of the United States, was confined to criminal cases exclusively; a decision

which leaves a large class of arbitrary legislative acts without the prohibitions of the constitution."[25] After noting that the *Calder* Court's limit was dictum,[26] Johnson offered a point-by-point refutation of the legal and historic claims advanced in its favor by Justice Chase in *Calder*.[27] Johnson also dismissed what he saw as the "great reason which influenced" *Calder*'s narrow construction of the ex post facto prohibition, namely that the justices "considered its application to civil cases as unnecessary, and fully supplied by the prohibition to pass laws impairing the obligation of contracts."[28] The belief, Johnson maintained, resulted from a stunted understanding of the gamut of retroactive laws adversely affecting individuals, beyond contracts:

> [T]he learned judges could not then have foreseen the great variety of forms in which the violations of private right have since been presented to this court. . . . This court has had more than once to toil up hill, in order to bring within the restriction on the states to pass laws violating the obligation of contracts, the most obvious cases to which the constitution was intended, to extend its protection; a difficulty, which it is obvious, might often be avoided, by giving to the phrase ex post facto its original and natural application.[29]

In ensuing years, references to ex post facto continued in the court's decisions, in the course of deciding matters not expressly concerning the prohibition, with Justice Johnson's critique of *Calder* going unmentioned. Indeed, in *Watson v. Mercer* (1834),[30] a case concerning a challenge to a land deed, the court expressly backed *Calder*'s criminal-centric view, stating:

> The constitution of the United States does not prohibit the states from passing retrospective laws generally; but only ex post facto laws. Now it has been solemnly settled by this court, that the phrase, ex post facto laws, is not applicable to civil laws, but to penal and criminal laws, which punish no party for acts antecedently done which were not punishable at all, or not punishable to the extent or in the manner prescribed. In short, ex post facto laws relate to penal and criminal proceedings which impose punishments or forfeitures, and not to civil proceedings which affect private rights retrospectively.[31]

Likewise, *Carpenter v. Pennsylvania* (1854),[32] a challenge to a state law retroactively changing estate tax law to the detriment of the petitioner, the court held that the ex post facto prohibition was not violated because it applies only in "a restricted sense, relating to criminal cases only."[33] In doing so, the court cited *Calder*, and, curiously, *Fletcher v. Peck*, which as noted seemingly adopted a broader view of ex post facto laws.

Civil War and Reconstruction

During and after the Civil War, which commenced in April 1861 and ended in Union victory in 1865, it was not uncommon for states to enact laws requiring "loyalty oaths," often referred to as "ironclad oaths," precluding Confederate sympathizers from voting, running for office, or engaging in specified occupations.[34] One such state was Missouri, which during the Civil War voted against secession, yet remained quite divided, with a secessionist government actually operating in exile (in Texas).

Toward the end of the war, Missouri voters approved an amended state constitution that required that an "Oath of Loyalty" be taken in order to be a qualified voter, hold office, or pursue a variety of occupations, including being an attorney or member of the clergy. In addition to denying participating "in armed hostility to the United States" the oath taker had to declare to never have "by act or word" asserted agreement with the rebels, sympathy for them, aided any of them in any manner, declared "disaffection to the government of the United States," or departed the state to avoid the draft.[35] Failure to take the oath or deceit in so doing, yet engaging in one of the occupations, resulted in a fine and/or imprisonment.[36]

In September 1865, Father John Cummings, a twenty-two or twenty-three-year-old duly ordained Catholic priest in Pike County, Missouri, refused to take the oath yet delivered mass and preached to his small congregation. One day later he was indicted by a local grand jury and arrested.[37] Refusals among clergy to take the oath were not uncommon at the time, nor were arrests. What distinguished Cummings, however, was his refusal to accept release on bail, and his insistence on pleading not guilty, based on his assertion that the oath was an infringement on his religious liberty.[38]

In a trial before a judge without a jury, Cummings admitted to the allegations in the indictment, was found guilty, and assessed a five hundred dollar fine; he refused to pay the fine, post bail for an appeal, or allow another to pay the fine on his behalf.[39] His conviction was upheld by the Missouri Supreme Court and the case headed to the US Supreme Court. The Archbishop of Missouri, opposed to the oath, financed the litigation as a test case to challenge its constitutionality.[40]

Over the course of four days in mid-March 1865 the court heard arguments in the case. Cummings was represented by David Dudley Field, a highly regarded lawyer of the time who, although a confidante of President Lincoln, took up Cummings's cause as the nation was roiled by postwar animosities.[41] Field argued that Missouri imposed a punishment for conduct not previously prohibited in that it "declared punishable or illegal to manifest, by act or word, sympathy with those who were drawn into the Rebellion."[42] He elaborated that

> [i]t would be strange, indeed, if a minister of the Gospel, whose sympathies are with all the children of men—the good and the sinful, the happy and the sorrowing— might not manifest such sympathy by an act of charity or a word of consolation. We will start, then, with the assumption that the act which the plaintiff in error is to affirm that he has not done was at that time lawful to be done.[43]

Cummings, Field concluded, was the subject of an invalid ex post facto law: he was "punished by deprivation of his profession, for an act not punishable when it was committed. . . ."[44]

Counsel for Missouri, defending the law, maintained that the amendment was a proper exercise of the state's police power authority to regulate professions. The amendment merely sought "to determine the qualifications for office and the conditions upon which its citizens may exercise their various callings and pursuits within its jurisdiction."[45]

In a 5-4 decision, issued on January 14, 1867 (reputedly "leaked" in advance by a sitting justice to Missouri partisans hoping to keep white suffrage intact[46]), the court in *Cummings v. Missouri* held that the constitutional amendment qualified as an ex post facto law (and bill of attainder), violative of Article I, section 10, of the Constitution. Remarkably, in light of modern expectations of judicial recusal, the majority opinion was authored by Justice Stephen J. Field, younger brother of chief counsel for petitioner Cummings, David Dudley Field.

Justice Field, a "Union Democrat" appointed by Lincoln and seated on the court in May 1863,[47] was a colorful individual, who rose to prominence in California during the gold rush.[48] The denial of a right to pursue an occupation was an occurrence familiar to Field. Before his appointment to the court, a rival had him disbarred as an attorney in California, and Field successfully argued to the California Supreme Court that he had a right to pursue a lawful calling and could not be deprived of the right without being provided notice and a hearing to contest his alleged misconduct.[49]

In *Cummings*, Justice Field rejected Missouri's claim that the matter should be resolved by deferring to its regulatory police power: "The question is not as to the existence of the power of the State over matters of internal police, but whether that power has been made in the present case an instrument for the infliction of punishment against the inhibition of the Constitution."[50] In a passage presaging another constitutional doctrine—substantive due process—for which his opinions as a whole are today best known,[51] Field then reasoned that the scope of activity identified in the oath lacked connection to an individual's fitness to engage in the occupations prohibited.[52]

Field then turned to the most important part of the decision, marking the first time that the court concluded that a particular sanction qualified as punishment under the Ex Post Facto Clause. According to Field and the *Cummings* majority:

> [t]he deprivation of any rights, civil or political, previously enjoyed, may be punishment, the circumstances attending and the causes of the deprivation determining this fact.... Disqualification from the pursuits of a lawful avocation, or from positions of trust, or from the privilege of appearing in the courts, or acting as an executor, administrator, or guardian, may also, and often has been, imposed as punishment.[53]

Field concluded that "[t]he disabilities created by the constitution of Missouri must be regarded as penalties—they constitute punishment."[54] He cited in support earlier English laws in this category, and noted the shared view expressed in famed eighteenth-century William Blackstone's *Commentaries*.[55] "[A]ll avocations, all honors, all positions, are alike open to every one," Field wrote, "and that in the protection of these rights all are equal before the law. Any deprivation or suspension of any of these rights for past conduct is punishment, and can be in no otherwise defined."[56] Punishment also "embrac[es] deprivation or suspension of political or civil rights."[57]

Having concluded that the disabilities were punitive, Field proceeded to address whether they were prohibited by the Constitution. He emphasized the context in which the amendment originated—during the Civil War in Missouri (a border state), a time of "fierce passions."[58] Reasoning that "[i]t would have been strange . . . had [the amended Missouri Constitution] not exhibited in its provisions some traces of the excitement amidst which the convention held its deliberations,"[59] Field wrote that the ex post facto and bill of attainder prohibitions in Article I were intended to apply in just such a situation: "It was against the excited action of the States, under such influences as these, that the framers of the Federal Constitution intended to guard."[60] In support, Field quoted Chief Justice Marshall's language in *Fletcher v. Peck* (1810):

> "Whatever respect might have been felt for the State sovereignties, it is not to be disguised that the framers of the Constitution viewed with some apprehension the violent acts which might grow out of the feelings of the moment; and that the people of the United States, in adopting that instrument, have manifested a

determination to shield themselves and their property from the effects of those sudden and strong passions to which men are exposed. The restrictions on the legislative power of the States are obviously founded in this sentiment; and the Constitution of the United States contains what may be deemed a bill of rights for the people of each State."[61]

On the substantive merits of the challenge, Field first concluded that the oath requirement constituted a bill of attainder, in that it retroactively presumed Cummings guilty of a crime without benefit of a judicial trial. It did not matter that the provision did not expressly deem Cummings guilty. This is because

> [t]he Constitution deals with substance, not shadows. Its inhibition was levelled at the thing, not the name. It intended that the rights of the citizen should be secure against deprivation for past conduct by legislative enactment, under any form, however disguised. If the inhibition can be evaded by the form of the enactment, its insertion in the fundamental law was a vain and futile proceeding.[62]

Field then addressed the ex post facto challenge, without initially specifically citing the *Calder* categories, concluding that the claim had merit. With regard to whether the disability imposed upon Cummings was based upon behavior that was not a crime when undertaken, Field answered in the affirmative. This was because "[i]t was no offence against any law to enter or leave the State of Missouri for the purpose of avoiding enrolment or draft in the military service of the United States, however much the evasion of such service might be the subject of moral censure."[63] Moreover, insofar as some of the acts specified by Missouri were offenses when undertaken, they incurred "further penalty," satisfying *Calder*'s prohibition of "impos[ing] additional punishment to that prescribed when the act was committed.'"[64] Finally, Field concluded that the provisions violated *Calder* category four, prohibiting changes in rules of evidence, stating that they

> subvert the presumptions of innocence, and alter the rules of evidence. . . . They assume that the parties are guilty; they call upon the parties to establish their innocence; and they declare that such innocence can be shown only in one way— by an inquisition, in the form of an expurgatory oath, into the consciences of the parties.[65]

That the punishment was imposed indirectly by "general provisions" was of no moment. This was because the Constitution intended to secure the liberty of the citizen, cannot be evaded by the form in which the power of the State is exerted. If this were not so, if that which cannot be accomplished by means looking directly to the end, can be accomplished by indirect means, the inhibition may be evaded at pleasure. No kind of oppression can be named, against which the framers of the Constitution intended to guard, which may not be effected [sic].[66]

"Under this form of legislation the most flagrant invasion of private rights, in periods of excitement," Field wrote, "may be enacted, and individuals, and even whole classes, may be deprived of political and civil rights."[67]

On the same day that it issued *Cummings*, January 14, 1867, the court issued its decision in *Ex Parte Garland*.[68] Like *Cummings*, *Garland* addressed a challenge to a loyalty oath, this time imposed by Congress. In July 1862, Congress passed a law requiring that individuals swear that they "neither sought nor accepted nor attempted to exercise the functions of any office whatever under any authority or pretended authority hostile to the United States." The oath was required before being eligible for federal government service (other than the president). In early 1865, Congress added that one could not appear as an attorney in federal court without executing the oath.

The latter provision affected Augustus Garland, a prominent lawyer who during the Civil War served in both the Confederate House of Representatives and the Confederate Senate. In the summer of 1865, President Andrew Johnson pardoned Garland for his support of the Confederacy, based upon his taking an oath that required only that he support the state and federal constitutions and all federal laws regarding the manumission of formerly enslaved persons. Despite the pardon, Garland was unable to practice law in federal courts because he was unable to take the broader oath required by Congress, containing the specific pledge that he had not aided an authority hostile to the United States. Garland presented his pardon to the Supreme Court and sought permission to practice without taking the oath.

As in *Cummings*, Justice Stephen Field wrote for the five-justice majority, and found the oath requirement, and its vocational prohibition, violative of the bill of attainder and ex post facto provisions. Like the Missouri oath, Field concluded, the federal oath

impos[ed] a punishment for some of the acts specified which were not punishable at the time they were committed; and for other of the acts it adds a new punishment to that before prescribed, and it is thus brought within the further inhibition of the Constitution against the passage of an ex post facto law.[69]

As in *Cummings*, the issue was not whether lawyer appearances in federal courts could be regulated by qualification, "but whether that power has been exercised as a means for the infliction of punishment, against the prohibition of the Constitution."[70] Congress, Field reasoned, imposed a retroactive punishment that "operate[d] as a legislative decree of perpetual exclusion. And exclusion from any of the professions or any of the ordinary avocations of life for past conduct can be regarded in no other light than as punishment for such conduct."[71]

Justice Samuel Miller wrote a dissent, joined by three of his brethren, applicable to both *Cummings* and *Garland*. The majority in both cases, Miller wrote, conceived of punishment only in a "loose sense," "as synonymous with chastisement, correction, loss, or suffering to the party supposed to be punished, and not in the legal sense, which signifies a penalty inflicted for the commission of crime."[72] To this, Miller added sardonically:

> And so, in this sence [sic], it is said that whereas persons who had been guilty of the offences mentioned in the oath were, by the laws then in force, only liable to be punished with death and confiscation of all their property, they are by a law passed since these offences were committed, made liable to the enormous additional punishment of being deprived of the right to practise [sic] law![73]

Indeed, Miller reasoned, applying the court's definition of punishment "would make a great number of laws, partaking in no sense of a criminal character, laws for punishment, and therefore ex post facto."[74] Miller offered by way of example a situation in which individuals afflicted with mental illness are subject to a new law requiring their "close confinement until their recovery is assured," asking

> [i]s it an ex post facto law? And, if not, in what does it differ from one? Just in the same manner that the act of Congress does, namely, that the proceeding is civil and not criminal, and that the imprisonment in the one case and the prohibition to practice law in the other, are not punishments in the legal meaning of that term.[75]

Post-*Cummings* and *Garland*

Despite Justice Miller's dissent, the court's broad definition of punishment held sway in later postwar decisions.[76] In *Pierce v. Carskadon* (1872), five years after *Cummings* and *Garland*, the court, in another opinion authored by Justice Field, relied on the decisions to invalidate on ex post facto grounds a

West Virginia law conditioning access to the civil justice system on the taking of an oath attesting to past loyalty.[77]

And in 1878, in *Burgess v. Salmon*,[78] the court, in an opinion authored by Justice Ward Hunt, unanimously invalidated on ex post facto grounds a non-oath-related law. In *Salmon*, the court addressed the constitutionality of a federal law, enforceable by civil suit, to collect a retroactively increased monetary tax on tobacco. The court held that the increased tax amount ($377.80) was punitive, averring that "the ex post facto effect of a law cannot be evaded by giving a civil form to that which is essentially criminal," and offering an analogy it thought dispositive of the question: "Had the proceeding . . . been taken by indictment instead of suit for the excess of the tax, and the one was equally authorized with the other, the proceeding would certainly have fallen within the description of an ex post facto law."[79]

Summary and Appraisal

As the foregoing highlights, during much of the nineteenth century the court, in a variety of contexts, over many decades, and with varied membership, exhibited a willingness to broadly interpret and vigorously apply the ex post facto prohibition. To be sure, upholding the rights of Confederate sympathizers was not well-received by many.[80] In granting relief, however, the court acted in a manner consistent with the purposes and concerns driving adoption of the Ex Post Facto Clause. Although the targets of retroactive laws might have differed—in the Framing Era, most often British loyalists, after the Civil War, Confederate sympathizers—in both contexts political actors were, as Chief Justice put in in *Fletcher v. Peck* (1810), seized by "feelings of the moment," the "sudden and strong passions to which men are exposed," and targeted individuals for past wrongs.

The court's decisions during the time were notable in two other chief respects. First, although they hewed to (or at least did not overtly question) the criminal-centric focus imposed by *Calder*, they embodied a broad conception of punishment, including government prohibitions to pursue a professional calling (*Cummings* and *Garland*) and a civil monetary tax (*Salmon*). Second, the court made clear that when determining whether a law is punitive in nature a court is to look past its formal designation or characterization. This is because, as the *Cummings* Court put it, the ex post facto prohibition "cannot be evaded by the form in which the power of the State is exerted."[81]

This is not to say, however, that the court's broad conception of punishment during the era was without limit. Indeed, in *Gut v. Minnesota* (1869),[82] in a unanimous decision authored by Justice Field, the court rejected an ex post facto challenge to a state constitutional amendment that retroactively changed the location of a criminal trial. Field reasoned that although the district in which a criminal trial is held is "[u]ndoubtedly . . . of the highest importance," it does not violate the ex post facto prohibition. This was because "[a]n ex post facto law does not involve, in any of its definitions, a change of the place of an alleged offense after its commission."[83]

4
Late Nineteenth Century to 1990

A Period of Retrenchment

If the bulk of nineteenth century Supreme Court case law was marked by an expansive view of the clause, subsequent case law has been of a considerably more restrictive nature. As before, the court maintained its position that only retroactive laws of a criminal nature were prohibited, although not without some ambivalence.[1] Its decisions, however, typically lack references to the grand purposes and motivating concerns of the clause, and lack the critical scrutiny manifest in decisions such *Cummings v. Missouri, Ex Parte Garland*, and Burgess *v. Salmon* (discussed in Chapter 3). This chapter examines this shift.

The chapter first examines the introduction of a new exception to ex post facto coverage, retroactive laws that are deemed "procedural" in nature, followed by a discussion of several decisions addressing challenges under *Calder* category three (retroactive increases in punishment). Next, discussion turns to the court's decisions regarding whether a particular retroactive sanction is punitive in nature, which in addition to adopting a more circumscribed view, entailed the emergence of a new analytic framework. Thereafter, the chapter examines several decisions in which the court introduced a new criterion for assessing whether the clause applies, asking whether the retroactive legal change deprived individuals of notice and who therefore relied to their detriment on preexistent law. Finally, attention centers on several decisions during the period addressing how a court determines whether a law is in fact retroactive in nature, an essential threshold requirement of any ex post facto challenge.

Coverage

The Supreme Court's landmark decision in *Calder v. Bull* (1798), Justice Samuel Chase's opinion in particular, articulated several basic criteria governing coverage of the clause. First, the clause is only triggered by retroactive

The Ex Post Facto Clause. Wayne A. Logan, Oxford University Press. © Oxford University Press 2023.
DOI: 10.1093/oso/9780190053505.003.0005

laws of a criminal nature, exclusive of laws that "mollify[y] the rigor of the criminal law."[2] Second, a law must fall within one or more of four categories Chase identified as falling "within the words and the intent of the prohibition":

> 1st. Every law that makes an action, done before the passing of the law, and which was innocent when done, criminal; and punishes such action. 2nd. Every law that aggravates a crime, or makes it greater than it was, when committed. 3rd. Every law that changes the punishment, and inflicts a greater punishment, than the law annexed to the crime, when committed. 4th. Every law that alters the legal rules of evidence, and receives less, or different, testimony, than the law required at the time of the commission of the offence, in order to convict the offender.[3]

Eighty later, in *Burgess v. Salmon* (1878),[4] the court also made clear that a court must look beyond labels that a government might attach to a particular law challenged, stating that "the ex post facto effect of a law cannot be evaded by giving a civil form to that which is essentially criminal."[5]

During the period examined in this chapter, 1880–1990, the court addressed no challenges falling in the first *Calder* category. The remaining three categories, however, afforded the justices ample opportunity to opine on the reach of the clause, sometimes granting, but far more often denying relief. The court also decided a line of cases addressing whether laws of a "procedural" nature are exempted from an ex post facto challenge, which will be examined first.

The "Procedural" Carveout

Laws making retroactive changes to the trial of criminal defendants would seem an obvious basis for mounting an ex post facto challenge. And indeed several such challenges were brought in the late 1800s.

The first, *Kring v. Missouri* (1883),[6] concerned a change in state law precluding a prosecution for first-degree murder after an individual pled guilty to a lesser homicide. Kring's case fit precisely within the law challenged: he was charged with first-degree murder, pled guilty to second-degree murder, and later successfully appealed his conviction. At his new trial he was convicted of first-degree murder and sentenced to death on the basis of a new law that removed the earlier prohibition for first-degree murder prosecution.[7]

The court, by a 5-4 vote, in an opinion authored by Justice Samuel Miller (who, as noted in Chapter 3, dissented in *Cummings* and *Garland*) reversed on ex post facto grounds, based on two *Calder* categories. First, the new Missouri law amounted to a change in a rule of evidence, category four. This was because

"conclusive evidence of innocence" of first-degree murder—Kring's conviction of a lower grade of homicide—was nullified by the new law.[8] Second, the
new law retroactively altered the quantum of punishment imposed on Kring,
category three; when initially convicted, based on his second-degree murder
guilty plea, he could not have been prosecuted for first-degree murder (and
sentenced to death).[9] Moreover, the court reasoned that the *Calder* categories
were not exhaustive, stating that "it is not to be supposed that [*Calder*] . . . undertook to define, by way of exclusion, all the cases to which the constitutional provision would be applicable."[10] In support, the court quoted from a
1809 lower court decision, *United States v. Hall*, authored by Justice Bushrod
Washington sitting as a trial judge, stating that an ex post facto law is one that
retroactively "*alters the situation of a party to his disadvantage*."[11]

Turning to the merits of the case, the court, citing *Calder*, *Cummings*, and
Garland as precedent, emphasized the need to employ a "liberal construction"
of the Ex Post Facto Clause, one "in manifest accord with the purpose of the
constitutional convention to protect the individual rights of life and liberty
against hostile retrospective legislation."[12] Consistent with this view, the court
rejected the assertion that the Missouri law was "procedur[al]" in nature and
categorically outside the ambit of ex post facto coverage.[13] "[A]s applied to a
criminal case, it is obvious that a law which is one of procedure may be obnoxious as an *ex post facto* law, both by the decision in [*Calder v. Bull*], and in
Cummings v. Missouri."[14] In support, the court rhetorically asked:

> Can the law with regard to bail, to indictments, to grand juries, to the trial jury, all
> be changed to the disadvantage of the prisoner by state legislation after the of-
> fence was committed, and such legislation not be held to be ex post facto because
> it relates to procedure . . . ?
>
> And can any substantial right which the law gave the defendant at the time to
> which his guilt relates be taken away from him by ex post facto legislation, because,
> in the use of a modern phrase, it is called a law of procedure? We think it cannot.[15]

Ultimately, the court held that the new Missouri law was invalid because it
unconstitutionally denied "the benefit which the previous law gave [Kring] of
acquittal of the charge of murder in the first degree, on conviction of murder
in the second degree."[16]

Only one year later, *Hopt v. Utah* (1884),[17] the court revised its view on retroactive "procedural" laws. Hopt was convicted of first-degree murder, and
his conviction was reversed on appeal.[18] He was retried and again convicted
of first-degree murder with the prosecution for the first time relying on the
testimony of a convict then serving time for murder, as permitted by an

intervening change in state law.[19] On appeal, Hopt challenged the testimony, arguing that at the time of his alleged offense, Utah law specified that felons were incompetent to testify in criminal trials.[20]

The court, in a unanimous decision authored by Justice John Marshall Harlan, held that retroactive application of the new law was permissible, reasoning that laws relating to witness competency did not come within the *Calder* categories.[21] In doing so, the court made no mention of the fourth *Calder* category barring "[e]very law that alters the legal rules of evidence, and receives less, or different, testimony, than the law required at the time of the commission of the offence, in order to convict the offender."[22] It also ignored the reality that Chief Justice Chase in *Calder* cited in his "instances" of ex post facto laws cases involving retroactive removal of the second witness requirement in treason prosecutions and those barring unsworn and interspousal testimony.[23]

According to the *Hopt* Court, "[s]tatutes which simply enlarge the class of persons who may be competent to testify in criminal cases are not *ex post facto* in their application to prosecutions for crimes committed prior to their passage."[24] Although the law broadened the permissible range of witnesses, it did not change "the quantity or degree of proof necessary to establish . . . guilt," and did not alter the requisite elements or facts necessary for guilt.[25] It thus fell within the category "relat[ing] to modes of procedure only, in which no one can be said to have a vested right, and which the state, upon grounds of public policy, may regulate at pleasure."[26]

Next, in a pair of decisions decided in 1898, the court again modified its stance, concluding that changes in procedural law can at times be improper. Such was the case in *Thompson v. Utah*.[27] Thompson killed a man when applicable law guaranteed a jury of twelve, but he was ultimately tried by a jury of eight, as permitted by a retroactive change in state law. Justice John Marshall Harlan, again writing for the court, concluded that the change in jury composition was of the problematic procedural kind condemned in *Kring*. The new law "materially impair[ed] the right of the accused to have the question of his guilt determined according to the law as it was when the offence was committed."[28] It could not "be said that the [law] . . . did not deprive [Thompson] of a substantial right involved in his liberty, and did not materially alter the situation to his disadvantage."[29] At the same time, however, Justice Harlan acknowledged the difficulty of applying the materiality test:

> The difficulty is not so much as to the soundness of the general rule that an accused has no vested right in particular modes of procedure, as in determining whether particular statutes by their operation take from an accused any right that was

regarded, at the time of the adoption of the Constitution, as vital for the protection of life and liberty, and which he enjoyed at the time of the commission of the offence charged against him.[30]

Roughly a week after deciding *Thompson v. Utah*, the court rejected an ex post facto challenge in *Thompson v. Missouri*.[31] Thompson was convicted of first-degree murder by means of strychnine poisoning.[32] At trial, the court admitted into evidence handwritten letters of Thompson so that they could be compared to an allegedly forged strychnine prescription. When the crime occurred such exemplars were inadmissible, but the Missouri legislature later passed a law allowing their consideration.[33] Thompson challenged the admission of the letters on ex post facto grounds.[34]

The court rejected the claim, reasoning that the legal change was procedural in nature.[35] Yet again writing for the court, Justice Harlan concluded that although *Calder* singled out for concern "legal rules of evidence," Thompson failed to show that he had "any vested right in the rule of evidence" applicable at the time of his offense, or that the new rule "entrenched upon any of the essential rights belonging to one put on trial for a public offence."[36] A criminal defendant "is not entitled of right to be tried in the exact mode, in all respects, that may be prescribed . . . at the time of the commission of the offence . . . so far as mere modes of procedure are concerned."[37] Justice Harlan added, however, that a procedural change could violate the clause when it "alters the situation of a party to his disadvantage," insofar as it affects a "substantial right."[38]

The substantive/procedural line-drawing challenge continued in the ensuing decades, assuming new forms. In *Beazell v. Ohio* (1925),[39] the court rejected a challenge to a law that retroactively altered the ability of codefendants to pursue separate trials. At the time of the defendants' offense, Ohio law expressly allowed for separate trials, but by the time of trial, the law had changed to permit separate trials only "for good cause shown."[40] After being tried jointly and convicted, the defendants challenged the law on ex post facto grounds.[41]

In a short opinion, authored by Justice Harlan Fiske Stone, the court unanimously rejected the claim. In doing so, the court used a novel formulation of the *Calder* categories. Rather than recounting the traditional four categories identified in *Calder*, the *Beazell* Court articulated a tripartite framework, which at once omitted the second and fourth *Calder* categories, and specified a new category concerning any "defense" retroactively withdrawn by law.[42] According to the court, an ex post facto law is one "which punishes as a crime an act previously committed, which was innocent when done; which makes more burdensome the punishment for a crime, after its commission, or which deprives one charged with crime of any defense available according to law the act was committed. . . ."[43]

The court then concluded that the change in Ohio law was a procedural one, affecting only how a defendant's trial was to be conducted.[44] The change did not deprive Beazell "of any defense previously available, nor affect the criminal quality of the act charged."[45] Nor did the change alter "the legal definition of the offense or the punishment to be meted out."[46] The law merely "restored a mode of trial deemed appropriate at common law, with discretionary power in the court to direct separate trials."[47]

The court again then equivocated, suggesting that some retroactive procedural changes might be problematic: "there may be procedural changes which operate to deny to the accused a defense available under the laws in force at the time of the commission of his offense, or which otherwise affect him in such a harsh and arbitrary manner as to fall within the constitutional prohibition."[48] However, "it is now well settled that statutory changes in the mode of trial or the rules of evidence, which do not deprive the accused of a defense and which operate only in a limited and unsubstantial manner to his disadvantage, are not prohibited."[49] Before concluding, the court again noted the obvious line-drawing challenge its decisions had created:

> Just what alterations of procedure will be held to be of sufficient moment to transgress the constitutional prohibition cannot be embraced within a formula or stated in a general proposition. The distinction is one of degree. But the constitutional provision was intended to secure substantial personal rights against arbitrary and oppressive legislation, and not to limit the legislative control of remedies and modes of procedure which do not affect matters of substance.[50]

A little over fifty years after *Beazell* came *Dobbert v. Florida* (1977),[51] another major decision concerning the substantive/procedural distinction. In *Dobbert*, when the defendant committed several killings in Florida state law provided that a capital defendant (1) would be sentenced to death unless a majority of the jury recommended life and (2) that the jury's decision was final.[52] After the killings, however, the Florida legislature adopted a new capital sentencing law, necessitated by the Supreme Court's ruling in *Furman v. Georgia* (1972) rendering the original Florida law (and the capital laws of other states) unconstitutional.[53] The new law provided for a separate sentencing proceeding, in lieu of the prior approach that consolidated the guilt-sentencing phase, and made the jury's life/death decision only advisory, permitting the trial court to override it.[54] Defendant's jury voted 10-2 to impose life and the trial court overrode the recommendation.[55] Contending that the new law deprived him of a substantial right to have the jury determine whether he was to live or die, defendant challenged the new law on ex post facto grounds.[56]

The court, by a 6-3 vote in an opinion authored by Justice William Rehnquist, concluded that the new law was procedural in nature and therefore rejected the claim.[57] Quoting from *Beazell*'s more limited tripartite scope of coverage,[58] the court stated that "[e]ven though it may work to the disadvantage of a defendant, a procedural change is not ex post facto."[59] The new law was "clearly procedural . . [it] simply altered the methods employed in determining whether the death penalty was to be imposed; there was no change in the quantum of punishment attached to the crime."[60] Quoting *Hopt*, the court stated that " '[t]he crime for which the present defendant was indicted, the punishment prescribed therefor, and the quantity or degree of proof necessary to establish his guilt, all remained unaffected by the subsequent statute.' "[61]

The court also reasoned that Dobbert was not disadvantaged by the change in law. This was so even though the prior law turned solely on the jury's life/ death decision, and that the jury in Dobbert's case voted for life (10-2), only to be overridden by the trial judge's decision that death was warranted. To the court, it "[could not] be said with assurance" that even under the old sentencing regime the jury would have returned a life sentence,[62] which the jury in fact did (under the new bifurcated law). Moreover, by empowering the trial court to override the jury's decision, along with other changes including allowing defendants to introduce mitigating evidence in a new post-guilt-sentencing phase, and providing for appellate review of the death decision, the new law actually afforded Dobbert "with more, rather than less, judicial protection."[63]

Thirteen years after *Dobbert* came *Collins v. Youngblood* (1990),[64] a decision cementing the court's procedural law exception. In *Collins*, the defendant was sentenced to a term of imprisonment and required to pay a fine, yet the fine was not authorized by law.[65] Under Texas law, the error entitled the defendant to a new trial, but while his habeas corpus petition was on appeal, the Texas legislature enacted a law expressly allowing appellate courts to reform "improper verdicts," obviating any need for remand.[66] The Texas Court of Criminal Appeals modified Collins's sentence and reinstated his prison term, leading to an ex post facto challenge.[67]

The court, by a 7-2 vote in yet another opinion authored by Justice Rehnquist (now chief justice), rejected the claim. The court concluded that "[t]he *Beazell* formulation is faithful to our best knowledge of the original understanding of the Ex Post Facto Clause: Legislatures may not retroactively [1] alter the definition of crimes or [2] increase the punishment for criminal acts."[68] In a footnote, the court acknowledged that *Beazell* had modified *Calder*, in particular omitting reference to changes to rules of evidence as being ex post facto, but inferred that "[a]s cases subsequent to *Calder* make clear, this language was not intended to prohibit the application of new evidentiary rules in trials for crimes committed before the changes."[69] The majority made no mention, however, of its omission of *Beazell*'s new third category, concerning retroactive deprivation of a defense.

Applying its two-category test, the court found no ex post facto violation, reasoning that the new law constituted a merely procedural change that (1) neither retroactively altered the definition of defendant's crime of conviction nor (2) retroactively increased its punishment.[70] Moreover, the court disavowed its prior view that changes in procedural law can implicate the Ex Post Facto Clause when they affect "substantial" rights or "matters of substance."[71] In doing so the court overruled *Kring v. Missouri* (1883)[72] and *Thompson v. Utah* (1898),[73] because their focus on "substantial protections" and "personal rights"[74] strayed from its two-category "analytical framework" and had "caused confusion."[75]

Collins was a major decision, for two chief reasons. First, the court seemingly truncated the four *Calder* categories to two.[76] And it did so while insisting that "the prohibition which may not be evaded is the one defined by the *Calder* categories,"[77] and relying on *Beazell v. Ohio*,[78] which it extolled as "faithful to [the Court's] best knowledge of the original understanding of the Ex Post Facto Clause,"[79] which itself had prescribed a three-category test.[80] To put this shift in perspective, *Calder* itself not only identified four categories, it also intimated even greater inclusiveness by stating that "all these, and similar laws, are manifestly unjust and oppressive."[81]

Second, *Collins* imposed a near-categorical exception for any retroactive change deemed procedural. Building upon its earlier statement in *Dobbert v. Florida* (1977) that a procedural change is permissible "[e]ven though it may work to the disadvantage of a defendant,"[82] the court broadly defined a procedural rule as one making "changes in the procedures by which a criminal case is adjudicated."[83] The *Collins* Court did, however, state that "simply labeling a law 'procedural,' a legislature does not thereby immunize it from scrutiny under the *Ex Post Facto* Clause . . Subtle *ex post facto* violations are no more permissible than overt ones."[84] Yet this caveat is less important than it might seem given the court's shift to a two-category test, prohibiting laws that "[1] retroactively alter the definition of crimes or [2] increase the punishment for criminal acts."[85] Thus, even though procedural rules are not categorically outside the scope of ex post facto protection,[86] the court stated that legal changes are permitted even when they burden "substantial protections" previously afforded.[87]

Imposing Greater Punishment (*Calder* Category Three): Conditions and Logistics

Calder category three prohibits a retroactive law "that changes the punishment, and inflicts a greater punishment, than the law annexed to the crime, when committed," a category preserved by *Collins*. The court's decisions during the time period focused upon in this chapter concerning what qualifies as a "greater punishment" arose in a variety of circumstances.

One recurring circumstance concerned whether conditions of confinement and methods of execution fall within the category. In its first decision, *In re Medley* (1890),[88] the court addressed a challenge to a new Colorado law requiring that individuals facing the death penalty be kept in solitary confinement until time of execution. With Justice Samuel Miller writing, the court by an 8-1 margin held that the shift to solitary confinement, which at the time of defendant's crime was neither authorized nor practiced, was "an additional punishment of the most important and painful character."[89] The court also found constitutional fault with another provision of the new law requiring that the precise date and time of execution be kept secret from the condemned individual. The change, Justice Miller wrote, produced "an immense mental anxiety amounting to a great increase of the offender's punishment."[90] "One of the most horrible feelings" experienced by those awaiting execution "is the uncertainty . . . which may exist for the period of four weeks, as to the precise time and execution shall take place."[91]

In subsequent decisions, however, the court made clear that not all changes to execution protocols and mechanics are problematic. In the same year that *In re Medley* was decided, the court in *Holden v. Minnesota*[92] held that changes to when and how hangings were to occur, the number and backgrounds of witnesses, and the exclusion of news reporters, were permissible because they were "regulations" that did not affect "substantial rights."[93] "Whether a convict, sentenced to death, shall be executed before or after sunrise, or within or without the walls of the jail, or within or outside of some other enclosure, and whether the enclosure within which he is executed shall be higher than the gallows, thus excluding the view of persons outside, are regulations that do not affect his substantial rights."[94]

Similarly, in *Rooney v. North Dakota* (1905),[95] the court unanimously rejected a challenge to several retroactive changes to the state's death penalty law. Writing for the court, Justice Harlan reasoned that one change—requiring that a condemned party be kept in "close confinement" for six to nine months, as opposed to being kept in a jail for three to six months—extended Rooney's life and was "favorable, rather than unfavorable to him"[96] As for the new "close confinement" requirement, it was permissible because, unlike solitary confinement (found problematic in *In re Medley*), it did not increase the punishment "in any substantial sense."[97] Finally, changing the location of the execution, from a county jail to the state penitentiary, was not problematic: "However material the place of confinement may be in case of some crimes not involving life, the place of execution, when the punishment is death ... is of no practical consequence to the criminal."[98]

In *Malloy v. South Carolina* (1915),[99] the court addressed whether changing the method of execution from hanging to electrocution presented ex post facto concern. The court rejected the challenge, reasoning that the change was based on "a well grounded belief that electrocution is less painful and more humane than hanging."[100] In short, "[t]he punishment was not increased, and some of the odious features incident to the old method were abated."[101]

As the foregoing survey suggests, the court was disinclined to find ex post facto fault with laws regulating the logistical incidents of punishment. The sole exception, *In re Medley* (1905), found that the use of solitary confinement and withholding information on the day and time of execution qualitatively—if not quantitatively—increased the punishment of a condemned killer.

Imposing Greater Punishment (*Calder* Category Three): Sentence Length

The court was far more receptive to claims based on alleged retroactive increases in sentence length.

In *Lindsey v. Washington* (1937),[102] the court unanimously condemned a new state law changing a maximum prison sentence of fifteen years to a mandatory sentence of fifteen years. The court acknowledged that it was possible that Lindsey could have been sentenced to fifteen years under the predecessor statute, but this was not dispositive. This was because "the ex post facto clause looks to the standard of punishment prescribed by a statute, rather than to the sentence actually imposed. The Constitution forbids the application of any new punitive measure to a crime already consummated, to the detriment or material disadvantage of the wrongdoer."[103]

Two other cases likewise granted relief in cases extending prison terms. In *Weaver v. Graham* (1981),[104] the court unanimously held that the retroactive cancellation of "gain time" for prisoners, based on good behavior, was invalid because it was "disadvantageous": it "reduce[d] the number of monthly gain-time credits available to an inmate . . . By definition, this reduction in gain-time accumulation lengthens the period that someone in petitioner's position must spend in prison."[105] Echoing the perspective adopted in *Lindsey*, the *Weaver* Court assessed the overall effect on individuals, not necessarily the petitioner, stating that the "inquiry looks to challenged provision, and not to any special circumstances that may mitigate its effect on the particular individual."[106]

In the other case, *Miller v. Florida* (1987),[107] the court unanimously held that the petitioner's sentence was impermissibly increased as the result of sentencing guidelines, enacted after his offense. Under the former sentencing regime, a presumptive range of three and one-half to four and one-half years in prison was in effect, subject to judicial departure based on demanding grounds, while under the new law seven years (which the petitioner received) was within the presumptive range. Citing *Weaver*, the court found that the new guideline made "'more onerous the punishment for crimes committed before its enactment.'"[108]

Taken together, *Lindsay* (1937), *Weaver* (1981), and *Miller* (1987)—all unanimous decisions by the court—highlight the relative ease with which *Calder* category three claims can be made. This is largely due to the fact that the claims concern quantitative changes in prison terms, which more easily lend themselves to establishing that an individual was materially disadvantaged.

Parameters of "Punishment"

As a result of *Calder*, an indispensable component of any successful ex post facto claim is that the challenged law is criminal or punitive in nature. *Calder* itself unfortunately shed no light on the taxonomic analysis; the change in probate law challenged in the case was plainly civil. Later cases, in the early mid-nineteenth century, were equally silent, but in the post-Civil War era, the analytic rubric for answering what will be called the "punishment question" began to take shape.

Most notably, as discussed in Chapter 3, in *Cummings v. Missouri* and *Ex Parte Garland*, both decided in 1867, the court was asked to determine whether a law precluding pursuit of a vocation based on prior conduct (sympathy for or involvement in the Confederacy) was punitive. After noting that governments possess the prerogative to regulate professions, the *Cummings* Court distinguished this authority from their power to punish, stating: "The question is not as to the existence of the power of the State over matters of internal police, but whether that power has been made in the present case an instrument for the infliction of punishment against the inhibition of the Constitution."[109] Fealty to the Confederate cause, the court reasoned, lacked any connection to fitness to engage in the specified vocations. The prohibition therefore

> reached the person, not the calling. It was exacted, not from any notion that the several acts designated indicated unfitness for the callings, but because it was thought that the several acts deserved punishment, and that for many of them there was no way to inflict punishment except by depriving the parties, who had committed them, of some of the rights and privileges of the citizen.[110]

The court thereafter deemed vocational disbarment, as well as "deprivation or suspension of political or civil rights,"[111] punitive in nature.

In addition to addressing the kinds of deprivations that qualify as punitive, *Cummings* provided a generous analytic framework for identifying punishment. The court emphasized the need to evaluate the legislative climate motivating the retroactive law challenged—"the circumstances attending and the causes of the deprivation."[112] In *Cummings*, the "circumstances" were the "fierce passions" of Radical Republican legislators, which the court weighed in finding that the occupational disbarments were punitive.[113]

The discussion will now pick up where *Cummings* and *Garland* left off, surveying the very substantial changes that followed.

Particular Disabilities

In *Hawker v. New York* (1898),[114] the court addressed a challenge to a New York law that made it a misdemeanor for a physician, after having been convicted of a felony, to practice medicine. Hawker, who had been convicted of performing an abortion (a felony at the time) over a decade before, was convicted under the new law after practicing medicine. Like Cummings and Garland before him, Hawker contended that the vocational prohibition was a punishment, retroactively enhancing the sentence he previously served.

By a 6-3 vote, with Justice David Brewer writing for the majority, the court rejected the claim, deeming the prohibition regulatory, not punitive, in character, and therefore a proper exercise of governmental police power. Brewer wrote that "[t]he state is not seeking to further punish a criminal, but only to protect its citizens from physicians of bad character. The vital matter is not the conviction, but the violation of law."[115] He distinguished *Cummings* and *Garland*, reasoning that the prohibitions deemed punitive there had no bearing on the petitioners' fitness to work in the professions prohibited.[116] The law challenged in *Hawker*, however, said nothing about character requirements and any negative presumption of poor character that might flow from a conviction.[117]

In his dissent, joined by Justices Peckham and McKenna, Justice John Marshall Harlan rejected the majority's conclusion that the statute imposed a character-related qualification, based upon a prior conviction, rather than an additional punishment for it. According to Harlan, the new law did "not deal with [Hawker's] present moral character. It seize[d] upon a past offense, and makes that, and that alone, the substantial ingredient of a new crime, and the conviction of it years ago the conclusive evidence of that new crime."[118] The new law, Harlan wrote, acted "directly upon and enhance[d] the punishment of the antecedently committed offense by depriving the person of his property and right, and preventing his earning his livelihood in his profession, only because of his past, and, in this case, expiated, offense against the criminal law."[119]

Today, well over a century after it was decided, *Hawker* remains a key precedent in what has turned out to be the court's now-decades long aversion for viewing civic and professional disabilities as punitive for ex post facto purposes.[120] In modern parlance, such disabilities are known as "collateral consequences," which are not deemed punishment but rather "civil" and "regulatory," and therefore lawfully imposed retroactively.[121]

Hawker's influence was evidenced in a considerable number of subsequent decisions concerning the nation's increasingly restrictive immigration laws. *Mahler v. Eby* (1924)[122] is emblematic of this shift. Petitioners there were immigrant "aliens" convicted in 1918 under the federal Selective Service Act, and later subject to deportation based on federal law amended in 1920.[123] They argued that the deportation was a punishment, retroactively imposed for their earlier conviction. In a unanimous decision, with Chief Justice William Howard Taft writing, the court rejected petitioners' ex post facto claim. The court stated that "deportation, while it may be burdensome and severe for the alien, is not punishment."[124] In enacting the 1920 law, Congress "was not increasing the punishment for the crimes of which petitioners had been convicted, by requiring their deportation. . . ."[125] Rather, citing *Hawker* in support, the government was exercising its sovereign police power.[126] Congress was "only seeking to rid the country of persons who had shown by their career that their continued presence here would not make for the safety or welfare of society."[127]

Subsequent decisions adhered to this view, including in relation to challenges brought amid increasing concern over the presence of former Communist Party members. In *Harisiades v. Shaughnessy* (1952),[128] the main petitioner was a legal resident alien from Greece who from 1925 to 1939 was a member of the party, and the US government sought to deport him several years later based on the Alien Registration Act of 1940. A 7-2 majority, in an opinion authored by Justice Robert Jackson, found no ex post facto problem.

Before getting to the merits of the case, the court stated that an ex post facto challenge was only actionable against a punishment and that deportation was not punishment, even though "[b]oth of these doctrines as original proposals might be debatable."[129] The court then refused to reconsider its designation of deportation as non-punitive,[130] a position that it reiterated in several other challenges by ex-Communist Party members in the 1950s.[131]

The majority's decision prompted a vigorous dissent by Justice Hugo Black, joined by fellow devout civil libertarian William O. Douglas,[132] which empha-sized the major negative personal consequences of deportation.[133] Five years after *Harisiades*, in *Lehman v. United States ex rel. Carson* (1957),[134] Black, in a concurring opinion joined by Douglas, wrote that

> [w]hat is being done to these respondents seems to me to be the precise evil the ex post facto clause was designed to prevent . . . To banish them from home, family, and adopted country is punishment of the most drastic kind whether done at the time they were convicted or later.[135]

Two years earlier, in *Marcello v. Bonds* (1955),[136] Douglas in a solo dissent stated that deportation

> may be as severe a punishment as loss of livelihood . . . [and may result] 'in loss of both property and life, or of all that makes life worth living.' I find nothing in the Constitution that exempts aliens from the operation of ex post facto laws . . . In the absence of a rational connection between the imposition of the penalty of de-portation and the present desirability of the alien as a resident in this country, the conclusion is inescapable that the Act merely adds a new punishment for a past of-fense. That is the injustice that the Ex Post Facto Clause was designed to prevent.[137]

In *Garner v. Board of Public Works of City of Los Angeles* (1951),[138] a city enacted a new law that conditioned continued employment on taking an oath and swearing out an affidavit attesting lack of involvement with the Communist Party. The court, by a 5-4 vote, rejected petitioners' ex post facto challenge, reasoning that the law was not retroactive in effect because prior law had similar coverage. The court's treatment of the petitioners' bill of attainder challenge, however, was more merit based, focusing on whether the challenged vocational prohibition was punitive. The *Garner* Court distinguished *Cummings* and *Garland*, citing *Hawker* and other decisions backing the power of governments to impose "reasonable qualifications" on employment.[139] The three dissenting Justices (Burton, Douglas, and Black) took strong issue with the majority's assessment that the deprivation was non-punitive, with Justice Black ending his dissent by stating the outcome "weaken[ed] one of the Constitution's great guarantees of individual liberty."[140]

An Analytic Framework Emerges

In addition to addressing whether particular disabilities qualify as punishment, the court, starting in the 1960s, issued several major decisions providing the first analytic rubric for answering the "punishment question." Before discussing the decisions, it is first necessary to consider a case decided in 1958—*Trop v. Dulles*[141]—which while not an ex post facto challenge, provided a key precedent for subsequent ex post facto-related decisions.

In *Trop*, the petitioner, who had been convicted by a military court of desertion during World War II, challenged a federal law allowing for his expatriation from the United States, arguing that stripping him of his citizenship violated the Eighth Amendment's prohibition of cruel and unusual punishment. In resolving the question, the five-member plurality first needed to determine whether the sanction was punitive, and it did so by anchoring its analysis in its ex post facto (and bill of attainder) jurisprudence. Writing for the plurality, Chief Justice Earl Warren stated that the court "generally based its determination upon the purpose of the [challenged] statute,"[142] adding in a footnote that "[o]f course, the severity of the disability imposed as well as all the circumstances surrounding the legislative enactment [are] relevant to this decision."[143] "If the statute imposes a disability for the purpose of punishment—that is, to reprimand the wrongdoer, to deter others, etc., it has been considered penal."[144] However, a statute is non-penal, Warren wrote, if it "imposes a disability, not to punish, but to accomplish some other legitimate governmental purpose."[145] With statutes having both a penal and non-penal effect, "the controlling nature of such statutes normally depends on the evident purpose of the legislature."[146]

Applying the foregoing, Warren concluded that the "purpose of taking away citizenship from a convicted deserter is simply to punish him. There is no other legitimate purpose that the statute could serve."[147] This purpose was distinct from that motivating deportation, an action by a sovereign based on unfitness of a noncitizen to remain in the country.[148] Warren thereafter found that depatriation was "cruel and unusual" under the Eighth Amendment, noting that it entailed "the total destruction of the individual's status in organized society. It is a form of punishment more primitive than torture, for it destroys for the individual the political existence that was centuries in the development."[149]

The *Trop* Court's focus on legislative purpose figured centrally in later cases concerning the ex post facto "punishment question." Two years later, *DeVeau v. Braisted* (1960)[150] addressed an ex post facto challenge against a New York State law banning anyone convicted of a felony from soliciting or receiving union dues. DeVeau, who had previously been convicted of a felony, argued that the prohibition punished him for his past conviction, a claim the court rejected. "The question in each case where unpleasant consequences are brought to bear upon an individual for prior conduct," Justice Felix Frankfurter wrote the five-member plurality, "is whether the legislative aim was to punish that individual for past activity, or whether the restriction of the individual comes about as a relevant incident to a regulation of a present situation, such as the proper qualifications for a profession."[151] Citing *Hawker*, the court held that the "proof was overwhelming" that the law challenged sought not to punish ex-felons "but to devise what was felt to be a much-needed scheme of regulation of the waterfront, and for the effectuation of that scheme it became important whether individuals had previously been convicted of a felony."[152]

Flemming v. Nestor (1960)[153] was decided that same year. Nestor challenged the loss of social security benefits he had accrued before being lawfully deported in 1956, based on his Communist Party membership in the 1930s. He claimed that he was unconstitutionally punished without a trial and that the deprivation of benefits was barred by the bill of attainder and ex post facto prohibitions.

By a 5-4 vote, with Justice John Marshall Harlan II (the grandson of John Marshall Harlan) writing for the majority, the court held that the deprivation of benefits was not punitive. Harlan reformulated the *Trop* test slightly as one focusing on the need to "discern the objects on which the enactment in question was focused."[154] Elaborating, he stated that punitiveness exists when the "source of legislative concern can be thought to be the activity or status from which the individual is barred."[155] If there is no "persuasive showing" of what *Cummings* called a purpose to " 'reach the person, not the calling,' "[156] the law is non-punitive. This is so "despite the often-severe effects such regulation has had on the persons subject to it,"[157] a statement the court qualified as it had in

Trop, but this time espousing the opposite view—that "the severity of a sanction is not determinative of its character as 'punishment.'"[158]

Building upon its purpose-based test, the court stated that "only the clearest proof could suffice to establish" an impermissible punitive intent, and that a "presumption of constitutionality" must inform the analysis, "forbid[ding] [a court] to lightly to choose that reading of the statute's setting which will invalidate it over which will save it."[159] Legislative intent was the focus, even though the court acknowledged that "[j]udicial inquiries into Congressional motives are at best a hazardous matter, and when that inquiry seeks to go behind objective manifestations it becomes a dubious affair indeed."[160]

The majority discerned no "punitive design" on the part of Congress: "the sanction is the mere denial of a noncontractual governmental benefit. No affirmative disability or restraint is imposed, and certainly nothing approaching the 'infamous punishment' of imprisonment."[161] And, unlike in *Cummings*, it could not be said that denying deportees social security benefits "bears no rational connection to the purposes of the legislation of which it is a part, and must therefore be taken as evidencing a Congressional desire to punish."[162]

Applying its "clearest proof" standard, the court found it impossible to find in the "meagre" legislative history of the challenged law "the unmistakable evidence of punitive intent which . . . is required before a Congressional enactment of this kind may be struck down."[163] Moreover, even if the history showed that Congress was concerned with the ground for deportation (previous Communist Party membership), "this, standing alone, would [not] suffice to establish a punitive purpose."[164] Such a situation "would still be a far cry" from a situation such as *Cummings* "where the legislation was on its face aimed at particular individuals."[165]

The majority's decision prompted three dissents (embodying the views of four dissenting justices), each condemning what was seen as the majority's significant departure from *Cummings* and *Garland*.[166] In his dissent, Justice Black wrote that the result "indicated the extent to which people are willing to go these days to overlook violations of the Constitution perpetrated against anyone who has ever innocently belonged to the Communist Party."[167] Black argued that Nestor was punished twice for being a Communist—first with his deportation and then denial of his accrued benefits earned over the years. Both were "in accord with the general fashion of the day—that is, is to punish in every way possible anyone who ever made the mistake of being a Communist in this country or who is supposed ever to have been associated with anyone who made that mistake."[168] On the ultimate question of whether Nestor was punished, Black wrote:

I think the Act does impose punishment even in a classic sense. The basic reason for Nestor's loss of his insurance payments is that he was once a Communist. This man, now 69 years old, has been driven out of the country where he has lived for 43 years to a land where he is practically a stranger, under an Act authorizing his deportation many years after his Communist membership. Now a similar ex post facto law deprives him of his insurance, which, while petty and insignificant in amount to this great Government, may well be this exile's daily bread. . . .[169]

Justice William Brennan, in a dissent joined by Chief Justice Warren and Justice Douglas, wrote at length as well. After noting that the laws challenged in *Cummings* and *Garland* were adopted when the nation was still gripped by the "fierce passions" of the Civil War, Brennan asserted that the court should not ignore that the law Nestor challenged was "enacted in a similar atmosphere. Our judicial detachment from the realities of the national scene should not carry us so far. Our memory of the emotional climate stirred by the question of communism in the early 1950s cannot be so short."[170]

Trop, DeVeau, and especially *Nestor* are important decisions because they shifted ex post facto analysis in a fundamental way by creating a new test—one focusing on legislative intent and purpose, not the nature or effect of a government-imposed disability. Although legislative purpose figured to some extent in prior decisions, certainly *Cummings* and *Garland*, the three later decisions made it a dominant threshold consideration. What's more, under *Nestor*, there must be the "clearest proof" of punitive legislative motivation, which must overcome a "presumption of constitutionality."

In one sense, the court's new standard was unremarkable: separation of powers obliges that courts show deference to legislative enactments,[171] and the "avoidance canon" similarly obliges that courts avoid invalidating laws on constitutional grounds when possible.[172] *Nestor,* with its "clearest proof" standard, is very significant because it transformed these premises into substantive constitutional law, formally imposing a heightened new burden in ex post facto challenges. As discussed in Chapter 6, both the demanding proof requirement and presumption of legitimacy are ill-suited to ex post facto claims, which concern laws having retroactive effect, a matter of major concern to the framers, a point emphasized by Justice Black in his *Nestor* dissent.[173]

The early 1960s witnessed yet another critically important development in the court's analytic approach to the punishment question. In *Kennedy v. Mendoza-Martinez* (1963),[174] the court addressed another part of the immigration law challenged in *Trop v. Dulles*, which also expatriated individuals, but for leaving the country to avoid the draft (as opposed to military desertion). The petitioners argued that their automatic depatriation without procedural protections violated the Fifth and Sixth Amendments of the Constitution.

A five-member majority of the court held that the depatriation was punishment, as found in *Trop*, not a non-criminal regulation exercised pursuant to congressional war and foreign affairs authority. The main opinion, authored by Justice Arthur Goldberg, which Justice Brennan joined in a concurring opinion as the fifth vote, stated that "[t]he punitive nature" of depatriation was "evident under the tests traditionally applied to determine whether an Act of Congress is penal or regulatory in character, even though in other cases this problem has been extremely difficult and elusive of solution."[175] He then articulated a seven-factor test that considers:

[1] whether the sanction involves an affirmative disability or restraint,

[2] whether it has historically been regarded as a punishment,

[3] whether it comes into play only on a finding of scienter,

[4] whether its operation will promote the traditional aims of punishment—retribution and deterrence,

[5] whether the behavior to which it applies is already a crime,

[6] whether an alternative purpose to which it may rationally be connected is assignable for it, and

[7] whether it appears excessive in relation to the alternative purpose assigned.[176]

Goldberg added that the factors "are all relevant to the inquiry, and may often point in differing directions."[177] "Absent conclusive evidence of congressional intent as to the penal nature of a statute, these factors must be considered in relation to the statute on its face."[178]

The court ultimately did not apply the foregoing test, although it was "convinced that application of the[] criteria to the face of the statutes support[ed] that they are punitive."[179] Rather, based on a lengthy analysis of the congressional record, considering both the predecessor and amended statute challenged, the court found what it considered "conclusive[]" and "unmistakable" evidence of punitive intent on the part of Congress.[180]

The *Mendoza-Martinez* test, although not actually applied in the decision bearing its name, and addressing whether a sanction is punitive such that the trial protections of the Fifth and Sixth Amendments must be provided, has become the benchmark in ex post facto challenges when deciding whether a sanction is punitive. Despite the court's insistence that its factors are " 'neither exhaustive nor dispositive,' " but are " 'useful guideposts,' "[181] the *Mendoza-Martinez* test is now the definitive framework for assessing whether the "effects" of a sanction are punitive for ex post facto purposes. The very significant shortcomings of the framework, combined with the threshold requirement (from *Nestor v. Flemming*) that a petitioner marshal the "clearest proof" that a retroactive law is intended to be punitive, are addressed at length in Chapter 6.

"Fair Notice" and Reliance as a Purpose

As discussed in Chapters 1 and 2, the framers of the Constitution included the Ex Post Facto Clause because of their concern over capricious or vindictive retroactive laws enacted in response to "feelings of the moment."[182] As Justice Chase put it in *Calder v. Bull* (1798), "the advocates of such laws were stimulated by ambition, or personal resentment and vindictive malice. To prevent such and similar acts of violence and injustice, . . . the federal and state legislatures were prohibited from passing any bill of attainder, or any ex post facto law."[183]

In 1977, in *Dobbert v. Florida*,[184] discussed earlier in another context, the Supreme Court introduced a new purpose supporting the ex post facto prohibition, providing a new consideration in assessing whether a retroactive criminal law is invalid. Dobbert, a defendant in a Florida capital murder prosecution, claimed that he suffered an ex post facto violation because at the time of the alleged murders no valid death penalty law was "in effect." This was because shortly after the killings the US Supreme Court declared in *Furman v. Georgia* (1972) that the death penalty as then applied was unconstitutional. A few months later, the Florida legislature enacted a new capital punishment law, which was used in defendant's 1974 capital trial, where he received the death penalty.

The court, with Justice Rehnquist writing for the 6-3 majority, rejected Dobbert's ex post facto argument, characterizing it as "sophistic," "highly technical," and "mock[ing] the substance of the Ex Post Facto Clause."[185] Citing as support one of its prior bankruptcy decisions,[186] the court reasoned that regardless of the constitutional invalidity of the law at the time of the killings, its existence in the Florida statutes "served as an 'operative fact' to warn the petitioner of the penalty that Florida would seek to impose upon him if he were convicted of first-degree murder."[187] The law, Justice Rehnquist wrote, "clearly indicated Florida's view of the severity of murder and of the degree of punishment which the legislature wished to impose upon murderers."[188] Its "existence on the statute books provided fair warning as to the degree of culpability which the State ascribed to the act of murder."[189]

Justice John Paul Stevens, in a dissent joined by Justices Brennan and Marshall, vigorously disputed the majority's use of "fair warning" and reliance as bases to reject the ex post facto challenge. After noting that the majority cited "not a single case involving the Ex Post Facto Clause" in support, Stevens wrote that the decision marked a "clear departure" from the court's ex post facto jurisprudence. In support, Stevens pointed to *Lindsey v. Washington* (1937) (discussed earlier), where the court found an ex post facto violation when the law in effect at the time of the offense authorized a maximum fifteen-year sentence, and the defendant was therefore aware of it being a possibility, but a new sentencing law mandated a fifteen-year term. According to Stevens, "[i]n the case before us the new standard created the possibility of a death sentence that could not have been lawfully imposed when the offense was committed. A more dramatically different standard of punishment is difficult to envision."[190]

Pivoting to his broader concern, Stevens opined that "[f]air warning cannot be the touchstone, for two reasons." First, it "does not provide a workable test for deciding particular cases . . . By what standard is the fairness of the warning contained in an unconstitutional statute to be judged? Is an itinerant, who may not have the slightest notion of what Florida's statute books contain, to be judged differently from a local lawyer?"[191] "A consistent application of that presumption would require the conclusion that neither the lawyer nor the itinerant had fair warning because both must also be presumed to know that the old Florida statute was a nullity."[192]

Second, Stevens objected to the majority's focus on notice, asserting that the "the Ex Post Facto Clause also provides a basic protection against improperly motivated or capricious legislation. It ensures that the sovereign will govern impartially and that it will be perceived as doing so."[193] Stevens reasoned that if the test "extend[ed] beyond this case, [it] would allow government action that is just the opposite of impartial. If that be so, the 'fair warning' rationale will defeat the very purpose of the Clause."[194] In support, Stevens noted that of the hundreds of condemned capital prisoners nationwide affected by *Furman*, none was resentenced to death.[195] Concluding, Stevens wrote that it was "distressing to witness such a demeaning construction of a majestic bulwark in the framework of our Constitution."[196]

On the merits, it is hard to say that Dobbert lacked notice that the Florida legislature's amended, constitutionally valid law, enacted after the killings, created a new criminal law prohibition; he was, of course, charged with homicide. Nor can it reasonably be said that Dobbert lacked notice that conviction could result in death, because at the time of the killings the death penalty loomed as a state option, as it did several years later when he was tried. In this sense, Justice Stevens's use of *Lindsey* as contrary precedent was not entirely convincing: when Lindsey committed his crime fifteen years was the maximum, whereas the amended law under which he was sentenced mandated a fifteen-year term.

The majority, however, did not use the foregoing approach; instead, it created a new stand-alone rationale, based on notice. The court elaborated on its new rationale not long thereafter in *Weaver v. Graham* (1981),[197] where the court by a unanimous vote invalidated on ex post facto grounds a law retroactively depriving inmates of "gain time" for good conduct. The court reasoned that the framers, by adopting the Ex Post Facto Clause, "sought to assure that legislative Acts give fair notice of their effect and permit individuals to rely on their meaning until explicitly changed."[198] The court then added that "[t]he ban also restricts governmental power by restraining arbitrary and potentially vindictive legislation,"[199] and appended a footnote stating that "the *ex post facto* prohibition also upholds the separation of powers by confining the legislature to penal decisions with prospective effect and the judicial and executive to applications of existing law."[200]

Six years later, in *Miller v. Florida* (1987),[201] the court solidified notice as a concern. Despite citing only a case decided a mere six years before (*Weaver*) in support, the unanimous court stated that "almost from the beginning" it had "recognized that central to the *ex post facto* prohibition is a concern for 'the lack of fair notice and governmental restraint when the legislature increases punishment beyond what was prescribed when the crime was consummated.'"[202] Invoking the notice rationale, the court unanimously held that retroactive imposition of a new Florida sentencing guideline increased the presumptive sentence for Miller and was invalid on ex post facto grounds. Citing *Dobbert* and *Lindsey* in support, the court rejected the government's argument that *Miller* was given "fair warning" because the sentencing statute provided for continuous review and possible recommend changes, stating that "[t]he constitutional prohibition against ex post facto laws cannot be avoided merely by adding to a law notice that it might be changed."[203]

The modern court's identification of notice as a value can only be interpreted as an instance of creative constitutional reasoning. Today, it not uncommon for judicial conservatives to assail "judicial activism," usually in response to the court interpreting a constitutional provision to identify and then protect an unremunerated right. For a conservative jurist such as Justice William Rehnquist (author of the *Dobbert* opinion) to engage in creative constitutionalism is ironic. Whether the innovation ultimately redounds to the benefit of citizens or the government, however, is unclear. In *Dobbert*, use of the notice rationale resulted in a government win, whereas the opposite was true in *Weaver* and *Miller*. What is significant is that the court, which otherwise very often professes to follow an "original understanding of the Ex Post Facto Clause,"[204] did not do so in *Dobbert*, and in the process created a new consideration for evaluating the validity of a retroactive criminal law.

Gauging Retroactivity

Before concluding, it is worth discussing the court's decisions during the era regarding whether a law is in fact retroactive, an essential aspect of an ex post facto challenge. Retroactivity, in a technical sense, is perhaps easy enough to define: in *Weaver v. Graham* (1981) the court defined it as when a law "changes the legal consequences of acts completed before its effective date."[205] For instance, with a crime such as burglary, which in general terms involves the unlawful entry of another's home with the intent to commit a felony inside, the crime occurs when those elements are satisfied; the crime is "completed" at a particular time.[206] Often, however, courts are presented with more complicated cases, which can turn on how they conceive of the crime in question and the provisions of the statutory code of which it is a part.[207]

Murphy v. Ramsey (1885)[208] is a case in point. In *Murphy*, petitioners challenged an 1882 federal law denying the right to vote to Utah polygamists, bigamists, and individuals who cohabited with more than one woman. The law, known as the Edmunds Act, was enacted amid strenuous debate over whether disenfranchisement was a lawful regulation of suffrage or qualified as punishment for ex post facto purposes.[209]

The unanimous court sidestepped the important civil liberties issue, doing so based on its view that the law was not retroactive in its effect. With respect to the cohabitation aspect, the court held that it pertained to a present and ongoing act. Polygamy and bigamy, on the other hand, were defined as a marriage to one or more others by someone who is already married, suggestive of a past act. The court, however, interpreted the law as one covering individuals who continued to be married to more than one person, which made the offense contemporaneous with disenfranchisement and therefore not ex post facto. In short, the court construed the law as prohibiting the act of remaining married (not being married) to more than one person: "The disfranchisement operates upon the existing state and condition of the person, and not upon a past offense."[210]

McDonald v. Massachusetts (1901)[211] further illustrates how judicial perspective, and method of interpretation, can affect ex post facto analysis on the retroactivity question. In *McDonald*, the petitioner challenged a new state law that enhanced the punishment of criminal recidivists for subsequent convictions, which he argued increased his punishment for already punished past convictions. The court unanimously rejected the claim, concluding that the enhanced "punishment is for the new crime only, but is the heavier if he is an habitual criminal . . . The statute, imposing a punishment on none but future crimes, is not ex post facto."[212]

In *Samuels v. McCurdy* (1925),[213] the court again addressed whether behavior that precedes a law, and continues after its enactment, is problematic for ex post facto purposes. *Samuels*, which arose in the Prohibition Era, held that the continued possession of outlawed liquor was the proper subject of criminalization. As Chief Justice William Howard Taft wrote for the unanimous court: "This law is not an ex post facto law. It does not provide a punishment for a past offense. It does not fix a penalty for the owner for having become possessed of the liquor. The penalty it imposes is for continuing to possess the liquor after the enactment of the law."[214]

As the outcomes in *Murphy*, *McDonald*, and *Samuels* make clear, retroactivity analysis is not always as clear-cut as might first appear, because it very much depends on how a court frames the temporal analysis. In *McDonald*, for instance, certainly from the petitioner's perspective, his past conviction functioned to enhance the sentence for his later conviction, but the court viewed his later enhanced sentenced as justified because his subsequent criminal activity was more culpable in light of the prior conviction.

Murphy and *Samuels* involved what might be called "continuing" offenses. Another example is the crime of conspiracy, which can spool out over an extended period of time and involve culpable acts or omissions by two or more parties. If an act or omission continues after the enactment or amendment of the challenged law, for instance, one increasing the punishment for conspiracy, the law is not problematic on ex post facto grounds.[215]

Related but distinct are "straddle crimes,"[216] those where "the defendant satisfies one or more elements of the crime before the date of enactment, and yet the crime is not fully completed—that is, all of the elements are not satisfied—until after the date of enactment."[217] Such offenses are not continuing in nature, but rather have elements occurring before and after an enactment, which the government must prove beyond a reasonable doubt. Professor Richard Broughton has written that the analysis turns on what Justice Chase intended when he used the words "action [] done" when describing *Calder* category one, which it will be recalled prohibits "[e]very law that makes an action, done before the passing of the law, and which was innocent when done, criminal; and punishes such action."[218] Under what Broughton calls the "completion approach," any element of the crime that occurs after the effective date of the law should not be deemed ex post facto. In such situations, courts properly find no ex post facto problem,[219] as the prohibition "bar[s] only legislation applied after the date of the offense, and the date of offense will always be the date on which the final element is satisfied."[220]

Summary and Conclusion

This chapter has traced the evolution of the court's interpretation and application of the Ex Post Facto Clause from the late nineteenth up to the final decade of the twentieth century. The many decisions, arising in distinct contexts, can be said to mark the maturation of ex post facto jurisprudence, which on the whole embodies a considerably more constricted view of the coverage of the clause compared to preceding decades. Although the court has insisted that that "[t]he ex post facto standard we apply today is constant,"[221] the judicial landscape canvassed here shows the contrary to be the case. Only in dissents does one see sentiments akin to those voiced by Justice Stephen Field, author of the majority opinions in *Cummings v. Missouri* (1867) and *Ex Parte Garland* (1867), who in 1883 wrote:

> I know, of course, that this court has, with the exception of two of its members, been entirely changed in its personnel since the *Cummings* Case was decided . . . I would fain hope, however, that this change may not lead to a change in the construction of clauses in the Constitution intended for the protection of personal rights . . . I am of [the] opinion that all the guarantees of the Constitution designed to secure private rights, whether of person or property, should be broadly and liberally interpreted so as to meet and protect against every form of oppression at which they were aimed, however disguised and in whatever shape presented. They ought not to be emasculated and their protective force and energy frittered away and lost by a construction which will leave only the dead letter for our regard when the living spirit is gone.[222]

The shift recognized by Justice Field is evidenced in the several distinct areas highlighted in this chapter. With scope of coverage, there has been an ebb and flow, mostly the former. For instance, in 1883 (*Kring v. Missouri*), the court cast the prohibition in broad terms—a violation occurs when a law retroactively "alters [a party's] situation to his disadvantage." Furthermore, the court must give the clause a "liberal construction," one "in manifest accord with the purpose of the constitutional convention to protect the individual rights of life and liberty against hostile retrospective legislation." And in 1898 (*Thompson v. Utah*), the court stated that to survive a challenge a retroactive law must "leave untouched all the substantial protections" enjoyed by a party. Roughly a century later, in 1990 (*Collins v. Youngblood*), however, the court disavowed *Kring* and *Thompson*, reasoning that they strayed beyond *Calder's* four categories. The court did so despite its obvious uneven fealty during the period to the four categories, variously omitting and adding categories, and identifying a new near-categorical exception to coverage of the clause (laws deemed "procedural" in nature).

During the period, the court also expounded on what it saw as the interests protected by the clause. In particular, the court newly identified notice (*Dobbert*, 1977)[223] and reliance (*Weaver*, 1981),[224] which, depending on how the court conceives of the legal change, can determine the outcome of challenges.

Finally, the period witnessed major changes on the key question of what qualifies as a punitive sanction. In decisions like *Hawker v. New York* (1898) and others addressing retroactive disabilities imposed upon former Communist Party members, the court exhibited a decidedly less critical view of retroactive laws compared to its earlier decisions, discussed in Chapter 3, such as *Cummings* (1867), *Ex parte Garland* (1867), and *Burgess v. Salmon* (1878). And, of critical importance, the court in the late 1950s and 1960s laid the groundwork for a new analytic rubric for the assessment of whether a particular sanction qualifies as punishment, the "intent-effects" test, imposing significantly greater burdens on a party bringing an ex post facto challenge.

Not surprisingly, the foregoing developments resulted in few wins for petitioners during the era. Indeed, of the multiple ex post facto challenges decided in the over one hundred-year period examined, only four had outcomes favoring petitioners (*Medley* (1890), *Lindsey* (1937), *Weaver* (1981), and *Miller* (1987)). All were challenges to indisputably criminal sanctions concerning *Calder* category three (enhancement of punishment),[225] which survived the era largely intact, without much elaboration or change.

5

The 1990s to the Present

Preceding chapters explored the Framing Era history of the Ex Post Facto Clause (Chapter 1); the Supreme Court's seminal 1798 decision interpreting the clause, *Calder v. Bull*, and subsequent critical reactions to it (Chapter 2); formative early-mid nineteenth century Supreme Court decisions, highlighting the court's willingness to broadly construe its protections (Chapter 3); and decisions from the late nineteenth century to 1990, in general marked by retrenchment, as well as the emergence of a "procedural" law exception, reliance and notice as a purpose, and a new analytic framework for addressing whether a retroactive law is criminal in nature (Chapter 4).

This chapter examines the next, most recent era of the Supreme Court's interpretation and application of the clause: the early 1990s to the present. Given its considerably shorter length, the period entails far fewer decisions from the court, yet contains some very important developments. Most notable is the Supreme Court's decidedly uncritical scrutiny of legislative enactments retroactively singling out disdained sub-populations for harsh retroactive sanctions. In this instance, previously convicted sex offenders bore the primary brunt of legislative attention.[1]

The laws assumed a variety of forms. With regularity, legislatures during the time increased prison sentences for newly convicted sex offenders and imposed more onerous new terms of community supervision.[2] However, in response to a series of widely reported sexual victimizations of children by previously convicted sex offenders, after their release from prison, legislatures also enacted significant new laws having retroactive effect. In two major decisions, *Kansas v. Hendricks* (1997) and *Smith v. Doe* (2003), the court rejected ex post facto challenges to, respectively, the likely lifetime "civil" confinement of previously convicted sex offenders, and the requirement that they register with police and provide personal identifying information (registration), which is then provided to the public (community notification). In each case, the court narrowly applied its "punishment question" analytic rubric (discussed in Chapter 4), which had the additional effect of limiting ex post facto challenges in lower courts to other post-conviction disabilities, known as collateral consequences, which in the 1990s were also

The Ex Post Facto Clause. Wayne A. Logan, Oxford University Press. © Oxford University Press 2023.
DOI: 10.1093/oso/9780190053505.003.0006

increasingly imposed on individuals previously convicted of crimes (not only sex offenders).[3]

The laws themselves were part of a broader nationwide shift toward "get tough" criminal justice policy.[4] During the time, political leaders unabashedly competed with one another to secure electoral benefit by enacting harsh laws targeting criminal offenders.[5] As a result, prison and jail populations swelled to unprecedented, world-leading proportions,[6] creating a penal system that would be utterly unrecognizable to the framers. Legislatures also enacted laws retroactively lengthening sentences and lessening availability of parole for inmates, which generated ex post facto challenges heard by the court. The challenges, which unquestionably concerned criminal laws within the potential protective scope of the clause (concerning *Calder* category 3), met with mixed results. The Supreme Court condemned retroactive sentencing changes (*United States v. Peugh*, 2013), but condoned retroactive changes in the availability of parole (*Garner v. Jones*, 2000).

Notably, amid the court's increasing tendency to read the clause narrowly, and deny relief, there were two exceptions, both 5-4 majorities, concerning ex post facto claims not often before the court. In the first, *Carmell v. Texas* (2000), the court, with arguably the most stalwart champion of the clause on the court in the modern era—Justice John Paul Stevens—writing for the majority, resuscitated *Calder* category four, prohibiting retroactive changes in evidence, which the court in two earlier decisions (*Beazell v. Ohio* (1925) and *Collins v. Youngblood* (1990)) seemingly had jettisoned. In the other, *Stogner v. California* (2003), the Supreme Court granted relief on the basis of *Calder* category two (concerning a law that "aggravates a crime, or makes it greater than it was when committed"), invalidating a state law retroactively extending an expired statute of limitations for a child sexual abuse prosecution.

The "Punishment Question" Redux: Convicted Sex Offenders

Although societal concern over sex offenders dates back to at least the 1930s, the 1990s marked a decided increase. In significant part, this shift was fueled by widespread media attention to several horrific sexual victimizations, typically of children. Researchers have since referred to the time as one of "moral panic," marked by a wave of harsh laws targeting previously convicted sex offenders.[7] Very often, the laws won quick approval by large legislative majorities or unanimous votes, without much if any debate, with legislators wary of being labeled "soft on crime" or, worse yet, "pro-sex offender."[8]

Involuntary Confinement

Kansas v. Hendricks (1997)

One strategy involved the involuntary confinement of previously convicted sex offenders, a strategy first used to target "sexual psychopaths" in the 1930s, which fell into disuse over time.[9] In 1990, Washington State was the first state to enact a new-generation law, but its law differed from predecessors in a significant respect. Rather than subjecting individuals to involuntary confinement in lieu of prison or jail, as in the past, Washington's law (targeting "sexually violent predators") authorized commitment in addition to, and after, incarceration.[10]

Kansas enacted a similar law. As in Washington, legislative interest there arose in the wake of a widely reported sexual offense by a previously convicted sex offender living in the community. The Kansas Sexually Violent Predator Act (SVPA), enacted in 1994, was retroactive in effect, impacting a Kansas inmate, Leroy Hendricks, who was then on the verge of release from prison. Hendricks had a lengthy history of sexual offending against children, but for reasons that remain unclear, was not subject when sentenced in 1984 to a lengthy term because of his status as a habitual felon.[11] Hendricks was the first individual to be subject to the SVPA and he challenged the law on several grounds, including substantive due process, ex post facto, and double jeopardy, arguing with respect to the ex post facto and double jeopardy claims that the potentially lifelong "care and treatment" he was to receive was punishment by another name.

In *Kansas v. Hendricks* (1997),[12] a five-member majority, in an opinion by Justice Clarence Thomas, concluded that the SVPA was constitutional in all respects. After rejecting the substantive due process challenge, the court turned its attention to the ex post facto and double jeopardy claims, focusing first on the threshold question of whether the SVPA was punitive. Relying on a prior decision assessing whether a statute is punitive for Fifth Amendment double jeopardy purposes,[13] the majority characterized the question of whether a sanction qualifies as punishment as being "first of all a question of 'statutory construction,'" and concluded that the SVPA was non-punitive on two bases: first, its "placement" in the Kansas probate code; and second, the Kansas legislature's description of the SVPA as a "civil commitment procedure." Under the court's facial mode of legislative analysis, the law plainly passed muster: "Nothing on the face of the statute suggests that the legislature sought to create anything other than a civil commitment scheme designed to protect the public from harm."[14]

Next, after noting that the "'civil label'" of a law "is not always dispositive,"[15] the court invoked the demanding *Nestor/Ward* standard (discussed in
Chapter 4) requiring that there exist "'the clearest proof' that 'the statutory
scheme [is] so punitive either in purpose or effect as to negate [the State's]
intention' to deem it 'civil.'"[16] "In those limited circumstances," the majority
wrote, "we will consider the statute to have established criminal proceedings
for constitutional purposes."[17]

The court concluded that Hendricks failed to satisfy this "heavy burden."[18]
In support of its conclusion, the court provided an extended discussion of
several, but not all, factors identified in *Kennedy v. Mendoza-Martinez* (1963)
(discussed in Chapter 4). "As a threshold matter," Justice Thomas wrote, the
SVPA "did not implicate either of the two primary objectives of criminal punishment: retribution or deterrence."[19] It was not retributive because it did not
"affix culpability for prior criminal conduct," despite its requirement that an
individual be "convicted of or charged with a sexually violent offense."[20] This
requirement, the court held, was employed solely for "evidentiary purposes,
either to demonstrate that a 'mental abnormality' exists or to support a finding
of future dangerousness."[21] That the SVPA was "'tied to criminal activity' was
'insufficient to render the [statute] punitive.'"[22] Nor did the SVPA require a
finding of scienter, another hallmark of the criminal law; rather, commitment
was based on the finding that an individual had a "mental abnormality" or
"personality disorder."[23] A deterrent purpose was not served because those
with a "mental abnormality" or "personality disorder" were "unlikely to be
deterred by the threat of confinement."[24]

The court also discounted the fact that Hendricks had been involuntarily
confined by the government, implicating the "affirmative disability or restraint" *Mendoza-Martinez* factor. Citing *United States v. Salerno* (1987),
which approved the preventive detention for a limited duration of pretrial
detainees under the federal Bail Reform Act of 1984, the court stated that
the mere fact that the SVPA imposed an "affirmative restraint" on Hendricks
did not make the law punitive. "The State may take measures to restrict the
freedom of the dangerously mentally ill. This is a legitimate non-punitive governmental objective and has been historically so regarded."[25]

The potentially indefinite duration of Hendricks's confinement did not
qualify as a punitive objective. In fact, "[f]ar from any punitive objective, the
confinement's duration is instead linked to the stated purposes of the commitment, namely, to hold the person until his mental abnormality no longer
causes him to be a threat to others."[26] Furthermore, because the SVPA provided for annual review of a predator's status, "commitment was only potentially indefinite," also indicative of a non-punitive purpose.[27]

Similarly, the court rejected Hendricks's argument that the array of procedural safeguards embodied in the SVPA, including the requirements that "predator" status be predicated on an initial finding of probable cause, and that commitment itself be based on proof beyond a reasonable doubt, made the SVPA punitive. According to the court, the procedural protections merely served to ensure that "only a narrow class of particularly dangerous individuals" be confined under the SVPA. "That Kansas chose to afford such procedural protections does not transform a civil commitment proceeding into a criminal prosecution," Justice Thomas reasoned.[28]

Finally, the court rejected the argument that the SVPA was punitive because it failed to ensure "treatment" for Hendricks's acknowledged pedophiliac condition. The court held that, even assuming the nonexistence or inefficacy of treatment opportunities, confinement is constitutionally acceptable when persons "pose a danger to others," as when government involuntarily confines "persons afflicted with an untreatable, highly contagious disease."[29] The court buttressed its conclusion with the observation that it was illogical to disallow confinement of the dangerously insane merely because no acceptable treatment was available. "To conclude otherwise would obligate a State to release certain confined individuals who were both mentally ill and dangerous simply because they could not be successfully treated for their afflictions."[30] Furthermore, even presuming that Hendricks was treatable, the SVPA was constitutional even if treatment was not its "overriding concern"; there was still "the possibility that an ancillary purpose of the [SVPA] was to provide treatment."[31]

Having established that commitment under the SVPA was non-punitive in nature, and analyzing why the particular other requirements for a Fifth Amendment double jeopardy claim were not satisfied, the majority honed in on Hendricks's ex post facto claim. Justice Thomas reiterated the majority's conclusion that the SVPA was non-punitive, which ruled out the claim as a threshold matter, and added that the law was not retroactive in effect. Rather, involuntary commitment under the law was based on current mental condition and likelihood to pose a future danger to the public. "To the extent that past behavior is taken into account, it is used, as noted above, solely for evidentiary purposes."[32] Concluding, Thomas enunciated an abbreviated and modified statement of *Calder*'s coverage, omitting the main claim that Hendricks's sentence was retroactively extended (*Calder* category 3), stating that "[b]ecause the Act does not criminalize conduct legal before its enactment, nor deprive Hendricks of any defense that was available to him at the time of his crimes, the Act does not violate the Ex Post Facto Clause."[33]

Justice Anthony Kennedy concurred in the result, providing the majority's necessary fifth vote. He acknowledged that "[i]f the object or purpose of the Kansas law has been to provide treatment but the treatment provisions were adopted as a sham or mere pretext, there would have been an indication of the forbidden purpose to punish."[34] Kennedy agreed with his four colleagues, however, that the SVPA did not present such a case, while noting that "[n]otwithstanding its civil attributes, the practical effect of the Kansas law may be to impose confinement for life."[35]

Justice Stephen Breyer, joined by Justices Stevens, Souter, and Ginsburg, dissented from the majority's conclusion that the SVPA did not constitute punishment, writing that the law "was not simply an effort to commit Hendricks civilly, but rather an effort to inflict further punishment upon him."[36] Breyer argued that the court was obliged to place "particular importance upon those features that would likely distinguish between a basically punitive and a basically nonpunitive purpose."[37] Under this view, the question deserving particular attention was whether the provision evidenced a "concern for treatment," as in *Allen v. Illinois*, the Fifth Amendment double jeopardy case relied upon by the majority.

Applying this standard, Breyer found several reasons to infer punitive purpose. First, the Kansas Supreme Court itself had determined that treatment was not a significant objective under the SVPA, a matter of record which he criticized the majority for ignoring.[38] Second, that Kansas designed the SVPA to provide "treatment" only after offenders completed their criminal sentences made clear that the state did not view treatment as an important objective. Furthermore, as of the time of Hendricks's commitment, Kansas had neither taken the necessary fiscal and practical steps to provide treatment, nor provided Hendricks with any treatment for his condition.[39] Third, the SVPA's failure to require the consideration of a less restrictive intervention (such as a halfway house) militated in favor of a punitive purpose.[40] Finally, of the seventeen other states with similar involuntary commitment statutes, only Kansas had the dual characteristics of delaying treatment and failing to offer a less restrictive placement, at least when such a post-confinement measure was imposed retroactively.[41]

Only at its end did Justice Breyer's dissent cite to *Kennedy v. Mendoza-Martinez*, as a seeming afterthought, noting that "one other case warrants mention." Paraphrasing its seven-factor test, he found the test satisfied, while acknowledging that the test was not dispositive, stating that "the added confinement the Act imposes upon Hendricks is basically punitive."[42]

Closing, Breyer emphasized that involuntary confinement, imposed prospectively, not retroactively, would not be problematic. The Ex Post Facto Clause in such a circumstance would

> not stand as an obstacle to achieving important protections for the public's safety; rather, it provides an assurance that, where so significant a restriction of an individual's basic freedom is at issue a State cannot cut corners. Rather, the legislature must hew to the Constitution's liberty-protecting line. *See The Federalist* No. 78, p. 466 (C. Rossiter ed., 1961) (A. Hamilton).[43]

Hendricks is a very important decision for several reasons. Jurisprudentially, it is important because it marked the first use of the court's now accepted analytic framework when answering the "punishment question" in ex post facto challenges: the "intent-effects" test. A court must first engage in a process of "statutory construction" to gauge whether the legislature intended the challenged law to be non-punitive in nature. If civil intent is discerned, analysis turns to whether the law is so punitive "either in purpose or effect" to negate the civil label, based on the factors identified in *Mendoza-Martinez* (1963). Finally, the threshold statutory construction conclusion that a law is civil in nature will be negated only if the "clearest proof" of punitiveness is shown, which is a "heavy burden." The majority announced this regime without any mention of the historic purposes of the Ex Post Facto clause, prescribing a constitutionally polyglot test borrowed from its several cases concerning the punishment question in the context of the Fifth and Sixth Amendments.[44]

More generally, on its merits the *Hendricks* analysis is problematic for several additional reasons. Foremost is that the majority ignored a basic teaching of its foundational ex post facto jurisprudence, reflected in *Cummings v. Missouri* (1867):[45] that a reviewing court, when assessing whether a particular sanction is punishment, be mindful of "the circumstances attending and the causes of the deprivation."[46] Almost a century later, in another ex post facto case, the court in *De Veau v. Braisted* (1960)[47] similarly recognized that a law must "be placed in the context of the structure and history of the legislation of which it is a part."[48]

If the *Hendricks* majority had considered the legislative background of the SVPA it would have been obliged to recognize that it was part of a larger package of harsh determinate sentencing laws increasing sentences for individuals convicted of sex offenses, especially those considered "predatory sex offenders."[49] These demonstrably criminal sanctions, however, targeted only future sex offenders, leaving unaddressed the population of offenders already imprisoned under older, more lenient indeterminate sentencing laws. One Kansas prosecutor summed up the legislative strategy as follows:

> It is not difficult to understand why legislators are reluctant to stop after simply increasing the criminal sentences that may be imposed on sex offenders in the future. Such laws will indeed punish and incapacitate future offenders and may deter some potential offenders from ever committing sex offenses. But it is difficult to inform constituents that there is nothing more that can be done to protect the public from past offenders who are now being or soon will be released from prison.[50]

The majority also ignored evidence in the record of plain expressions of punitive intent in the legislative evolution of the SVPA, a great deal of which emanated from key players in the legislative process. For instance, in testifying before the Kansas legislature on behalf of the SVPA, Kansas Attorney General Robert Stephan stated:

> Most new laws against criminal conduct tend to provide punishment after the victimization has occurred. Senate Bill 525 will act prospectively and be preventive of criminal conduct and not just punitive. You have a rare opportunity to pass a law that will keep dangerous sex offenders confined past their scheduled prison sentence. As I am convinced none of them should ever be released, I believe you, as legislators, have an obligation to enact laws that will protect our citizens through incapacitation of dangerous offenders.[51]

Stephan's successor, Attorney General Carla Stovall, described the SVPA's goal as keeping sexual offenders "locked up indefinitely"[52] because Kansas could not "open [its] prison doors and let these animals back into [its] communities."[53] Extensive testimony indicated that the law would very likely result in indefinite confinement, rather than treatment in the hope of release.[54] The reasons for this ranged from the practical reality that mental health professionals would be reluctant to certify that offenders could ever be safely returned to the community,[55] to the acknowledged lack of effective treatment in Kansas for pedophiles.[56] In the prior state court challenge to the SVPA, the Kansas Supreme Court deemed the SVPA punitive in nature, and characterized the legislature's "treatment" motivation as "somewhat disingenuous,"[57] an inference buttressed by the fact that commitment (and hence "treatment") occurred only when the "predator" faced imminent release from prison.[58]

Ultimately, the SVPA became law amid a landslide of support.[59] The Kansas House approved the legislation 101-23 and the Senate 40-0, in a single day,[60] largely due to the efforts of a task force assembled in the wake of a widely

reported rape and murder of a woman by a recently paroled convicted sex offender. The task force included the following members: the mother, father, and
sister of the victim; Kansas Attorney General Robert Stephan; a local district
attorney; law enforcement personnel; the State Victims' Rights coordinator;
parole board members; probation officers; legislators; and several concerned
citizens. It did not include any mental health professionals.[61] When one task
force member was confronted with the reality that commitment would de
facto amount to a life term, because effective treatment was lacking, their response was "So be it."[62]

Finally, as noted, the *Hendricks* majority ignored, or at least skirted, the
Kansas Supreme Court's evaluation of the purpose driving its own legislature.
The Kansas Supreme Court, when addressing Hendricks's substantive due
process claim earlier in the litigation,[63] found it "clear that the primary objective of the Act is to continue incarceration and not to provide treatment."[64]
Rather than defer to the express finding, the majority instead focused on the
Kansas court's use of "segregation" at one point in its opinion (as opposed
to its repeated use of "incarceration"). The majority's neglect of the Kansas
Supreme Court's authoritative understanding deviated from well-settled case
law: that "in applying the ex post facto prohibition of the Federal Constitution
to state laws, [the Court] accepts the meaning ascribed to them by the highest
court of the state."[65]

Altogether, the record in *Hendricks* provided strong reason to be wary of
accepting the Kansas legislature's assurance that it was seeking only to "treat,"
not punish, previously convicted sexual offenders, amid legislators' undisguised disdain for the "predators" targeted.[66] The court's lack of sensitivity for
legislative context contrasts sharply with that evinced in *Cummings v. Missouri*
(1867),[67] where the court emphasized the context in which the challenged
law—one that barred Confederate sympathizers from certain professions—
during the Civil War in Missouri (a border state) and immediately thereafter,
as a time of "fierce passions."[68] The court noted that "[i]t would have been
strange . . . had [the provision] not exhibited in its provisions some traces of
the excitement amidst which the convention held its deliberations,"[69] and
stated that the ex post facto prohibition was intended to apply in just such a
situation: "It was against the excited action of the States, under such influences
as these, that the framers of the Federal Constitution intended to guard."[70]

At a minimum, as suggested by Justice Breyer in his *Hendricks* dissent, the
court should have been obliged to "place particular importance upon those
features that would likely distinguish between a basically punitive and basically nonpunitive purpose."[71] Tellingly, as Breyer observed, those confined under the law were held in the psychiatric wing of a prison hospital,

where prisoners and committees were housed together, neither receiving treatment.[72]

When Leroy Hendricks was convicted and sentenced Kansas could have, in the words of one Kansas Supreme Court justice, kept him in prison "until he exhaled his last breath and his spirit departed this earth . . ."[73] Local prosecutors, however, elected not to pursue that path, and the Kansas Legislature, on the eve of Hendricks's release from prison enacted the SVPA, a "gap-filling" strategy,[74] likely ensuring his lifelong involuntary confinement. In deeming the SVPA non-punitive, the court refused to acknowledge, let alone weigh, the clear indicia of punitive purpose and effect of the SVPA. In doing so, as Justice Breyer put it, the state "cut corners" and failed to "hew to the Constitution's liberty-protecting line."[75]

Finally, Hendricks has major practical importance because it today serves as a constitutional benchmark. After Hendricks, courts frequently invoke the fact that the Supreme Court found non-punitive a law imposing likely lifelong involuntary confinement as a basis for finding other less impactful sanctions non-punitive.[76] Also, the Kansas Legislature, by labeling the SVPA as a "civil commitment" law and ensconcing it in the probate code, provided a road map for other legislatures wishing to disguise provisions of their own.

Seling v. Young (2001)

Four years after Hendricks, the Supreme Court addressed another ex post facto challenge to involuntary confinement, this time from Washington State. In Seling v. Young (2001),[77] the court addressed a narrow but important question: whether a law, previously deemed civil by a reviewing court, for double jeopardy and ex post facto purposes, could become punitive over time when the state fails to provide treatment?

By a 8-1 vote, the court, with Justice Sandra Day O'Connor writing for the majority, held that on the "assumption" that a law was non-punitive (based on Hendricks and the Washington State Supreme Court's prior holding), a challenge to how the law is implemented—an "as applied" challenge—"would prove unworkable."[78] This was because "confinement is not a fixed event," in that it "extends over time under conditions that are subject to change . . . The civil nature of a confinement scheme cannot be altered based merely on vagaries in the implementation of the authorizing statute."[79] An as-applied analysis, O'Connor wrote, "would never conclusively resolve whether a particular scheme is punitive and would thereby prevent a final determination of the scheme's validity."[80] Justice O'Connor concluded by noting that the court did not have before it a question of "the relevance of conditions of confinement to a first instance determination,"[81] having earlier noted that she did "not deny that some of respondent's allegations are serious."[82]

Justice Scalia, joined by Justice Souter, concurred in the result, and endorsed the view that a law once deemed civil for double jeopardy and ex post facto purposes cannot later be transformed into a punitive one because of the way it is implemented. According to Justice Scalia:

> The short of the matter is that, for Double Jeopardy and Ex Post Facto Clause purposes, the question of criminal penalty vel non depends upon the intent of the legislature; and harsh executive implementation cannot "transfor[m] what was clearly intended as a civil remedy into a criminal penalty," any more than compassionate executive implementation can transform a criminal penalty into a civil remedy.[83]

In a footnote, Justice Scalia added that because the Ex Post Facto Clause expressly prohibits "pass[ing]" ex post facto laws, a limit on legislative action, "the irrelevance of subsequent executive implementation to" assessing legislative intent "is, if anything, even clearer."[84] Scalia also rejected the majority opinion's intimation that actual conditions of confinement and implementation could have relevance to the analysis of whether a law is civil or criminal "in the first instance."[85]

Justice Thomas also concurred in the result, but voiced an even greater aversion for analytic consideration of how a statute is implemented. Like Scalia, he argued that judicial determination of whether a statute is civil or criminal is to be determined by examining the "statute on its face," without consideration of how the statute has been implemented.[86]

The sole dissent was lodged by Justice Stevens, who vigorously challenged his colleagues' refusal to consider Young's allegations regarding confinement conditions. While acknowledging that the civil/criminal nature of a statute is "initially one of statutory construction,"[87] Stevens argued that conditions should play a role in the constitutional inquiry, regardless of whether the statute was initially deemed civil by a court.[88] In assessing whether a law is "'so punitive in purpose *or effect*,'" and asking whether there exists the "'clearest proof'" that a nominally civil law is criminal in nature, Stevens argued, the court had "consistently looked to the conditions of confinement as evidence of both the legislative purpose behind the statute and its actual effect.... [T]he question whether a statute is in fact punitive cannot always be answered solely by reference to the text of the statute."[89]

Seling is a narrow but potentially quite significant decision. The court considered a "punitive-as-applied" ex post facto challenge categorically unworkable, when a law is initially deemed civil in nature, because conditions of confinement can change over time, making it impossible to "conclusively resolve whether a particular scheme is punitive."[90] Although the court was correct in its recognition that conditions can and do change, and as Justice Scalia noted in his concurrence the Clause speaks of the "pass[ing]" of a law, Justice Stevens was also correct in his recognition that assessment of the "effects" of a nominally civil law must be considered in an ex post facto challenge. Indeed, it remains unclear how the "intent-effects" test can be applied if a court cannot assess how a law is applied to individuals—its "effects" (a point elaborated upon in Chapter 6). Furthermore, the position adopted in *Seling*, vis-à-vis the assessment of whether a sanction is punitive, is curiously at odds with the court's approach to whether a sentence is enlarged by a retroactive law (*Calder* category three), which as discussed later, *Garner v. Jones* (2000) a year earlier held requires assessment of a law's "practical implementation."

Ultimately, refusing to consider how a law is actually implemented, whatever its "facial" intent, certainly makes it more difficult to satisfy the already demanding "clearest proof" standard. It also allows a government to do an end run of the Ex Post Facto Clause: the legislature can enact a nominally civil law, and then, with a wink and nod, have the law implemented in a punitive manner, without violating the clause. And even if a law's actual implementation were considered, and punitive characteristics are discerned, the demanding "clearest proof" requirement provides a daunting hurdle to surmount.

Registration and Community Notification

Smith v. Doe (2003)

The 1990s witnessed the emergence of another novel social control method targeting convicted sex offenders, after they have "done their time": laws requiring that they register with government authorities, by providing and updating identifying information (e.g., their home address, description of any vehicles), which is then provided to the public at-large in the name of public safety (usually via internet websites). Although registration laws targeting convicted individuals more generally existed to some extent since the 1930s, they were largely ignored until the 1990s when, much as with involuntary confinement, several high-profile sexual victimizations of children by convicted sex offenders enraged the public.[91] Washington State again was at the forefront of innovation, enacting not only a registration law, but for the first time also a law allowing for registry information to be shared with local communities. Often named after particular child victims, with New Jersey's Megan's Law (enacted in 1994) being the best known, sex offender registration and notification (SORN) laws were in effect nationwide by the late 1990s, usually passed in rapid-fire succession with little debate.[92]

In 2003, in *Smith v. Doe*,[93] the Supreme Court addressed an ex post facto challenge against one state's law, that of Alaska. Alaska's Sex Offender Registration Act (SORA) required that individuals convicted of specified sex offenses register with authorities for between fifteen years and their lifetime, depending on their offending history, and provide a broad array of information, including body features (e.g., scars and tattoos), vehicle information, residential and work addresses, conviction history, and a photo. They were required to verify the information at least annually, and update it in the event of any changes, and threatened with criminal prosecution if they failed to comply. Authorities provided registrants' information to the community members in the hope that they would protect themselves against possible further sex offenses by the registrants. Petitioners, two individuals subject to the law, who were convicted and released from prison prior to the law's effective date in 1994, and required to verify their registry information on a quarterly basis, argued that the requirements and negative effects of SORA were punitive, in violation of the Ex Post Facto Clause.

By a 6-3 vote, with Justice Anthony Kennedy writing for the majority, the court found that the law did not qualify as punishment and rejected the challenge. Citing *Hendricks*, the court applied what it termed its "well established" framework for analysis (despite only being created four years before, in 1997, when *Hendricks* was decided), first asking whether the legislature intended the challenged law to be a civil, non-punitive regulatory scheme.[94] If deemed civil, the court must then assess whether the scheme is " 'so punitive either in purpose or effect as to negate [the State's] intention' to deem it 'civil.' "[95] And, because the Court will " 'ordinarily defer to the legislature's stated intent,' "[96] only the " 'clearest proof' will suffice to override legislative intent and transform what has been denominated a civil remedy into a criminal penalty."[97]

Engaging the first step, the majority concluded that Alaska intended the law to further public protection, which like in *Hendricks*, was a " 'legitimate nonpunitive governmental objective.' "[98] It was of no moment, Justice Kennedy wrote, that public protection was also a purpose of the state's criminal justice system; the state's "pursuit of it in a regulatory scheme does not make the objective punitive."[99] The registration provision was codified in the state's "Health, Safety, and Housing Code," but the notification provision was in the criminal code. After acknowledging that " 'location and labels of a statutory provision do not by themselves transform a civil remedy into a criminal one,'"[100] the court concluded that the location of notification in the criminal code was "not sufficient to support a conclusion that the legislative intent was punitive."[101] The court also concluded that the procedures and requirements of SORA were consistent with the state's intent to create a civil, non-punitive regulatory regime.[102]

Turning to the effects of the law, the court—for the first time, and in its most thorough fashion to date—relied upon the analytic framework provided in *Kennedy v. Mendoza-Martinez* (1963),[103] discussed in Chapter 4. Justice Kennedy stated that the test's "factors, which migrated into our ex post facto case law from double jeopardy jurisprudence, have their earlier origins in cases under the Sixth and Eighth Amendments, as well as the Bill of Attainder and the Ex Post Facto Clauses."[104] "Because the *Mendoza-Martinez* factors are designed to apply in various constitutional contexts, we have said they are 'neither exhaustive nor dispositive,' but are 'useful guideposts.'"[105] The court, thereafter singled out five of the seven factors as "most relevant" to its analysis, in slightly rephrased form:

> whether, in its necessary operation, the regulatory scheme: [1] has been regarded in our history and traditions as a punishment; [2] imposes an affirmative disability or restraint; [3] promotes the traditional aims of punishment; [4] has a rational connection to a nonpunitive purpose; or [5] is excessive with respect to this purpose.[106]

Regarding the first factor, the court rejected respondents' argument that registration and notification, especially the latter, resembled colonial public-shaming punishments, stating that "the stigma of Alaska's [SORA] results not from public display for ridicule and shaming but from the dissemination of accurate information about a criminal record, most of which is already public."[107] While the court acknowledged that public dissemination of registrants' information could have adverse personal consequences, the court reasoned that

> the State does not make the publicity and the resulting stigma an integral part of the objective of the regulatory scheme . . . The purpose and the principal effect of notification are to inform the public for its own safety, not to humiliate the offender. Widespread public access is necessary for the efficacy of the scheme, and the attendant humiliation is but a collateral consequence of a valid regulation.[108]

The court also found that SORA did not impose an affirmative disability or restraint, the second factor, in part because its restrictions did not resemble imprisonment, which the court referred to as the "paradigmatic affirmative disability or restraint."[109] Moreover, the periodic verifications and updates required by the law did not have to be made in person, and under SORA, unlike the acknowledged punitive restraints of probation and parole, individuals were free to move, live, and work wherever they wished with no supervision.[110]

With respect to whether the law advanced a "traditional aim of punishment," the third factor, the court acknowledged that SORA promoted some traditional aims, such as deterrence, but explained that "any number of governmental programs might deter crime without imposing punishment."[111] Nor did the law have a retributive purpose, based on the associated increased onerousness of provisions with criminal history, because the requirements were "reasonably related to the danger of recidivism, and this is consistent with the regulatory objective."[112]

Turning to the fourth factor, whether SORA had a rational connection to a non-punitive purpose, which for unspecified reason it called "a '[m]ost significant' factor,'"[113] the court concluded that there was such a connection, and rejected respondents' argument that a connection was lacking because the law applied without making any assessment of the future dangerousness of individuals targeted.[114] After noting that "[a] statute is not deemed punitive simply because it lacks a close or perfect fit with the nonpunitive aims it seeks to advance,"[115] the court reasoned that it was rational for the Alaska legislature to use a conviction-based approach given the "grave concerns over the high rate of recidivism among convicted sex offenders and their dangerousness as a class."[116] The majority stated that just as in *Hawker v. New York* (1898), discussed in Chapter 4, where the court concluded that criminalizing the practice of medicine based on a prior felony conviction was not punitive, "[t]he State's determination to legislate with respect to convicted sex offenders as a class, rather than require individual determination of their dangerousness, does not make the statute a punishment under the *Ex Post Facto Clause*."[117]

The majority also rejected the argument that SORA was excessive because (1) registration was of extended duration, citing the "'frightening and high'" rate of sex offender recidivism;[118] and (2) registry information was disseminated statewide (indeed, worldwide) via the internet, because the state website was passive, requiring a viewer to access information, and the mobility of the state's population.[119] Ultimately, the majority stated, fit need not be exact:

> The excessiveness inquiry of our ex post facto jurisprudence is not an exercise in determining whether the legislature has made the best choice possible to address the problem it seeks to remedy. The question is whether the regulatory means chosen are reasonable in light of the nonpunitive objective. The Act meets this standard.[120]

The majority concluded with a brief treatment of the remaining two *Mendoza-Martinez* factors: whether the law comes into play on the basis of a finding of scienter and whether the behavior to which it applies is already a crime. The two factors were

> of little weight in this case. The regulatory scheme applies only to past conduct, which was, and is, a crime. This is a necessary beginning point, for recidivism is the statutory concern. The obligations the statute imposes are the responsibility of registration, a duty not predicated upon some present or repeated violation.[121]

Summarizing its conclusion regarding the effects part of the "intent-effects" test, the court stated that "[o]ur examination of the Act's effects leads to the determination that respondents cannot show, much less by the clearest proof, that the effects of the law negate Alaska's intention to establish a civil regulatory scheme."[122]

Justice Thomas concurred. Echoing his concurrence in *Seling v. Young* (discussed above), he agreed with the outcome but wrote separately to emphasize his position that judicial analysis of whether a statute is civil or criminal is determined solely on face of the statute: "the obligations created by the statute."[123] Therefore, he would not have taken into account whether the dissemination of registrants' information on the state website rendered SORA punitive because internet notification was technically not required by SORA.[124]

Justice Souter, in another concurrence, also agreed with the result but expressed his concern with the analytic rubric used by the majority. He maintained that the answer to the threshold question of whether the Alaska Legislature intended SORA to be non-punitive was unclear,[125] and that the demanding "clearest proof" standard is appropriate only when the assessment "clearly points in the civil direction."[126] Souter noted that SORA was not expressly designated as a civil regime, unlike in *Hendricks* and other cases, "which have relied heavily on the legislature's stated label in finding civil intent,"[127] and thought that SORA had both civil and criminal characteristics.[128]

Turning to step two, concerning the law's "purpose and effects," Souter took a more critical view than Justice Kennedy in his majority opinion, noting that while securing public safety is a "fundamental regulatory goal," that "it would be naïve to look no further, given pervasive attitudes toward sex offenders."[129] Also, because SORA used past conviction

> as the touchstone, probably sweeping in a significant number of people who pose no real threat to the community, serves to feed suspicion that something more

than regulation of safety is going on; when a legislature uses prior convictions to impose burdens that outpace the law's civil aims, there is room for serious argument that the ulterior purpose is to revisit past crimes, not prevent future ones.[130]

Finally, Souter pointed to the "severity of the burdens imposed" by SORA, discounting the majority's conclusion that the state was simply making public information available to community members. Rather, doing so resembled the traditional punishment of shaming, resulting in an array of negative consequences, including possible harassment, physical harm, and loss of employment.[131]

Ultimately, in Souter's view, the civil and criminal indicia were in "roughly equipoise," and "[c]ertainly, the formal evidence of legislative intent does not justify requiring the 'clearest proof' of penal substance in this case."[132] However, "what tip[ped] the scale" for Justice Souter was "the presumption of constitutionality normally accorded a State's law. That presumption gives the State the benefit of the doubt in close cases like this one, and on that basis alone I concur in the Court's judgment."[133]

Three justices dissented. In his dissent, Justice Stevens contended that SORA violated due process, and that it was punitive for ex post facto purposes. Unlike the laws challenged in *Hendricks* and other cases cited by the majority in support, under SORA a criminal conviction was both "a *sufficient* and a *necessary* condition of the sanction."[134] Stevens, moreover, used his dissent as an opportunity to condemn the court's punishment question jurisprudence more generally, and its application to SORA in particular, stating:

No matter how often the Court may repeat and manipulate multifactor tests that have been applied in wholly dissimilar cases involving only one or two of these three aspects of these statutory sanctions, it will never persuade me that the registration and reporting obligations that are imposed on convicted sex offenders and on no one else as a result of their convictions are not part of their punishment. In my opinion, a sanction that (1) is imposed on everyone who commits a criminal offense, (2) is not imposed on anyone else, and (3) severely impairs a person's liberty is punishment.[135]

In her dissent, joined by Justice Breyer, Justice Ginsburg echoed Souter's view that the "clearest proof" standard should not be applied because it was unclear whether the legislature intended SORA to be civil or punitive.[136] Instead, she advocated that the court "neutrally evaluate the act's purpose and effects," per the *Mendoza-Martinez* factors, which persuaded her of the punitive nature of

SORA. "What ultimately tip[ped] the balance," given what Ginsburg saw as a legitimate civil-regulatory purpose (public safety), was "the Act's excessiveness in relation to its nonpunitive purpose."[137] This was because SORA applied to all convicted sex offenders, without any individualized risk determination, and particular registration and information verification requirements were not tied to individual risk.[138] Finally, what Ginsburg saw as "meriting heaviest weight" in the punitiveness assessment, SORA did not allow for early termination of registration, based on rehabilitation.[139]

Smith, the latest decision from the court on the punishment question, is of enormous importance. In practical terms, the court's finding that the Alaska SORA was a civil-regulatory regime has served as precedent for multiple state and lower federal courts to reject ex post facto challenges to sex offender registration and community notification laws, including against newer laws of a more onerous nature (e.g., requiring in-person information verification),[140] and other laws retroactively imposing harsh sanctions on convicted sex offenders (e.g., where they can live, lifetime electronic monitoring).[141]

Smith also proved a milestone in ex post facto doctrine. In addition to reaffirming the intent-effects test, and the required burden to muster the "clearest proof" that a facially civil law is punitive in effect, outlined in *Hendricks* (1997), *Smith* was the first case where the court invoked and fully relied upon and addressed the multifactor *Mendoza-Martinez* test (at least five of its seven factors).

The three dissenting justices—Stevens, Ginsburg, and Breyer—applied the *Mendoza-Martinez* factors and reached the opposite conclusion of the majority. Stevens in particular remained unconvinced of the validity of the factors, "[n]o matter how often the Court may repeat and manipulate" the factors.[142] Also, Souter, in his concurrence, in language reminiscent of Justice Brennan's dissent in *Flemming v. Nestor* (1960)[143] criticizing the majority's disregard of the 1950s political climate in which the law challenged targeting former Communist Party members was enacted,[144] wrote that it "serves to feed suspicion that something more than regulation of safety is going on; when a legislature uses prior convictions to impose burdens that outpace the law's civil aims, there is room for serious argument that the ulterior purpose is to revisit past crimes, not prevent future ones."[145] Finally, three justices—Souter (concurring) and Ginsburg and Breyer (dissenting)—condemned the "clearest proof" requirement, advocating that the demanding standard only be employed when legislative civil intent is clear. These and other points are elaborated upon in Chapter 6.

Sentencing

Over the years, the court has frequently entertained challenges to laws ret-roactively changing sentences imposed on individuals convicted of crimes. Such challenges implicate *Calder* category three (proscribing "[e]very law that changes the punishment, and inflicts a greater punishment, than the law annexed to the crime, when committed"). As Chapter 4's survey of earlier twentieth-century decisions highlighted, such challenges enjoy higher rates of litigation success compared to *Calder*'s other three categories.

This subsection will examine two distinct junctures within the broader cate-gory of sentencing: "front-end" and "back-end." The former considers changes to sentencing guidelines, typically created by legislatures or commissions. "Back-end" laws concern changes to parole eligibility and deprivation of "gain time" and other forms of credit earned by inmates, having the poten-tial effect of extending periods of confinement. Discussion will also focus on so-called straddle offenses (briefly discussed in Chapter 4), those involving behavior that possibly comes within the ambit of an amended law resulting in a lengthier sentence.

Back-End

In earlier era decisions, the court addressed laws retroactively altering methods of punishment (e.g., how the death penalty was administered)[146] and those that functioned to increase sentence lengths imposed by courts.[147] In the 1990s, a time of "get tough" sentencing reform, the court addressed challenges to retroactive modifications to the ability of individuals to secure early release from confinement.

California Department of Corrections v. Morales (1995)[148] concerned a state law that retroactively changed when certain prisoners (persons convicted of more than one killing) could be considered for parole release—from an an-nual basis to up to three years.[149] By a 7-2 vote, the court rejected the chal-lenge, with Justice Thomas writing for the majority. The new law, Justice Thomas reasoned, was unlike prior successful claims against retroactive sen-tence changes (*Lindsey*, 1937; *Weaver*, 1981; and *Miller*, 1987), which had the "effect of enhancing the range of available prison terms."[150] The law *Morales* challenged merely "'alter[ed] the method to be followed' in fixing a parole re-lease date under identical substantive standards."[151] Moreover, the decreased number of required parole hearings created "only the most speculative and attenuated possibility . . . of increasing the measure of punishment for covered crimes, and such conjectural effects" did not present ex post facto difficulty.[152]

In a footnote, the majority expressly rejected the contention that changes in punishment are ex post facto if they produce "some ambiguous sort of 'disadvantage.'"[153] For the clause to apply, the petitioner must show "a sufficient risk of increasing the measure of punishment attached to the covered crimes."[154] Extending ex post facto coverage to laws having only conceivable risk of enhancing punishment would require the judiciary to be charged "with the micromanagement of an endless array of legislative adjustments of parole and sentencing procedures."[155] Such "changes might create some speculative, attenuated risk of affecting a prisoner's actual term of confinement by making it more difficult for him to make a persuasive case for early release, but that fact alone cannot end the matter for ex post facto purposes."[156]

With the foregoing, the court provided a new test—"sufficient risk of increasing the measure of punishment." But it failed to define the test's parameters, contenting itself with its conclusion that the law challenged created "only the most speculative and attenuated possibility," adding that any "conjectural effects" were insufficient to "satisfy any threshold we might establish under the Ex Post Facto Clause."[157]

Justice Stevens, joined by Justice Souter, dissented. After noting that the court had "consistently condemned laws falling in [*Calder* category three]," and that "[i]n light of the importance the Framers placed on the Ex Post Facto Clause, [the Court had] always enforced the prohibition against retroactive enhancement scrupulously,"[158] Stevens argued that the challenged law raised ex post facto concern because it singled out a subgroup of individuals: those (like Morales) convicted of more than one homicide. *Contra* the majority's acceptance of the view that the law was motivated by cost savings, Stevens inferred that the California legislature had a vindictive motivation, noting that the targeted subgroup was very small, and that the law was part of a national trend seeking harsher penalties and conditions of confinement. He wrote that

The danger of legislative overreaching against which the Ex Post Facto Clause protects is particularly acute when the target of the legislation is a narrow group as unpopular (to put it mildly) as multiple murderers. There is obviously little legislative hay to be made in cultivating the multiple murderer vote. For a statute such as the 1981 amendment, therefore, the concerns that animate the Ex Post Facto Clause demand enhanced, and not (as the majority seems to believe) reduced, judicial scrutiny.[159]

Although expressing no explicit disagreement with the "sufficient risk" standard, Stevens disagreed with the majority's conclusion that a retroactive increase in Morales's case was "speculative," arguing that the majority itself engaged in speculation, for instance, concerning the parole prospects of Morales and others like him. Stevens concluded by stating that "[t]o engage in such pure speculation while condemning respondent's assertion of increased punishment as 'speculative' seems to me not only unpersuasive, but actually perverse."[160]

Two years later, in *Lynce v. Mathis* (1997),[161] the court addressed a Florida law permitting the retroactive cancellation of early release credits earned by prisoners.[162] Lynce earned the credits and was released, only to be rearrested when, in response to public outcry,[163] a new law rescinded the prior grant of credit for certain inmates (including those convicted of attempted murder, such as Lynce).[164]

In addressing Lynce's ex post facto challenge, the unanimous court stated that "the Constitution places limits on the sovereign's ability "to use its lawmaking power to modify bargains it has made with its subjects,"[165] and looked to the "objective" effects of the legal change: whether the retroactive cancellation of the credits lengthened his incarceration.[166] With Justice Stevens writing, the court found the test satisfied, given that Lynce was rearrested after having been released.[167]

Unlike the lost "opportunity" and "speculative" lengthening of imprisonment contested in *Morales*, Lynce obviously experienced greater punishment (as he was re-imprisoned), justifying relief.[168] The state attempted to distinguish *Weaver v. Graham* (1981) (discussed in Chapter 4) on the ground that it involved "good time" credits earned by a prisoner, whereas credits earned by Lynce were conferred by the state to alleviate overcrowding. The court dismissed that distinction, stating "in *Weaver*, we relied not on the subjective motivation of the legislature in enacting the . . . credits, but rather on whether objectively the new statute 'lengthen[ed] the period that someone in petitioner's position must spend in prison.' "[169]

Justice Thomas, joined by Justice Scalia, authored a separate concurring opinion. Thomas wrote that whether a law retroactively increases punishment "is often a close question," but that unlike in *Morales* the increase in *Lynce* was neither "speculative" nor "attenuated."[170] He concurred "[u]nder these narrow circumstances," but expressly stated that he did not agree with the majority's discussion of *Weaver v. Graham*, decided before he was a justice, which invalidated retroactive change in the availability of credits, signaling his presumed disagreement with the result.[171] "The present case," Thomas stated, "involves not merely an effect on the availability of future release credits, but the retroactive elimination of credits already earned and used."[172]

Three years after *Lynce*, in *Garner v. Jones* (2000),[173] the court significantly altered its analytic methodology. In *Garner*, as in *Morales*, the court addressed a retroactive change in the frequency of parole hearings, increasing the wait period from three to eight years. Unlike in *Morales*, where the court asked whether there was a "sufficient risk" of a sentence increase, in *Garner* the six-member majority posed the question as whether the new law created a "significant risk" of prolonging an individual's incarceration.[174]

Garner also marked another important change. For the first time, the court explicitly looked beyond the statute challenged, creating a two-step test: "When the [challenged] rule does not by its own terms show a significant risk [of prolonging punishment], the respondent must demonstrate, by evidence drawn from the rule's practical implementation by the agency charged with exercising discretion, that its retroactive application will result in a longer period of incarceration than under the earlier rule."[175] Unless the face of the provision convinces the court "by its own terms" of a "significant risk" of increase, the party challenging it "must show that as applied to his own sentence the law created a significant risk of increasing his punishment."[176] The court remanded the case for further factual development, stating that the analysis of the lower court "failed to reveal whether the amendment [to the challenged rule], in its operation, created a significant risk of increased punishment for respondent."[177]

The shift to a two-step analysis, the first facial, the second as-applied, is at odds with express language in *Weaver v. Graham* (1981)[178] where a unanimous court stated that "[t]he inquiry looks to the challenged provision, and not to any special circumstances that may mitigate its effect on the particular individual."[179] Use of an as-applied test is also at odds with the court's conclusion one year later, in *Seling v. Young* (2001),[180] that the "punishment question" is determined on the face of a statute, not how it was applied to a particular individual. Why, indeed whether, different tests should be used to assess the "punishment question" (*Seling*) and whether a law "inflicts a greater punishment" (*Garner*, concerning *Calder* category three) remains unclear.

It also remains unclear whether the analytic model used in *Garner* applies only to challenges concerning discretionary parole. The court emphasized that "the presence of discretion does not displace the Ex Post Facto Clause's protections," but then added that "the idea of discretion is that it has the capacity, and the obligation, to change and adapt based on experience."[181] This qualifying language, and the court's statement that the "whole context" of parole is discretionary, suggest that future ex post facto challenges to retroactive parole changes will face a tough uphill climb.[182] Importantly, moreover, *Garner*'s "significant risk" standard has been applied by lower courts outside the parole context,[183] and the court itself more recently (*Peugh v. United States* (2013), discussed later), concerning a retroactive change to the federal sentencing guidelines (a "front-end" sentencing question), used both "sufficient" (*Morales*) and "significant" risk (*Garner*).[184]

Finally, *Garner* imposed a higher burden on a challenger in another respect. The *Garner* Court ultimately stated that a challenger "must show that as applied *to his own sentence* the law created a significant risk of increasing his punishment."[185] In prior cases, the court insisted that only the face of the statute be considered, raising the possibility that some but not all individuals affected would experience a recognized punishment increase.[186]

None of the aforementioned changes was noted by the *Garner* dissent, authored by Justice Souter, joined by Justices Stevens and Ginsburg.

Front-End

Until the latter part of the twentieth century, individuals convicted in state and federal courts typically were subject to what was known as indeterminate sentencing. Legislatures would prescribe a sentence range for particular crimes (e.g., ten to twenty years for an armed robbery), a court would impose the sentence, and a parole board or other entity would decide if and when an individual would be released (on the "back-end"). In the 1980s, however, an important shift began to occur. The federal government and states, in a "get tough" era,[187] began gravitating toward fixed, determinate sentences, often complemented by guidelines that courts would use to determine the more precise terms individuals would serve. The guidelines considered things such as any prior criminal history of the defendant, whether physical harm resulted from the crime, loss of money, etc.

In *Miller v. Florida* (1987),[188] discussed in Chapter 4, the court addressed a retroactive change adopted by Florida to its sentencing guidelines. The sentencing court applied the amended guidelines, increasing Miller's presumptive sentence to the lengthier new end of the range. The Supreme Court invalidated the change on ex post facto grounds. The court reasoned that in order to impose the petitioner's actual sentence under the preexisting guidelines, the sentencing judge would have been required to provide clear and convincing reasons for this higher sentence, but because the sentence imposed was within the new guidelines range it required no explanation and was unreviewable.[189] The fact that the guidelines "create[d] a high hurdle that must be cleared before discretion can be exercised" was sufficient to qualify as a retroactive increase in sentence.[190]

The guidelines regime adopted by Florida was one of many adopted by states. A higher profile effort was embarked upon by Congress, culminating in the 1984 Sentencing Reform Act. The act eliminated parole in the federal system and directed a newly created entity, the US Sentencing Commission, to promulgate guidelines for federal courts to apply when sentencing. For some twenty years, the guidelines were considered binding, consistent with the avowed legislative purpose of limiting the sentencing discretion of federal judges and the disparate sentences they often imposed.[191] In a landmark decision, *United States v. Booker* (2005),[192] however, the court deemed the guidelines "advisory" in nature, with the court later stating that the sentencing range for particular defendants should serve as the "starting point," subject to deviation above or below based on reasons specifically stated by the court.[193]

Eight years later, in *Peugh v. United States* (2013),[194] the court addressed a challenge to the federal guidelines. Peugh and several others were convicted in federal court of banking-related fraud schemes. Peugh argued that he should be sentenced under the 1998 version of guidelines, in effect at the time of his offenses, rather than the 2009 version in effect at the time of sentencing (in May 2010). Because the two versions yielded significantly different results for his applicable guidelines sentencing range, Peugh argued, using the later version violated the Ex Post Facto Clause.

By a 5-4 vote, the court, with Justice Sonia Sotomayor writing for the majority, granted relief. In doing so, the court rejected the government's argument that the higher sentence was permissible because it was the result of only "advisory," not legally binding guidelines (per *Booker*). Next, the court reasoned that *Miller* was not dispositive because the "hurdles" imposed on the sentencing judge in *Miller* were more restrictive than the "gentler checks" in the challenged law, which militated in favor of "more within-Guidelines sentences."[195] After citing evidence showing that sentences imposed were actually most often within guideline ranges, despite their advisory nature, the court concluded that the guidelines were the "lodestone" of federal sentencing, creating a "sufficient" or "significant" risk of a higher sentence.[196] The difference with *Miller*, in short, was one of degree, not kind.[197]

Thereafter, in a part of the opinion (III-C) in which Justice Kennedy did not join (meaning that Justice Sotomayor spoke for only four justices—herself, Ginsburg, Breyer, and Kagan), Sotomayor emphasized that the court's holding was "consistent with basic principles of fairness that animate the *Ex Post Facto* Clause. The framers considered *ex post facto* laws to be 'contrary to the first principles of the social compact and to every principle of sound legislation.' . . . The Clause ensures that individuals have fair warning of applicable laws and guards against vindictive legislative action."[198] Furthermore, "[e]ven where these concerns are not directly implicated . . . the Clause also safeguards 'a fundamental fairness interest . . . in having the government abide by the rules of law it establishes to govern the circumstances under which it can deprive a person of his or her liberty or life.'"[199]

Subjecting Peugh to a higher recommended sentence (from thirty to thirty-seven months to seventy–eighty-seven months) raised ex post facto concern, with one effect being an increase in the pressure to plead guilty, which data suggested did not disappear because the range was advisory.[200] Nor did it matter that as a formal matter the Sentencing Commission was "insulated from legislative interference," as the government argued, because "the coverage of the *Ex Post Facto* Clause is not limited to legislative acts."[201]

In his dissent, Justice Thomas, in part joined by Chief Justice Roberts and Justices Scalia and Alito, concluded that the guidelines change did not warrant ex post facto relief. Thomas first provided an extensive review of what he viewed as the limited practical impact of *Booker* on the sentencing discretion of federal judges, and distinguished *Miller*, reasoning that the law invalidated there significantly limited a court's discretion to impose less than an increased sentence.[202] Because the statutory sentencing range (as opposed to the guidelines range) in *Peugh* remained the same from the time of the petitioner's offense to the time of his sentencing, and because the advisory guidelines sentencing range did not—in the prohibitory language of *Calder v. Bull* (1798)—retroactively "affix" a new punishment, his sentence under the newer guidelines did not offend the Ex Post Facto Clause.[203]

In an interesting and potentially more important part of his dissent, in which he wrote only for himself, Justice Thomas stated that the majority's opinion "demonstrates the unworkability of our *ex post facto* jurisprudence."[204] In particular, he claimed that the assessment of whether a risk of increased punishment is "sufficient" had "devolved into little more than an exercise in judicial intuition."[205] As is often his wont in constitutional cases more generally, Justice Thomas urged that the court "return to the original meaning of the Clause as stated in Justice Chase's classic *Calder* formulation," which prohibits only retroactively increased punishment "'annexed to the crime.'"[206] "Under this view, courts must compare the punishment affixed to the crime at the time of the offense with the punishment affixed at the time of sentencing. If the latter is harsher than the former, the court must apply the punishment in effect at the time of the offense."[207]

The *Morales* "sufficient risk" standard, Justice Thomas wrote, improperly focuses on the "sentence the defendant *might* receive, rather than on the punishment 'annexed to the crime.'"[208] According to Thomas, who in a footnote wrote "[a]s the author of *Morales*, failure to apply the original meaning was an error to which I succumbed,"[209] "nothing in the text or history of the Ex Post Facto Clause suggests that it should hinge on the expectations that prisoners and defendants have about how many days they will spend in prison."[210] "Retroactive laws that merely create a *risk* that a defendant will receive a higher sentence . . . do not implicate traditional *ex post facto* concerns. An individual . . . may *hope* to receive a lenient sentence, and he may even have good reasons for expecting leniency. But he does not have any guarantees."[211] Justice Thomas continued:

> The law provides the defendant with only one assurance: He will be sentenced within the range affixed to his offense by statute. Legal changes that alter the likelihood of a particular sentence within the legally prescribed range do not deprive people of notice and fair warning, or implicate the concerns about tyranny that animated the adoption of the *Ex Post Facto* Clause.[212]

Because the statutory range of sentence in Peugh's case remained the same, the guidelines change only affected the "*likelihood*" of a particular sentence within the range, obliging rejection of the ex post facto challenge.

Justice Alito, joined by Chief Justice Roberts and Justice Scalia, agreed with Justice Thomas's conclusion that retroactive application of the guidelines did not satisfy the *Morales* "sufficient risk" test.[213] He stated, however, that he did "not have occasion in this case to reconsider that test's merits or its relation to the original understanding of the Clause."[214]

In the final analysis, it is difficult to determine the importance of *Peugh* vis-à-vis *Calder* category three (i.e., whether a retroactive law "inflicts a greater punishment"). When the votes are counted, five justices seemingly backed use of both the *Morales* "sufficient risk" and the *Garner* "significant risk" of greater punishment test (Sotomayor, Breyer, Ginsburg, Kagan, and Kennedy, who concurred with that part of Justice Sotomayor's opinion).

As discussed, Justice Thomas expressly rejected any "risk"-based test, focusing on whether the statutory punishment "annexed" to a crime increased, perhaps suggesting that only statutory law, not parole and sentencing guidelines, matter. Three other dissenters—Justices Alito and Scalia and Chief Justice Roberts—demurred on the question. With subsequent changes in the court's membership, it remains to be seen whether Justice Thomas's narrower view will ultimately prevail.

The Special Case of "Straddle" Offenses

To violate the ex post facto prohibition, it is of course essential that a law be retroactive in its operation. Generally speaking, a law is retroactive if it is passed, takes effect, or is amended after the commission of the offense in question. Courts look to the date of the offense, not the time of the trial, conviction, or sentencing of an individual.[215] The question, as the Supreme Court put it in *Weaver v. Graham* (1981),[216] is whether the challenged law "changes the legal consequences of acts completed before its effective date."[217]

As discussed in Chapter 4, a new law that increases the penalty for a crime based on a prior conviction is not violative of the clause. This is because, as the court stated in *McDonald v. Massachusetts* (1901),[218] the enhanced "punishment is for the new crime only, but is the heavier if he is an habitual criminal . . . The statute, imposing a punishment on none but future crimes, is not ex post facto."[219] The court reiterated its position several decades later in *Gryger v. Burke* (1948),[220] stating that the enhanced penalty "is not to be viewed as either a new jeopardy or additional penalty for the earlier crimes. It is a stiffened penalty for the latest crime, which is considered to be an aggravated offense because a repetitive one."[221]

Chapter 4 also discussed the timing of retroactivity. In that regard, it was noted that in *Samuels v. McCurdy* (1925)[222] the court concluded that continuing offenses, which begin and persist at least until the time of the new law, are not ex post facto.[223] Continuing offenses are distinct from "straddle" offenses, which one commentator defined as those "involv[ing] a single crime, but elements of that crime are satisfied both before and after a new law either aggravates the crime or increases the punishment for its completion."[224] Chapter 4 examined how straddle offenses can implicate *Calder* category one claims (outlawing retroactive crime creation). Here, focus is on the possible sentence-enhancement ramifications of straddle offenses (*Calder* categories two and three).

The connection between straddle offenses and sentencing is illustrated by how courts apply the US Sentencing Guidelines when two or more offenses occur over a period of time when the guidelines increase penalties for the offenses. As with *Calder* category one claims, concerning when an act is "completed" (see Chapter 4), with offenses that straddle old and newer versions of the guidelines, application of the newer version is permitted.[225] Similarly, the guidelines operate under a provision known as the "one-book rule," which instructs that if "the defendant is convicted of two offenses, the first committed before, and the second after, a revised edition of the Guidelines Manual became effective, the revised edition of the Guidelines Manual is to be applied to both offenses."[226] If a court is considering application of different versions of the guidelines, it should choose one version, which should be applied "in its entirety."[227] However, the guidelines also provide that "[i]f the court determines that the use of the Guidelines Manual in effect on the date that the defendant is sentenced would violate the Ex Post Facto Clause of the United States Constitution, the court shall use the Guidelines Manual in effect on the date that the offense of conviction was committed."[228]

How the foregoing impacts a particular sentence can depend on whether offenses, committed pre- and post-guideline revision, are "grouped." Almost all federal courts follow the approach of the First Circuit Court of Appeals in *United States v. Pagán-Ferrer* (2013),[229] where the defendant was convicted of civil-rights violations and obstruction of justice for lying to investigators in 2008 (post-amendment) about a 2003 assault (pre-amendment). The court upheld the heightened sentence, reasoning as follows:

> The Sentencing Guidelines' one book and grouping rules placed [the defendant] on notice that if he committed a closely related offense in the future, his sentence for both offenses would be calculated pursuant to the Guidelines in effect at the time of that later, related offense conduct. . . . Accordingly, the change in [the defendant's] offense level is properly viewed not as a consequence of an ex post facto violation, but as the direct result of his decision to engage in closely related offense conduct [after the amendment].[230]

In a later decision, *United States v. Mantha* (2019),[231] the First Circuit attached importance to the grouping of offenses in *Pagán-Ferrer* and the role it played in satisfying ex post facto notice concern. Emphasizing that the defendant's offenses were unrelated and spanned a considerable period of time, the court found notice problematic. The court added that the enhanced sentence also violated the ex post facto concern for fundamental fairness. "Simply telling a person that those rules may change should not suffice to circumvent the ex post facto bar. Otherwise, that bar could be effectively eliminated altogether by the enactment of a broad, catch-all caveat."[232] In so holding, the court aligned itself with the views of all but one other federal appellate court deciding the issue.[233]

The Resuscitation of *Calder* Category Four

In the court's landmark decision *Calder v. Bull* (1798),[234] Justice Chase identified four kinds of retroactive laws within the scope of the Ex Post Facto

Clause, specifying the fourth category as "[e]very law that alters the legal rules of evidence, and receives less, or different testimony, than the law required at the time of the commission of the offence, in order to convict the offender."[235] Two of the court's major decisions, however, *Beazell v. Ohio* (1925) and *Collins v. Youngblood* (1990), discussed in Chapter 4, seemingly disavowed category four as a basis for ex post facto challenge. This was so despite Chase's express identification of the category in his *Calder* list and concern expressed elsewhere in his *Calder* opinion over retroactive provisions that "change the rules of evidence, for the purpose of conviction."[236]

The viability of category four was directly before the court in *Carmell v. Texas* (2000).[237] *Carmell* involved yet another challenge to a law retroactively affecting sex offenders. At the time Carmell allegedly sexually abused his stepdaughter, Texas law specified that a person could not be convicted on the basis of uncorroborated testimony of a victim who was the age of his daughter. Later, Texas amended its law to allow convictions based on the uncorroborated testimony of any victim who, like his daughter, was less than eighteen at the time of the offense. The trial court applied the new law, allowing the stepdaughter to testify without corroboration. Carmell was convicted and challenged the retroactive application of the new law on ex post facto grounds, arguing that the change violated *Calder*'s fourth category.

In a highly unusual assemblage of liberal and conservative justices,[238] the court affirmed the existence of the fourth *Calder* category and held that the amended Texas law violated it. Writing for the 5-4 majority, Justice Stevens concluded that the new law "changed the quantum of evidence necessary to sustain a conviction; under the new law, petitioner could be (and was) convicted on the victim's testimony alone, without any corroborating evidence."[239] Stevens reasoned that "[r]equiring only the victim's testimony to convict, rather than the victim's testimony plus other corroborating evidence is surely 'less testimony required to convict' in any straightforward sense of those words."[240]

Justice Stevens's opinion for the Court began by tracing the provenance of the *Calder* categories, citing *Calder*'s reliance on eighteenth-century authorities William Blackstone and Richard Wooddeson, and their nineteenth-century successors Joseph Story and James Kent. Of particular note was the 1695 case of Sir John Fenwick, cited by the authorities, and which Justice Chase cited in *Calder* as an example of the fourth category. Fenwick was a Jacobin thought to have conspired with others to overthrow King William III. At the time of the alleged betrayal, English law required two witnesses to support any high treason conviction, which served to bar Fenwick's prosecution. Fenwick, however, was ultimately tried and convicted under a new law that eschewed the two-witness requirement.[241] Stevens reasoned that with Fenwick and Carmell alike a new law retroactively allowed the government to convict on "less than the previously required quantum of evidence."[242]

"The fourth category, so understood," Stevens wrote, "resonates harmoniously with one of the principal interests that the Ex Post Facto Clause was designed to serve, fundamental justice."[243] Allowing retroactive reduction in the amount of evidence needed to convict "is as grossly unfair as, say, retrospectively eliminating an element of the offense, increasing the punishment for an existing offense, or lowering the burden of proof."[244] Echoing the view he expressed for the majority in *Lynce v. Mathis* (1997),[245] Stevens wrote that "[t]here is plainly a fundamental fairness interest, even apart from any claim of reliance or notice, in having the government abide by the rules of law it establishes to govern the circumstances under which it can deprive a person of his or her liberty or life."[246] The clause, in short, prohibits the government from refusing, "after the fact, to play by its own rules, altering them in a way that is advantageous only to the State, to facilitate an easier conviction."[247]

Next, after again surveying historical sources in support of the "accuracy of the fourth category as an original matter,"[248] Stevens addressed the government's claim that the court had jettisoned the fourth *Calder* category in *Beazell v. Ohio* (1925) and *Collins v. Youngblood* (1990). Noting the inconsistency in *Collins* between its insistence that the *Calder* categories provide "the 'exclusive definition' of ex post facto laws," and its questionable assertion that *Beazell*'s truncated summary of the categories was a "faithful" interpretation of the "original understanding" of the Ex Post Facto Clause,[249] Stevens reaffirmed the existence of the fourth category. Calling the *Collins* Court's treatment of the issue "cryptic," he reasoned that if *Collins* had intended to discard the fourth category (itself not implicated under the *Collins* facts) it would not "have done so in a footnote . . . [T]his Court does not discard longstanding precedent in this manner."[250]

Justice Stevens next at length explained how the amended law changed the sufficiency of the evidence required to convict, rather than modified the competency of witnesses to testify. The latter was allowed in *Hopt v. Utah* (1884), where the court rejected a challenge to the retroactive removal of a rule prohibiting a convicted felon to testify, which Stevens characterized as a witness competency rule. The law Carmell challenged differed—it did not "simply enlarge the class of persons who may be competent to testify" or "remove existing restrictions" on the competency of potential witnesses.[251] Rather, like the newly enacted law imposed on Fenwick, it concerned the sufficiency of the evidence necessary for the government to meet its burden of proof.[252] *Hopt* itself "expressly distinguished witness competency laws from those laws that 'alter the degree, or lessen the amount or measure, of the proof which was made necessary to conviction when the crime was committed.' "[253] Justice Stevens elaborated on the distinction he saw between the two types of rules, again emphasizing the clause's core concern over unfairness:

> [A] sufficiency of the evidence rule resonates with the interests to which the Ex Post Facto Clause is addressed in a way that a witness competency rule does not. In particular, the elements of unfairness and injustice in subverting the presumption of innocence are directly implicated by rules lowering the quantum of evidence required to convict. Such rules will always run in the prosecution's favor, because they always make it easier to convict the accused. This is so even if the accused is not in fact guilty, because the coercive pressure of a more easily obtained conviction may induce a defendant to plead to a lesser crime rather than run the risk of conviction on a greater crime. Witness competency rules, to the contrary, do not necessarily run in the State's favor. A felon witness competency rule, for example, might help a defendant if a felon is able to relate credible exculpatory evidence.[254]

Justice Ginsburg authored a lengthy dissent, joined by Chief Justice Rehnquist and Justices O'Connor and Kennedy. She disputed the majority's conclusion that the Texas law was a "sufficiency of the evidence rule," arguing that it was functionally equivalent to the witness competency law upheld in *Hopt v. Utah*.[255]

Moreover, the amended law did not transgress any of the values protected by the clause. Fair notice was not violated because Carmell "had ample notice that the conduct in which he engaged was illegal. He certainly cannot claim to have relied in any way on the pre-amendment version [of the law]. He tendered no reason to anticipate that [his stepdaughter] would not report the assault within the outcry period, nor any cause to expect that corroborating evidence would not turn up sooner or later."[256] Nor, Ginsburg reasoned, was there evidence of legislative vindictiveness or arbitrariness: she saw no evidence that the "Texas Legislature intended to single out this defendant or any class of defendants for vindictive or arbitrary treatment. Instead, the amendment . . . simply brought the rules governing certain victim testimony in sexual offense prosecutions into conformity with Texas law governing witness testimony generally."[257]

Ginsburg also maintained that the fourth category of *Calder* had been nullified by *Beazell* and *Collins*, and reasoned that the four-category definition of ex post facto laws in *Calder* was dictum altogether, as *Calder* involved a civil statute, not a criminal one.[258] Further, she noted that Justices Iredell and Paterson in their *Calder* concurring opinions "gave no hint" that they considered rules of evidence to fall within the scope of the Ex Post Facto Clause.[259] Although Justice Stevens's majority opinion provided "an impressive-looking" array of cases in support of its view of the fourth category's vitality, the cases cited "simply quoted or paraphrased Chase's enumeration, a mechanical task that naturally entailed a recitation of the fourth category."[260] Also, none of the cases cited depended on the fourth category for the judgment the court reached,[261] and the only two other previous cases invoking the fourth category—*Kring v. Missouri* (1883) and *Thompson v. Utah* (1898)—were overruled by *Collins v. Youngblood* (1990).[262] Finally, Ginsburg objected to the majority's use of Fenwick's case as precedent, stating that the amended Texas law was "nothing like the two-witness rule on which Fenwick vainly relied"[263] and explained why this was so.

Carmell is a notable decision for several reasons. First and most obvious, the court resuscitated *Calder's* fourth category, which *Beazell* and *Collins* had seemingly disavowed.[264] Second, the court provided a newly formulated articulation of a basic value protected by the Clause—"fundamental fairness" (earlier voiced by Stevens in *Lynce*, and later relied upon by four Justices in *Peugh*), which, while "not a doctrine unto itself, invalidating laws under the Ex Post Facto Clause by its own force,"[265] takes its place alongside other interests the clause serves (fair notice, reliance, concern over vindictive legislation, separation of powers). On the narrow question of whether the challenged Texas law impermissibly affected the sufficiency of the evidence, as contended by the five-member majority, or was a permissible witness competency rule (like that previously upheld in *Hopt v. Utah*), as contended by the dissent, there remains room for reasonable minds to disagree, as the well-reasoned arguments advanced by both sides attest.

The Solidification of *Calder* Category Two

In *Stogner v. California* (2003),[266] the court addressed a claim based on the second *Calder* category, another category also seemingly abandoned by the court in *Beazell v. Ohio* (1925) and *Collins v. Youngblood* (1990), which proscribes "[e]very law that aggravates a crime, or makes it greater than it was when committed,"[267]

Stogner was still yet another case involving sex offenders. In 1998, Stogner was indicted for sexually abusing children between 1955 and 1973. Until 1993, California law provided a three-year statute of limitations, which by 1998 had long since expired with respect to Stogner's alleged wrongdoing. A 1993 amendment and another in 1996 allowed time-barred prosecutions regarding child sexual abuse to be brought.[268] The question before the court was whether the Ex Post Facto Clause was violated by California's effort to revive previously time-barred prosecutions.

The court, with Justice Breyer writing for the five-justice majority, concluded that the amendment ran afoul of *Calder*'s second category. As a general matter, Justice Breyer wrote, retroactively permitting time-expired prosecutions

> threaten[ed] the kind of harm that . . . the Ex Post Facto Clause seeks to avoid. Long ago the Court pointed out that the Clause protects liberty by preventing governments from enacting statutes with "manifestly unjust and oppressive" retroactive effects. Judge Learned Hand later wrote that extending a limitation period after the State has assured "a man that he has become safe from its pursuit . . . seems to most of us unfair and dishonest."[269]

In such a situation, "the government has refused 'to play by its own rules'"[270] and betrayed the interests protected by the clause. The new law also deprived Stogner of "fair warning" because he might have otherwise sought to preserve exculpatory evidence.[271] Moreover, if such a law were constitutionally condoned, legislatures would be permitted "to pick and choose when to act retroactively," risking both "'arbitrary and potentially vindictive legislation,' and erosion of the separation of powers."[272]

Second, Justice Breyer reasoned that the law fell "literally" within the second *Calder* category, noting that Justice Chase in *Calder*, in describing prohibited laws more generally, included new laws that "inflicted punishments, where the party was not, by law, liable to any punishment."[273] Focusing on this language in tandem with the actual language of the second category specified in *Calder*, Breyer concluded that the new law "aggravate[d]" Stogner's alleged crime because at the time of its amendment Stogner was not "liable to any punishment."[274] This understanding of the second category, in turn, clarified its distinctive place in the *Calder* framework:

> So to understand the second category (as applying where a new law inflicts a punishment upon a person not then subject to that punishment, to any degree) explains why and how that category differs from both the first category (making criminal noncriminal behavior) and the third category (aggravating the punishment).[275]

Breyer added that the new law also ran afoul of *Calder* category four, concerning changes to rules of evidence affecting the quantum of evidence needed to convict, which the court in *Carmell* condemned. This was because a statute of limitations "reflects a legislative judgment that, after a certain time, no quantum of evidence is sufficient to convict. . . . And that judgment typically rests, in large part, upon evidentiary concerns—for example, concern that the passage of time has eroded memories or made witnesses or other evidence unavailable."[276] Breyer also discussed at length the historical aversion for revival of expired statutes of limitation, citing Congress's rejection of such laws as applied to Confederates in the Reconstruction Era for treason prosecution, and condemnation of the laws by courts and commentators down the years.[277]

After an extended discussion of historical sources, Breyer addressed the dissent's assertion that it was not "unfair, in any constitutionally relevant sense," for California "to prosecute a man for crimes committed 25 to 42 years earlier when nearly a generation has passed since the law granted him an effective amnesty."[278] Breyer considered the law constitutionally invalid because it violated "significant reliance interests" and ignored "a predominating constitutional interest" in governmental fairness, which outweighed the competing governmental interest in prosecuting a decades-old allegation of child sexual abuse.[279]

The four-justice dissent, authored by Justice Kennedy, joined by Chief Justice Rehnquist, and Justices Scalia and Thomas, contended that the "Court's stretching of *Calder*'s second category contradicts the historical understanding of that category, departs from established precedent, and misapprehends the purpose of the Ex Post Facto Clause."[280] The second category prohibited only "those retroactive statutes which 'affect the criminal quality of the act charged [by] chang[ing] the legal definition of the offense.'"[281] The law challenged only altered the time period during which Stogner could be prosecuted; it did not change the criminal quality of his conduct.[282] Even the supplemented description of the second category used by the majority was inapt, Justice Kennedy reasoned, because it embodied what Justice Chase saw as wrongful laws passed by the British Parliament, and was not intended "as a definitive description of the laws prohibited" by the clause.[283] After disputing that the law was unfair, and noting social science findings highlighting the reasons behind delayed reporting of sexual abuse among children, Kennedy wrote that the majority's "opinion harms not only our ex post facto jurisprudence but also these and future victims of child abuse."[284]

Much like *Carmell*, which also entailed very scholarly majority and dissenting opinions laden with judicial and historical sources, *Stogner* provided the court with an opportunity to expand its focus beyond its typical diet of *Calder* category one and three challenges (the latter, mainly).

It arguably did so, however, by in the dissent's words "forc[ing]" the challenged law into *Calder*'s second category.[285] Recognizing that the law did not fit the precise language of the category in Calder's actual list—"2nd. Every law that aggravates a crime, or makes it greater than it was, when committed"— the majority resorted to language elsewhere in Chase's *Calder* opinion condemning a law that "'inflict[s] punishments, where the party was not, by law, liable to any punishment.'" Whether one is persuaded by the majority or dissent,[286] *Stogner* is a good example of the difficulties posed by the need to fit a challenged law into one of the procrustean four *Calder* categories, a matter addressed in Chapter 7.

Summary

Although spanning a mere thirty years, the era examined in this chapter witnessed some very significant developments. Most recently, the court signaled an inclination toward granting relief, at times by unusual liberal-conservative coalitions of justices (*Carmell*) or razor-thin five-justice majorities (*Stogner, Peugh*). *Carmell* and *Stogner* in particular signal an insistence that a government play "by its rules" and honor "fundamental fairness" when enacting criminal provisions. It was this same concern that prompted Justice Hugo Black, a leading civil libertarian and author of several decisions in the mid-twentieth century invoking the clause to grant relief, to insist that "the Government should turn square corners in dealing with the people."[287] More narrowly, *Carmell* and *Stogner* resulted in the rebirth of two long-ignored categories of the four identified by *Calder*.

Yet, as the foregoing also highlights, from the 1990s to today the court has imposed significant limits on the reach of the clause. This shift is most notable with what has been referred to here as the "punishment question"—how courts evaluate the critically important matter of whether a retroactive law is criminal in nature, the threshold requirement for an ex post facto challenge. In three cases, all addressing retroactive laws targeting previously convicted sex offenders, an especially reviled subpopulation,[288] the court rejected challenges and imposed significant hurdles. In *Kansas v. Hendricks* (1997) and *Seling v. Young* (2001), with potentially lifelong involuntary confinement, and later in *Smith v. Doe* (2003), with registration and community notification, the court held that laws enacted to promote public safety, and which imposed very significant burdens on those targeted, were valid civil regulations, not punishment. Taken together, the three cases marked a significant step in the evolution of the "punishment question," imposing a demanding standard that is used to this day.

Finally, during the period examined the court issued several decisions concerning sentencing, implicating *Calder* category three, which prohibits "[e]very law that changes the punishment, and inflicts a greater punishment, than the law annexed to the crime, when committed." With "back-end" retroactive sentencing laws in particular, which affect potential loss of parole eligibility, good time credits, and the like, the court muddied the doctrinal waters, variously referring to the burden as needing to show "sufficient" and "significant" likelihood of a sentence increase.

6

Recasting the "Punishment Question"

Although unequivocal in its prohibition—providing that neither states nor Congress "shall" pass ex post facto laws—the Ex Post Facto Clause has been treated by the Supreme Court in a distinctly equivocal way. Indeed, the uncertainty was apparent from the very outset, when in *Calder v. Bull* (1798) Justice Samuel Chase, whose opinion is now seen as containing the principal holdings of the decision, wrote that "naked and without explanation" the prohibition "is unintelligible, and means nothing."[1] Chase nevertheless stated that "ex post facto" laws have a "technical meaning," which "had been in use long before the Revolution, and had acquired an appropriate meaning, by Legislators, Lawyers, and Authors."[2] Chase concluded that only retroactive criminal (not civil) laws come within its scope, and identified four categories of laws as constitutionally problematic, noting that "all these, and similar laws, are manifestly unjust and oppressive."[3]

Since 1798, the Supreme Court has significantly added to this basic constitutional scaffolding through the "accretion of case law."[4] As the preceding chapters highlight, at times the court has embraced a broad understanding of the clause, and rigorously enforced its prohibitions; at other times, especially in the last several decades, the court has adopted a decidedly more cramped view, rejecting challenges to very burdensome retroactive laws. Taken together, the court's decisions have a distinctly ad hoc quality, marked by the creation and application of new and varied analytic tests, often from disparate constitutional areas, that lack theoretical grounding.[5]

This chapter addresses perhaps the foremost problematic aspect of the court's modern ex post facto doctrine—what has been referred to here as the "punishment question": how a court determines whether a provision is punitive, and therefore criminal in nature, a threshold requirement imposed by *Calder* for any successful challenge. Doctrine concerning the issue is problematic, not only for its indeterminacy and malleability, but more importantly because it diverges from the animating concerns of the clause and its basic structural purposes in the nation's constitutional democracy. The chapter begins with discussion of these purposes, which will inform the suggested ways in which the punishment question can be recast.

The Ex Post Facto Clause. Wayne A. Logan, Oxford University Press. © Oxford University Press 2023.
DOI: 10.1093/oso/9780190053505.003.0007

Structural Constitutional Purposes

As Chapter 1 highlighted, the framers adamantly opposed ex post facto laws and were acutely aware of the tendency of legislatures to enact them. Indeed, several delegates at the Constitutional Convention thought that such laws were so inherently problematic that it was unnecessary to expressly prohibit them in the Constitution. Oliver Ellsworth of Connecticut, a future US Supreme Court Chief Justice, reasoned that "there was no lawyer, no civilian who would not say that ex post facto laws were void of themselves. It cannot then be necessary to prohibit them."[6] Daniel Carroll of Maryland, however, maintained that "[e]xperience overruled all other calculations" and that "in whatever light [ex post facto laws] might be viewed by civilians or others, the State Legislatures had passed them, and they had taken effect."[7] Ultimately, the prevailing view was expressed by Hugh Williamson of North Carolina: that "[s]uch a prohibitory clause is in the Constitution of North Carolina ... [and] it has done good there & may do good here, because the Judges can take hold of it."[8]

When the time came to lobby for state ratification of the Constitution, the ex post facto prohibition assumed prime significance. In the *Federalist Papers*, James Madison described ex post facto laws as "contrary to the first principles of the social compact, and to every principle of sound legislation"[9] and argued that the prohibition of them, along with bills of attainder and those impairing the obligation of contracts, constituted a

> bulwark in favor of personal security and private rights ... The sober people of America are weary of the fluctuating policy which has directed the public councils. They have seen with regret and indignation that sudden changes and legislative interferences, in cases affecting personal rights, become jobs in the hands of enterprising and influential speculators, and snares to the more industrious and less informed part of the community.[10]

Alexander Hamilton, in another *Federalist Papers* entry, considered the ex post facto prohibition among the "greate[st] securities to liberty and republicanism [the Constitution] contains."[11] "[Ex post facto laws] have been, in all ages, the favorite and most formidable instruments of tyranny."[12]

Early decisions of the Supreme Court echoed these sentiments. Of the ex post facto laws passed by the British Parliament, Justice Chase in *Calder v. Bull* (1798)[13] wrote that "[w]ith very few exceptions the advocates of such laws were stimulated by ambition, or personal resentment, and vindictive malice.

To prevent such, and similar, acts of violence and injustice, I believe, the federal and state legislatures, were prohibited from passing any bill of attainder; or any ex post facto law."[14] Chase then zeroed in on what he saw as the "plain and obvious meaning and intention of the prohibition":

> that the Legislatures of the several states, shall not pass laws, after a fact done by a subject, or citizen, which shall have relation to such fact, and shall punish him for having done it. The prohibition considered in this light, is an additional bulwark in favour of the personal security of the subject, to protect his person from punishment by legislative acts, having a retrospective operation.[15]

A few years later, Chief Justice John Marshall in *Fletcher v. Peck* (1810)[16] again emphasized the framers' concern over the abusive proclivities of legislatures, especially in states, writing for the unanimous court that:

> Whatever respect might have been felt for the state sovereignties, it is not to be disguised that the framers of the constitution viewed, with some apprehension, the violent acts which might grow out of the feelings of the moment; and that the people of the United States, in adopting that instrument, have manifested a determination to shield themselves and their property from the effects of those sudden and strong passions to which men are exposed. The restrictions on the legislative power of the states are obviously founded in this sentiment; and the constitution of the United States contains what may be deemed a bill of rights for the people of each state.[17]

In 1827, in *Ogden v. Saunders*,[18] Justice Bushrod Washington focused on what he saw as the practical political reason behind the ex post facto prohibition:

> Why did the authors of the constitution turn their attention to this subject, which, at the first blush, would appear to be peculiarly fit to be left to the discretion of those who have the police and good government of the State under their management and control? The only answer to be given is, because laws of this character are oppressive, unjust, and tyrannical; and, as such, are condemned by the universal sentence of civilized man. The injustice and tyranny which characterizes ex post facto laws, consists altogether in their retrospective operation, which applies with equal force, although not exclusively, to bills of attainder.[19]

Recent decisions of the court echo this recognition of the structural constitutional purposes of the Ex Post Facto Clause. One, which aligns with its placement in Article I of the Constitution (which specifies the powers and limits of the legislative branch), is that it "restricts governmental power by restraining arbitrary and potentially vindictive legislation" and guards against "legislative abuses."[20] In doing so, the court noted in *Carmell v. Texas* (2000),[21] the clause helps ensure "fundamental fairness," in that ex post facto laws have one thing in common: "In each instance, the government refuses, after the fact, to play by its own rules, altering them in a way that is advantageous only to the State, to facilitate an easier conviction."[22] Justice John Paul Stevens, writing for the majority in *Carmell*, stated that "[t]here is plainly a fundamental fairness interest . . . in having the government abide by its own rules of law it establishes to govern the circumstances under which it can deprive a person of his or her liberty or life."[23] Stevens earlier evoked this same concern when he wrote for the unanimous court in *Lynce v. Mathis* (1997)[24] that "the Constitution places limits on the sovereign's ability to use its lawmaking power to modify bargains it has made with its subjects."[25] "The specific prohibition on ex post facto laws is . . . one aspect of the broader constitutional protection against arbitrary changes in the law."[26]

The clause guards against this unfairness. It does not prohibit passage of arbitrary or vindictive laws generally, but only those that are arbitrary or vindictive due to their retroactive force. With retroactivity, legislators can single out already identified parties who are disfavored (and who cannot change their past actions),[27] confident in the knowledge that the electorate will back them.[28] Functionally, the clause prevents legislators from politically benefiting themselves,[29] by requiring that if punitive laws are to be enacted, they must apply prospectively,[30] targeting only future (not yet identified) individuals.[31] Recently, Justice Neil Gorsuch noted that the expectation that laws apply prospectively "prevents majoritarian legislatures from condemning disfavored minorities for past conduct they are powerless to change."[32]

In this sense, the clause functions as what Professor Adrian Vermeule (borrowing from legal philosopher John Rawls) has termed a "veil of ignorance" rule, which help suppress "self-interested [political] decision making."[33] According to Professor Vermeule:

> The simplest tactic for introducing uncertainty is to entrench a constitutional requirement that rules be prospective—enacted in advance of the events they govern. The power of retroactive legislation, for example, enables legislators to identify the winners and losers from proposed policies—to know who will bear costs and benefits as well as what those costs and benefits will be. The opportunities for legislative self-dealing are obvious if legislators can match up identified winners and losers with past or future friends and enemies, respectively. Under a prospectivity requirement, however, legislators are hard put to match up consequences with allegiances, because prediction is intrinsically more difficult and less certain than

backward-looking observation, and because targets who know of the law will be able to steer clear of its prohibitions.[34]

The clause also helps ensure the separation of governmental powers. As the court stated in *Weaver v. Graham* (1981),[35] the clause "upholds the separation of powers by confining the legislature to penal decisions with prospective effect."[36] The ex post facto prohibition prevents legislatures from intruding upon a judicial prerogative—determining liability and imposing punishment on the basis of past conduct. In this respect, it is worth noting, the Ex Post Facto Clause differs from the Bill of Attainder Clause, also in Article I. The Bill of Attainder Clause bars state or federal legislation "that appl[ies] either to named individuals or to easily ascertainable members of a group in such a way as to inflict punishment on them without a judicial trial."[37] It thus honors separation of power concerns by barring legislative usurpation of judicial authority in individual cases.[38] The Ex Post Facto Clause bars retroactive criminal laws of general effect, a kind of lawmaking that is especially vulnerable to separation of powers abuse.[39]

A third and final purpose of the clause is to guard against retroactive laws depriving individuals of notice, undercutting their ability to rely on the law to guide their actions. Only in 1977 in *Dobbert v. Florida* did the court expressly identify notice as a concern,[40] but it since has often been invoked.[41] Notice of a legal change would be important, for instance, to an "indigent defendant engaged in negotiations that may lead to an acknowledgment of guilt and a suitable punishment."[42] Notice and frustration of reliance is also at issue when a legislature retroactively criminalizes previously innocent conduct,[43] implicating *Calder* category number one.

However, the concern arguably is not so much at issue in other contexts. Scholars, for instance, have long noted that the severity of punishment actually plays little role in deterring criminal activity,[44] which militates against notice being a concern when a punishment is retroactively increased (*Calder* category three, a common basis for ex post facto challenge). Similarly, notice is of little moment when a legislature retroactively alters the amount of imprisonment served by an inmate, such as by reducing "gain time" (condemned in *Weaver v. Florida* (1981)). Nor is notice likely to figure when a legislature retroactively alters a rule of evidence (*Calder* category four). In *Carmell v. Texas* (2000),[45] the court inferred, quite reasonably, that it was unlikely that the petitioner, when engaging in his alleged sexual abuse of a minor, relied to his detriment on a rule of evidence. Ultimately, governmental fairness, not notice, was what drove the *Carmell* Court's decision to invalidate the law challenged: "[t]here is plainly a fundamental fairness interest, even apart from any claim of reliance or notice, in having the government abide by the rules of law it establishes to govern the circumstances under which it can deprive a person of his or her liberty or life."[46] Finally, a basic practical reason limits the constitutional importance of notice. As the court put it in *Miller v. Florida* (1987),[47] "[t]he constitutional prohibition against *ex post facto* laws cannot be avoided merely by adding to a law notice that it might be changed."[48]

* * *

As the preceding makes clear, over the decades several important values and purposes of the clause have been identified, with the Supreme Court attaching varying degrees of importance to them. Overall, it can be said that concern over arbitrary or vindictive legislation, and its attendant fundamental unfairness, and to a lesser extent separation of powers and notice, are the predominant concerns. At its core, the clause guards against the "hydraulic pressures"[49] periodically affecting legislatures, which can drive them to enact burdensome retroactive laws at the expense of disfavored individuals "of the moment."[50] These recognitions, however, shed little light on how courts are to identify an unconstitutional ex post facto law in a principled manner. To simply say, as one Supreme Court Justice (in)famously did with regard to pornography in 1964, "I know it when I see it,"[51] is not a sufficient basis for resolving ex post facto challenges. This is especially so given the range of retroactive impediments imposed by modern-day legislatures of a nonphysical and "quasi-criminal" nature,[52] which the framers could not have imagined.

The discussion now turns to the key threshold question addressed in ex post facto challenges: whether a retroactive law is punitive (and therefore criminal) in nature.

Origins of the Punishment Question

Since *Calder v. Bull* (1798), the Ex Post Facto Clause has only prohibited retroactive laws of a criminal nature. During the century after *Calder*, the court used a decidedly non-formalistic analytic framework when deciding whether a law was criminal in nature. *Cummings v. Missouri* (1867),[53] which addressed an ex post facto challenge against a Civil War-era provision adopted in Missouri denying Confederate sympathizers the ability to pursue a profession, is illustrative. In addressing the challenge, the court adopted a broad understanding of what qualifies, stating that "[t]he deprivation of any rights, civil or political, previously enjoyed, may be punishment, the circumstances attending and the causes of the deprivation determining this fact."[54] "Any deprivation or suspension of any of these rights for past conduct is punishment, and can in no otherwise defined."[55] The Ex Post Facto Clause, Justice Field wrote for the court, was "intended to secure the liberty of the citizen ... [and] cannot be evaded by the form in which the power of the State is exerted."[56] Only a view years later, the court recognized the "liberal construction" it had provided the clause, "a construction in manifest accord with the purpose of the constitutional convention to protect the individual rights of life and liberty against hostile retrospective legislation."[57]

In subsequent decades, however, the court came to adopt a decidedly more formalistic, less generous analytic approach in ex post facto cases. A key shift occurred in *Flemming v. Nestor* (1960),[58] involving an ex post facto challenge lodged by another disdained group, of a different era—Communist Party sympathizers. In *Nestor*, the court introduced a new requirement, and burden, for challengers to surmount. In rejecting Nestor's ex post facto challenge to a law depriving him of earned Social Security benefits, a 5-4 majority of the court held that the "clearest proof" must exist contradicting a legislature's ostensible civil purpose in enacting a law.[59]

Another key development came in *Kennedy v. Mendoza-Martinez* (1963),[60] which actually involved a challenge based on the Fifth and Sixth Amendments, concerning a federal law that stripped several World War II draft evaders of their citizenship without providing them procedural protections. In addressing whether the deprivation of citizenship constituted the imposition of punishment, without affording procedural protection, the court again focused on legislative purpose, this time concluding that Congress intended to punish the petitioners. Although resolved on that basis, the court in dictum proceeded to provide a seven-factor test, patched together without comment with citations to *Cummings* and *Nestor* and several non-ex post facto cases,[61] saying of the factors that "are all relevant to the inquiry, and may often point in differing directions."[62]

The next formative decision came in *United States v. Ward* (1980),[63] which addressed whether a nominally civil penalty was criminal in nature for purposes of the Fifth Amendment's privilege against self-incrimination. In *Ward*, the court combined *Nestor* and *Mendoza-Martinez* to create what today is known as the "intent-effects" test. Under the test, it first must be determined whether the legislature intended the challenged law to be civil or criminal in nature, a question of "statutory construction."[64] A reviewing court must determine whether the legislature "indicated either expressly or impliedly a preference for one label or the other."[65] It must "consider the statute's text and its structure to determine the legislative objective,"[66] and "considerable deference must be accorded to the intent as the legislature has stated it."[67] If the court determines that the legislature had punitive intent, the analysis is complete and the law is classified as criminal in nature.[68]

If the law is determined to be non- punitive in intent, a court will then consider whether it is so punitive either in purpose or effect as to negate that intention. On this question, a court is to consider the seven factors set forth in *Mendoza-Martinez*:

[1] whether the sanction affirmatively disables or restrains those subject to it; [2] whether the sanction has been historically regarded as a punishment; [3] whether the sanction was imposed only on a finding of scienter; [4] whether the sanction's operation promotes the traditional aims of punishment: retribution and deterrence; [5] whether the behavior to which the sanction applies is already a crime; [6] whether the sanction has a rational connection to a nonpunitive purpose; and [7] whether the sanction appears excessive in relation to the nonpunitive purpose.[69]

After considering the effects, a court will grant relief only if the challenging party provides "the clearest proof" (per *Nestor*) negating the civil intent discerned as a threshold matter.[70]

The foregoing evolution is reflected in current ex post facto doctrine, which assumed substantial form first in *Kansas v. Hendricks* (1997) and later *Smith v. Doe* (2003). In *Hendricks*, a 5-4 decision, the court rejected an ex post facto challenge against the Kansas "Sexually Violent Predator Act" (SVPA), which resulted in the potentially lifelong involuntary confinement of a convicted sex offender, based on a law enacted after he committed his crime, and near the end of his prison sentence. The court first engaged in what will be referred to as "step one," assessing whether the legislature intended to enact a civil law. "If so, [the court will] ordinarily defer to the legislature's stated intent."[71] This manifest intent will be overridden only if the party challenging the statute provides "the clearest proof" that the law is so punitive either in purpose or effect as to negate the government's civil intent.[72] The latter analysis, which the *Hendricks* Court did not fully undertake,[73] entails what will be called "step two," based on analysis of the *Mendoza-Martinez* factors.

In *Smith v. Doe* (2003),[74] a 6-3 decision, the court rejected an ex post facto challenge to another law targeting previously convicted sex offenders: one retroactively imposing possible lifelong registration and community notification. *Smith,* in addition to conducting a step one analysis, more fully applied the *Mendoza-Martinez* test, and today serves as the court's primary exposition of the punishement question.

Step One: Legislative Intent

Step one is problematic for several significant reasons. First, discerning legislative intent is notoriously difficult.[75] As the court itself recognized in *Nestor*, "[j]udicial inquiries into [legislative] motives are at best a hazardous matter."[76] This is not only because of the difficulty of ascertaining, with any degree of certainty, the view(s) of a multi-member entity such as a legislature.[77] Even more important, the inquiry itself is at odds with the basic ex post facto tenet, expressed in *Cummings v. Missouri* (1867),[78] that the Ex Post Facto Clause was "intended to secure the liberty of the citizen . . . [and] cannot be evaded by the form in which the power of the State is exerted."[79] Twenty years later, in *Burgess v. Salmon* (1878),[80] the court emphasized that the clause could not be evaded by ascribing civil form to what is "essentially criminal."[81]

Suspicion over legislative labels is even more justified today, a time when legislatures are presumably mindful of the importance of labels.[82] Situating a new law in, say, the probate code and describing it as a "civil" procedure, as Kansas did with its SVPA law, exemplifies why labels should not govern.[83] The *Hendricks* majority concluded that "[n]othing on the face of the statute" suggested that the Kansas Legislature intended to impose an additional punishment,[84] notwithstanding the punitive political climate in which the SVPA originated, recounted in Chapter 5.

By conceiving of its task as solely one of "statutory construction," regardless of the context in which the law originated and the event(s) motivating it,[85] the *Hendricks* Court ignored a basic teaching—to quote the *Cummings* Court again: that "[t]he deprivation of any rights . . . may be punishment, the circumstances attending and the causes of the deprivation determining this fact."[86] Almost a century later, in another ex post facto case, the court in *De Veau v. Braisted* (1960)[87] similarly recognized that a challenged law must "be placed in the context of the structure and history of the legislation of which it is a part."[88] As Justice Souter said in *Smith v. Doe* (2003) of Alaska's avowed non-punitive intent in enacting its registration and community notification law, "it would be naive to look no further, given pervasive attitudes toward sex offenders."[89]

Even more problematic, in its effort to label the SVPA, the *Hendricks* Court embraced a very broad understanding of governmental regulatory (i.e., non-punitive) purpose. In the majority's view, when government seeks to "protect the health and safety of its citizens," it does so as an exercise of its civil "regulatory power," not "to add to the punishment."[90] Protecting public health and safety, however, is of course also a foremost purpose of the criminal justice system; both are embodied in governmental police power authority.[91] As constitutional law scholar Christopher Tiedeman noted in 1896,[92] using an example of police power authority strikingly similar to the facts of *Hendricks*: "The confinement of a violent lunatic is as defensible as the punishment of a criminal. The reason for both police regulations is the same, viz.: to insure the safety of the public . . ."[93]

Justice Stephen Breyer, in his *Hendricks* dissent, joined by three of his colleagues, condemned the broad view adopted by the majority, noting that commitment and incarnation of an individual seek and secure the same end.[94] The court itself recognized this roughly thirty years before, in *United States v. Brown* (1965),[95] which concerned a Bill of Attainder challenge, stating that "[o]ne of the reasons society imprisons those convicted of crimes is to keep them from inflicting future harm, but that does not make imprisonment any the less punishment."[96]

In short, concluding that a government has a non-punitive intent when it acts in the name of protecting public safety papers over the expansive, not always distinct components of governmental police power authority. Under the view adopted in *Hendricks*, would a law retroactively requiring the physical castration or whipping of a previously convicted male sex offender be considered a civil sanction, if the legislature says it is being done in the name of "protect[ing] the health and safety" of the public?

Exacerbating matters, the court has been inconsistent in its treatment of a discrete but significant aspect of its "statutory construction." In particular, the court has varied in how it assesses instances where a retroactive law provides procedural protections usually reserved for criminal cases. In *Smith*, the court deemed it important that the Alaska registration and community notification law did "not require the procedures adopted to contain any safeguards associated with the criminal process," leading it to "infer that the legislature envisioned the [law's] implementation to be civil and administrative."[97] Whereas in *Hendricks* the SVPA's inclusion of protections (e.g., proof beyond a reasonable doubt and provision of counsel for indigents) failed to militate in favor of the law being deemed punitive. Rather, the majority reasoned that the protections "demonstrate[d] that the Kansas legislature has taken great care to confine only a narrow class of particularly dangerous individuals, and then only after meeting the strictest procedural standards."[98]

Despite the foregoing concerns, a court's initial finding of non-punitive intent has major importance. This is because it can be overcome only if a very high standard of proof is satisfied: the petitioner must establish by the "clearest proof that the statutory scheme [is] so punitive either in purpose or effect as to negate [the State's] intention to deem it civil,"[99] based on step two, which is discussed next.

Step Two: Analysis of *Mendoza-Martinez* Factors

Conceivably, the second step of the analysis, which considers the "purpose and effect" of the challenged provision,[100] based on the multifactor *Mendoza-Martinez* framework, might ameliorate the court's label fetishism.[101] In *Smith v. Doe* (2003),[102] the court referred to the second step as a "useful framework" that "migrated" into its ex post facto jurisprudence from double jeopardy jurisprudence and originated "in cases under the Sixth and Eight Amendments, as well as the Bill of Attainder and Ex Post Facto Clauses."[103] Thereafter, echoing the view it expressed a decade before in *Austin v. United States* (1993), that the *Mendoza-Martinez* framework should be cabined to the Fifth and Sixth Amendment context in which it originated,[104] the *Smith* Court stated that because its factors originated from and are designed "to apply in various constitutional contexts," they are " 'neither exhaustive nor dispositive' . . . but are 'useful guideposts.' "[105] Today, however, the *Mendoza-Martinez* framework is always used to resolve ex post facto claims, and its factors are regarded as both exhaustive and dispositive. This is problematic for several reasons.

First and foremost, the framework, which as noted earlier was dictum because it was not even applied in *Mendoza-Martinez* (the law was deemed punitive on the basis of legislative intent), functions as an indeterminate grab bag of factors, which have never been ascribed relative weight or importance.[106] Although *Smith* instructed that the factors "are 'useful guideposts,' "[107] " 'neither exhaustive nor dispositive,' "[108] it also referred to the sixth factor (whether the sanction has a "rational connection to a nonpunitive purpose") as "a 'most significant' factor" in its analysis.[109] Lower courts have since ascribed most prominent weight to one or more other factors,[110] and varied in their approach to weighing the factors. A panel of the US Third Circuit Court of Appeals, for instance, recently rejected an ex post facto challenge stating that a law "need not be wholly nonpunitive to survive . . . it need only be mostly nonpunitive."[111] Meanwhile, the Louisiana Supreme Court rejected a federal ex post facto challenge because a law had a "predominantly nonpunitive" intent and effect.[112] As one commentator recently said of the *Mendoza-Martinez* factors:

the idea of a disability or restraint was correctly taken from *Cummings* and subsequent cases, but nowhere did those cases require the deprivation to be an *affirmative* one. The ideas of historical consideration and excessiveness . . . were entirely from dicta in earlier cases—and the same cases had often expressly rejected the idea that punishments *had* to be traditional or severe. The ideas of scienter and application to criminal act came out of a line of jurisdictional and tax cases that prior courts had considered irrelevant to constitutional questions—not from the more relevant *Cummings/Garland* rule that punishment had to be in response to past acts regardless of their character.[113]

A second problem with the *Mendoza-Martinez* factors is that they require highly subjective assessments by courts. Testament to this fact is that in *Smith* three of the nine justices (arguably four, including Justice Souter's ambivalent concurrence) disagreed on the punitive nature of the registration and notification law challenged; further disagreement was evident in the views of federal judges earlier in the progression of the case.[114] More recent litigation concerning laws retroactively requiring that convicted sex offenders wear global positioning satellite (GPS) tracking devices exhibits similar variation.[115]

The indeterminacy is not surprising when one considers the individual factors themselves. The first factor asks, "whether the sanction affirmatively disables or restrains those subject to it." As an initial matter, it should be noted that the factor is suspect given that fines, a long-standing sanction used by the criminal justice system, do not impose what one would generally consider an affirmative disability or restraint.[116] Moreover, even under the most cramped understanding of the factor it would seem that the involuntary confinement of Leroy Hendricks in a secure facility, likely for his lifetime, would readily qualify. Not so, according to the five-member *Hendricks* majority, which, in a notable instance of circular reasoning, dismissed the claim by stating that "[t]he State may take measures to restrict the freedom of the dangerously mentally ill. This is a legitimate non-punitive governmental objective and has been historically so regarded."[117] Predictably, the court's ultimate finding that the Kansas SVPA was non-punitive has since served as a constitutional benchmark for lower courts to reject ex post facto challenges against sanctions not involving physical restraint, such as lifelong required wearing of a GPS tracking device[118] and residence restrictions imposed on previously convicted sex offenders.[119]

Smith, which involved a challenge to a law retroactively singling out previously convicted sex offenders for registration and community notification (SORN), for a minimum of fifteen years and potentially life, highlights another problem with the factor. To the *Smith* majority, the fact that SORN did not impose "physical restraint" was key because it did "not resemble the punishment of imprisonment, which is the paradigmatic affirmative disability or restraint."[120] Nor was SORN, as a formal matter, an aspect of probation or supervised release (its targets were "off paper"), which the court has traditionally recognized as a punitive.[121] The *Smith* majority also dismissed as "minor" the many significant nonphysical burdens of SORN for registrants, such as the requirement that they confirm their registry information every three months and alert authorities of any changes in the interim.[122] With its stunted view the court ignored a basic teaching of its prior holding in *Collins v. Youngblood* (1990):[123] that a retroactive law is ex post facto if it makes "more burdensome the punishment for a crime,"[124] without consideration of degree of the burden imposed. It also ignored its decisions where retroactively imposed non-carceral burdens were deemed punitive (e.g., *Cummings v. Missouri*).

At least as important, *Smith* failed to take account of a critically important shift in correctional strategies that has occurred in recent years, of which SORN is a notable part. The constant legal requirement to personally certify at specified intervals the accuracy of registry information (including the car one drives, and home, school, and work addresses), and provide updates regarding any changes (such as growing a beard or driving a different car), under threat of prosecution for failing to do so, represents a unique encumbrance.[125] Surely no less consequential are the negative consequences flowing from community notification, whereby the information is publicly disseminated by government-run websites and other means, and is intended to allow community members to monitor registrants, which can result in harassment, job loss, forced residential moves, and vigilantism.[126]

By viewing such consequences as mere unintended byproducts of disseminated public information, a non-punitive "legitimate governmental objective," the *Smith* majority failed to recognize that SORN achieves a "hidden custody" of those it targets.[127] By design, SORN seeks to achieve the controlling surveillance effect of Jeremy Bentham's Panopticon, with its central tower and inspector's lodge.[128] Like the Panopticon, notification endeavors to make those subject to it feel that they are being watched,[129] what philosopher Michel Foucault described as "a state of conscious and permanent visibility that assures the automatic functioning of power. So to arrange things that the surveillance is permanent in its effects, even if it is discontinuous in its action."[130] SORN and Bentham's Panopticon refrain from use of physical irons yet they both succeed in imposing disciplinary control over their targets.[131] In short, the court, in drawing a constitutional line, should have exhibited greater awareness of the ongoing evolution toward non-carceral social control methods,[132] such as lifelong satellite tracking by the required wearing a GPS device and registration and community notification of individuals previously convicted of crimes (which many jurisdictions have extended to encompass non-sex offenders).

The second factor—whether "the sanction has been historically regarded as a punishment"—is also problematic. Justice Kennedy, writing for the majority in *Smith v. Doe*, explained that a "historical survey [of punishment] can be useful because a state that decides to punish an individual is likely to select a means deemed punitive in our tradition."[133] Historical connection is important, he suggested, "so that the public will regard it as such."[134]

There are three chief problems with the factor. First, the court has failed to specify the relevant historical period that should serve as a reference point—English common law, colonial America, Greek or Roman times? Use of prisons, as we know them today, emerged in prevalence as a punishment strategy only in the early-mid 1800s. If that is too late a frame of reference, a multi-decade prison term would not qualify as punishment, an odd result to be sure. Likewise, probation and supervised release, which as noted the *Smith* Court acknowledged constituted punishment, took root in the United States only in the mid to late nineteenth century.[135] Still yet, should the reference period be based on a particular jurisdiction's historical practices, as one court suggested?[136] And what falls within the parameters of "our tradition"? These questions remain unanswered.

Second, relatedly, the factor is assessed at such a high degree of generality that it does not likely serve Justice Kennedy's goal that the "public will regard [the challenged sanction] as [punishment]."[137] Beyond the death penalty, physical flogging, incarceration, and shaming in pillory, historical metrics can lack heuristic value, as the *Smith* Court's failure to discern the close parallel of SORN with colonial era shaming practices attests.

To the majority, SORN was a strategy of " 'fairly recent origin,' "[138] and did not constitute "traditional" punishment.[139] Historical parallel with colonial era public shaming, despite "[a]ny initial resemblance," was "misleading." This was because colonial practices involved physical pain, "face-to-face shaming or [physical expulsion] from the community," which SORN did not.[140] Moreover, with SORN stigma resulted "not from public display for ridicule and shaming but from the dissemination of accurate information about a criminal record,"[141] and the government was not responsible for any adverse personal consequences, including ostracism, loss of employment, or vigilantism.[142] "In contrast to the colonial shaming punishments," the *Smith* majority reasoned, "the State does not make the publicity and the resulting stigma an integral part of the objective of the regulatory scheme."[143] Posting registrants' identifying information on a government-operated website, including a current photo, home and work address information, identifying bodily marks, and criminal history, was "more analogous to a visit to an official archive of criminal records than it is to a scheme forcing an offender to appear in public with some visible badge of past criminality."[144]

The *Smith* majority was correct in concluding that the public shaming and ostracization that occurs with SORN is not the same as the colonial face-to-face variety; nor are the bodies of registrants physically acted upon, as in a colonial era town square pillory. Rather, with SORN the shaming is today primarily achieved by the internet, with its power to disseminate worldwide information regarding individuals, who are branded as "sexual offenders" or "sexual predators." As Justice Souter stated in his *Smith* concurrence:

> While the Court accepts the State's explanation that the Act simply makes public information available in a new way, the scheme does much more. Its point, after all, is to send a message that probably would not otherwise be heard, by selecting some conviction information out of its corpus of penal records and broadcasting it with a warning. Selection makes a statement, one that affects common reputation and sometimes carries harsher consequences, such as exclusion from jobs or housing, harassment, and physical harm.[145]

Even more problematic, the shaming is not for a limited period of time (as in colonial days), but very often for one's lifetime (even for non-lifetime registrants, given the indelibility of the internet, especially regarding non-governmental websites). And, because of the global reach of the internet, the branding follows registrants wherever they go (unlike in colonial days).

At the same time, the *Smith* Court erred in its characterization of community notification, conceiving of it simply as the provision of neutral information to the public. As noted by the New Hampshire Supreme Court:

> If the registry were truly just about making criminal records more easily available to the public, then all such records would be available. Instead, only certain offenders are listed on the website. This "[s]election makes a statement." [Smith, 538 U.S. at 109 (Souter, J., concurring).] . . . [T]he mere fact that certain individuals are on the list signals that they are worthy of such recognition. The act also makes the information readily and instantly accessible to anyone who wants it, which is not often the case for other public information and records.[146]

The court added, with respect to the unhelpful historical analogy used by the US Supreme Court in *Smith*, that:

We must recognize that our world has changed. The purpose of colonial shaming was to punish the offender by holding the offender out to the community as someone to be shunned or ridiculed. However, shaming also served to notify the community of the crime committed and the individual who committed it, so that members of the community could protect themselves. The act does the equivalent in our modern times. Our communities have grown, and in many ways, the internet is our town square. Placing offenders' pictures and information online serves to notify the community, but also holds them out for others to shame or shun.[147]

In short, as Professor Seth Kreimer observed of modern shaming sanctions, "[n]o one doubts that Hester Prynne's scarlet letter provided more than neutral information, or that the effort of Senator Joseph McCarthy to 'expose' the background of his political opponents was not simply public education."[148]

A third reason the "historically regarded as punishment" factor is problematic is that it is inherently static and atavistic; like the first factor, it ignores the evolving range of burdensome government social control strategies. A principal characteristic of this shift is a focus on the prevention of potential future crime and the reduction of criminal risk, what Professors Malcom Feeley and Jonathan Simon in 1992 called a "new penology" based on actuarial risk.[149] The Kansas SVPA law addressed in *Kansas v. Hendricks* and the Alaska SORN law addressed in *Smith v. Doe* exemplify this shift. They number among an expanding category of newly conceived "pre-crime restraints,"[150] which the second factor by definition ignores.

Very recently, in another constitutional context, the Supreme Court recognized the problem of using historical practices as a comparative baseline to resolve modern-day constitutional questions. In a case challenging the authority of police to search an individual's cell phone without a warrant, the Court in *Riley v. California* (2014)[151] reasoned that likening the massive information storage capacity of a modern cell phone to items like a bag or purse is "like saying a ride on horseback is materially indistinguishable from a flight to the moon. Both are ways of getting from point A to point B, but little else justifies lumping them together."[152] The same criticism applies to the second *Mendoza-Martinez* factor.

The third and fifth *Mendoza-Martinez* factors are related; the third asks, "whether the sanction was imposed only on a finding of scienter," and the fifth asks "whether the behavior to which the sanction applies is already a crime." Both seem sensible factors in assessing whether a law is punitive, but the Supreme Court disagreed in *Smith* and *Hendricks*, cases where the parties had been convicted of crimes (requiring scienter) before the laws were enacted. The *Hendricks* Court concluded that the SVPA used prior conviction "solely for evidentiary purposes, either to demonstrate that a 'mental abnormality' exists or to support a finding of future dangerousness."[153] Meanwhile, in *Smith* the court reasoned that both factors were "of little weight,"[154] stating "[t]he regulatory scheme applies only to past conduct, which was, and is, a crime."[155] A prior conviction "is the necessary beginning point, for recidivism is the statutory concern,"[156] the Court stated, and "[t]he obligations the statute imposes are the responsibility of registration, a duty not predicated upon some present or repeated violation."[157] What the court meant by the first clause in the foregoing sentence is unclear. The latter clause moreover, misapprehends what was challenged: *currently being subject* to the consequences of SORN, based on a past conviction.

A more accurate understanding of the two factors, one consistent with the precedents cited in *Mendoza-Martinez* itself for their existence, concerns whether application of the sanction depends on past misconduct requiring scienter (i.e., purpose or intent)—the most common mental state for a crime. Justice Souter, concurring in *Smith*, was correct in concluding that the Alaska SORN law used "past crime as the touchstone," which "serve[d] to feed suspicion that something more than regulation of safety [was] going on; when a legislature uses prior convictions to impose burdens that outpace the law's stated civil aims, there is room for serious argument that the ulterior purpose is to revisit past crimes, not prevent future ones."[158] Justice Ginsburg in her *Smith* dissent, joined by Justice Breyer, agreed with Justice Souter.[159] Justice Stevens, in his solo dissent in *Smith*, similarly observed that a criminal conviction was "both a *sufficient* and a *necessary* condition for the sanction."[160]

State supreme courts, interpreting ex post facto provisions in their state constitutions, have agreed with Justice Stevens. The Indiana Supreme Court, for instance, in *Wallace v. State* (2009),[161] in considering the array of offenses triggering registration in its state SORN law found that while a few were strict liability in nature (i.e., lacked scienter), the "overwhelming[]" number required a finding of scienter for conviction.[162] Regarding the fifth *Mendoza-Martinez* factor, the *Wallace* Court noted that state law required a "conviction" and reasoned that "it is the determination of guilt of a sex offense, not merely the fact of the conduct and potential for recidivism, that triggers the registration requirement." Ultimately, the court concluded, "[b]ecause it is the criminal conviction that triggers obligations under the Act," analysis favored a punitive finding, just as with the third factor.[163] Decisions of other state supreme courts reflect the same understanding and have reached the same conclusion with respect to their SORN laws.[164] In cases involving non-SORN ex post facto challenges, state courts have followed the same analytic approach.[165]

Again, on its face, the fifth factor—whether the challenged sanction is triggered by behavior that "is already a crime"—would seem eminently sensible. Yet, the more precise question for ex post facto purposes is whether the challenged sanction is triggered by a *conviction*, as *Wallace v. State* reasoned. The third factor—asking whether a sanction is imposed only on a finding of scienter—is problematic because it is under inclusive. Scienter, basically requiring knowing, criminal intent, is indeed the norm for criminal liability, but liability can of course also turn on strict liability (e.g., statutory rape) and non-intentional misconduct (e.g., involuntary manslaughter). However, in the end, it is unclear whether the two factors have much if any importance. As the US Court Appeals for the Fifth Circuit recently stated in rejecting a federal ex post facto claim against a retroactive felon disenfranchisement law, the fact that a sanction "may be 'tied to criminal activity' is 'insufficient to render the statut[e] punitive.'"[166]

Factor four asks whether the law's "operation will promote the traditional aims of punishment—retribution and deterrence."[167] This factor would seem easy enough to apply, as retribution and deterrence are familiar penological purposes. However, the matter is complicated from the start because, as the court has recognized, deterrence "may serve civil as well as criminal goals."[168] For instance, a civil monetary penalty for illegal dumping of waste seeks to deter, but so does a criminal fine, and governments in recent decades have increasingly used such quasi-civil sanctions.[169] In *Smith*, Justice Kennedy wrote for the Court that "[t]o hold that the mere presence of a deterrent purpose renders such sanctions 'criminal' . . . would severely undermine the Government's ability to engage in effective regulation."[170] Presence of a deterrent purpose, in short, is not dispositive because it "proves too much."[171]

The court's interpretation of the factor and the language it used to convey it prompts several questions. For one, how can deterrence have any significance, militating in favor of finding a punitive purpose, if laws can have a deterrent purpose without, as *Smith* put it, "imposing punishment"? Also, what precisely did the court mean when it said that the presence of a deterrence purpose "prove[d] too much"—what was proved too much: that the law had a punitive aim? And what did the court mean when it minimized the "mere presence" of a deterrence purpose? Was it suggesting that the purpose is irrelevant or that its presence must be considered against another purpose? The former would annul this component of factor four. The latter is not consistent with the factor itself, which simply asks whether the challenged law "promote[s]" a traditional aim of punishment, containing no comparative element (unlike factors six and seven).

That leaves retribution as the sole recognized purpose distinguishing a criminal from a civil sanction. And yet in *Hendricks*, the court found that a retributive purpose was absent from a law entitled the "Sexually Violent Predator Act," which permitted potentially lifelong involuntary confinement; was the centerpiece of a package of get-tough laws targeting convicted sex offenders; and had a legislative record clearly manifesting retributive intent (as discussed in Chapter 5). Similarly, in *Smith*, the court downplayed the central role that public blame plays in retribution,[172] prompting Justice Ginsburg in dissent to note that the SORN law challenged imposed "onerous and intrusive obligations on convicted sex offenders" and subjected them "to profound humiliation and community-wide ostracism."[173]

More generally, by focusing solely on retribution and deterrence, the court failed to recognize other "traditional aims" of the criminal justice system, which it has had no difficulty identifying before.[174] First and most obvious, it ignored incapacitation, which one would think would have figured in the court's analysis of the law challenged in *Hendricks*. The *Hendricks* majority gave incapacitation a nod yet dismissed it saying that "incapacitation may be a legitimate end of the civil law."[175] As noted, the court also ignored prior clear language in *United States v. Brown* (1965),[176] a Bill of Attainder challenge, which recognized incapacitation as a prime goal of the criminal justice system because it prevents detained individuals "from inflicting future harm."[177] In short, as one commentator correctly observed, the *Hendricks* Court wrongly conceived of incapacitation as an "alternative to punishment, as opposed to a specific form of it."[178]

The court also ignored the traditional penal aim of rehabilitation. Although it has recently gone out of fashion, rehabilitation—since the origin of the US prison system in the early 1800s—has served as an avowed goal of corrections. The *Hendricks* Court identified rehabilitation as at least an "ancillary goal" of the Kansas SVPA,[179] yet made no mention of its role in assessing whether it was punitive.

Ultimately, even presuming that only retribution and deterrence are the sole recognized "traditional aims," uncertainties reign. *Smith* seemingly requires that a court answer what the *primary* aim of a law is, which is quite different from the actual phrasing of the *Mendoza-Martinez* factor—simply whether the sanction "promote[s] a traditional aim of punishment." Or perhaps the standard is that the promotion of *any* civil purpose is sufficient to classify the sanction as non-punitive? Such an interpretation would also seem consistent with *Smith*.[180]

The sixth factor, which considers "whether the sanction has a rational connection to a nonpunitive purpose," appears repetitive of the fourth factor ("traditional aim[]"). In *Smith*, the court termed it "a 'most significant' factor" in its analysis,[181] although as noted earlier it is unclear whether the singling out of the factor pertained only to deciding the *Smith* challenge in particular, or applies more generally. Also, neither *Smith* nor the court's earlier decision in *United States v. Ursery* (1996),[182] a Double Jeopardy case, from which it drew the "most significant" factor language, stated why the factor was "most significant." Why would it be, compared to, say, the first factor—whether the sanction affirmatively disables or restrains those subject to it? The latter would appear a better candidate for preeminence, from a civil liberty perspective. Moreover, although the *Smith* Court used "a" rather than "the" in conjunction with "significant factor," *Ursery* used neither grammatical article, employing the phrase "[m]ost significant is that. . . ." Not surprisingly, lower courts relying on *Smith* have variously employed "a" and "the,"[183] and as noted earlier have designated other factors as having paramount importance.

Finally, the seventh factor—"whether the sanction appears excessive in relation to the nonpunitive purpose"—is problematic for its inherent subjectivity: How is "excessive[ness]" to be determined? *Smith* ultimately made clear that the seventh factor analysis itself should be quite permissive. This is because assessing excessiveness "is not an exercise in determining whether the legislature has made the best choice possible to address the problem it seeks to remedy. The question is *whether the regulatory means chosen are reasonable* in light of the nonpunitive objective."[184] So conceived, the framework bears a striking resemblance to the "rational basis" test,[185] the least demanding, most deferential scrutiny courts more generally use in assessing the constitutional propriety of social and economic legislation, again a judicial perspective at odds with the structural role and purpose of the clause.

For the reasons discussed, the *Mendoza-Martinez* framework is problematic for multiple reasons. It is inherently indeterminate test and contains readily manipulable factors, which are repetitive[186] and selectively relied upon, and require normative judgments without guidance on how the factors are to be weighed.[187] Even the Supreme Court has admitted this indeterminacy, admonishing that the *Mendoza-Martinez* factors "are all relevant to the inquiry, and may point in different directions."[188] As two commentators recently observed of the *Mendoza-Martinez* analysis:

> In every case of its application, the judge ends up with a mixture of yes and no answers to each of the seven factors and must ultimately determine whether the sanction at hand is civil or criminal based upon her own valuation of each factor and its relative weight. Inevitably, the Court resorts to tautological reasoning: it purports to define as criminal, and thus order heightened procedural safeguards

for[,] sanctions that serve primarily to punish, when, as a matter of fact, the punitive purpose ascribed to the sanction rests upon some intuition regarding the
procedural safeguards that the sanction merits. In other words, the purported test
does no more than restate the underlying issue, rather than lead to the answer[189]

Nor did the *Smith* Court make clear whether the "effects" of a law are to be
assessed singly and in isolation, or cumulatively, although it would appear
that the former approach was employed.

Uncertainty Regarding Consideration of "Effects"

Exacerbating matters, uncertainty exists regarding the fundamental question
of which if any "effects" can be considered by courts when applying the two-
step "intent-effects" test. This is because of *Seling v. Young* (2001),[190] which
the court decided between *Hendricks* (1997) and *Smith* (2003). In *Seling*,
discussed in Chapter 5, the court rejected an "as applied" ex post facto challenge to a Washington State sex offender involuntary commitment statute
"nearly identical" to that upheld in in *Hendricks*. *Seling* held that when a law is
deemed civil, as the Washington Supreme Court had previously concluded regarding its state law, the initial civil showing "cannot be altered based merely
on vagaries in the implementation of the authorizing statute."[191] Properly
read, the five-Justice *Seling* majority held that "effects" are to be disregarded
only when the law in question has previously been deemed civil (as in *Seling*
itself).[192]

Concurring opinions of justices in *Seling*, however, have muddied the water.
Justice Scalia, joined by Justice Souter, agreed that a law initially declared civil
cannot later be transformed into a punitive one because of the way that it is
implemented.[193] In a footnote, Justice Scalia added that because the Ex Post
Facto Clause expressly prohibits "pass[ing]" ex post facto laws, a limit on legislative action, "the irrelevance of subsequent executive implementation to"
assessing legislative intent "is, if anything, even clearer."[194] Scalia also rejected
the majority's view that actual conditions of confinement and implementation
might have relevance to the analysis of whether a law is civil or criminal "in
the first instance."[195] In yet another concurring opinion, Justice Thomas (with
no one joining) made the latter point even more forcefully. He asserted that
an "implementation-based challenge to a facially civil statute" was not proper
in principle, even in the first instance. Only the effect(s) authorized by the
"face of the statute" are relevant.[196] Justice Thomas reiterated this view in his
Smith concurrence, stating that effects beyond "obligations actually created

by the statute" must be ignored (in *Smith*, internet notification, not expressly required by the statute).[197]

Troublingly, lower courts are showing an inclination to embrace the view of Justices Thomas, Scalia, and Souter. The US Ninth Circuit Court of Appeals, for instance, in *Does v. Wasden* (2020)[198] stated that "ex post facto claims based on the punitive effect of purportedly civil statutes cannot be construed as 'as-applied' challenges."[199] The Supreme Court of Maine, in *State v. Letalien* (2009),[200] likewise categorically precluded as-applied ex post facto challenges. Other courts have adopted a similarly narrow view.[201]

In addition to being inconsistent with the *Seling* majority opinion, and being at odds with other aspects of ex post facto analysis (e.g., when a sentence is allegedly lengthened due to a change in parole procedure, which is conceived "as applied to [a petitioner's] own sentence"),[202] the narrow view is contrary to the court's own precedent. *Smith v. Doe* itself involved an "as applied" challenge to an Alaska law,[203] made no mention of *Seling* (decided only two years before), and stated that analysis of the *Mendoza-Martinez* factors must assess "how the effects of the [law] are felt by those subject to it,"[204] the impact of the law "as to them."[205] Applying these precepts, the US Sixth Circuit Court of Appeals in *Does v. Snyder* (2016)[206] invalidated on ex post facto grounds Michigan's SORN law (which also entailed residence exclusion laws), noting that the plaintiffs "had trouble finding a home in which they c[ould] legally live or a job where they c[ould] legally work," and "those Plaintiffs who ha[d] children (or grandchildren)" were prevented "from watching them participate in school plays or on school sports teams" or from "visiting public playgrounds with their children for fear of 'loitering.'"[207] In short, ex post facto challenges are very commonly lodged as "as applied," not facial, challenges.[208]

If the narrow view prevails it would be a very significant development for ex post facto doctrine. Regarding an ex post facto challenge as always "facial" in nature can be outcome determinative because a litigant must establish that "no application of the statute would be constitutional."[209] An as applied challenge, however, "does not contend that a law is unconstitutional as written but that its application to a particular person under particular circumstances deprived that person of a constitutional right."[210] Although in recent years, courts, including the Supreme Court, have jousted over the importance of labeling a challenge as one type or another, it is accepted that facial challenges are "disfavored"[211] and more difficult to sustain.[212]

As a practical matter, the narrow view would introduce significant confusion into analysis of a law's "effects," step two of modern ex post facto analysis. How is a court to distinguish consideration of what the New Jersey Supreme

Court recently referred to as a law's "real world effects,"[213] stemming from what *Smith* called its "necessary operation," from constitutionally irrelevant effects? A good example concerns the well-documented homelessness often experienced by sex offender registrants, which is exacerbated by laws prohibiting where they can lawfully live (e.g., within 2000' of a school or playground). Homelessness is not a specified goal of SORN laws but it regularly occurs. Or, what if a new residence exclusion law makes it a crime for a registrant to live in an area where he rents or owns a home but a non-home owning registrant does not experience this impact? Is the distinct burden experienced by the homeowner constitutionally irrelevant? And what of harassment and vigilantism experienced by some but not all registrants, or a particular registrant's loss of a job due to a public protest at his workplace? Such "effects," again, are not expressly ordained by statute, even though they occur with regularity.[214]

Ultimately, refusal to consider such effects will make it even more difficult for petitioners to satisfy the demanding "clearest proof" standard, which is discussed next.

"Clearest Proof" Requirement

Another problematic aspect of modern era ex post facto doctrine is the requirement that a litigant establish by the "clearest proof" that a purportedly civil law is actually punitive in its effects. The party challenging a law bears the "heavy burden" of satisfying the demanding standard.[215] In *Hudson v. United States* (1997),[216] which addressed whether particular sanctions were punitive under the Double Jeopardy Clause, Justice Souter noted the increasing use of quasi-criminal sanctions and warned us "to be wary" of presuming that use of the clearest proof requirement "is likely to be as rare in the future as it has been in the past."[217] His words were prescient. Much as the *Mendoza-Martinez* factors have become mainstays, not mere nonexclusive "guideposts," the clearest proof standard is now a mainstay of punishment question analysis.

The first concern with the "clearest proof" requirement is uncertainty over when the demanding standard should be used. In *Smith*, Justice Souter in his concurring opinion reaffirmed his position that the "heightened burden makes sense only when the evidence of legislative intent clearly points in the civil direction,"[218] a view shared by Justice Ginsburg in her *Smith* dissent (joined by Justice Breyer).[219] Only a minority of courts, however, agree with Justices Souter, Ginsburg, and Breyer.[220] And even then uncertainty reigns because judges on the same court can disagree over whether non-punitive legislative intent is "clear[]."[221]

Second, as discussed in Chapter 4, the clearest proof test, with its "heavy burden," is problematic because it wrongly superimposes on substantive ex post facto doctrine what is a generally operative judicial presumption—that legislation enjoys a presumption of constitutionality.[222] As a consequence, the Ex Post Facto Clause, which was included in Article I to guard against legislative abuses and protect individual liberty, has been largely sapped of its vitality.[223] As Justice Stevens observed in his dissent in *California Department of Corrections v. Morales* (1995), "the concerns that animate the Ex Post Facto Clause demand enhanced, and not . . . reduced, judicial scrutiny."[224]

From the framers' perspective, we can safely assume that Justice Souter's anemic suspicion in *Smith* that perhaps "something more than regulation of safety is going on" when a legislature retroactively singles out for lifelong harsh treatment convicted sex offenders[225]—a reviled subpopulation[226]—would come as a disappointment. That the abdication of enhanced judicial scrutiny should occur with the Ex Post Facto Clause, one of the few specified limitations on the legislative branch identified in the Constitution,[227] and one of the select few liberty-protecting provisions in the Constitution itself (as opposed to the Bill of Rights), is especially problematic.[228]

Finally, it is worth noting that the clearest proof standard is notably absent from the proof regime the court has prescribed for challenges brought under the Bill of Attainder Clause and the Contracts Clause, the two other chief prohibitions on legislative power specified in Article I, section 10.[229] The absence of the requirement regarding bill of attainder, which also turns on whether a law is punitive in nature, especially underscores the irregularity of its presence in ex post facto doctrine.

The Punishment Question in State Courts

Although it is commonly thought that federal courts have exclusive say over federal constitutional questions, this is not the case. With federal constitutional law, the US Supreme Court does indeed have final say on its interpretation and application. As a result, for example, the court's decision in *Smith v. Doe* (2003) and its analytic regime dictate how federal trial courts and federal circuit courts of appeal interpret and apply the federal Ex Post Facto Clause. State courts, which also entertain federal constitutional law challenges,[230] must also defer to US Supreme Court decisions on federal constitutional questions.

State courts, however, also have a form of constitutional authority that federal courts—even the US Supreme Court—do not: they have final say over the interpretation and application of their own state constitutional provisions.[231] Almost all states have an ex post facto provision in their state constitution (Appendix B provides a list), several of which predated the US Constitution and influenced adoption of a federal counterpart (see Chapter 1).[232] Typically, the language contained in state ex post facto provisions mirrors in material part language in the US Constitution.[233] When this occurs, state courts usually adopt an *in pari materia* approach, referred to "lock stepping," resulting in state doctrine tracking federal doctrine.[234]

However, several state supreme courts, independently applying their own state constitutional ex post facto provisions, have taken a broader view.[235] The separation is evidenced in state court invalidation of sex offender registration and notification (SORN) laws.[236] Perhaps the most notable instance is the 2008 decision by the Alaska Supreme Court in *Doe v. State*.[237] In *Doe*, the court addressed a state ex post facto challenge to the same SORN law earlier upheld by the US Supreme Court in *Smith v. Doe* (2003), but granted relief based on its identically worded state ex post facto provision. It did so by applying the same analytic regime prescribed by the court in *Smith*, including the multifactor *Mendoza-Martinez* framework,[238] but exercised its independent authority to interpret and apply its own ex post facto provision.[239] In so concluding, the Alaska Supreme Court "disagree[d], respectfully but firmly" with the *Smith* majority, adding that it viewed its decision as "consistent with. . . the compelling comments of dissenting [Justices Stevens and Ginsburg] in *Smith*."[240]

Other state supreme courts have also granted relief on the basis of their state ex post facto constitutions, impliedly but not expressly deeming their provisions to be of broader reach.[241] The New Hampshire Supreme Court, for instance, granted a state ex post facto challenge using the *Smith* regime, stating that "[a]lthough the State and Federal Constitutions afford the same protection against *ex post facto* laws," it had "the responsibility to make an independent determination for the protections afforded in the New Hampshire Constitution.'"[242] Unlike the US Supreme Court in *Smith*, which made no mention of the important matter, the New Hampshire Supreme Court emphasized that the inquiry regarding effects "'cannot be answered by looking at the effect of any single provision in the abstract'"; rather, a court "must consider the effect of all the provisions 'and their cumulative impact upon the defendant's rights.'"[243]

The Oklahoma Supreme Court, also using the *Smith* regime, emphasized that "we are not limited in our interpretation of Oklahoma's constitution" and found its SORN law (complemented by residence limits) punitive, relying in significant part on the *Smith* dissents and stating that the legislature had unconstitutionally "continued to move the finish line" for those targeted.[244] The highest courts of Maine[245] and Pennsylvania[246] have held that their SORN laws are punitive under both their own constitutions and the US Constitution.[247]

Although it can be the case that the SORN laws challenged differ from the Alaska law upheld in *Smith*, for instance requiring periodic in-person (as opposed to mail or electronic) verification of registry information,[248] it is evident that many state courts undertake a more rigorous evaluation of the effects of laws than that in *Smith*, more in keeping with the constitutional "bulwark" envisioned by the framers and consistent with the court's formative nineteenth-century case law.

Proposed Test

Having dedicated so much time to critiquing the Supreme Court's current approach to answering the "punishment question," the time has come for a proposed alternative. And none too soon. Despite the core importance of the Ex Post Facto Clause in the nation's constitutional order, and more than two centuries after its adoption, a reliable, definitive test for deciding the threshold question for its application is lacking. We know this because the Supreme Court itself in *Smith v. Doe* (2003) stated that the core component of punishment question analysis, the factors specified in *Mendoza-Martinez*, are only " 'useful guideposts' " that are " 'neither exhaustive nor dispositive.' "[249]

Presuming that the Ex Post Facto Clause will continue to concern only retroactive laws of a criminal nature (a matter re-examined in Chapter 7), the definitional task is a considerable one.[250] Compared to the punishment question, the related *enhancement* of punishment question (*Calder* category three, discussed in Chapter 5)—itself beleaguered by several basic uncertainties—is a model of clarity and consistency. The contrast in significant part is explained by the fact that enhancement of a sentence—which is concededly penal— often lends itself to a more quantitative analysis.[251] Whether a sanction is punitive depends on evaluation of the seven *Mendoza-Martinez* factors, with penological theory figuring centrally, which itself is not amenable to "formulaic definition,"[252] complicated by the fact that sanctions can serve both punitive and non-punitive purposes.

The Supreme Court has emphasized that the reach of a constitutional provision should turn on the "reasons" it was included in the Constitution and "the evils it was designed to eliminate."[253] Recognition of the need for such tailoring was evident in *Smith v. Doe*, when the court wrote that the *Mendoza-Martinez* framework provides only "useful guideposts" because it "migrated into" the court's ex post facto doctrine from other constitutional areas and its factors "are designed to apply in various constitutional contexts."[254]

Although tailoring is evident in many constitutional contexts in which the punishment question arises,[255] a particularly noteworthy instance is found in the court's case law concerning the Bill of Attainder Clause (BOAC), which is considered the constitutional "twin" of the Ex Post Facto Clause.[256] As noted earlier, a bill of attainder, which like an ex post facto law is banned in both sections 9 and 10 of Article I, is "a law that legislatively determines guilt and inflicts punishment upon an identifiable individual without provision of the protections of a judicial trial."[257] In *Carmell v. Texas* (2000),[258] the court recognized the "kinship between bills of attainder and ex post facto laws,"[259] which is evident in the numerous challenges invoking both clauses, dating back most notably to the Confederate "loyalty oath" cases of *Cummings v. Missouri* (1867)[260] and *Ex parte Garland* (1867).[261]

As noted, application of the BOAC prohibition also turns on whether the law challenged is punitive,[262] and like the Ex Post Facto Clause, which resists evasion "by the form in which the power of the State is exerted,"[263] the BOAC "deals with substance not shadows. Its inhibition was levelled at the thing not the name."[264] In the last several decades, however, the analytic framework for answering the punishment question in the two constitutional contexts has experienced a marked separation. *Brown v. United States* (1965)[265] was a key decision in this evolution. In *Brown*, the court invalidated on BOAC grounds a law making it a crime for a Communist Party member to serve as an officer or employee of a labor union. Tracing the historical events giving rise to the inclusion of the BOAC in the Constitution,[266] the court stated that while historical instances of attainders provided some guidance, "the proper scope of the Bill of Attainder Clause, and its relevance to contemporary problems, must ultimately be sought by attempting to discern the reasons for its inclusion in the Constitution, and the evils it was designed to eliminate."[267] The BOAC, the *Brown* Court stated, "was intended not as a narrow, technical (and therefore soon to be outmoded) prohibition. . . ."[268] Quoting *Cummings*, the court stated that the "deprivation of any rights, civil or political, previously enjoyed," could constitute a bill of attainder, depending on "the circumstances attending and the causes of the deprivation[.]"[269]

The *Brown* Court also adopted a broad understanding of penal purposes, compared to the limited view expressed in *Kansas v. Hendricks* (1997) and *Smith v. Doe* (2003). The court stated that "[p]unishment serves several purposes; retributive, rehabilitative, deterrent—and preventive," not only retribution and deterrence.[270] Moreover, in contrast to the *Hendricks* and *Smith* view of prevention as being regulatory (i.e., non-penal), the *Brown* Court recognized that "[o]ne of the reasons society imprisons those convicted of crimes is to keep them from inflicting future harm, but that does not make imprisonment any the less punishment."[271]

This same insistence on constitutional purpose, generous construction, and temporal flexibility was evidenced in the court's next BOAC decision, *Nixon v. Administrator of General Services* (1977).[272] In *Nixon*, the court rejected a BOAC claim brought by President Richard Nixon against the federal Presidential Recordings and Materials Preservation Act, which allowed the government to take custody of his presidential papers and materials, preventing their possible destruction. Nixon sued to enjoin implementation of the act, arguing inter alia that it singled him out for retroactive "punishment" in violation of the BOAC. Although the court rejected the challenge, it recognized that its BOAC cases provided a "broad and generous meaning to the constitutional protection against bills of attainder."[273] The court added that its "treatment of the scope of the Clause has never precluded the possibility that new burdens and deprivations might be legislatively fashioned that are inconsistent with the bill of attainder guarantee."[274]

Seven years after *Nixon*, *Selective Service System v. Minnesota Public Interest Research Group (MPIC)*[275] addressed whether retroactive application of the federal Military Selective Service Act, which denied financial aid to students who evaded the Vietnam War draft, constituted a bill of attainder. After canvasing several of its prior BOAC decisions, the court provided the following test for determining whether a law constitutes punishment under the BOAC:

(1) "whether the challenged law falls within the historical meaning of legislative punishment";
(2) whether the law, "viewed in terms of the type and severity of burdens imposed, reasonably can be said to further nonpunitive purposes"; and
(3) "whether the legislative record evinces a congressional intent to punish."[276]

Applying the tripartite framework, the court concluded that the law challenged did not "inflict punishment within the meaning of the Bill of Attainder Clause."[277]

Drawing from the court's decisions, punishment question analysis in a BOAC challenge is animated by several principles:

(1) "the proper scope of the [BOAC], and its relevance to contempo-
    rary problems, must ultimately be sought by attempting to discern
    the reasons for its inclusion in the Constitution, and the evils it was
    designed to eliminate" (*Brown*);
(2) the BOAC "was intended not as a narrow, technical (and therefore soon
    to be outmoded) prohibition" (*Brown*);
(3) in interpreting the BOAC, a court is to be mindful that "[p]unishment
    serves several purposes; retributive, rehabilitative, deterrent—and pre-
    ventive" (*Brown*);
(4) "treatment of the scope of the [BOAC] has never precluded the possi-
    bility that new burdens and deprivations might be legislatively fashioned
    that are inconsistent with the bill of attainder guarantee" (*Nixon*); and
(5) the Court has provided a "broad and generous meaning to the consti-
    tutional protection against bills of attainder" (*Nixon*).

Because the BOAC and the Ex Post Facto Clause share the basic constitutional pedigree and purpose of guarding against arbitrary and abusive
legislative enactments,[278] adopting the same analytic rubric for answering
the punishment question is sensible. However, while an improvement over
ex post facto doctrine, the three-part BOAC test enunciated by the court in
MPIC is not free of problems.

To start, the first BOAC test factor—whether the law "falls within the historical meaning of legislative punishment"—suffers from the same problematic historically hidebound view as *Mendoza-Martinez* and can be explained
away (as in *Smith v. Doe*, distinguishing the obvious historical parallel of
SORN with colonial era shaming). As important, the first factor is contrary to
three of the several key BOAC principles identified above:

(1) *Nixon*'s recognition that "treatment of the scope of the [BOAC] has never
    precluded the possibility that new burdens and deprivations might be legis-
    latively fashioned that are inconsistent with the bill of attainder guarantee";
(2) *Brown*'s statement that "the proper scope of the [BOAC], and its rel-
    evance to contemporary problems, must ultimately be sought by
    attempting to discern the reasons for its inclusion in the Constitution,
    and the evils it was designed to eliminate"; and
(3) *Brown*'s insistence that the BOAC "was intended not as a narrow, tech-
    nical (and therefore soon to be outmoded) prohibition."

The second BOAC factor—asking whether the law "viewed in terms
of the type and severity of burdens imposed, reasonably can be said to

further nonpunitive purposes"—suffers from the same indeterminacy of the *Mendoza-Martinez* "effects" test, in particular its factors (1), (4), (6), and (7). However, consideration of the "type and severity of burdens imposed" by a challenged law has obvious importance to the assessment of whether a law is punitive. In *Cummings*, interpreting both the BOAC and the Ex Post Facto Clause, the court stated that "[t]he deprivation of any rights, civil or political, previously enjoyed, may be punishment. . . ."[279]

The *Cummings* Court conceptualization obviously covers a lot of territory. One resource to lend further specificity lies in yet another kindred constitutional area—the "antiretroactivty presumption," which the Supreme Court applies when addressing statutes of uncertain temporal scope,[280] in the absence of "unambiguously instructed retroactivity."[281] The presumption has obvious parallel to ex post facto doctrine (less so BOAC doctrine, which does not technically require that a law be retroactive).[282] Indeed, in *Johnson v. United States* (2000),[283] which involved an initial ex post facto challenge that was ultimately resolved by determining that the federal law challenged was not retroactive in its application, the court stated that the Ex Post Facto Clause "raises to the constitutional level one of the most basic presumptions of our law: legislation, especially of the criminal sort, is not to be applied retroactively."[284]

The court's decisions applying the anti-retroactivity presumption provide useful insight into the kinds of burdens warranting attention. In *Vartelas v. Holder* (2012),[285] which addressed whether Congress intended an immigration law to apply retroactively, the court, invoking principles dating back to the early nineteenth century, stated that the anti-retroactivity presumption arises when retroactive application of a law would take away or impair vested rights acquired under existing law, or create a new obligation, impose a new duty, or attach a new disability.[286] The assessment of whether a law should be applied retroactively, the court stated in *Martin v. Hadix* (1999),[287] ultimately "demands a commonsense, functional judgment about 'whether the new provision attaches new legal consequences to events completed before its enactment.'"[288]

Finally, the third BOAC factor—asking whether the legislative record evinces a legislative motivation to punish—also warrants attention, despite the misgivings earlier identified regarding the undertaking, especially as practiced in *Kansas v. Hendricks*. Laws do not originate in a vacuum; what the *Cummings* Court termed "the circumstances attending and the causes of the deprivation"[289] should figure in the determination of whether a law is punitive. In *Cummings*, the court addressed a state constitutional provision adopted toward the end of the Civil War in Missouri (a border state). "It would have been strange," the court observed, "had [the amended Missouri Constitution] not exhibited in its provisions some traces of the excitement amidst which the convention held its deliberations."[290] In *Nixon*, the court undertook an extensive examination of the legislative record, finding no punitive purpose in a BOAC challenge. This absence, the court found, distinguished *Nixon* from its prior decision in *United States v. Lovett* (1946) where it found a bill of attainder,[291] in which "a House Report expressly characterized individuals as 'subversive ... and ... unfit ... to continue in Government employment.'"[292] The *Nixon* Court, however, was at pains to make clear that a "formal legislative announcement of moral blameworthiness or punishment" was not a prerequisite to concluding that the enactment constituted a bill of attainder.[293]

In short, with ex post facto doctrine, as with BOAC, a court should consider what *Cummings* called the "circumstances" in which the challenged law came into existence. Evidence of vindictiveness and/or disdain for a targeted population or past behavior, and any occurrences propelling the law in question, should be accorded importance. As Chief Justice John Marshall long ago advised, "[w]here the mind labours to discover the design of the legislature, it seizes everything from which aid can be derived."[294]

Taken together, the approach suggested here can be summarized as follows. A court should first examine the legislative record and context in which the challenged law arose for evidence of punitive motivation, notwithstanding any express legislative espousal of non-punitive intent. Next, the impact of the law on those targeted should be analyzed, considering the "type and severity of the burden imposed,"[295] including the deprivation of "any rights, civil or political, previously enjoyed,"[296] and whether the law "'tak[es] away or impai[rs] vested rights acquired under existing laws, or creat[es] a new obligation, impos[es] a new duty, or attac[hes] a new disability, in respect to transactions or considerations already past.'"[297] Importantly, ultimately, when evaluating Ex Post Facto Clause challenges, courts, as with BOAC challenges, should heed *Nixon*'s command that the clause be provided a "broad and generous meaning," and be mindful, as *Brown* put it, "of the reasons for its inclusion in the Constitution, and the evils it was designed to eliminate" and not conceived "as a narrow technical (and therefore soon to be outmoded) prohibiton."

There is much to be said in favor of leaving the test at that—as with BOAC doctrine, not requiring any further analysis, certainly not use of a "clearest proof" standard, with its "heavy burden" of proof. A court should approach the challenged law as it would any other constitutional challenge—with a presumption of constitutionality.[298]

In the alternative, the framework might require an additional step that would raise the bar for an effective challenge. In particular, the framework could create a rebuttable presumption that the law is punitive, imposing on the government the burden to negate the presumption.

The shift in burden from the law's challenger to the government would not be unprecedented: it occurs in challenges brought under the Contracts Clause. Like the Ex Post Facto Clause and the BOAC, the Contracts Clause is one of the few categorical prohibitions on legislation contained in the body of the Constitution, in Article I, section 10.[299] The framers included each prohibition based on recent experience,[300] with the Contracts Clause the experience being widespread efforts by state legislatures, dominated by debtors or their advocates, to repudiate or beneficially alter contracts with creditors.[301] James Madison in the *Federalist Papers*[302] and Chief Justice John Marshall in *Fletcher v. Peck* (1810)[303] spoke of the Ex Post Facto Clause, the BOAC, and the Contracts Clause collectively, as protections against governmental police power authority overreach. From early on, the court held that the Contracts Clause applied to public and private contracts alike.[304]

Although today Contracts Clause doctrine is less robust than in the late eighteenth and nineteenth centuries,[305] its current analytic framework is important to the discussion here because it still reflects the framers' acute concern over abusive legislation. In a Contracts Clause challenge, a reviewing court first asks "'whether the state law has operated as a substantial impairment of a contractual relationship.'"[306] If so, the state must identify "'a significant and legitimate public purpose'" for the impairment, and ensure that the impairment "is drawn in an 'appropriate' and 'reasonable' way to advance" that purpose.[307] If the state is not a contracting party, the "courts properly defer to legislative judgment as to the necessity and reasonableness of a particular measure,"[308] using a standard of review amounting to something somewhat more demanding than the rational basis test customarily used in constitutional challenges to economic legislation.[309]

However, a "stricter standard" of review is required when a state government is a contracting party. When the state substantially impairs its obligations under a contract in which it is a party, the Supreme Court has stated that less deference is owed because concern exists that legislators will seek to advance the "State's self-interest" in modifying or rescinding its obligations.[310] Although the matter is not entirely free of doubt, language in the court's decisions[311] and the reasoning of most state and lower federal appellate courts addressing the issue[312] impose on the government the burden of showing that the substantial impairment is both reasonable and necessary.[313]

The Ex Post Facto Clause guards against this same self-interested legislative behavior. *Carmell v. Texas* (2000), discussed in Chapter 5, is illustrative. In *Carmell*, the court backed an ex post facto challenge against a retrospective change in state evidence law removing the requirement that a victim's sexual assault allegation be corroborated by another party, not the victim alone, which effectively reduced the amount and kind of evidence required to convict. Interpreting the fourth *Calder* category, the *Carmell* Court held that while changes in evidentiary rules are not always improper, a change is improper if it does so only "in a way that is advantageous only to the State."[314] Rule changes that lower the amount of evidence needed to convict are improper, Justice Stevens wrote for the court, inasmuch as they "*always* run in the prosecution's favor because they always make it easier to convict the accused."[315]

Shifting to the government the burden to rebut an inference of punitiveness in ex post facto doctrine would mark a radical shift: no longer would an individual need to satisfy the burdensome "clearest proof" standard; instead, the government would be required to rebut the presumption of punitiveness raised. In doing so, the analytic framework would align with the framers' suspicion of retroactive laws, and allow the clause to serve as the "bulwark" envisioned by James Madison and other framers.

Summary

Use of the new framework suggested would have several benefits. First, unlike current doctrine,[316] it would serve the basic structural purposes of the Ex Post Facto Clause as a check on the "sudden and strong passions" that can result in the enactment of "arbitrary and vindictive" retroactive laws. Second, consistent with the framers' skepticism over legislative propensities, the framework adopts a functional approach consistent with the recognition that the Ex Post Facto Clause was "intended to secure the liberty of the citizen . . . [and] cannot be evaded by the form in which the power of the State is exerted."[317] Finally, by abandoning the "clearest proof" burden, or by imposing on the state the burden to justify what appears to be a punitive law, the framework will allow the Ex Post Facto Clause to serve its intended structural purpose,[318] allowing courts, in Professor Richard Fallon's words, to "implement the Constitution."[319]

Independent of its substantive merits, the shorter, more specific framework is preferable because it can better provide ex ante guidance to legislatures in their lawmaking efforts. Historically, the Ex Post Facto Clause operated as a legislative lodestar, perhaps most notably after the Civil War when Radical Republicans in Congress cited it as a reason for not enacting a law reviving time-barred prosecutions of Confederates for treason.[320] Many years ago

Professor Paul Brest recognized the "practical problems that confront a legislator whose constitutional obligations conflict with the political demands of his office," noting that "[p]erhaps it is naive to assume that the Constitution will often prevail when political interests are threatened."[321] Whether the suggested framework will actually have the salutary goal sought, of course, remains to be seen; however, as the Supreme Court stated with regard to its anti-retroactivity presumption, in *Landgraf v. USI Film Products* (1994),[322] doing so will hopefully better achieve the "virtue of giving legislators a predictable background rule against which to legislate."[323]

Conclusion

The temptation for Congress and state legislatures to pass burdensome retroactive laws is age-old and, if recent history is to serve as a guide, will not abate any time soon. The Ex Post Facto Clause, as Chief Justice Marshall observed not long after the nation's formation, was designed to guard against such laws, inspired by the "feelings of the moment" and the "sudden and strong passions" that can beset legislative bodies.[324]As Justice Stephen Breyer recognized in his dissent in *Kansas v. Hendricks* (1997), the clause "provides an assurance that, where so significant a restriction of an individual's basic freedoms is at issue, a [legislature] cannot cut corners. Rather, the legislature must hew to the Constitution's liberty-protecting line."[325] It is hoped that the overhaul suggested in this chapter—concerning what has become a major barrier to successful challenges against burdensome retroactive laws—will help resuscitate and fortify the liberty-protecting constitutional line that the clause was intended to provide.

7
Broadening the Scope of Coverage

The preceding chapters surveyed the Framing Era history and intended purposes of the Ex Post Facto Clause; the Supreme Court's decision in *Calder v. Bull* (1798), the reigning precedent interpreting the clause, and criticisms of it; decisions by the court in subsequent decades regarding the scope and application of the clause; and the ways in which the court's decisions have often strayed from the meaning and purpose of the clause, regarding the "punishment question" in particular, and the how this can be remedied. This chapter addresses four other key issues concerning the coverage of the clause.

The first concerns whether the clause should prohibit both retroactive civil and criminal laws, not only the latter. As Chapters 1 and 2 recount, the court's conclusion in *Calder v. Bull* that the clause only applies to criminal laws has long been contested. The accumulated history provides the basis for the provocative possibility of expanding its reach. Doing so would align with calls by "originalists" to interpret and apply the Constitution's provisions in a way that is consistent with its understanding during the Framing Era. It would also have significant practical benefit, including avoiding the need to engage in the "punishment question" addressed at length in Chapter 6. There are, however, potential downsides to expansion; for instance, should all, or only some, retroactive civil laws be banned? These and other issues are explored.

Next, the discussion turns to disavowing another long-accepted benchmark for the application of the clause: that a challenged law falls within at least one of the four categories of laws specified in *Calder*. As with the limit to criminal cases, history suggests that the reach of the clause was not so limited. Also, as noted in Chapter 2, the court's specification of the four categories, contained in Justice Chase's opinion for the *Calder* Court, was judicial dictum, and therefore not precedential. Finally, although the court has often reverently cited the categories as definitive, it also has variously stated, added to and truncated the list; moreover, language in *Calder* itself seemed to leave the door open to other kinds of laws. Abandoning the requirement would have the benefit of obviating the need for courts to undertake the procrustean task of fitting a challenged law into a category, and expand the

The Ex Post Facto Clause. Wayne A. Logan, Oxford University Press. © Oxford University Press 2023.
DOI: 10.1093/oso/9780190053505.003.0008

reach of protection for individuals. But, as with expansion to civil laws, it carries risks, which will be examined.

The chapter then considers whether the specific prohibition in the clause regarding an ex post facto "[l]aw" extends beyond legislative enactments. Suffice it to say, the framers lived before the rise of the administrative state, a time when government agencies frequently promulgate rules, regulations, and guidelines that have very significant consequences for individuals. In an important decision, *Bouie v. City of Columbia* (1964),[1] the court held that the Due Process Clause of the Fourteenth Amendment, not the Ex Post Facto Clause, prevents retroactive application of a judicial construction of a law that expands its retroactive reach. However, as will be seen, for better or worse the Supreme Court has seen fit to interpret the term "[l]aw" broadly, encompassing provisions not strictly emanating from legislatures, in contrast to its proclivity to otherwise interpret coverage of the clause narrowly (viz.: criminal laws, limited to the four categories identified in *Calder*).

Finally, the chapter addresses whether the court should continue to except laws deemed "procedural" from the coverage of the clause. The exception, which was created by the court only in the mid to late twentieth century, lacks historical pedigree, and creates similar (if not greater) line-drawing challenges for courts, and should be abandoned.

The chapter closes with a discussion of the many critically important shifts occurring in the nation's political order, and the role and function of its three branches of government, which together heighten the importance of the changes suggested.

Expansion Beyond Criminal Laws

In *Calder v. Bull* (1798),[2] Justice Samuel Chase, whose opinion is thought to have the main precedential force of the four opinions written by justices in the case, stated that the Ex Post Facto Clause prohibited only retroactive criminal (not civil) laws. After stating that the "ex post facto" prohibition "necessarily requires some explanation," he provided what he saw as the "plain and obvious meaning and intention of the prohibition" from "within the words and meaning" of the Constitution:

> that the Legislatures of the several states, shall not pass laws, after a fact done by a subject, or citizen, which shall have relation to such fact, and shall punish him for having done it. The prohibition considered in this light, is an additional bulwark in

favour of the personal security of the subject, to protect his person from punishment by legislative acts, having a retrospective operation.[3]

Elaborating, Chase wrote that the clause was not "inserted to secure the citizen in his private rights, of either property, or contracts. . . ."[4] Other prohibitions contained in Article I, section 10 (such as concerning the impairment of contracts) concerned civil matters, whereas the ex post facto prohibition was intended to "secure the person of the subject from injury, or punishment, in consequence of such law."[5]

In defense of his view, Chase noted that "[t]he expressions 'ex post facto laws,' are technical, they had been in use long before the Revolution, and had acquired an appropriate meaning, by Legislators, Lawyers, and Authors."[6] Two of the three other justices writing also saw the prohibition as affecting only retroactive criminal provisions. Justice William Paterson stated that the words ex post facto "must be taken in their technical, which is also their common and general, application, and are not to be understood in their literal sense," which encompassed retroactive laws more generally.[7] Justice James Iredell wrote that

> the true construction of the prohibition extends to criminal, not to civil, cases. It is only in criminal cases, indeed, in which the danger to be guarded against, is greatly to be apprehended . . . The policy, the reason and humanity, of the prohibition, do not, I repeat, extend to civil cases, to cases that merely affect the private property of citizens.[8]

The fourth justice writing an opinion in *Calder*, William Cushing, seemingly did not directly speak to the issue.[9]

Despite the apparent confidence of the justices, the actual historical record, surveyed in Chapter 1, makes clear that the delegates at the Philadelphia Convention were, at a minimum, divided on the question of whether "ex post facto" laws covered both civil and criminal provisions. George Mason voted against the ex post facto ban because he worried that its coverage of civil laws, which might at times be beneficial, would be unwise.[10] James Madison's comments usually, though not always, suggested that he understood the prohibition to cover both civil and criminal laws.[11]

Later, debates in the state ratifying conventions, which Madison later in life believed key to understanding the Constitution,[12] similarly undercut confidence in the criminal-centric view. In Virginia, Edmund Randolph (then also serving as governor) maintained that ex post facto laws covered only criminal laws, but the four other delegates addressing the ex post facto prohibition believed it encompassed civil and criminal laws.[13] James Iredell, a North Carolina State Convention delegate, seemingly adopted a broad view, notwithstanding his subsequent opinion in *Calder*.[14] And in New York's fractious convention, an amendment was proposed that would specifically limit the ex post facto prohibition to criminal laws but the proposal failed.[15]

As Chapter 2 demonstrated, *Calder's* criminal-centric view was doubted by several justices not long after *Calder*. Most notably, in a "Note" attached to his concurring opinion in *Satterlee v. Matthewson* (1829),[16] Justice William Johnson provided an extensive, point-by-point refutation of *Calder's* criminal-centric view and the historic and jurisprudential sources advanced by Justice Chase in its support. Shortly thereafter, Joseph Story, both a Supreme Court Justice and a highly respected constitutional scholar of his time, wrote in his *Commentaries on the Constitution* (1833) that "ex post facto laws, in a comprehensive sense, embrace all retrospective laws, whether they are of a civil or criminal nature." Story wrote that if the question of the applicable scope of the clause was assessed in a case of first impression, before *Calder*, Johnson's analysis and conclusions in *Satterlee* "would be entitled to grave consideration."[17]

In later years, several of the court's decisions suggested operation of broader coverage. Most notably, the court upheld ex post facto challenges in *Cummings v. Missouri* (1867)[18] and *Ex parte Garland* (1867),[19] invalidating government prohibitions to pursue a profession (clergy and attorney, respectively), and in *Burgess v. Salmon* (1878),[20] invalidating a monetary tax and penalty that were imposed retroactively on a shipment of tobacco. Subsequently, justices concurring or dissenting in decisions voiced their disagreement with the criminal-centric focus of *Calder*.[21]

A key aspect of the ongoing debate has been how ex post facto laws were viewed in the Framing Era. In *Collins v. Youngblood* (1990),[22] citing the opinions in *Calder*, the court confidently stated that "[a]s early opinions in this court explained, 'ex post facto law' was a term of art with an established meaning at the time of the framing of the Constitution."[23] Today, as Chapter 2 discussed at length, to the extent this assessment is accurate, the scholarly consensus is that ex post facto laws were then understood to encompass both civil and criminal laws, whether under a "technical" understanding, the focus of Justice Chase in *Calder*, or understanding within the general lay public. As noted by historian Leonard Levy, *Calder's* narrow view of the ex post facto prohibition "was more innovative than it was an accurate reflection of the opinions of the Framers and ratifiers. . . . [T]he history of the framing and ratification of the ex post facto clauses simply do not bear out the opinions in *Calder v. Bull*. The court in that case reinvented the law on the subject."[24]

The modern consensus could have significant bearing on the continued precedential status of *Calder*'s criminal-centric limit. Today, well over two hundred years after the Constitution was drafted and ratified by the states, debate continues over how its text should be interpreted and applied. Two of the primary camps are "living constitutionalists" and "originalists." The former camp regards provisions of the Constitution as drawing their meaning over time and in accord with possibly changing norms, typically resulting in new or expanded protections. Originalists, especially those of the current dominant view attaching paramount importance to how text was publicly understood (versus what the framers might have subjectively intended),[25] believe that if the meaning of a text can be "fixed" when it was drafted and ratified, then its interpretation should be bound by that meaning.[26]

Original public meaning, in short, is "the meaning that a reasonable and informed member of the public would have ascribed to [text] at the time of its promulgation."[27] In support of the view, Professor Lawrence Solum, one of its leading proponents, recently wrote that

> [g]iven that the constitution aims to communicate to the public (but also to officials including judges, legislators, and executive officers), the drafters of the constitutional text needed to write a document that had a publicly accessible meaning, using words and phrases in their ordinary senses and limiting technical language and terms of art to limited instances that could be identified by the public.[28]

Solum adds that "[t]technical meanings that are apparent on the face of the text, given the context of constitutional communication, are permissible. Hidden technical meanings are not."[29]

And what of "ex post facto"? The opinions of two of the four justices writing substantive opinions in *Calder* (Chase and Paterson, but not Iredell, or Cushing, whose short cryptic opinion is difficult to fathom) provide some insight. Again, Chase wrote that "[t]he expressions 'ex post facto laws,' are technical, they had been in use long before the Revolution, and had acquired an appropriate meaning, by Legislators, Lawyers, and Authors."[30] Paterson wrote that the terms "must be taken in their technical, which is also their common and general, application, and are not to be understood in their literal sense."[31] It would thus appear that ex post facto was at once a "technical" expression, understood by those learned in the law, and one understood by the general public. In other words, the expression does not contain what Professor Solum would call "[h]idden technical meanings." Yet, at least since Justice William Johnson's extended critique in *Satterlee v. Matthewson* (1829), compelling reason exists to believe that *Calder* represents a very early example of what has been disparaged as poorly executed "law office history."[32]

Originalism, however, influences more than *interpretation* of constitutional text; it addresses, as it must, *construction* of text—in effect, how it is to be applied.[33] In *Calder*, Justice Chase's opinion for the court arguably engaged in both enterprises. He first concluded that ex post facto coverage only extends to criminal laws and then supported his position by invoking the framers' purpose in adopting the clause: prohibiting unjust retroactive laws, not all retroactive laws.[34] If by construction one means enforcement of a rule "to preserve or promote the values the constitutional text is understood to serve," as two leading originalists posit,[35] Justice Chase got it wrong. The framers made abundantly clear their desire to prohibit retroactive legislative abuses more generally, and the clause should be construed in a manner that is consistent with this liberty-protecting value, much as the court has done with its constitutional "twin," the Bill of Attainder Clause (as discussed in Chapter 6).

Overruling a landmark decision like *Calder* would obviously be a significant development. The doctrine of stare decisis promotes important goals,[36] and even on the rare occasion that the court has acknowledged the dispute over *Calder*'s criminal-centric view, it has remained steadfast in its refusal to reconsider it.[37] The position aligns with the view that it is more important for a legal question to be "settled" than be "right."[38] The court, moreover, has stated that a departure from precedent "demands special justification."[39] "[S]omething more than 'ambiguous historical evidence' is required" before the court will " 'flatly overrule a number of major decisions,' "[40] and "the strength of the case for adhering to such decisions grows in proportion to their 'antiquity.' "[41] As the court put it in *Galvan v. Press* (1954),[42] despite the compelling critique of Justice Johnson in *Satterlee*, "[i]t would be an unjustifiable reversal to overturn a view of the Constitution so deeply rooted and so consistently adhered to."[43]

However, perhaps to a greater extent than ever before, the historical evidence favoring a broader scope might serve as a catalyst for change. This is because today, despite the typically distinct views of living constitutionalists and originalists more generally, members of both camps, and those in between, attribute importance to Framing Era history to some extent.[44] Moreover, because adherents of "living constitutionalism" are often inclined to be more protective of personal liberty and civil rights, abandoning *Calder*'s criminal-centric focus would likely have appeal.

For originalists, for whom historical understanding has particular importance, broadened reach should have obvious allure, even though they often have a more circumscribed view of civil rights and liberties. The question is complicated, however, by the fact that originalists can differ in their view of what if any deference should be paid to judicial precedent, especially from around the time of the Framing Era, such as *Calder* (decided in 1798).[45] Some originalists maintain that wrongly decided precedent, from any era, is undeserving of deference. As Professor Michael Stokes Paulsen reasoned, "stare decisis, understood as a theory of adhering to prior judicial precedents that are contrary to the original public meaning, is completely irreconcilable with originalism."[46] Justice Clarence Thomas, who long ago signaled his willingness to reconsider the criminal-centric coverage mandated by *Calder*,[47] recently announced his willingness to overrule "demonstrably erroneous precedent,"[48] adding that "[t]his view of *stare decisis* follows directly from the Constitution's supremacy over other sources of law—including our own precedents."[49] Justice Neil Gorsuch, also a staunch originalist, recently opined that *stare decisis* "isn't supposed to be the art of methodically ignoring what everyone knows to be true."[50] Others, including the late Justice Antonin Scalia, show greater deference to precedent that is inconsistent with original understanding.[51]

For its part, the court, with its increasingly conservative membership in recent years, has shown a distinct willingness to overrule precedent based on originalist reasoning.[52] This willingness is complemented by two acknowledged principles: that stare decisis plays a diminished role in deciding constitutional questions[53] and that it is "at its nadir in cases" implicating "fundamental constitutional protections,"[54] a reality borne out by the court's recent abandonment of several constitutional precedents.[55] With *Calder* in particular, not only is a constitutional right in question, but the court might be swayed by the argument that its criminal-centric holding was in fact judicial dictum. This is because, as noted in Chapter 2, the challenged legal action in the case was technically a judicial act (it resulted from the Connecticut legislature sitting in a judicial capacity, granting a new trial), not a "law" that was "pass[ed]" within coverage of the clause.[56] Moreover, the very nature of the opinions issued by the *Calder* Justices arguably undercuts the decision's precedential status. As the US Eighth Circuit Court of Appeals recently observed, "it is instructive to note that Justice Chase's opinion in *Calder* was written in the period in which each Justice gave his opinion seriatim. Thus, it is not a Supreme Court holding that would be included in the definition of 'clearly established Federal law.'"[57]

In short, unlike other constitutional expressions, such as "commerce," where scholars continue to debate original meaning,[58] ample historical evidence would support a change of course with "ex post facto."[59] Further militating in favor of broadening the scope is the basic point that Article I itself draws no express distinction between civil and criminal enactments, a recognition finding favor among constitutional textualists (who often share originalist views).[60] If such a broadening comes to pass, ironically, originalism[61]—significantly shaped by conservatives in response to perceived liberal judicial activism resulting in expanded personal rights[62]—could be the impetus for a broader, pro-civil liberties use of the Ex Post Facto Clause as a limit on the exercise of legislative authority.[63]

Broadening the reach of the ex post facto prohibition would have significant benefits. Perhaps most significant, it would obviate the judicial need to decide whether a provision is civil or criminal in nature. As discussed at length in Chapter 6, use of the indeterminate *Mendoza-Martinez* factors and the "clearest proof" standard is problematic for multiple reasons. Abandoning the line drawing it entails will save considerable judicial resources and avoid the need for courts to engage in the often unconvincing doctrinal gymnastics the test requires, such as evidenced by the majority in *Smith v. Doe* (2003).[64] It would also free legislatures from the unseemly felt need to camouflage sanctions with meaningless labels and "civil" window dressing in order to rebuff ex post facto challenges.[65]

In addition to the foregoing, overruling the criminal-centric view would be in keeping with broader shifts in governance since *Calder*, in particular use of sanctions that make line-drawing problematic. As Justice William Johnson noted in 1829, in *Satterlee v. Mathewson*,[66] the holding in *Calder* "leaves a large class of arbitrary legislative acts without the prohibitions of the constitution,"[67] which "the learned judges [in *Calder*] could not then have foreseen . . ."[68] What was true in 1829 is much more so today, as the scope of legislative activity has expanded exponentially over time with governments frequently enacting retroactive sanctions that betray simple binary categorization. As Justice Neil Gorsuch recently said of this hybridization:

> today's civil laws regularly impose penalties far more severe than those found in many criminal statutes . . . Ours is a world filled with more and more civil laws bearing more and more extravagant punishments. Today's "civil" penalties include confiscatory rather than compensatory fines, forfeiture provisions that allow homes to be taken, remedies that strip persons of their professional licenses and livelihoods, and the power to commit persons against their will indefinitely. Some of these penalties are routinely imposed and are routinely graver than those associated with misdemeanor crimes—and often harsher than the punishment for felonies.[69]

There are, however, several arguments in favor of preserving *Calder*'s criminal-centric focus. First and perhaps foremost, the narrow focus can be thought justified because of the unique nature of the criminal law, a domain where eighteenth-century legal scholar Richard Wooddeson said, "justice wears her sternest aspect."[70] Criminal law not only imputes the greatest stigma.[71] It also is distinct for its comprehensive effect; as legal philosopher Lon Fuller observed, "[o]f all branches of law, criminal law is most obviously and directly concerned with shaping and controlling human conduct."[72]

The unique political dynamic of criminal lawmaking further distinguishes it from other legislative undertakings. As Professor William Stuntz noted, "[i]f there is any sphere in which politicians would have an incentive simply to please the majority of voters, it's criminal law."[73] For legislators, proposing and voting for criminal laws affords an irresistible chance to align themselves with the victims of crime and against the criminal element, a dynamic accentuated by the soundbite modus operandi of the modern media.[74] Moreover, as noted previously, legislating in the criminal law arena bears little risk for politicians because those caught up in the criminal justice system very often lack political influence. As Professor Harold Krent recognized, "[l]egislators need not fear that enacting most criminal measures will dry up campaign coffers. Throughout history, criminal offenders have been from the poorest strata in society. . . . Nor will legislators necessarily lose votes if they are insensitive to the needs of convicted felons. Felons often cannot vote. . . ."[75] Given these realities, singling out retroactive criminal laws for prohibition, not civil ones, is justified because the ballot box can more possibly protect against governmental arbitrariness in the civil context.[76]

A second concern with expanding the clause relates to what is called the "anti-redundancy" canon of interpretation—that the Constitution should be interpreted in a manner that avoids rendering a provision redundant.[77] The concern figured centrally in Justice Chase's opinion in *Calder*, where he reasoned that broad coverage of the Ex Post Facto Clause would render the Contracts Clause, also in Article I, section 10, "unnecessary and, and, therefore improper."[78] However, as Justice Johnson recognized in 1829 the expanse of harmful retroactive civil enactments has surpassed the limited reach of the Contracts Clause, an assessment certainly no less accurate today. For evidence of this one need only consider the retroactive laws challenged in *Smith v. Doe* (sex offender registration and community notification) and *Kansas v. Hendricks* (involuntary indefinite commitment)—neither strategy related to contracts in any way.

Furthermore, even in the event of overlap, redundancy is not uncommon in the Constitution: for example, several provisions address retroactivity,[79] discrimination against individuals based on religion,[80] and confiscation of property.[81] Also, as even a cursory review of the court's ex post facto case law reveals, in many instances (e.g., *Cummings v. Missouri* (1867)) both the Bill of Attainder Clause and Ex Post Facto Clause served as the basis for challenge, prompting no concern from the court.

Finally, concern exists that broadening the scope of the clause might hamstring the ability of governments to enact beneficial civil laws.[82] As noted earlier, this was a major worry of George Mason at both the Philadelphia and Virginia Conventions, such that he urged that the clause be removed altogether from the Constitution. James Madison shared this concern, as did Justice Chase in *Calder* who asserted that expansion would "greatly restrict the power of the federal and state legislatures; and the consequences of such a construction may not be foreseen."[83] Today, support for this concern is borne out by an academic literature extolling the potential benefits of retroactive civil lawmaking, for instance, by protecting or providing remedies to consumers and investors.[84]

Means exist, however, that will allow expansion of the ex post facto prohibition without curbing possibly salutary retroactive laws. Most instructive, is the large body of case law generated by state courts interpreting the many state constitutions barring retroactive civil provisions.[85] According to one recent survey, ten states contain a limit on retroactive civil legislation,[86] and their state court decisions illustrate how the boundaries of the prohibition can be delineated. For instance, the Ohio Supreme Court, interpreting its provision barring "retroactive laws," has stated that

> critical inquiry of the constitutional analysis is to determine whether the retroactive statute is remedial or substantive. A purely remedial statute does not violate [the provision], even when it is applied retroactively. On the other hand, a retroactive statute is substantive—and therefore unconstitutionally retroactive—if it impairs vested rights, affects an accrued substantive right, or imposes new or additional burdens, duties, obligations, or liabilities as to a past transaction.[87]

Other state courts adopt a similar test for deciding when a retroactive civil law is unconstitutional.[88]

In short, if the court overrules *Calder* and expands coverage to retroactive civil and criminal laws alike, it will not need to write on a blank constitutional slate. Although it is usually the case that states tie interpretation of their constitutional provisions to federal constitutional analogs, the states have decades, and in some instances centuries, of wisdom to impart regarding how this doctrinal shift can take shape.[89]

Expanding Beyond *Calder*'s Four Categories

Presuming *Calder*'s narrow, criminal-centric reading survives, another question ripe for possible consideration is whether the four categories of retroactive criminal laws *Calder* prohibited should be expanded. As described by Justice Chase, the four categories are:

> 1st. Every law that makes an action, done before the passing of the law, and which was innocent when done, criminal; and punishes such action. 2nd. Every law that aggravates a crime, or makes it greater than it was, when committed. 3rd. Every law that changes the punishment, and inflicts a greater punishment, than the law annexed to the crime, when committed. 4th. Every law that alters the legal rules of evidence, and receives less, or different, testimony, than the law required at the time of the commission of the offence, in order to convict the offender.[90]

There are four chief problems with the limit.

First, much like the criminal-centric holding of *Calder*, the limits prescribed by the categories lack support in the historical record. As Professor Oliver Field noted decades ago, the Philadelphia Constitutional Convention debates contain "not a single mention of the practice of the British Parliament to which Justice Chase referred" in support of the specified categories.[91] To make matters worse, the early English parliamentary practices that did occur lend themselves to varied interpretation regarding their fit with the *Calder* categories, as the lengthy jousting of the majority and dissenting opinions in *Carmell v. Texas* (2000)[92] and *Stogner v. California* (2003)[93] (discussed in Chapter 5) attest.

Second, the court's treatment of the categories over time has been anything but consistent. In *Calder*, Justice Chase identified four categories of particular "instances" of ex post facto laws, but added that "these and similar laws" were of concern.[94] Since then, the court has characterized the categories as being constant and sacrosanct.[95] But not always. In *Collins v. Youngblood* (1990),[96] for instance, the majority condemned earlier decisions for taking what it saw as undue liberty with the scope of *Calder*, but specified a new category (defenses), deleted two others (relating to rules of evidence and "aggravation"), and ultimately endorsed what is basically a two-category standard.[97] And it did so while insisting that "the prohibition which may not be evaded is the one defined by the *Calder* categories."[98] Sixty-five years before, in *Beazell v. Ohio* (1925),[99] a decision upon which the *Collins* Court heavily relied, and extolled as "faithful to [the Court's] best knowledge of the original understanding of the Ex Post Facto Clause,"[100] the court used a three-part test.[101]

And only in 2000, with *Carmell v. Texas,* did the court rely upon the fourth category (regarding rules of evidence) to decide a case, after it had seemingly pared down the list to three categories, and it was not until 2003, in *Stogner v. California*, that the court ascribed constitutional meaning and weight to the second category, which previously had been thought by some as redundant of the third category.[102] Even further back in time, Justice Paterson in *Calder* recognized the closely related nature of the first three categories, writing that "[t]he enhancement of a crime, or penalty, seems to come within the same mischief as the creation of a crime or penalty; and therefore they may be classed together."[103]

Also, despite the court's professed reverence for the four categories its decisions have been notably slipshod in describing them. Recently, in *United States v. Peugh* (2013),[104] for instance, the court addressed whether a retroactive change in the federal sentencing guidelines was post facto, posing the question as (with text italicized for emphasis):

> whether there is an ex post facto violation when a defendant is sentenced under Guidelines promulgated *after he committed his criminal acts* ["acts" is a term used in category one] and the new version provides a higher applicable Guidelines sentencing range than the version in place at the *time of the offense* ["offense" is a term more or less synonymous with "crime," used in categories two and three].[105]

Although the foregoing conflation might seem unimportant, this is not always necessarily so. *Commonwealth v. Rose,*[106] decided by the Pennsylvania Supreme Court in 2015, is illustrative. In *Rose,* defendant assaulted the victim in 1993, when the maximum punishment for third-degree murder was twenty years' imprisonment. The victim remained in a coma after the assault and did not die until fourteen years later (in 2007), during which time the Pennsylvania legislature (in 1995) increased the maximum punishment to forty years imprisonment. The court confronted a basic framing question under the third *Calder* category, which highlights the semantic distinction noted. If the date of the criminal "act" was relevant to the analysis, then the later change in punishment was ex post facto. If, however, the relevant time was occurrence of the "crime, when committed" (i.e., the time when the elements of murder, which requires a death, are met), then the increase in punishment was constitutional because it occurred before the death.

The majority in *Rose* adopted the former view, concluding that the punishment increase denied the defendant of notice and was fundamentally unfair.[107] A dissenting justice argued, with reason, that there was no *Calder* category three violation because the crime charged—third-degree murder—by definition required a death, which occurred before the sentence increase.[108] As the court stated in *Weaver v. Graham* (1981),[109] the critical question when assessing a third category claim is "whether the new provision imposes a greater punishment after the *commission of the offense*,"[110] not simply that an act, which is one element of a crime, occur.[111]

A third reason to abandon the categories is that they impose upon courts the procrustean task of fitting a law into one of the limits.[112] By its very nature, the task is contrary to the basic animating purpose of the clause, which is "to secure the liberty of the citizen, [and which] cannot be evaded by the form in which the power of the State is exerted."[113] The court's decision in *Stogner* is illustrative of the shortcoming, where the five-member majority struggled to situate (the dissent fairly used the term "forc[e]") a law reviving an expired statute of limitation within the *Calder* categories, ultimately having to resort to Justice Chase's "alternative description" of the second *Calder* category.[114]

The court's approach, it is worth noting, is at distinct odds with that taken with the Bill of Attainder Clause (BOAC), which as discussed in Chapter 6 is regarded as the constitutional "twin" of the Ex Post Facto Clause. Rather than adhering to a "narrow historic reading" of attainder, which at common law pertained exclusively to capital sanctions, the court has given the BOAC a "broad and generous meaning,"[115] covering any "legislative punishment, of any form or severity, of specifically designated persons or groups."[116] Moreover, rather than adopting a historically static view of what can qualify, as it has with the Ex Post Facto Clause, the court has emphasized that its "treatment of the scope of the [Bill of Attainder] Clause has never precluded the possibility that new burdens and deprivations might be legislatively fashioned that are inconsistent with the bill of attainder guarantee."[117]

Finally, the four-category limit is problematic for several technical reasons. The first is that, like *Calder*'s limit to retroactive criminal laws, its categories are dictum. As Justice Ginsburg wrote in her *Carmell v. Texas* (2000) dissent, joined by three of her colleagues, "Justice Chase's formulation [of the categories] was dictum ... because *Calder* involved a civil statute and the court held that the statute was not ex post facto for that reason alone."[118] Second, also as with *Calder*'s criminal-centric focus, it can be argued that the seriatim nature of Justice Chase's lead opinion for the court lacks precedential value, and the opinions of the other three justices writing (Iredell, Paterson, and Cushing) made no mention of the categories.[119] Finally, it can be argued that the categories themselves are mere "gloss" imposed by the court on the Constitution, and therefore unworthy of deference.[120]

Extending Coverage Beyond "Laws"

A third coverage question concerns the kinds of retroactive legal interventions potentially prohibited by the clause. The text of both sections 9 and 10 in Article I prohibits the "pass[age]" of an "ex post facto Law." A law, as customarily understood, is passed by the legislative branch (not the judicial or executive branch),[121] a view shared by both William Blackstone in his *Commentaries* and James Madison and Alexander Hamilton in the *Federalist Papers*.[122] Moreover, both the federal (section 9) and state (section 10) ex post facto prohibitions are ensconced in Article I, which governs the legislative branch. Finally, as often noted in this volume, there is no mistaking that concern over legislative abuses in particular motivated inclusion of the clause in the Constitution.

Although *Calder v. Bull* (1798)[123] muddied this basic point early on, by addressing an ex post facto claim against a "resolution or law" issued by the Connecticut Legislature acting in its capacity as an appellate court,[124] later decisions from the court made clear that the clause only concerns legislative enactments. *Bouie v. City of Columbia* (1964)[125] illustrates this point, where the court held that a retroactive judicial enlargement of a statutorily codified crime was not a "law" within coverage of the Ex Post Facto Clause, but rather was subject to challenge under the Due Process Clause of the Fourteenth Amendment.[126]

Importantly, however, a proviso attaches to the basic principle that the clause only concerns legislative enactments. Although as a general matter no distinction exists between the coverage of the ex post facto prohibition directed at state legislatures and Congress, it is often overlooked that a significant distinction exists regarding the range of legislative activity regulated. In an important article, Professor Nicholas Rosenkranz closely analyzed the verbiage and structure of sections 9 and 10, observing that they "are identical in subject matter but different in *subject*."[127] This is because the Constitution requires that in the federal government "[a]ll legislative Powers" be vested in Congress, whereas it does not require that state legislative power be vested entirely in legislatures, as a technical matter. The only requirement for states is that they have a "Republican Form of Government" (see Article V, section 4), meaning that they can delegate legislative authority as they see fit.[128]

As a result, Rosenkranz maintains, the range of governmental actors regulated by the clause is broader vis-à-vis the states: the entity "must be a state actor exercising legislative power, but it need not be a state legislature."[129] The court recognized this difference in *Ross v. Oregon* (1913),[130] noting that the section 10 state-related ex post facto prohibition reaches "every form in which the legislative power of a state is exerted, whether it be a constitution, a constitutional amendment, an enactment of the legislature, a bylaw or ordinance of a municipal corporation, or a regulation or order of some other instrumentality of the state exercising delegated legislative authority."[131]

In retrospect, this explained the court's exercise of constitutional authority in *Cummings v. Missouri* (1867),[132] where it invalidated on ex post facto grounds a Missouri constitutional amendment retroactively barring the petitioner from practicing his profession (the priesthood). So too in *Duncan v. Missouri* (1894),[133] where the court later rejected on the merits an ex post facto challenge against a retroactive change in the Missouri Constitution concerning the number of judges that were to decide a criminal case. The broader prohibitory scope of state legislative enactments aligns with the patent concern among the framers over state legislative abuses, as opposed to Congress, as manifest in the longer list of prohibitions contained in section 10 compared to section 9 (see Chapter 1).

The broader reach of the state prohibition has considerable practical significance. Coverage of state constitutional provisions in particular is important in light of the common state practice of allowing voters to approve constitutional amendments (numbering twenty-four states at last count).[134] Often originating in the Progressive Era, in an effort to sidestep the representative legislative process and wrest control from oligarchs and plutocrats, today the initiatives very often address criminal justice matters and are susceptible to the same inflammatory influences affecting legislatures that the Ex Post Facto Clause is designed to guard against.[135] The broader scope is also significant because it encompasses the legislative activities of municipal governments, which play an increasingly important role in criminal lawmaking, especially with respect to ordinances concerning low-level criminal offenses.[136]

Although the federal prohibition is narrower, it has also been applied outside the strict rubric of "laws."[137] Evidence for this is found in changes made to the US Sentencing Guidelines. The guidelines originated in the 1980s, a time marked by widespread concern (among liberals and conservatives alike) over sentencing disparities believed to result from the exercise of excessive discretion by federal trial judges.[138] To develop the guidelines, Congress, as part of the Sentencing Reform Act of 1984, created the US Sentencing Commission, an independent entity within the judicial branch directed to collect sentencing data, formulate general interpretive policy and commentary, and ultimately devise sentences for crimes based on use of an elaborate grid.[139] Per the Sentencing Reform Act, any change adopted by the commission became law effective after 180 days, unless affirmatively rejected by Congress.[140] The unusual hybrid nature of the commission raised a separation of powers concern, which the Supreme Court addressed in *Mistretta v. United States* (1989).[141] In *Mistretta*, the court, over Justice Scalia's dissent disparaging the commission as a "sort of junior-varsity Congress,"[142] upheld its constitutionality, concluding that Congress had established sufficient standards for the exercise of the authority delegated to the commission and that its existence did not violate separation of powers.[143]

Plainly, the commission was not something within the contemplation of the framers of the Constitution, yet the heightened sentences it prescribed, imposed on criminal conduct occurring before enactment, generated ex post facto claims in federal courts.[144] Early decisions sought guidance in *Miller v. Florida* (1987),[145] which as discussed in Chapter 5, involved a challenge to a state sentencing guideline system that retroactively increased the presumed sentencing range imposed on the defendant. The guidelines were recommended by a legislatively created commission, approved by the Florida Supreme Court, and ultimately adopted by the state legislature.[146] The *Miller* Court found that "the revised sentencing law is a law enacted by the Florida legislature, and it has the force and effect of law," setting the stage for its ultimate conclusion that its retroactive application was unconstitutional on ex post facto grounds.[147] In so deciding, the court distinguished lower federal appellate court decisions finding that federal parole guidelines were not "laws" for ex post facto purposes because they only provided a framework for the exercise of discretion.[148]

After *Miller*, federal circuit courts of appeal typically found that retroactive application of the federal guidelines was problematic.[149] A rare exception was a concurring opinion by Seventh Circuit Court of Appeals Judge Frank Easterbrook, who in *United States v. Seacott* (1994)[150] observed:

> The federal guidelines differ from the Florida sentencing guidelines addressed in *Miller v. Florida* . . . Florida authorized its supreme court to adopt rules that would become effective "only upon the subsequent adoption by the Legislature of legislation implementing the guidelines as then revised." Fla. Stat. § 921.001(4)(b). This made the state's sentencing guidelines "laws" for constitutional purposes, the Court concluded . . . We know from *Mistretta*, however, that the federal guidelines are judicial products . . . that they are rules rather than "laws."[151]

So matters stood until the court decided in *United States v. Booker* (2005)[152] that the US Sentencing Guidelines were no longer mandatory, but rather were "advisory."[153] The shift prompted many courts to conclude, as the Seventh Circuit Court of Appeals Judge Richard Posner put it in *United States v. Demaree* (2006),[154] that the clause "should apply only to laws and regulations that bind rather than advise."[155] Other circuit courts disagreed, however, obliging the Supreme Court to resolve the dispute in *United States v. Peugh* (2013).[156]

Peugh was sentenced under the 2009 version of the guidelines, rather than the 1998 version in effect at the time of his offenses, and challenged his significantly higher sentence under the 2009 version on ex post facto grounds. The court held that the sentence was invalid and provided some informative insights into its view of ex post facto coverage. Writing for herself and four of her colleagues (Justices Ginsburg, Breyer, Kennedy, and Kagan), Justice Sotomayor rejected the government's argument that the now-advisory nature of the guidelines deprived them of the status of a " 'law' within the meaning of the *Ex Post Facto* Clause."[157] In another part of her opinion, which only three justices joined (save Justice Kennedy), comprising less than a majority, Sotomayor wrote more expansively:

> We are therefore not persuaded by the argument advanced by the Government and also suggested by the dissent that the animating principles of the Ex Post Facto Clause are not implicated by this case. *While the Government argues that the Sentencing Commission is insulated from legislative interference, our precedents make clear that the coverage of the Ex Post Facto Clause is not limited to legislative acts,* see Garner, 529 U.S., at 247 (recognizing that a change in a parole board's rules could, given an adequate showing, run afoul of the Ex Post Facto Clause).[158]

Citation of *Garner* was curious because it involved a challenge to a state rule enlarging intervals for parole consideration, which the state board of probation and parole amended pursuant to authority expressly delegated by the legislature,[159] which as discussed earlier is consistent with the broader reach of the state prohibition in Article I, section 10. Nevertheless, the court in *Peugh* concluded that the guidelines were within the scope of the clause.

In sum, with respect to both ex post facto prohibitions in Article I, courts will address claims against a "law" as well as, as the court put it in *Miller*, enactments that have the "force and effect of law."[160] This is important because, as discussed later, executive branch entities, part of the "administrative state," have come to play a significant role in devising and implementing criminal justice policy.

Abandon the "Procedural" Exception

A final matter deserving attention concerns the court's special treatment of laws deemed "procedural" (as opposed to "substantive") in nature. The *Calder* Court made no mention whatsoever of the distinction, nor does the clause itself, yet *Beazell v. Ohio* (1925)[161] briefly alluded to it and *Dobbert v. Florida* (1977)[162] and *Collins v. Youngblood* (1990)[163] explicitly recognized it. In *Dobbert*, which rejected an ex post facto challenge to changes in Florida's capital punishment scheme, the court made clear that "[e]ven though it may work to the disadvantage of a defendant, a procedural change is not ex post facto."[164] *Collins* rejected a challenge to a Texas law that allowed reformation of an improper jury verdict without the necessity of remand for retrial because it was a "procedural change."[165] But *Collins* also stated that "by simply labeling a law 'procedural' a legislature[] does not thereby immunize it from scrutiny under the Ex Post Facto Clause."[166]

To an extent, the procedural exception is sensible as a practical matter. As Justice John Marshall Harlan noted in *Gibson v. Mississippi* (1896),[167] "[t]he inhibition upon the passage of ex post facto laws does not give a criminal a right to be tried, in all respects, by the law in force when the crime charged was committed."[168] In this light, the court was correct in *Gut v. Minnesota* (1870)[169] when it rejected an ex post facto challenge to a law retroactively changing judicial district boundaries that allowed for a change of venue for a criminal trial. Likewise, in *Duncan v. Missouri* (1894)[170] the court properly rejected an ex post facto challenge concerning a retroactive change in the number of appellate judges on a panel deciding a case.

However, the line drawing regarding what qualifies as a procedural as opposed to substantive law introduces the same line-drawing difficulty plaguing other areas of legal doctrine. As Supreme Court itself has noted, "[t]he line between 'substance' and 'procedure' shifts as the legal context changes. 'Each implies different variables depending upon the particular problem for which it is used.'"[171] In *Miller v. Florida* (1987),[172] the court acknowledged that the effort to distinguish procedural changes for ex post facto purposes has "prove[d] elusive."[173] Illustrative of this difficulty, before *Carmell v. Texas* (2000)[174] resuscitated the fourth *Calder* category (concerning changes to rules of evidence), retroactive changes to evidentiary laws were regularly deemed procedural in nature and upheld.[175]

In principle, much as with the *Calder* categories discussed earlier, the line-drawing necessitated by the procedural exception is contrary to the court's insistence that the Ex Post Facto Clause "cannot be evaded by the form in which the power of the State is exerted."[176] Functionally, the procedural exception has resulted in creation of an amorphous catch-all category beyond the scope of the clause,[177] without constitutional support. Its continued existence serves to incentivize legislatures to shroud retroactive legal changes in procedural window dressing, much as the limit of coverage to retroactive criminal provisions has incentivized legislatures to camouflage punitive laws as regulatory ones. Abandoning the exception will avoid this unseemly sleight of hand, save judicial resources, and anchor analysis in the structural constitutional purpose of the clause.

Coda

The preceding pages here and in Chapter 6 make the case for a reinvigorated approach to the protective coverage of the clause. In advancing this vision, a key point has been that in critical ways modern-day understanding of the structural role of the clause in the nation's constitutional democracy is at odds with Framing Era history. Simply as a constitutional matter, this fidelity is important because, much as the Supreme Court has said with regard to the Fourth Amendment, in the Bill of Rights, the clause should "provide at a minimum the degree of protection it afforded when it was adopted."[178]

The case for reinvigoration, however, does not rest solely on history. As important, reinvigoration is warranted by the many very significant developments since 1787 in the nation's social, political, economic, and institutional landscape, which have at once validated the framers' concerns and magnified the need for the changes urged.

One fundamental change concerns a radical shift in the national zeitgeist. At the nation's origin, prisons, to the very modest extent they existed, were "houses of correction" that sought to rehabilitate offenders, during short periods of incarceration.[179] Starting in late twentieth century, however, this orientation experienced radical change. As the 1960s "war on poverty" gave way to the "war on crime" and the "war on drugs," policy and practice became far more punitive. The American body politic was (and remains) gripped by a kind of populism unimaginable to the framers—one especially focusing on crime, criminal offenders, criminal victims, and crime control. As Professor Jonathan Simon recounts in his insightful book *Governing Through Crime: How the War on Crime Transformed American Democracy and Created a Culture of Fear* (2007), starting in the 1980s criminal justice assumed a preeminent place in American politics and being "tough on crime" became a sine qua non of political success. Other scholars, such as Marie Gottschalk in her book *Caught: The Prison State and the Lockdown of American Politics* (2016), have chronicled the many social, political and economic factors that combined to make the United States a world leader in incarceration.

Michelle Alexander, in her acclaimed book *The New Jim Crow: Mass Incarceration in the Age of Color Blindness* (2012), highlighted the critically important role that race has played in this shift, resulting in today's markedly higher comparative imprisonment rates among African Americans. More recently, James Forman, in *Locking Up Our Own: Crime and Punishment in Black America* (2017), a book providing a case study of the punitive crime control policies in 1980s Washington, DC, a predominantly African American jurisdiction, showed that punitiveness has not been limited to white political elites. During the time, the news media and popular culture created and fed the public's fear and demonization of criminal offenders, at once reflecting retributive impulses of political leaders and spurring them on, as chronicled in *Incarceration Nation: How the United States Became the Most Punitive Democracy in the World* (2016) by Peter Enns.

As noted, a key component of the "get tough" shift was the increasing role of victims, who as Jonathan Simon observed have served "in a real sense [as] the representative subjects of our time."[180] Simon's point is borne out by the torrent of laws enacted in the 1990s retroactively targeting previously convicted sex offenders, such as registration and community notification. In state legislatures and Congress, the memory of victims, almost always young white females,[181] figured prominently in legislative proceedings, and laws were frequently eponymously titled in their honor (with "Megan's Law" being the most familiar). The strategy proved highly successful: putting victims' faces on initiatives humanized and accentuated the urgency of enactment. As Representative William Martini (R-NJ) stressed in urging adoption of the federal Megan's Law in 1996: "We must not allow this little girl's life to be taken in vain."[182] Any opponents risked being portrayed not only as "soft on sex offenders," but also "anti-victim," or, even more deleterious, "anti-this victim."

At the same time, quick and often unanimous passage of the laws was ensured by another modern-day form of political personalization—the overt demonization of offenders. Again, individuals convicted of sexual offenses figured prominently, variously referred to as "beast[s]," "monster[s]," and the "human equivalent of toxic waste."[183] As Congressman Randall "Duke" Cunningham (R-CA) vividly framed the issue in 1996: "perhaps a sexual predator's life should be just a little more toxic than someone [else's] in the American citizenry."[184]

In short, powerful forces have combined to create a political landscape very distinct from that of the framers.[185] As a result of these shifts, today, unlike the nation's origin, when no criminal justice "system" as such existed,[186] we have a "prison industrial complex," accounting for major parts of state, local, and federal budgets, with strong support from both major political parties.[187] The nation's incarceration rate—measured as the proportion of the population held in state and federal prisons plus local jails—increased nearly fivefold from 1972 (161 per 100,000) to its peak in 2007 (760 per 100,000).[188] Since then rates have fallen, but the United States comfortably retains its status as world leader in incarceration,[189] a function of policy more than crime rates, which have fallen over the years.[190]

Burgeoning prison and jail populations, however, have been only the most salient (and expensive) manifestations of the shift toward punitive politics and policies. Alongside growth of the "carceral state,"[191] since the 1980s legislatures have enacted a torrent of laws imposing disabilities and burdens independent of incarceration.[192] Collectively, the laws are known as "collateral consequences" of conviction, such as laws subjecting convicted sex offenders to indeterminate involuntary commitment, lifelong GPS monitoring, and registration and community notification. Other common collateral consequences include loss of eligibility for student loans and public housing; termination of disability and welfare benefits; limits on where one can live or visit; loss of eligibility for occupational or professional licenses; debarment from particular jobs; and registration and community notification (for conviction of nonsexual offenses). Convicted individuals also can lose the right to vote, serve on a jury, possess a firearm, and hold public office, and face deportation (if a noncitizen). The ability to adopt, be a foster parent, and retain custody of children can also be adversely affected. And on top of it all, jurisdictions often require those targeted to pay associated costs (e.g., for GPS monitoring).[193]

The sanctions attach to convictions for felonies and misdemeanors alike, imposing burdens that very often last lifetimes and which can, in practical terms, be far more impactful than the direct consequences of conviction, such as a finite period of incarceration or probation or parole conditions. Typically, moreover, the consequences have nationwide effect, following those targeted if they change state residence,[194] and are piled onto the many informal collateral consequences of conviction, such as prospective employers being reluctant to hire and landlords being averse to rent to previously convicted individuals.[195] Collateral consequences also have serious negative impact on families, including children and other dependents.[196]

Progeny of the ancient doctrines of "outlawry" and "civil death," stripping convicted individuals of all political, civil, and legal rights,[197] collateral consequences were in such disfavor by 1983 that the American Bar Association predicted that they would soon meet their demise.[198] However, the prediction proved wrong, when collateral consequences roared back to life starting in the late 1980s,[199] with state and federal codes containing over forty thousand as of 2016.[200]

The penchant for collateral consequences underscores a broader transformation in the nation's regard for those convicted of crime. Today, Judge (later Justice) Benjamin Cardozo's statement in 1936 that "[p]ersons convicted of crime . . . are not outcasts, nor are they to be treated as such"[201] seems a quaint reminder of a bygone past.[202] As Michelle Alexander has written:

> Criminals, it turns out, are the one social group in America we have permission to hate. In "colorblind" America, criminals are the new whipping boys. They are entitled to no respect and little moral concern. . . . [C]riminals today . . . [are] deserving of our collective scorn and contempt . . . Hundreds of years ago, our nation put those considered less than human in shackles; less than one hundred years ago, we relegated them to the other side of town; today we put them in cages. Once released, they find that a heavy and cruel hand has been laid upon them.[203]

The sentiment was on full display in the Supreme Court's decision in *Smith v. Doe* (2003),[204] where the court rejected an ex post facto challenge to retroactive imposition of lifelong registration and community notification, with its "public shame," "humiliation," and "social ostracism."[205]

The foregoing changes, while critically important, are not the sole forces accounting for the markedly distinct modern landscape, compared to the late 1700s. Institutional changes among the branches of government have heightened the need for a more robust Ex Post Facto Clause. One major change concerns the legislative branch. Unlike in the Framing Era, when criminal laws were a product of judge-made common law, criminal laws today are almost exclusively the product of legislation. Already predisposed to harsh policies, for reasons discussed, modern-day legislators are pushed further in that direction by an array of powerful interests, including prosecutor organizations, correctional officer and law enforcement unions, and private businesses, which stand to financially profit from punitive policies.[206] These forces, which of course did not exist in the Framing Era, meet with little resistance, as groups advocating less punitive approaches, such as Families Against Mandatory Minimums and public defender organizations, speak to sparsely populated legislative hearing rooms, if they are included in the process at all.

Major changes have of course also come to the executive branch. Public prosecutors, which did not exist in recognizable form at the nation's origin, today play a foremost role in the criminal justice process. Their discretionary authority regarding whether and what criminal charges to file drives justice system outcomes.[207] Although federal prosecutors are appointed and serve at the pleasure of the president, state and local prosecutors, who handle the vast majority of the nation's criminal cases, and are typically subject to popular election, have strong reason to appear tough on crime (especially if they aspire to higher political office, which is commonly the case).[208] Prosecutors, as William Stuntz pointed out, figure centrally in policymaking, playing a synergistic role with legislative branch actors. "[T]he story of American criminal law," Stuntz observed, "is a story of tacit cooperation between prosecutors and legislators, each of whom benefits from more and broader crimes . . . Prosecutors are better off when criminal law is broad than when it is narrow. Legislators are better off when prosecutors are better off. The potential for alliance is strong, and obvious."[209]

Prosecutors, however, are not the only executive branch actors coming to play a critical role in modern-day criminal justice policy—executive branch agencies have come to play a major role. For instance, in 1897, well before the rise of the modern administrative state, the US Supreme Court concluded in *In re Kollock*[210] that the Constitution does not prohibit Congress from assigning to an agency the power to prescribe elements of a criminal offense.[211] In 1991, in *Touby v. United States*,[212] the court allowed a delegation of authority to the US Attorney General to determine which drugs appear on the "schedules" of controlled substances under the Controlled Substances Act, making them subject to criminal prosecution. And, in 2019, in *Gundy v. United States*,[213] the court upheld the very substantial delegation of congressional authority to the US Attorney General, part of the US Department of Justice, to determine whether and how the requirements of the federal Sex Offender Registration and Notification Act were to be retroactive in effect.[214]

This story of legislative and executive branch ascendance contrasts with a corresponding diminution in the role played by the judiciary. One notable example is found in the context of the US Sentencing Guidelines, adopted by Congress in 1987, discussed earlier. The Guidelines were the result of a politically bipartisan coalition in Congress seeking to limit the sentencing discretion of federal judges.[215] Several years in the making, the provisions achieved their goal of achieving greater uniformity in sentences, but in doing so allocated major discretionary authority to prosecutors (and probation officials, themselves often fellow executive branch actors).[216] The same scenario played out in the many states adopting sentencing guidelines in recent decades.[217]

Another manifestation of diminution in judicial authority, and corresponding diminution in ability to check legislative and executive actors, concerns the rise in plea bargaining. Today, unlike in the Framing Era, criminal cases are overwhelmingly resolved by guilty pleas (over 90 percent), based on agreements negotiated by prosecutors and defense counsel. Criminal litigation has effectively become an administrative process, with prosecutors serving as administrative adjudicators.[218] As a result, juries—despite being guaranteed both in the Constitution (Article III, section 2) and the Bill of Rights (the Sixth Amendment)—no longer play a central role in criminal cases, removing an important institutional check on the application of criminal laws.[219] And, in a plea-dominated system, judges are tasked with only ensuring that pleas themselves are voluntary, knowing, and factually based.[220]

Another critically important way in which the institutional landscape differs concerns the increasingly less rigorous interpretive method used by courts with criminal laws. Unlike courts that well into the nineteenth century read criminal statutes narrowly and in favor of criminal defendants, modern courts, embracing "textualism" and "purposivism," seek to be "faithful agents" of legislatures.[221] This has had the effect of facilitating, rather than curbing, the punitive impulses of legislatures. As Professors Andrew and Carissa Hessick have observed, historically courts were "quite aggressive, deliberately developing doctrines designed to interpret criminal laws in a way that favored criminal defendants."[222] Courts both strictly construed laws to avoid their extension beyond their literal terms and narrowly applied the literal terms of statutes in favor of defendants.[223]

Courts over time have also been less inclined to vigorously apply the rule of lenity, which requires that ambiguous criminal laws be construed narrowly in favor of defendants. The rule was never questioned by the framers[224] but today is rarely employed.[225] The shift is especially problematic in modern times, as legislatures have (either purposefully or inadvertently) enacted very broad and imprecise criminal laws.[226] The turn away from the rule of lenity not only has paved the way for more convictions. It has afforded yet more charging discretion to prosecutors, executive branch actors, and removed an obstacle to the modern legislative penchant for punitiveness.

Suffice it to say, early twenty-first century America differs in myriad ways from the late eighteenth century when the Ex Post Facto Clause was adopted. The framers could not have envisioned the advent of cars, computers, and the twenty-four-hour news cycle. But more important, they could not have imagined the colossus that is the modern criminal justice system, nor the important changes occurring within and among the three branches of government they enshrined, and the checks and balances the respective branches are expected to exercise. What they would recognize, however, is the modern legislative penchant to single out disdained individuals (today, very often persons previously convicted of crimes) for burdensome retroactive laws, and the need for a rejuvenation in the protective scope of the clause.

Conclusion

That the body of the Constitution contains not one, but two, prohibitions of ex post facto laws, limiting the retroactive lawmaking wherewithal of Congress and state legislatures,[227] makes clear the framers' considerable concern over such laws. Ten years after being ratified, however, the actual scope of the prohibition came into question. This is because in *Calder v. Bull* (1798) the Supreme Court limited the clause to criminal laws, of four particular kinds, conclusions which in addition to lacking historical support, arguably lacked precedential value. Later, disagreement has arisen over what qualifies as a "law" for ex post facto purposes, and application of a new carve-out in coverage regarding retroactive "procedural" provisions. This chapter has examined these important disputes and urged that the Ex Post Facto Clause have a more robust protective scope, one consistent with its animating purpose and the critical role it was intended to play in the nation's constitutional order, which changes occurring over the centuries have made all the more important.

8
Global Perspectives

This chapter, the volume's last, situates the Ex Post Facto Clause within the broader global context of human rights protection. Discussion begins with examination of an event marking the high-water mark of worldwide public attention to the ex post facto prohibition: the international criminal tribunals targeting German and Japanese leaders for their atrocities during World War II. The prosecutions not only provided opportunities to see vivid film and photo imagery of alleged war criminals being held to account, along with extensive testimony and documentation attesting to their misdeeds. They also proved a legal landmark, both for the international forum they created and their application of arguably newly created and retroactively applied criminal laws. Concern over the latter in particular inspired inclusion of ex post facto prohibitions in formative postwar instruments such as the Universal Declaration of Human Rights, adopted by the United Nations in 1948. The chapter then turns to a discussion of the many ex post facto provisions now contained in national constitutions throughout the world and in the charters of modern-day war tribunals. The chapter concludes with discussion of yet another international human rights value garnering particular attention after the war, human dignity, and how it aligns with, and can inform, understanding and enforcement of the Ex Post Facto Clause in the United States

The International Emergence of Ex Post Facto Principles

The first half of the twentieth century experienced two cataclysmic world wars, which in addition to causing incalculable human suffering and loss, had a major impact on international law. Historically, in the wake of war, the losing party was subject to a variety of adverse consequences, including forced monetary compensation and prosecution by individual nations.[1]

The horrific tactics and massive carnage of World War I, however, marked a shift in approach. After the war's conclusion, in 1919, the Paris Peace Conference appointed a multinational Commission on the Responsibility

The Ex Post Facto Clause. Wayne A. Logan, Oxford University Press. © Oxford University Press 2023.
DOI: 10.1093/oso/9780190053505.003.0009

of the War and Enforcement of Penalties. The commission recommended appointment of a three-judge tribunal that would apply "the principles of the law of nations as they result from the usages established among civilized peoples, from the laws of humanity and from the dictates of public conscience."[2]

The United States dissented from the recommendation for a number of reasons, including that no international statute or convention made a violation of the laws or customs of war an international crime.[3] The US position was that the application of a new international criminal law and associated penalty would violate ex post facto principles[4] and that there existed "'no fixed and universal standard of humanity.'"[5] Later, the Versailles Peace Treaty provided that the Allies were to "publicly arraign [German Kaiser Wilhelm] . . . for a supreme offense against international morality and the sanctity of treaties."[6] Ultimately, however, the effort foundered because the Netherlands, where Wilhelm had fled, refused to extradite him to the Allies, citing as one of its reasons that the acts alleged did not violate international law.[7] The German government, meanwhile, refused to surrender its nationals accused of war crimes, and conducted trials internally, which did not result in widespread lability or severe punishments.[8]

In the 1920s, proposals were advanced to create an international criminal code and court, but none came to fruition. In 1928, however, fifteen nations, including the United States, Germany, Italy, France, Japan, and the United Kingdom, signed the Kellogg-Briand Peace Pact, which outlawed the use of war as an instrument of national policy and called upon signatories to settle their disputes by peaceful means. The pact took the important step of condemning war as a foreign policy tool, yet its lack of explicit penalty or enforcement mechanism caused it to have little more than aspirational rhetorical importance.[9]

So matters stood when World War II and its new shocking atrocities by the Nazis and their Axis allies came into focus. After the war, with Hitler and his successor Joseph Goebbels having committed suicide, the victorious Allies saw three options for dealing with remaining German leaders: summary punishment (including execution), trial, or release, with the latter considered "unthinkable."[10]

Initially, the United States agreed with Prime Minister of the United Kingdom Winston Churchill's proposal of summary execution but by 1945 sided with the Soviet position that trial of the major German war criminals in an international court was the preferable course of action.[11] A trial, unlike extrajudicial execution, would align with the Allies' avowed adherence to the rule of law, providing a sharp contrast with the Third Reich.[12]

In the summer of 1945, representatives of the United States, France, Britain, and the Soviet Union met in London to devise plans. They faced daunting challenges: never before had an international trial of individuals for war crimes been undertaken. Aside from resolving basic questions such as the roles of defense counsel, prosecutors, and judges, and the rules of evidence for conducting the trials, the conferees had to decide the criminal offenses on which the prosecutions would be based.[13] What was known as the London Charter (adopted in August 1945) identified the crimes within the tribunal's jurisdiction, which fell into three main categories: "crimes against peace," "war crimes," and "crimes against humanity."

The conferees debated whether the specified crimes were ex post facto and therefore illegal. A French delegate at the London conference, Professor Andre Gros, maintained that there was no preexisting international legal prohibition of the crimes, to which British conferee Sir David Maxwell Fyfe replied "We declare what international law is . . . there won't be any discussion of whether it is international law or not."[14] Even though three decades earlier the United States had objected to the legality of charging Germans with war crimes and crimes against humanity,[15] it supported the prosecutions. Supreme Court Justice Robert Jackson, on leave from the court for the proceedings, maintained that it was critically important "to win the trial on the ground that the Nazi war was illegal," and to establish that the German launching of aggressive war constituted an international war crime.[16]

A four-count indictment issued on October 6, 1945, charging twenty-two defendants variously with four counts:

1. conspiracy to wage aggressive war;
2. planning, preparing, initiating or waging aggressive war;
3. commission of war crimes; and
4. perpetrating crimes against humanity.[17]

A main focus was the allegation concerning aggressive war, which the charter provided little definitional guidance on other than that it was "the supreme international crime differing from other war crimes in that it contains within itself the accumulated evil of the whole."[18]

The trials, which were presided over by four judges of the Allied powers, began in Nuremberg, Germany, in November 1945 and lasted for nine months. Among the defendants prosecuted were high-ranking Nazis such as Herman Goering, Albert Speer, and Rudolph Hess. Ultimately, after considering extensive evidence (much of it coming from Nazi records) and hearing from multiple witnesses (including survivors of Nazi atrocities), three defendants were found not guilty, seven were found guilty and sentenced to prison terms, and twelve were sentenced to death by hanging.[19]

During and after the trials intense debate occurred among the world's leading jurists, lawyers, and academics over whether the bases for criminal conviction were ex post facto.[20] Professor Hans Kelsen, for instance, wrote that the tribunal simply sought to "veil the arbitrary character of the acts of a sovereign law-maker."[21] "A retroactive law providing for punishment of acts which were illegal though not criminal at the time they were committed, seems . . . to be an exception to the rule against *ex post facto* laws."[22] It was also suggested by some that the United States and its Allies tacitly condoned German invasions of other nations by failing to raise contemporaneous diplomatic objections, which also arguably undercut German awareness of their alleged criminal misconduct.[23]

Domestically, in Germany the ex post facto prohibitions had taken a telling course. Although constitutional and statutory ex post facto protection had been in existence since at least 1871, the Third Reich suspended the prohibitions, as notably evidenced by a 1933 statute that retroactively imposed the death penalty for those supposedly involved in the infamous Reichstag fire.[24] Thereafter, in June 1935, per a decree by Hitler, the German Code was amended to read: "Any person who commits an act which the law declares to be punishable or which is deserving of penalty according to the fundamental conceptions of the penal law and sound popular feeling, shall be punished."[25] Defending the latter enactment, the president of the Academy of German Law, Hans Frank, stated:

> By means of . . . [this law], the liberal foundation of the old penal code "no penalty without a law" was definitely abandoned and replaced by the postulate, "no crime without punishment," which corresponds to our conception of the law.
>
> In the future, criminal behavior, even if it does not fall under formal penal precepts, will receive the deserved punishment if such behavior is considered punishable according to the healthy feelings of the people.[26]

The Allies, as part of their occupation of Germany at the war's end, rescinded the changes.[27]

In his opening remarks at the trial, Justice Robert Jackson, serving as chief prosecutor for the United States, downplayed the lack of specific preexisting law, and highlighted what he saw as the necessary evolutionary character and plasticity of international law, stating:

Unless we are prepared to abandon every legal principle of growth for International Law, we cannot deny that our own day has the right to institute customs and to conclude agreements that will themselves become sources of a newer and strengthened International Law. International Law is not capable of development by the normal processes of legislation for there is no continuing international legislative authority. Innovations and revisions in International Law are brought about by the actions of governments designed to meet a change in circumstances . . . The fact this that when the law evolves by the case method, as did the Common Law and as international law must do if it is to advance at all, it advances at the expense of those who wrongly guessed and learned too late their error. The law, so far as International Law can be decreed, had been clearly pronounced when these acts took place.[28]

The tribunal endorsed Jackson's view, concluding that the provisions of the London Charter were an "expression of international law existing at the time [of the Charter's] creation,"[29] such as the Kellogg-Briand Peace Pact of 1928 (noted earlier), which Germany signed, and which resolved to settle disputes by peaceful means. Although the tribunal acknowledged that the pact itself did not make violation of its terms an international crime, it reasoned that international law "is not static, but by continual adaptation follows the needs of a changing world,"[30] and the criminal prohibition of aggressive war was demanded by "the conscience of the world."[31] The tribunal also rejected the argument that international law was solely concerned with the actions of sovereign states, not individuals. It stated that the principle that "international law imposes duties and liabilities upon individuals as well as upon states has long been recognized."[32]

The Nuremberg Tribunal proved a major landmark in the history of international law. As Robert Jackson put it in his opening statement, "That four great nations, flushed with victory and stung with injury stay the hand of vengeance and voluntarily submit their captive enemies to the judgment of the law is one of the most significant tributes that Power has ever paid to Reason."[33] However, many critics maintained that the trials were simply a form of victors' justice, having only a patina of lawfulness, and that claims of wrongdoing could be lodged against the Allies for their alleged wrongdoing (e.g., the bombing of German cities). As Professor Dina McIntyre put it in 1962, although the tribunal was intended as a refutation of "might makes right," "it was the 'might' of the Allies . . . that made the Charter, Trial and Judgment of Nuremberg 'right.'"[34] With respect to the use of the Kellogg-Briand Pact as precedent for the convictions, Professor Sheldon Glueck wrote in 1946:

> [T]he fact that the contracting Parties to a treaty have agreed to render aggressive war illegal does not necessarily mean that they have decided to make its violation an international crime. Even an international contract and one dealing with a subject so vital to the survival of nations as the [Pact] is not a penal statute; and the remedy for breach of contract does not consist of prosecution and punishment of the guilty party, but rather of obtaining compensation for its breach.[35]

Although debate continues to this day over the lawfulness of the tribunal, one can scarcely argue that the Nazi defendants lacked notice of the basic criminality of their actions or that their being held to individual account was morally unfair. As one commentator observed:

> The crimes with which the Nuremberg defendants were charged—including murder, torture, and enslavement, carried out on an enormous scale—were so clearly criminal under every domestic legal system in the world that it could hardly be said that the prospect of criminal liability for them was unpredictable. Ultimately, the *nullum crimen* principle turns on fairness to the defendant; . . . it cannot be said that the Nuremberg war crimes proceedings compromised that fairness.[36]

Bernard Meltzer, who served on the Nuremberg prosecutorial trial team, shortly after the verdict voiced a widely held view:

> To shield the Nazi leaders by applying a principle [ex post facto] designed to protect men who acted without knowledge of their culpability would involve a monumental perversion of justice. The mechanical application of a Latin phrase, however important the values it enshrines, would not be permitted to victimize the moral sense of the peoples of the world.
>
> Nuremberg does not in this view stand or fall on the validity of the charge that the penalization of aggressive war had an ex post facto aspect . . . [I]t is more important to condemn and punish [the action of the Nazis] than to follow literally the principle against retroactivity.[37]

Nevertheless, it is hard to avoid the conclusion that the specific crimes charged lacked prior fixed legal specification and definition.[38] Reduced to their basic form, the competing views regarding the legality of the Nuremberg convictions could be boiled down to two schools of thought: pragmatic-natural law (backers of the tribunal) and legal positivism (the tribunal's critics).

Natural law philosophy dates back to the Greeks, but later most notably Italian theologian and philosopher Thomas Aquinas (1225–1274), and after him Dutch international law theorist Hugo Grotius (1583–1645), and English philosophers Thomas Hobbes (1588–1679) and John Locke (1632–1704). Natural law essentially posits that just laws can be "discovered" or "found," but not "created" by enacted human law. Law can result from an evolutionary process but reflects universal and absolute norms and principles of the law of nature or human reason.[39]

Positive law is most commonly associated with British jurist John Austin (1790–1859). Professor William Bosch, summarizing Austin's views, explains that positivism defines "law as a regulation established by a political superior, non-compliance with which called for a definite punishment."[40] "Regulations not imposed by the political superior or which had no definite sanction, such as rules of honor, customs, and much of international 'law,' were . . . part of positive morality, but not positive law." Furthermore, "unenforceable international legal codes were for Austin merely expressions of tender persuasions, pious hopes, and traditional mythologies."[41]

To a positive law adherent, the tribunal's use of the Kellogg-Briand Peace Pact of 1928 as precedent was unjustified. Critics suggested that when the pact was signed only the Americans possibly believed it enunciated a legal basis for liability, and even this arguably was suspect given the US government's purported acquiescence in German aggressions, especially early in the war (e.g., against Czechoslovakia and Poland).[42] Nor did any world leaders or organizations specifically urge the criminality of aggressive war, which again some contended had been undertaken at times by the Allies.[43] Furthermore, the Peace Pact was devoid of legal bearing because it lacked the necessary prerequisite of being enacted by a supranational authority. "If such an accepted power with competence over all nations did not exist," Professor Bosch writes, "then there was no arbitrator, no one with the right and duty to bring alleged outlaw states before the bar of world justice."[44] Ultimately, "[b]oth friend and foe [of the Tribunal] agreed that the Tribunal was a concrete expression of the pragmatic and natural law philosophies. The Austinian consistently affirmed that the trials were a chimera, a natural-law myth which cloaked a reality far different from what the Tribunal purported to be."[45]

Indeed, arguably, the tribunal's reasoning in support of the convictions was paradoxical. It averred that the ex post facto prohibition was merely "in general a principle of justice," not an enforceable limit on sovereignty."[46] Yet it felt obliged to address ex post facto concern by invoking positive law (especially the generalized prohibitions contained in the Kellogg-Briand Peace Pact of 1928).[47]

In the wake of the Nuremberg Tribunal, and subsequent criminal trials in Germany and Tokyo (the latter targeting Japanese alleged war criminals),[48] many notable figures weighed in on the issue of retroactive criminalization. US Senator Robert Taft (R-Ohio), the son of former Supreme Court Chief Justice and President William Howard Taft, and known as "Mr. Republican," delivered a widely reported speech at Keyon College in October 1946 asserting that the trials were lawless because they "violate[d] that fundamental principle of American law that a man cannot be tried under an ex post facto statute . . . About this whole judgment there is the spirit of vengeance, and vengeance is seldom justice. The hanging of the 11 men convicted [Herman Goering took his own life post-trial] will be a blot on the American record which we shall long regret."[49] Supreme Court Justice William O. Douglas wrote that "the crime for which the Nazis were tried ["aggressive war"] had never been formalized as a crime with the definiteness required by our legal standards, or outlawed with a death penalty by the international community. By our standards that crime arose under an *ex post facto* law. Goering et al. deserved severe punishment. But their guilt did not justify us in substituting POWER for PRINCIPLE."[50]

Federal Judge Charles E. Wyzanski, Jr., spoke to the ex post facto concern in greater detail:

> There is no convention or treaty which places obligations explicitly upon an individual not to aid in waging an aggressive war. Thus, from the point of view of the individual, the charge of a "crime against peace" appears in one aspect like a retroactive law. At the time he acted, almost all informed jurists would have told him that individuals who engaged in aggressive war were not in the legal sense criminals.[51]

Echoing the principled concerns of others, Wyzanski condemned the legal foundation of the tribunal on even more fundamental and unequivocal terms, writing that

> [t]he feeling against a law evolved after the commission of an offense is deeply rooted . . . The antagonism to ex post facto laws is not based on a lawyer's prejudice encased in a Latin maxim. It rests on the political truth that if a law can be created after an offense, then power is to that extent absolute and arbitrary. To allow retroactive legislation is to disparage the principle of constitutional limitation. It is to abandon what is usually regarded as one of the essential values at the core of our democratic faith.[52]

The legacy of the tribunal is a complex one. In the United States, the trials received a mainly approving response from the public and political leaders. Universal condemnation of Nazi atrocities and the desire for their punishment, and the fact that defendants received a lengthy trial (with a record ultimately comprising forty-two volumes),[53] largely overshadowed critical views of the tribunal's legality.[54]

Indeed, it has been said that ex post facto concern was "a fetish only of American lawyers. European legal experts who opposed Nuremberg did not give great weight to the principle. Other lawyers pointed out that it was neither enforced in common law courts nor a necessary rule in international law."[55] As of 1946, Professor Kenneth Gallant observed, many nations lacked "constitutional provisions that on their face required non-retroactivity of crimes and punishments. . . . [O]ne certainly could not say that non-retroactivity in criminal law was a worldwide standard."[56]

The high-profile, hotly disputed legality of the tribunal, and the Nazis' own repudiation of the legality principle, however, proved to have significant longer-term impact—it catapulted concern over ex post facto laws to international prominence.[57] So did the International Tribunal for the Far East (a.k.a. the Tokyo War Crimes Tribunal), which from 1946–1948 prosecuted leading Japanese officials. In contrast to the Nuremberg Tribunal, which was unanimous in its agreement on the legality of the proceedings, the justices in Tokyo (numbering eleven, as opposed to the four in Nuremberg) were sharply divided, with Justice Pal of India in particular condemning the retroactive creation of crimes,[58] further fueling international interest in explicitly enshrining the ex post facto prohibition as an international human right.[59]

Ex Post Facto Principles in the Modern World Order

International Agreements

The seminal development on the international stage was the adoption by the United Nations General Assembly in December 1948 of the Universal Declaration of Human Rights. Article 11(2) of the Declaration provides that "[n]o one shall be held guilty of any penal offence on account of any act or omission which did not constitute a penal offence, under national or international law, at the time it was committed. Nor shall a heavier penalty be imposed than the one that was applicable at the time the penal offense was committed."[60]

The declaration was adopted without opposition (but with eight abstentions),[61] and its prohibitions are repeated using the same or similar language in the International Covenant on Civil and Political Rights,[62] the European Convention on Human Rights,[63] and the American Convention on Human Rights.[64] The Rome Statute of the International Criminal Court also prohibits retroactive creation of a crime (*nullum crimen sine lege*), but does not expressly prohibit a retroactive increase in penalty (*nulla poena sine lege*).[65] The same approach is reflected in the United Nations Convention on the Rights of the Child.[66]

National Constitutions

Today, virtually all nations prohibit ex post fact laws in some shape or form on some legal basis.[67] The list includes those without a provision in the immediate aftermath of World War II,[68] and those that rejected it at some point in the twentieth century (e.g., Soviet Union/Russia).[69] As noted by Judge Theodor Meron, the prohibition "is a fundamental principle of criminal justice and a customary, even peremptory, norm of international law that must be observed in all circumstances by national and international tribunals."[70]

Based on his comprehensive survey, current as of October 2007, Professor Kenneth Gallant reports that approximately 84 percent of United Nations members (162 of 192) prohibit only retroactive crimes (*nullum crimen*) in their constitutions,[71] and that 76 percent (147 of 192) in their constitutions ban both retroactive crime creation and increased punishment (*nulla poena*).[72] Many nations have constitutions that expressly incorporate international human rights instruments that contain prohibitions, without mentioning each right separately, or have both a specific prohibitory provision and incorporate international human rights law.[73] Altogether, all but two UN members (Bhutan and Brunei) require nonretroactivity of crimes and punishments to some extent by means of constitutional provision, statute, international treaty, or some combination thereof.[74]

Among provisions targeting both retroactive crimes and punishments, a common approach is patterned after the Universal Declaration of Human Rights, which prohibits (1) conviction for "any penal offense on account of any act or omission which did not constitute a penal offense, under national or international law, at the time it was committed"; and (2) imposition of "a heavier penalty . . . than the one that was applicable at the time the penal offense was committed." Bespeaking its universality, as indicated, the article covers "national or international "law."[75] The extra-domestic scope evidenced in the declaration is found in many constitutions. The Canadian Constitution's Charter of Rights and Freedoms, for instance, requires that an act or omission "constitute[s] an offence under Canadian or international law or was criminal according to the general principles of law recognized by the community of nations."[76]

Another common feature requires that the law in question be published or promulgated in some way, for instance by statute or regulation, an approach reflected in the French Declaration of the Rights of Man and of the Citizen (1789): "no one shall suffer punishment except it be legally inflicted in virtue of a law passed and promulgated before the commission of the offense."[77] Professor Gallant notes that this kind of provision serves three important policies:

> [First,] [t]he requirement of legislative action and publication ensures notice and accessibility of the law . . . A second policy is ensuring that there actually is a law (i.e., that the requirements for making a legal rule binding the populace have actually been met). . . . Finally, this type of provision now protects democratic governance in many places. Where the legislature is democratically chosen, this type of provision ensures that criminal law is created by the institution of representative democracy.[78]

War crimes and crimes against humanity are often singled out as an exception. The Constitution of Albania, for instance, provides: "No one may be charged or declared guilty of a criminal offense that was not considered as such by law at the time of its commission, with the exception of cases, that at the time of their commission, according to international law, constitute war crimes or crimes against humanity."[79] The Maldives and Yemen reference both Sharia and "law."[80] The ex post facto prohibitions are recognized by authoritarian governments as well (e.g., Oman), whether by decree, proclamation, order, or statute.[81]

Several national constitutions have broad retroactivity prohibitions not limited to crimes or criminal punishment (akin to some American state constitutions, as discussed in Chapter 7). The Costa Rican Constitution, for instance, provides that "[n]o law shall have retroactive effect to the detriment of any person whatsoever of his acquired property rights"[82] and "[n]o one shall be made to suffer a penalty except for a crime, unintentional tort or misdemeanor punishable by previous law. . . ."[83] In Mozambique, "laws may have retroactive effect only where this is to the benefit of citizens and other legal persons."[84]

Many constitutions, however, are specifically limited to criminal cases. The Constitution of Myanmar, for instance, provides that "[n]o Penal law shall be enacted to provide retrospective effect."[85] Venezuela has an unusual provision stating that "[n]o legislative provision will have retroactive effect, except when it imposes a minor penalty."[86] Similarly, the Israeli penal law prohibits retroactive increase in a penalty but specifies that "updating the amount of a fine is not deemed setting a more severe penalty."[87]

Only a few nations, those with historic ties to the United States, use the phrase "ex post facto" in their constitutions (the Philippines, the Marshall Islands, Micronesia, and Liberia).[88] The Constitution of the Philippines provides that "[n]o *Ex Post Facto* Law . . . shall be enacted,"[89] and that of Micronesia provides that "[a] bill of attainder or ex post facto law may not be passed."[90] The Marshall Islands Constitution, however, is more detailed, stating that "[n]o person shall be subjected to ex post facto punishment—such as punishment in excess of that validly applicable at the time the act in question was committed, or punishment imposed by a procedure less favorable to the accused than that validly applicable at the time the act was committed."[91] The Liberian Constitution provides double coverage of a sort stating that "[n]o person shall be made subject to any law or punishment which was not in effect at the time of commission of an offense, nor shall the Legislature enact any bill of attainder or ex post facto law."[92]

Importantly, some constitutions make the ban conditional. For example, in Canada, where as noted the charter prohibits retroactive crime creation, the prohibition can be overridden[93] when the government identifies a pressing and substantial objective.[94] In El Salvador, the constitution provides that "laws shall not have retroactive effect, except in matters of public order and in penal matters if the new law is favorable to the offender."[95] In Greece, retroactive "security measures" are a permissible exception to the otherwise categorical ban.[96]

Experience in Nepal is illustrative of the impact such a condition can have. In *Chandra Bijaya Shah and Others*,[97] the Supreme Court of Nepal addressed the case of those allegedly involved in several June 1985 bombings targeting the government. At the time no law in force specifically criminalized the incidents. Also, one part of the constitution (in effect since 1962) expressly prohibited retroactive crime creation and sentence enhancement,[98] yet another provided that "[l]aws may be made for the sake of public good to regulate or control the exercise of fundamental rights," with "preservation of the security of Nepal" and "the maintenance of law and order" being among the exceptional conditions.[99] After the bombings, and the arrest of the defendants, a new law with expressly retroactive force concerning the bombings took effect, and the defendants were convicted.

Relying on the exceptional condition provision, the Nepal Supreme Court upheld the constitutionality of the new law and the convictions, emphasizing that the preamble of the challenged law expressly stated that it was enacted for the public good and cited the constitutional provision containing the exception provision.[100]

The doctrine of parliamentary sovereignty can also have significant influence. In the United Kingdom (England, Scotland, Wales, and Northern Ireland), which lacks a codified written constitution, the doctrine allows for ex post facto laws[101] (even though the United Kingdom is a signatory of the European Convention on Human Rights,[102] which contains an ex post facto prohibition[103]). In Sierra Leone, where the constitution bans retroactive crime creation and sentence enhancement, the Privy Council in *Akar v. Att'y Gen. of Sierra Leone* (1969)[104] stated that "it is open to the legislature to enact [retroactive] legislation as long as this is expressly stated on the particular legislation. Where such intentions are expressed in clear and definite words they must be applied by the Court regardless of the wisdom or desirability of exercising such powers."[105]

Finally, it should not be ignored that even in nations where express constitutional provisions exist (without conditional exceptions), their impact can be less than dispositive. A case from Indonesia underscores this point. In the *Masykur Abdul Kadir Case*,[106] an individual involved in the Bali terrorist bombings in October 2002 was convicted and sentenced pursuant to a law enacted after the bombings. The Indonesia Constitution provides that the "right not to be tried under a law with retrospective effect" is a "human right[] that cannot be limited under any circumstances."[107] By a 5-4 vote, the Constitutional Court of Indonesia deemed the law unconstitutional, emphasizing the provision's unequivocal prohibition. The court noted that while international treaties allow for an exception for genocide and crimes against humanity, the bombing with its many fatalities, while deplorable, did not so qualify, meaning that killings must be redressed by preexisting law. The court stated that "the principle [of retrospectivity] was breached . . . during the Nuremberg Trials. But, . . . this was an exception and was motivated by very strong desires to punish Nazi cruelty."[108] So things stood, until there came an unusual development. After the decision, several members of the court's majority announced that the decision would not operate retroactively upon the defendant. In the words of two commentators, "the decision, whilst binding, only prevents future investigations . . . It would not, therefore, impact upon convictions that that have already been obtained."[109]

International Criminal Tribunals and Courts

Ex post facto principles also figure in provisions governing international criminal courts addressing wrongdoing in the former Yugoslavia, Rwanda, Sierra Leone, and Iraq. The courts recognize the rule of *nullum crimen sine lege* without explicit provision in their governing law. The Rome Statute of the International Criminal Court (ICC) is illustrative.[110] Also, three of the international courts (Kosovo, East Timor, and Cambodia) embrace ex post facto principles by reference to international humanitarian law documents, and the East Timor court explicitly incorporated it into its governing law.[111] The Iraqi Tribunal incorporated the principles by reference to Iraqi domestic law.[112]

The United Nations Human Rights Committee (HRC) has addressed challenges to retroactive crime creation and sentence enhancement. In one well-known case, in 1980, the HRC applied the International Covenant on Civil and Political Rights (ICCPR), discussed earlier, to grant relief to an individual convicted under a law of Uruguay that retroactively criminalized membership in "subversive organizations."[113] Later, in *A.R.S. v. Canada* (1981),[114] the HRC addressed an instance where the government retroactively increased the mandatory supervision of parolees, denying relief under the ICCPR on the rationale that there was no penalty increase "as it was a 'measure of social assistance intended to provide for the rehabilitation of the convicted person, in his own interest.'"[115]

In *M. v. Germany* (2009),[116] the European Court of Human Rights addressed a claim under Article 7, section 1, of the Convention for the Protection of Human Rights and Fundamental Freedoms, which bans retroactive crime creation and sentence enhancement. The plaintiff, a German citizen with a history of serious criminal activity and mental illness, was convicted in 1986 of attempted murder and robbery and sentenced to a five-year prison term, followed by another five-year term in preventive detention. Thereafter, the German Criminal Code was amended allowing for preventive detention for an unlimited period of time, which the plaintiff challenged.

The court concluded that the retroactive extension of preventive detention violated Article 7, in a decision distinctly unlike that of the US Supreme Court in *Kansas v. Hendricks* (1997),[117] discussed at length in Chapters 5 and 6, which upheld a law retroactively allowing the indefinite involuntary confinement of "sexually violent predators." The court rejected the German government's labeling of preventive detention as civil and emphasized that the new law was triggered by an underlying criminal conviction.[118] The court identified several factors to be considered when assessing whether the detention was penal in nature, the first being "whether the measure in question is imposed following conviction for a 'criminal offence,'"[119] and others being "the characterization of the measure under domestic law, its nature and purpose, the procedures involved in its making and implementation, and its severity."[120] After emphasizing that it "must remain free to go behind appearances and assess for itself whether a particular measure amounts in substance to a 'penalty' within the meaning of this provision,"[121] the court considered the "realities of the situation of persons in preventive detention,"[122] and concluded that there was no substantial difference between a prison sentence and that of a preventive detention order,[123] including a lack of meaningful treatment.[124] The retroactive abolition of the ten-year maximum term of preventive detention, in short, violated Article 7 of the Convention for the Protection of Human Rights and Fundamental Freedoms prohibiting imposition of "a heavier penalty" than that applicable at the time the offense was committed.[125]

Ex Post Facto Principles and "Human Dignity"

One final basis for comparative reference is the emergence of human dignity in the pantheon of international rights.[126] Much as with the worldwide proliferation of ex post facto protections, a major catalyst in the recognition of human dignity was its inclusion in 1948 in the Universal Declaration of Human Rights (UDHR), which enshrined "the dignity and worth of the human person."[127] Today, human dignity is a mainstay of international human rights documents.[128] The Charter of Fundamental Rights of the European Union declares, for example, "Human dignity is inviolable. It must be respected and protected."[129]

Many national constitutions also reference dignity.[130] India's Constitution, for instance, provides that the nation "resolve[s] . . . to secure to all its citizens . . . fraternity assuring the dignity of the individual and the unity and integrity of the Nation."[131] Similarly, South Africa's Constitution states that "[e]veryone has inherent dignity and the right to have their dignity respected and protected."[132] "Human dignity," observes Luis Barroso, of the Brazilian Constitutional Court, "has become a central and recurrent concept in the reasoning of supreme courts and constitutional courts throughout the world."[133] Similarly, Professor Michael Rosen notes that dignity "is central to modern human rights discourse, the closest thing that we have to an internationally accepted framework for the normative regulation of political life, and it is embedded in numerous constitutions, in international conventions and declarations."[134]

Human dignity initially surfaced in US Supreme Court opinions in the 1940s.[135] One of the first references came in a dissent by Justice Frank Murphy in the court's infamous decision *Korematsu v. United States* (1944),[136] which condoned the involuntary internment of Japanese Americans during World War II.[137] Soon thereafter, in *Carter v. Illinois* (1946),[138] the majority invoked the concept in a case concerning a criminal defendant's right to counsel, opining that states have latitude in the "methods and practices by which crime is brought to book, so long as they observe those ultimate dignities of man which the United States Constitution assures."[139] Not long thereafter came another reference, from Supreme Court Justice Robert Jackson.[140] In the case, *Brinegar v. United States* (1949),[141] Jackson, not long after he returned from his service as chief prosecutor in Nuremberg, dissented from the majority's approval of a warrantless search of a car, writing that police searches and seizures of citizens was

> one of the first and most effective weapons in the arsenal of every arbitrary government. And one need only briefly to have dwelt and worked among a people possessed of many admirable qualities but deprived of these rights to know that the human personality deteriorates and dignity and self-reliance disappear where homes, persons and possessions are subject at any hour to unheralded search and seizure by the police.[142]

Since the 1940s, human dignity has played a central role in the court's constitutional jurisprudence. According to one study, the term "dignity" appears in over nine hundred opinions of the court.[143] Over time, the court has come to regard "dignity as a distinct and core value,"[144] which while not expressly found in the constitution or its amendments,[145] qualifies as a "fundamental" constitutional value.[146] Human dignity has been invoked by liberal and conservative justices alike (although the latter with less vigor).[147]

Although dignity very often figures in civil cases, such as those concerning Fourteenth Amendment rights to equal protection and privacy (e.g., the right to marry), the court's criminal cases offer multiple examples of its invocation. One of the more notable instances is found in *Lawrence v. Texas* (2003),[148] which in invalidating a law criminalizing consensual homosexual sodomy stated that the law degraded "the dignity of the persons" charged and convicted.[149] Dignity frequently figures in death penalty decisions,[150] and the court has stated more generally that "[t]he basic concept underlying the Eighth Amendment is nothing less than the dignity of man."[151] Dignity has also recently figured in decisions concerning search and seizure (Fourth Amendment), coercive police interrogation (Fifth Amendment), the right to represent oneself in a criminal trial (Sixth Amendment), and poor prison conditions (Eighth Amendment, again).[152]

Testament to the increasing salience of dignity,[153] the nation's leading organization of judges and lawyers, the American Bar Association, in 2019 unanimously adopted a resolution recognizing human dignity as "foundational to a just rule of law" and urging governments to "ensure that 'dignity rights'—the principle that human dignity is fundamental to all areas of law and policy—be reflected in the exercise of their legislative, executive, and judicial functions."[154] Dignity has also figured in the work of prominent legal scholars seeking to temper the harshness of US penal policies, including Professors James Whitman,[155] Jonathan Simon,[156] and Carol Steiker.[157]

A core principle of human dignity derives from the work of eighteenth-century German philosopher Immanuel Kant,[158] who posited that "to treat people with dignity is to treat them as autonomous individuals able to choose their destiny."[159] Kant articulated a "formula of ends": individuals should always be treated "as an end, never as a mere means,"[160] a view that aligns with a main concern motivating the framers' inclusion of the Ex Post Facto Clause in the Constitution. As discussed in Chapter 6, the clause does not prohibit the passage of arbitrary or vindictive legislation generally, but only that which is arbitrary or vindictive because of its retroactive force. With retroactive laws, legislators can single out already identified parties who are disfavored,[161] confident in the knowledge that the voting public will back them.[162] The clause thus prevents legislators from politically benefiting themselves[163]—treating those targeted as instrumental means and objects. The clause requires that if punitive laws are to be enacted, they must apply prospectively, targeting only future (i.e., not yet identified) criminals.

Barring retroactive laws also serves another basic Kantian concern: ensuring the decision-making autonomy of individuals and the capacity for self-determination.[164] Retroactive creation of a crime, or enhancement of a sentence, the former perhaps especially, introduces unexpected negative consequences for past acts.[165] It thus "disrupts the expectations people have formed on the basis of existing law and the actions they have taken in the expectation that the law will be applied to determine the legal consequences of contemplated actions is the law standing at the time the action is taken."[166] In 1964, legal scholar Lon Fuller elaborated on the connection between dignity and the necessity of a knowledge basis to inform individual action, which is jeopardized by retrospective laws:

> To embark on the enterprise of subjecting human conduct to rules of necessity a commitment to the view that man is, or can become, a responsible agent, capable

of understanding and following rules, and answerable for his defaults. Every departure from the principles of a law's inner morality is an affront to man's dignity as a
responsible agent. To judge his actions by unpublished or retrospective laws . . . is
to convey to him your indifference to his powers of self-determination.[167]

More recently, Supreme Court Justice Antonin Scalia relied on this connection in his dissent in *Indiana v. Edwards* (2008),[168] where the majority denied
a legally competent but mentally ill defendant the right to represent himself at
trial, when he spoke of "the supreme human dignity of being master of one's
fate rather than a ward of the State—the dignity of individual choice."[169]

Respect for human dignity also aligns with fundamental fairness, another
ex post facto concern. Laws transgressing the ex post facto prohibition, the
Supreme Court in *Carmell v. Texas* (2000)[170] recognized, have one thing in
common: "In each instance, the government refuses, after the fact, to play by
its own rules, altering them in a way that is advantageous only to the State,
to facilitate an easier conviction."[171] Justice John Paul Stevens, writing for
the court, stated that "[t]here is plainly a fundamental fairness interest . . . in
having the government abide by its own rules of law it establishes to govern
the circumstances under which it can deprive a person of his or her liberty or
life."[172] Stevens earlier evoked this same rule of law concern when he wrote for
the unanimous court in *Lynce v. Mathis* (1997)[173] and noted that "[t]he specific prohibition on ex post facto laws is . . . one aspect of the broader constitutional protection against arbitrary changes in the law."[174]

Despite these parallels, US ex post facto doctrine fails to reflect several core
values of human dignity, as evidenced by comparison to how it is conceived
by courts outside the United States. A good example is found in Germany,
which adopted its modern constitution in the wake of Nazi atrocities, the
Third Reich's mistreatment of Jews in particular.[175] The German Basic Law
of 1949 declared that human dignity shall be "inviolable"[176] and the German
Constitutional Court has described human dignity as the foundation of all
basic rights.[177] Among other safeguards, it protects a right to the protection of
personality, which in turn protects a right of informational self-determination.
As Professor Edward Eberle has written, the right ensures personal control
over "such matters as how to present one's self in society, including control
over one's words, images, portraits, reputation, and critically in the computer
age, control over access to and use of personal information."[178]

German courts have vigorously enforced the right. In one decision, for
instance, the *Census Act Case of 1983*,[179] the Federal Constitutional Court
addressed a challenge to a law requiring citizens to divulge to the government
information such as their method of transportation to work, occupation, and

work hours. The court held that it must protect the individual "from the un-limited collection, storage, use, and transmission of personal data as a con-dition for free personality development under modern conditions of data processing."[180]

In another decision, *Lebach*,[181] an individual received significant media at-tention after his conviction for serving as an accessory to an armed robbery, and a German television station sought to present a documentary showing his name and photograph and providing other details about him. He sued to enjoin the broadcast based on his right of personality and human dignity. In granting relief, the German Constitutional Court stated, "The rights to the free development of one's personality and human dignity secure for everyone an autonomous sphere in which to shape one's private life by developing and protecting one's individuality." The court added that as the public's interest in the crime subsides with the passage of time, "the criminals' 'right to be left alone' fundamentally increases in importance . . ."[182]

The foregoing perspective stands in stark contrast to that common to US law, as reflected in the Supreme Court's decision in *Smith v. Doe* (2003).[183] In *Smith*, discussed at length in Chapters 5 and 6, the court by a 6-3 vote condoned the publication on a government internet website of personal identifying and locational information regarding individuals previously convicted of sexual offenses, ostensibly to allow community members to take self-protective measures. In concluding that the law was not punitive in its intent or effects the court discounted the dignitary loss experienced by the petitioners. To the majority, the nation's criminal justice "system does not treat dissemination of truthful information in furtherance of a le-gitimate governmental objective as punishment . . ."[184] "The publicity may cause adverse consequences for the convicted defendant" but it was permis-sible because the state did not "make the publicity and the resulting stigma an integral part of the objective of the regulatory scheme."[185] Echoing this sentiment, Chief Justice William Rehnquist said from the court's bench during the oral argument in *Smith* that the retroactively targeted individuals "deserve[d] stigmatization."[186]

Lebach and *Smith* reflect strikingly different views of how informational disclosure impacts human dignity. When comparing the United States and Continental Europe with regard to privacy policy more generally, it is impor-tant to recognize the latter's much more protective stance concerning indi-vidual informational privacy (e.g., the European Union's recognized "right to be forgotten").[187] Even so, the negligible weight the *Smith* majority accorded the petitioners' interest in not being publicly shamed (before the world, po-tentially for their lifetimes), and the court's prioritization of government interest over the negative effects imposed on individuals, represents a notably stark contrast.

Ultimately, while US constitutional law more generally parallels the increasing worldwide focus on human dignity,[188] it remains to be seen whether human dignity will come to figure explicitly in its Ex Post Facto Clause doctrine. To date, the Eighth Amendment's Cruel and Unusual Punishment Clause and the Fourteenth Amendment's Due Process and Equal Protection Clauses might fairly be called "Dignitary Clauses."[189] For reasons discussed, to this category we might reasonably add the Ex Post Facto Clause.

Conclusion

This chapter has sought to contextualize the book's primary focus: the understanding and application of US domestic law regarding the Constitution's Ex Post Facto Clause. The chapter traced the modern global history of the ex post facto prohibition, in its various forms, from Nuremberg onward, in constitutions and international governance. The instances surveyed, while by no means exhaustive, highlight the relative robustness of US doctrine. Unlike several nations, for instance, in the United States no provision is made for conditions that allow for exceptions to be made for retroactive criminal laws. Yet the survey also highlights ways in which US domestic law is less protective, for instance, regarding the principle of human dignity, which can help aid in eventual fulfillment of the aims of the US Constitution's Ex Post Facto Clause.

U.S. Supreme Court Ex Post Facto (and Related) Decisions

Calder v. Bull, 3 U.S. (3 Dall.) 386 (1798)
Fletcher v. Peck, 10 U.S. (6 Cranch) 87 (1810)
Watson v. Mercer, 33 U.S. 88 (1834)
Baltimore & S. R. Co. v. Nesbit, 51 U.S. 395 (1850)
Carpenter v. Pennsylvania, 58 U.S. 456 (1855)
Locke v. New Orleans, 71 U.S. 172 (1867)
Cummings v. Missouri, 71 U.S. 277 (1867)
Ex Parte Garland, 71 U.S. 333 (1867)
Gut v. State, 76 U.S. 35 (1869)
Burgess v. Salmon, 97 U.S. 381 (1878)
Kring v. Missouri, 107 U.S. 221 (1882), rev'd, *Collins v. Youngblood*, 497 U.S. 37 (1990)
Hopt v. Utah, 110 U.S. 574 (1884)
Murphy v. Ramsey, 114 U.S. 15 (1885)
In re Medley, 134 U.S. 160 (1890)
Holden v. Minnesota, 137 U.S. 483 (1890)
Cook v. United States, 138 U.S. 157 (1891)
Duncan v. Missouri, 152 U.S. 377 (1894)
Gibson v. Mississippi, 162 U.S. 565 (1896)
Hawker v. New York, 170 U.S. 189 (1898)
Thompson v. Utah, 170 U.S. 343 (1898), rev'd, *Collins v. Youngblood*, 497 U.S. 37 (1990)
Thompson v. Missouri, 171 U.S. 380 (1898)
Neely v. Henkel, 180 U.S. 109 (1901)
McDonald v. Massachusetts, 180 U.S. 311 (1901)
Mallett v. North Carolina, 181 U.S. 589 (1901)
Reetz v. Michigan, 188 U.S. 505 (1903)
Rooney v. North Dakota, 196 U.S. 319 (1905)
Kentucky Union Co. v. Kentucky, 219 U.S. 140 (1911)
Johannessen v. United States, 225 U.S. 227 (1912)
Luria v. United States, 231 U.S. 9 (1913)
Ross v. Oregon, 227 U.S. 150 (1913)
Bugajewitz v. Adams, 228 U.S. 585 (1913)
Malloy v. South Carolina, 237 U.S. 180 (1915)
Frank v. Mangum, 237 U.S. 309 (1915)
Chicago & A.R. Co. v. Tranbarger, 238 U.S. 67 (1915)
Bankers Trust Co. v. Blodgett, 260 U.S. 647 (1923)
Mahler v. Eby, 264 U.S. 32 (1924)
Samuels v. McCurdy, 267 U.S. 188 (1925)
Beazell v. Ohio, 269 U.S. 167 (1925)
Lindsey v. Washington, 301 U.S. 397 (1937)
United States v. Powers, 307 U.S. 214 (1939)

Gryger v. Burke, 334 U.S. 728 (1948)
Harisiades v. Shaughnessy, 342 U.S. 580 (1952)
Galvan v. Press, 347 U.S. 522 (1954)
Marcello v. Bonds, 349 U.S. 302 (1955)
De Veau v. Braisted, 363 U.S. 144 (1960)
Flemming v. Nestor, 363 U.S. 603 (1960)
Konigsberg v. State Bar of California, 366 U.S. 36 (1961)
Bouie v. City of Columbia, 378 U.S. 347 (1964)
Marks v. United States, 430 U.S. 188 (1977)
Splawn v. California, 431 U.S. 595 (1977)
Dobbert v. Florida, 432 U.S. 282 (1977)
Portley v. Grossman, 444 U.S. 1311 (1980)
Weaver v. Graham, 450 U.S. 24 (1981)
Miller v. Florida, 482 U.S. 423 (1987)
Collins v. Youngblood, 497 U.S. 37 (1990)
Cal. Dep't of Corr. v. Morales, 514 U.S. 499 (1995)
Lynce v. Mathis, 519 U.S. 433 (1997)
Garner v. Jones, 529 U.S. 244 (2000)
Carmell v. Texas, 529 U.S. 513 (2000)
Johnson v. United States, 529 U.S. 694 (2000)
Smith v. Doe, 538 U.S. 84 (2003)
Stogner v. California, 539 U.S. 607 (2003)
Peugh v. United States, 569 U.S. 530 (2013)

State and District of Columbia Constitutional Provisions

ALABAMA

Ala. Const. Art. I, § 22

"That no ex post facto law, nor any law, impairing the obligations of contracts, or making any irrevocable or exclusive grants of special privileges or immunities, shall be passed by the legislature; and every grant or franchise, privilege, or immunity shall forever remain subject to revocation, alteration, or amendment."

ALASKA

Alaska Const. Art. I, § 15

"No bill of attainder or ex post facto law shall be passed. No law impairing the obligation of contracts, and no law making any irrevocable grant of special privileges or immunities shall be passed. No conviction shall work corruption of blood or forfeiture of estate."

ARIZONA

Ariz. Const. Art. 2, § 25

"No bill of attainder, ex-post-facto law, or law impairing the obligation of a contract, shall ever be enacted."

ARKANSAS

Ark. Const. Art. 2, § 17

"No bill of attainder, ex post facto law, or law impairing the obligation of contracts shall ever be passed; and no conviction shall work corruption of blood or forfeiture of estate."

CALIFORNIA

Cal. Const. Art. 1, § 9

"A bill of attainder, ex post facto law, or law impairing the obligation of contracts may not be passed."

COLORADO

Colo. Const. Art. 2, § 11
"No ex post facto law, nor law impairing the obligation of contracts, or retrospective in its operation, or making any irrevocable grant of special privileges, franchises or immunities, shall be passed by the general assembly."

CONNECTICUT

Does not have a provision. *See* Abed v. Commissioner of Correction, 682 A.2d 558, 562 (Conn. Ct. App.), *cert. denied*, 684 A.2d 707 (1996).

DELAWARE

Does not have a provision. (The state formerly had a "retrospective" provision, but omitted it. Neil Colman McCabe & Cynthia Ann Bell, *Ex Post Facto Provisions of State Constitutions*, 4 EMERGING ISSUES ST. CONST. L. 133, 137 n.1 (1991)).

DISTRICT OF COLUMBIA

D.C. Code Art. 1 Bill of Rights, § 14
"Bills of attainder and ex post facto laws are prohibited."

FLORIDA

Fla. Const. Art. 1, § 10
"No bill of attainder, ex post facto law or law impairing the obligation of contracts shall be passed."

GEORGIA

Ga. Const. Art. I, § I, ¶ X
"No bill of attainder, ex post facto law, retroactive law, or laws impairing the obligation of contract or making irrevocable grant of special privileges or immunities shall be passed."

HAWAII

Does not have a provision. (The state formerly had a "retrospective" provision, but omitted it. Neil Colman McCabe & Cynthia Ann Bell, Ex Post Facto Provisions of State Constitutions, 4 EMERGING ISSUES ST. CONST. L. 133, 137 n.1 (1991)).

IDAHO

Idaho Const. Art. 1, § 16
"No bill of attainder, ex post facto law, or law impairing the obligation of contracts shall ever be passed."

Idaho Const. Art. XI, § 12

"The legislature shall pass no law for the benefit of a railroad, or other corporation, or any individual, or association of individuals retroactive in its operation, or which imposes on the people of any county or municipal subdivision of the state, a new liability in respect to transactions or considerations already past."

ILLINOIS

Ill. Const. Art. 1, § 16

"No ex post facto law, or law impairing the obligation of contracts or making an irrevocable grant of special privileges or immunities, shall be passed."

INDIANA

Ind. Const. Art. 1, § 24

"No ex post facto law, or law impairing the obligation of contracts, shall ever be passed."

IOWA

Iowa Const. Art. 1, § 21

"No bill of attainder, ex post facto law, or law impairing the obligation of contracts, shall ever be passed."

KANSAS

Does not have a provision.

KENTUCKY

Ky Const. § 19, ¶ 1

"No ex post facto law, nor any law impairing the obligation of contracts, shall be enacted."

LOUISIANA

La. Const. Art. 1, § 23

"No bill of attainder, ex post facto law, or law impairing the obligation of contracts shall be enacted."

MAINE

Me. Const. Art. 1, § 11

"The Legislature shall pass no bill of attainder, ex post facto law, nor law impairing the obligation of contracts, and no attainder shall work corruption of blood nor forfeiture of estate."

MARYLAND

Md. Const. Art. 17
"That retrospective Laws, punishing acts committed before the existence of such Laws, and by them only declared criminal are oppressive, unjust and incompatible with liberty; wherefore, no ex post facto Law ought to be made; nor any retrospective oath or restriction be imposed, or required."

MASSACHUSETTS

Mass. Const. pt. 1, Art. XXIV
"Laws made to punish for actions done before the existence of such laws, and which have not been declared crimes by preceding laws, are unjust, oppressive, and inconsistent with the fundamental principles of a free government."

MICHIGAN

Mich. Const. Art. 1, § 10
"No bill of attainder, ex post facto law or law impairing the obligation of contract shall be enacted."

MINNESOTA

Minn. Const. Art. 1, § 11
"No bill of attainder, ex post facto law, or any law impairing the obligation of contracts shall be passed, and no conviction shall work corruption of blood or forfeiture of estate."

MISSISSIPPI

Miss. Const. Art. 3, § 16
"Ex post facto laws, or laws impairing the obligation of contracts, shall not be passed."

MISSOURI

Mo. Const. Art. I, § 13
"That no ex post facto law, nor law impairing the obligation of contracts, or retrospective in its operation, or making any irrevocable grant of special privileges or immunities, can be enacted."

MONTANA

Mont. Const. Art. II, § 31
"No ex post facto law nor any law impairing the obligation of contracts, or making any irrevocable grant of special privileges, franchises, or immunities, shall be passed by the legislature."

NEBRASKA

Neb. Const. Art. 1, § 16
"No bill of attainder, ex post facto law, or law impairing the obligation of contracts, or making any irrevocable grant of special privileges or immunities shall be passed."

NEVADA

Nev. Art. 1, § 15
"No bill of attainder, ex-post-facto law, or law impairing the obligation of contracts shall ever be passed."

NEW HAMPSHIRE

N.H. Const. Pt. 1, Art. 23
"Retrospective laws are highly injurious, oppressive, and unjust. No such laws, therefore, should be made, either for the decision of civil causes, or the punishment of offenses."

NEW JERSEY

N.J. Const. Art. 4, § 7, ¶ 3
"The Legislature shall not pass any bill of attainder, ex post facto law, or law impairing the obligation of contracts, or depriving a party of any remedy for enforcing a contract which existed when the contract was made."

NEW MEXICO

N.M. Const. Art. II, § 19
"No ex post facto law, bill of attainder nor law impairing the obligation of contracts shall be enacted by the legislature."

NEW YORK

Does not have a provision.

NORTH CAROLINA

N.C. Const. Art. I, § 16
"Retrospective laws, punishing acts committed before the existence of such laws and by them only declared criminal, are oppressive, unjust, and incompatible with liberty, and therefore no ex post facto law shall be enacted. No law taxing retrospectively sales, purchases, or other acts previously done shall be enacted."

NORTH DAKOTA

N.D. Const. Art. 1, § 18
"No bill of attainder, ex post facto law, or law impairing the obligations of contracts shall ever be passed."

OHIO

Ohio Const. Art. II, § 28
"The general assembly shall have no power to pass retroactive laws, or laws impairing the obligation of contracts; but may, by general laws, authorize courts to carry into effect, upon such terms as shall be just and equitable, the manifest intention of parties, and officers, by curing omissions, defects, and errors, in instruments and proceedings, arising out of their want of conformity with the laws of this state."

OKLAHOMA

Okla. Const. Art. 2, § 15
"No bill of attainder, ex post facto law, nor any law impairing the obligation of contracts, shall ever be passed. No conviction shall work a corruption of blood or forfeiture of estate: Provided, that this provision shall not prohibit the imposition of pecuniary penalties."

OREGON

Or. Const. Art. I, § 21
"No *ex-post facto* law, or law impairing the obligation of contracts shall ever be passed, nor shall any law be passed, the taking effect of which shall be made to depend upon any authority, except as provided in this Constitution; provided, that laws locating the Capitol of the State, locating County Seats, and submitting town, and corporate acts, and other local, and Special laws may take effect, or not, upon a vote of the electors interested."

PENNSYLVANIA

Pa. Const. Art. 1, § 17
"No *ex post facto* law, nor any law impairing the obligation of contracts, or making irrevocable any grant of special privileges or immunities, shall be passed."

RHODE ISLAND

R.I. Const. Art. 1, § 12
"No ex post facto law, or law impairing the obligation of contracts, shall be passed."

SOUTH CAROLINA

S.C. Const. Art. 1, § 4
"No bill of attainder, ex post facto law, law impairing the obligation of contracts, nor law granting any title of nobility or hereditary emolument, shall be passed, and no conviction shall work corruption of blood or forfeiture of estate."

SOUTH DAKOTA

S.D. Const. Art. VI, § 12
"No ex post facto law, or law impairing the obligation of contracts or making any irrevocable grant of privilege, franchise or immunity, shall be passed."

TENNESSEE

Tenn. Const. Art. I, § 11
"That laws made for the punishment of acts committed previous to the existence of such laws, and by them only declared criminal, are contrary to the principles of a free Government; wherefore no Ex [sic] post facto law shall be made."

TEXAS

Tex. Const. Art. 1, § 16
"No bill of attainder, ex post facto law, retroactive law, or any law impairing the obligation of contracts, shall be made."

UTAH

Utah Const. Art. 1, § 18
"No bill of attainder, ex post facto law, or law impairing the obligation of contracts shall be passed."

VERMONT

Does not have a provision.

VIRGINIA

Va. Const. Art. 1, § 9
"That excessive bail ought not to be required, nor excessive fines imposed, nor cruel and unusual punishments inflicted; that the privilege of the writ of habeas corpus shall not be suspended unless when, in cases of invasion or rebellion, the public safety may require; and that the General Assembly shall not pass any bill of attainder, or any ex post facto law."

WASHINGTON

Wash. Const. Art. 1, § 23
"No bill of attainder, ex post facto law, or law impairing the obligations of contracts shall ever be passed."

WEST VIRGINIA

W. Va. Const. Art. 3, § 4
"The privilege of the writ of habeas corpus shall not be suspended. No person shall be held to answer for treason, felony or other crime, not cognizable by a justice, unless on presentment or indictment of a grand jury. No bill of attainder, ex post facto law, or law impairing the obligation of a contract, shall be passed."

WISCONSIN

Wis. Const. Art. 1, § 12
"No bill of attainder, ex post facto law, nor any law impairing the obligation of contracts, shall ever be passed, and no conviction shall work corruption of blood or forfeiture of estate."

WYOMING

Wyo. Const. Art. 1, § 35
"No ex post facto law, nor any law impairing the obligation of contracts, shall ever be made."

Notes

Introduction

1. For discussion of the shift and the potent political forces driving it, see RACHEL E. BARKOW, PRISONERS OF POLITICS: BREAKING THE CYCLE OF MASS INCARCERATION (2019); KATHERINE BECKETT, MAKING CRIME PAY: LAW AND ORDER IN CONTEMPORARY AMERICAN POLITICS (1997); JONATHAN SIMON, GOVERNING THROUGH CRIME: HOW THE WAR ON CRIME TRANSFORMED AMERICAN DEMOCRACY AND CREATED A CULTURE OF FEAR (2007).

2. Of this responsiveness, eighteenth-century English philosopher Jeremy Bentham recognized that "legislators and men in general are naturally inclined" to extreme harshness, because "antipathy, or a want of compassion for individuals who are represented as dangerous and vile, pushes them onward to an undue severity." Jeremy Bentham, *Principles of Penal Law*, pt. II, book I, ch. 6, in THE WORKS OF JEREMY BENTHAM 401 (John Bowring ed. 1843) (1962). Bentham further recognized that penal laws are systematically biased toward severity because "[w]hat is too little is more clearly observed than what is too much." *Id.*

3. *See generally* JOHN PRATT, PENAL POPULISM (2007). "Popular punitivness" is another phrase used to describe the shift. *See also* Donald Braman, *Punishment and Accountability: Understanding and Reforming Criminal Sanctions in America*, 53 UCLA L. REV. 1143, 1183–86 (2006) (surveying use of the phrase).

4. Technically, the correct Latin phrasing is "ex postfacto." Charles Sweet, Note, 34 LAW QUARTERLY REV. 8 (1918).

5. U.S. Const. art. I, §9, cl. 3 ("No . . . ex post facto Law shall be passed [by Congress]."); *id.* at §10, cl. 1 ("No State shall . . . pass any . . . ex post facto Law."). Throughout the book the two clauses collectively will be referred to as the clause, except in the rare circumstance that discussion requires specification of one or the other.

6. "Retroactive" and "retrospective" are often used interchangeably when referencing the Ex Post Facto Clause. With respect to the basic definition, the US Supreme Court has stated that an ex post facto law is one that is "retrospective, that is, it must apply to events occurring before its enactment." Weaver v. Graham, 450 U.S. 24, 29 (1981). An ex post facto law "changes the legal consequences of acts completed before its effective date." *Id.* at 31.

   Legal philosophers have dedicated considerable attention to the possible differences between retroactive and retrospective laws. *See, e.g.*, CHARLES SAMPFORD, RETROSPECTIVITY AND THE RULE OF LAW 10–23 (2006); Neil Duxbury, *Ex Post Facto Law*, 58 AM. J. JURIS. 135, 158–61 (2013); Daniel E. Troy, *Toward a Definition and Critique of Retroactivity*, 51 ALA. L. REV. 1329 (2000). Even in this literature, Professor Sampford has written, the distinction "lacks normative and practice significance" and "is not as important as ordinarily assumed." SAMPFORD, *supra*, at 21, 22.

7. THE FEDERALIST NO. 84, at 511–12 (Alexander Hamilton) (Clinton Rossiter ed., 1961).

8. *Id.* at 511 (Alexander Hamilton)

9. *Id.*, No. 44, at 282 (James Madison).

10. *Id.* at 282–83.

11. 3 U.S. (Dall.) 386 (1798).

12. *Id.* at 389 (Chase, J.).

13. 10 U.S. (6 Cranch) 87 (1810).

14. *Id.* at 137–38 (Marshall, C.J.).

15. 71 U.S. (4 Wall.) 277 (1867).

16. *Id.* at 322.

17. *Id.* at 329.

18. *See generally* Kenneth Mann, *Punitive Civil Sanctions: The Middleground Between Criminal and Civil Law*, 101 YALE L.J. 1795, 1849–52 (1992).

19. United States v. Jones, 565 U.S. 400, 411 (2012) (emphasis in the original). *See also id.* at 406 (quoting Kyllo v. United States, 533 U.S. 27, 34 (2001) ("we must 'assure preservation of that degree of privacy against government that existed when the Fourth Amendment was adopted.'").

20. St. Regis Paper Co. v. United States, 368 U.S. 208, 229 (1961) (Black, J., dissenting).

Chapter 1

1. Robert G. Natelson, *Statutory Retroactivity: The Founders' View*, 39 IDAHO L. REV. 489, 499–500 (2003) (citing and translating Dig. 1.3.22 (Ulpianus, Ad Editum 35) ("Cum lex in praeteritum quid indulget, in futurum vetat.").

2. Elmer E. Smead, *The Rule Against Retroactive Legislation: A Basic Principle of Jurisprudence*, 20 MINN. L. REV. 775, 776 & n.5 (1936).

3. WILLIAM BLACKSTONE, COMMENTARIES ON THE LAWS OF ENGLAND *46 (1765).

4. Jerome Hall, *Nulla Poena Sine Lege*, 47 YALE L.J. 165, 165–70 (1937).

5. *The [Philadelphia] Freeman's Journal, Or, the North-American Intelligencer* 2 (Sept. 7, 1785) (under pen name Rusticus), available at https://infoweb.newsbank.com/apps/rea dex/?p=EANX. According to Professor William Crosskey, the item was published and disseminated in various states at the time. William W. Crosskey, *The True Meaning of the Constitutional Prohibition of Ex-Post-Facto Laws*, 14 U. CHI. L. REV. 539, 541 (1947).

6. 4 JOURNALS OF THE CONTINENTAL CONGRESS 1774–1789, at 357–58 (Worthington C. Ford ed., 1904). *See also* GORDON S. WOOD, THE CREATION OF THE AMERICAN REPUBLIC 1776–1787, at 131–32 (1969).

7. James E. Hergert, *The Missing Power of Local Governments: A Divergence between Text and Practice in Our Early State Constitutions*, 62 VA. L. REV. 999, 1000 (1976).

8. As one historian put it:

> The long period of colonial development had been characterized by a struggle between the colonial assemblies and the governor, the one representing the people, the other the Crown. . . . This struggle had demonstrated the value of written charters and documents as a safeguard against arbitrary government. Time and again the colonists had appealed to their charters and the great documents of the English constitution against the invasion of their rights, and in many cases their appeal had been successful. . . . This law . . . would serve as a check not only upon the officers of the government, but also upon the people in the exercise of their sovereign power, and thus give protection to the people and stability to their political institutions.

> The people looked upon constitutions as shields against the abuses of those entrusted with political power, for they not only specified what powers the officers might exercise, but also set limits beyond which they might not go. If the constitution were written, the people would know what those powers and limits were and could check the officials should they abuse them.

FLETCHER M. GREEN, CONSTITUTIONAL DEVELOPMENT IN THE SOUTH ATLANTIC STATES, 1776–1860: A STUDY IN THE EVOLUTION OF DEMOCRACY 51–52 (1971). *See also* Muller v. Oregon, 208 U.S. 412, 420 (1908) (noting that "it is the peculiar value of a written constitution that it places in unchanging form limitations upon legislative action, and thus gives a permanence and stability to popular government which otherwise would be lacking."); Marbury v. Madison, 5 U.S. (1 Cranch) 137, 176–77 (1803) (Marshall, C.J.) ("The powers of the legislature are defined, and limited; and that those limits may not be mistaken, or forgotten, the constitution is written. . . . Certainly all those who have framed written constitutions contemplate them as forming the fundamental and paramount law of the nation, and consequently the theory of every such government must be, that an act of the legislature, repugnant to the constitution, is void. This theory is essentially attached to a written constitution, and is consequently to be considered, by this court, as one of the fundamental principles of our society."); Nikolas Bowie, *Why the Constitution Was Written Down*, 71 STAN. L. REV. 1397 (2019).

9. Gordon S. Wood, Foreword, *State Constitution-Making in the American Revolution*, 24 RUTGERS L.J. 911, 917 (1993).

10. WILLI PAUL ADAMS, THE FIRST AMERICAN CONSTITUTIONS: REPUBLICAN IDEOLOGY AND THE MAKING OF STATE CONSTITUTIONS IN THE REVOLUTIONARY ERA 61–66 (1980).

11. Robert F. Williams, *The State Constitutions of the Founding Decade: Pennsylvania's Radical 1776 Constitution and Its Influence on American Constitutionalism*, 62 TEMP. L. REV. 541, 544–45 (1998) ("The real controversies over the first state constitutions had little to do with rights. What was at stake was how the new state governments would be structured and which groups in society would have the dominant policy-making role under the new governments. The question of rights as we think of them today was not at the forefront of these debates.").

12. Cummings v. Missouri, 71 U.S. (4 Wall.) 277, 323 (1867).

13. 1 JOSEPH STORY, COMMENTARIES ON THE CONSTITUTION OF THE UNITED STATES 239 (1833).

14. That other early state constitutions did not expressly prohibit ex post facto laws should not be interpreted as any condonation of them. As historian Jonathan Gienapp has observed, Revolutionary and Framing Era actors were devout adherents of natural law, "pre-existing, universal, unchanging, and divinely sanctioned." Jonathan Gienapp, *Written Constitutionalism, Past and Present*, 39 LAW & HIST. REV. 321, 339 (2021). "The constitutional text was presumed to be embedded within a broader web of fundamental law that was not, by definition, exclusively textual in nature," including abhorrence of ex post facto laws. *Id.* at 342 & 344–45. Gienapp adds that

> the first declaration of rights that accompanied several of the state constitutions were understood to *declare* rather than *create* fundamental rights. That only about half of the new states compiled these declarations confirms as such. Citizens of New Jersey or South Carolina would have been shocked to learn that they lacked the fundamental rights that had been codified in Virginia or Delaware.

Id. at 343 (emphasis in original).

15. Dan Friedman, *Tracing the Lineage: Textual and Conceptual Similarities in the Revolutionary-Era State Declarations of Rights of Virginia, Maryland, and Delaware*, 33 RUTGERS L.J. 929, 958 (2002). It seems that Virginia, in devising its Declaration of Rights, earlier considered, and rejected, use of the term in a draft provision, apparently at the urging of Patrick Henry. *Id.* at 958 n.118. Virginia's draft provided: "That laws having retrospect to crimes, and punishing offences, committed before the existence of such laws, are generally oppressive, and ought to be avoided." VA. CONST., decl. of rts., art. 9 (May 27, 1776, draft).

16. MD. CONST. of 1776, decl. of rts., art. XV, reprinted in 1 B. POORE, FEDERAL AND STATE CONSTITUTIONS, COLONIAL CHARTERS, AND OTHER ORGANIC LAWS OF THE UNITED STATES 818 (2d ed. 1878).

17. *See* N.C. CONST. of 1776, decl. of rts., art. XXIV, reprinted in 2 B. POORE, *supra* note 16, at 1410.

18. MASS. CONST. of 1780, pt. 2, decl. of rts., art. XXIV, reprinted in 1 B. POORE, *supra* note 16, at 959.

19. DEL. CONST., decl. of rts., sect. 11 (Sept. 11, 1776, draft).

20. N.H. CONST. OF 1784, pt. 1, art. XXIII.

21. For a very helpful overview of the convention, *see* Gregory E. Maggs, *A Concise Guide to the Records of the Federal Constitutional Convention of 1787 as a Source of the Original Meaning of the U.S. Constitution*, 80 GEO. WASH. L. REV. 1707 (2012) [hereinafter *Concise Guide-Federal*].

22. 1 THE RECORDS OF THE FEDERAL CONSTITUTION OF 1787, at 15 (Max Farrand ed., 1937) [hereinafter FARRAND'S RECORDS]; *see also* Vasan Kesavan & Michael S. Paulsen, *The Interpretive Force of the Constitution's Secret Drafting History*, 91 GEO. L.J. 1113 (2003).

23. CLINTON ROSSITER, 1787: THE GRAND CONVENTION 142–43 (1966).

24. 1 FARRAND'S RECORDS, *supra* note 22, at xiii–iv. For a more positive account of *Jackson's Journal*, which had a very interesting post-convention history, *see* Mary S. Bilder, *How Bad Were the Official Records of the Federal Constitution?*, 80 GEO. WASH. L. REV. 1620 (2012).

25. DREW R. MCCOY, THE LAST OF THE FATHERS: JAMES MADISON AND THE REPUBLICAN LEGACY 163–70 (1989).

26. *See* DAVID B. ROBERTSON, THE CONSTITUTION AND AMERICA'S DESTINY 22 (2005) (describing Madison's *Notes* as "the most complete and reliable record of the proceeding"). The *Notes* were republished in various publications over time, including in FARRAND'S RECORDS. Louis J. Sirico, Jr., *The Supreme Court and the Constitutional Convention*, 27 J. L. & POLITICS 63, 68–69 (2011).

27. *See, e.g.*, MARY S. BILDER, MADISON'S HAND: REVISING THE CONSTITUTIONAL CONVENTION 141 (2015) (stating that Madison's notes from August 22 to September 17, when the ex post facto debates occurred, are "particularly unreliable"). In a more recent work Professor Bilder states that

> beginning with August 22, Madison's notes present a significant problem. Madison served on multiple committees in late August, and also became sick. Whatever rough notes he took during the proceedings after that date were not written up during the summer of 1787. Instead, the section of Madison's notes from August 22 to the end of the convention was likely written two years later, in the winter and spring of 1789–90, when Madison knew that Thomas Jefferson finally would return to the United States from France.

Mary S. Bilder, *Madison's Notes Don't Mean What Everyone Says They Mean*, THE ATLANTIC, Dec. 22, 2019. Bilder relates that Madison had told Jefferson that he planned to share his notes with Jefferson and "the most visible difference between the original sections and these later ones is that in the original sections, Madison did not write his own name out. He wrote, instead, 'M.' Later, when finishing the manuscript for Jefferson, Madison consistently wrote his name as 'Madison.'" *Id.*

28. LEONARD W. LEVY, ORIGINS OF THE BILL OF RIGHTS 287 (1999); James H. Hutson, *The Creation of the Constitution: The Integrity of the Documentary Record*, 65 TEX. L. REV. 2, 25 (1986); Maggs, *Concise Guide-Federal, supra* note 21, at 1742. For a particularly critical re-assessment of Madison's role in the framing and his unjustified "hagiographical" account of the proceedings, *see* David Schwartz & John Mikhail, *The Other Madison Problem*, 89 FORDHAM L. REV. 2033 (2021).

29. *See generally* FORREST MCDONALD, NOVUS ORDO SECLORUM: THE INTELLECTUAL ORIGINS OF THE CONSTITUTION (1985); JACK N. RAKOVE, ORIGINAL MEANINGS: POLITICS AND IDEAS IN THE MAKING OF THE CONSTITUTION (1996); ROSSITER, *supra* note 23.

30. 2 FARRAND'S RECORDS, *supra* note 22, at 375.

31. *Id.*

32. *See id.* at 376 ("The first part of the motion relating to bills of attainder was agreed to nem[ine] contradicente."). The source, *Madison's Notes*, then cryptically reports at the bottom of the page: "(the proceedings on this motion involving the two questions on 'attainders & ex post facto laws.' are not so fully stated in the printed Journal.)." *Id.*

33. *See* Suzanna Sherry, *The Founders' Unwritten Constitution*, 54 U. CHI. L. REV. 1127, 1157 (1987) ("All the delegates who spoke explicitly or implicitly regarded [an] ex post facto law as a violation of natural law, and most of them thought it unnecessary to include such a basic natural law principle in the written constitution. . . ."). *See also, e.g.,* Thomas Jefferson, *Letter to Isaac McPherson*, August 13, 1813, available at Founders Online, https://found ers.archives.gov/documents/Jefferson/03-06-02-0322 ("The sentiment that ex post facto laws are against natural right is so strong in the United States, that few, if any, of the State constitutions have failed to proscribe them."). For a brief overview of the influence on the framers of natural law theorists such as Locke and Grotius, *see* Daniel Lambright, Comment, *Man, Morality, and the United States Constitution*, 17 U. PA. J. CONST. L. 1487 (2015).

34. *See* 2 FARRAND'S RECORDS, *supra* note 22, at 376. "Gouverneur" was his mother's maiden name and was his actual first name and did not signify a title of office.

35. *Id.*

36. *Id.*

37. As historian Jonathan Gienapp observed, "[t]he debate . . . presupposed that some things would be part of the Constitution regardless of what was enacted. The Constitution's 'ex post facto' clause was a paradigmatic example of non-constitutive text." Gienapp, *supra* note 14, at 345; *see also id.* at 345 n.95 ("Founding-Era Americans assumed that long-standing common law rights (including prohibitions against ex post facto laws but also the right to habeas corpus and jury trial) were already inherent in the social contract on which the polity was based."). Gienapp observes that Ellsworth and Wilson "assumed that the Constitution that they were making would be embedded in a wider field of general fundamental law, composed of a diverse array of materials—some expressed, some not; some positively enacted, some already part of the social contract—none of which could easily be separated from the rest. Indeed, this *had* to be the case for their comments to make sense." *Id.* at 345 (footnote omitted) (emphasis in original). *See also* ROBERT COVER,

JUSTICE ACCUSED: ANTISLAVERY AND THE JUDICIAL PROCESS 25–30 (1975) (noting that framers were both adherents of natural law and constitutional positivists).

38. MCDONALD, *supra* note 29, at 59.

39. One motivation for including the ex post facto provision, as noted later in the text, was to provide a basis for judicial enforcement of the prohibition, but another was possibly that doing so served the "educative function that declarations of rights served in guiding political officials and shaping public opinion—goals that undergirded most calls for a declaration of rights during the ensuing ratification controversy." Jud Campbell, *Judicial Review and the Enumeration of Rights*, 15 GEO. J. L. & PUB. POL'Y 569, 580 (2017).

40. 2 FARRAND'S RECORDS, *supra* note 22, at 376.

41. *Id.*

42. *Id.*

43. New Hampshire, Massachusetts, Delaware, Maryland, Virginia, South Carolina, and Georgia. *Id.* at 369.

44. Connecticut, New Jersey, and Pennsylvania. *Id.*

45. *Id.*

46. *Id.* New York delegates Robert Yates and John Lansing, Jr. departed the convention on July 10, 1787, leaving only Alexander Hamilton to represent New York. Because Hamilton could not by himself represent New York, the state was without a vote on matters coming before the convention. Maggs, *Concise Guide-Federal, supra* note 21, at 1716.

47. *See* Robert C. Palmer, *Obligations of Contracts: Intent and Distortion,* 37 CASE W. RES. L. REV. 631, 641–42 (1986) (discussing original draft Articles XII and XIII generated August 6, 1787).

48. 2 FARRAND'S RECORDS, *supra* note 22, at 439.

49. Douglas Kmiec & John McGinnis, *The Contract Clause: A Return to the Original Understanding,* 14 HASTINGS CONST. L. Q. 525, 529–30 (1987).

50. *See* 2 FARRAND'S RECORDS, *supra* note 22, at 439 ("Mr. King moved to add[] in the words used in the Ordinance of Cong[ress] establishing . . . a prohibition on the States to interfere in private contract"). *See also* Kmiec & McGinnis, *supra* note 49, at 529–30 (noting that the entry "strongly suggests that the Contract Clause was modeled on this ordinance— the Ordinance of the Northwest Territory—which Congress had established under the authority of the Articles of Confederation just six weeks before.").

51. 2 FARRAND'S RECORDS, *supra* note 22, at 440.

52. *Id.*

53. *Id.*

54. *Id.*

55. *Id.* at 440 & n.19.

56. *Id.*

57. In favor: New Hampshire, New Jersey, Pennsylvania, Delaware, North Carolina, South Carolina, and Georgia; against: Connecticut, Maryland, and Virginia. (Massachusetts apparently did not vote.) *Id.* at 436 & 440. Interestingly, while the vote margins were the same regarding the ex post facto limits on states and Congress, the composition of the tallies varied. Virginia and Maryland voted in favor of the federal ban but against the state ban, whereas Pennsylvania and New Jersey voted against the federal ban but in favor of the state ban. And Massachusetts voted in favor of the ban on Congress but did not vote on the state ban.

58. *Id.* at 448–49.
59. *Id.* at 547.
60. It also seems that James Wilson, although not a formal member, also participated in the committee's work. William Michael Treanor, *The Case of the Dishonest Scrivener: Gouverneur Morris and the Creation of the Federalist Constitution*, 120 MICH. L. REV. 1, 8 (2021).
61. 2 FARRAND'S RECORDS, *supra* note 22, at 619. *See also* CHARLES WARREN, THE MAKING OF THE CONSTITUTION 556–57 (1928).
62. 2 FARRAND'S RECORDS, *supra* note 22, at 617. Farrand notes that Mason may have moved only for reconsidering the clause, rather than striking it. *Id.* at 617 n.12. Mason's papers indicate that he made two motions, first as to Congress, then as to the states, both "refused." George Mason, *Mason's Memorandum Notes on Proposed Changes in the Committee of Style Report*, 983–84 in 3 THE PAPERS OF GEORGE MASON 983–84 (Robert A. Rutland ed., 1970).
63. 2 FARRAND'S RECORDS, *supra* note 22, at 617.
64. *Id.*
65. *Id.*
66. *Id.* at 640. Farrand relates that "this was written by Mason on the blank pages of his copy of the draft of September 12." *Id.* at 637 n.21. Mason identified his failed effort to limit the prohibition to criminal cases as a reason for his ultimate refusal to back the Constitution. *Id.* at 636.
67. *Id.* at 643.
68. *The Constitution: How Did It Happen?*, NAT'L. ARCHIVES, https://www.archives.gov/founding-docs/constitution/how-did-it-happen#:~:text=After%20three%20hot%20summer%20months,in%20less%20than%20four%20days (last visited Sep. 23, 2019).
69. 2 FARRAND'S RECORDS, *supra* note 22, at 577.
70. *Id.* at 596–97.
71. *Id.* at 571. The *Official Journal* entry similarly used active voice. 1 THE DEBATES IN THE SEVERAL STATE CONVENTIONS ON THE ADOPTION OF THE FEDERAL CONSTITUTION, at 257 (Jonathan Elliot ed., 1836) [hereinafter ELLIOT'S DEBATES] (noting that it was moved, second, and voted in the affirmative to insert "The legislature shall pass no bill of attainder, nor ex post facto laws"), available at https://memory.loc.gov/cgi-bin/query/r?ammem/hlaw:@field(DOCID+@lit(ed0011)).
72. 2 FARRAND'S RECORDS, *supra* note 22, at 596.
73. Perhaps foremost is the Contracts Clause, which was voted down on the convention floor, only to make its way into the draft document provided by the committee, and approved by delegates. Dean Michael Treanor maintains that the explanation for the clause's re-emergence lies in Morris' preference and the committee members' reaction to delegate Dickinson's view that ex post facto applied only to criminal, not also civil, laws. Treanor, *supra* note 60, at 63–64. *See also* MCDONALD, *supra* note 29, at 270–74 (further speculating on reasons behind the ultimate inclusion of the Contacts Clause).
74. For an interesting discussion of the document's use of the passive voice, in particular regarding the ex post facto prohibitions and which branch of government is regulated, *see* Nicholas Q. Rosenkranz, *The Objects of the Constitution*, 63 STAN. L. REV. 1005, 1019–21 (2011).
75. Often referred to as constitutional "twins" of one another, the ex post facto and bill of attainder prohibitions, while distinct, exercise complementary protective coverage. As Professor Akhil Amar has written:

> In the absence of companion [ex post facto] ban, a legislature seeking to target a specific victim could simply reverse engineer an attainder by substituting a precise description of the victim's past (and wholly innocent) conduct for his proper name. The gross injustice of such legislative trickery . . . prompted the Federalists to ban all such practices, state as well as federal.

Akhil R. Amar, America's Constitution: A Biography 125 (2005).

76. 2 Farrands Records, *supra* note 22, at 376.

77. *Id.* at 435.

78. W.W. Thornton, *Ex Post Facto Laws and Bills of Attainder*, 5 Crim. L. Mag. 325, 326 (1884).

79. *See* McDonald, *supra* note 29, at 269–70.

80. *Id.* at 268–70. For further discussion of the possible reasons why the delegates left Congress free of the contracts-related prohibition, *see* Michael W. McConnell, *Contract Rights and Property Rights: A Case Study in the Relationship Between Individual Liberties and Constitutional Structure*, 76 Calif. L. Rev. 267 (1988); Robert C. Palmer, *Obligations of Contracts: Intent and Distortion*, 37 Case W. Res. L. Rev. 631 (1986).

81. *See* McDonald, *supra* note 29, at 270 ("The other new restrictions were designed exclusively to prevent infringement upon property rights by the legislatures. Specifically, the states are forbidden to coin money, to emit bills of credit, to make anything but gold or silver coin legal tender in payment of debts, and to pass any law impairing the obligation of contracts.").

82. *See id.* at 155–57 (surveying instances such as confiscation of property and laws staying execution of debts owed to Loyalists).

83. Madison's concerns shifted over time, undergirding his transformation from devout Federalist during the Framing Era, in favor of a strong national government, to a Jeffersonian Republican in later years. As Professors Schwartz and Mikhail have observed:

> Rather than a deep constitutional thinker and authoritative oracle, Madison might be better regarded as—in Rakove's apt phrase—"a politician thinking" and in particular, one often thinking up constitutional arguments to win the dispute of the moment without due regard for their longer- term implications. . . .
>
>   Based on what he took to be the greatest policy challenge at a particular moment in time, he devised a structural remedy or interpretive "principle," only to abandon that idea when changed circumstances converted his former solution into a problem. When the challenge in 1787 was (in his view) faction-dominated state legislatures running rampant with debt relief laws, paper money issues, and other statutes that threatened "different kinds of property," the solution was an extended republican government with a national legislative veto over state laws. When the challenge in 1798 was a faction- dominated national legislature overreaching by enacting the Alien and Sedition Acts on the basis of implied national powers, the solution was, in effect, the reverse: a state legislative veto over national laws. When the challenge was a Federalist administration creating a national bank and embracing Hamilton's ideas about political economy in 1791, the solution was to appeal to a government of limited and enumerated powers. But when the challenge was the desperate need for a national bank to reign in rampant currency nonconformity in 1816, Madison created an exception to limited enumerated powers in cases where the violation of that principle lasted long enough to furnish a different constitutional interpretation. Finally, when the challenge in the 1830s was a state inappropriately (in Madison's view) using this veto against a national policy that did not rise to the level of the Alien and Sedition Acts, the solution was to claim that his 1798 position on federal-state relations was being misconstrued.

Schwartz & Mikhail, *supra* note 28, at 2082 (footnotes omitted).

84. THE FEDERALIST NO. 44, at 279 (James Madison) (Clinton Rossier ed., 1961). Of note, delegate Eldridge Gerry earlier in the convention voiced a differing view regarding the need to regulate state legislatures versus Congress. Gerry, in responding to why the ex post facto provision first debated applied only to Congress, stated that the risk of ex post facto laws "was greater in the National than the State Legislature, because the number of members in the former being fewer, they were on that account the more to be feared." 2 FARRAND's RECORDS, *supra* note 22, at 375.

85. 1 ANNALS OF CONGRESS 458 (June 8, 1789) (James Madison) (J. Gales ed. 1834). *See also* McConnell, *supra* note 80, at 392 (stating that under Madison's view, laws impairing contracts "are particularly likely to be adopted—and likely to be particularly egregious—at the state level, where factions (such as the debtor class) might well seize the machinery of government for their own advantage."); *id.* at 279 (stating that "[t]he omission of a contracts clause from section 9 is too obvious to be anything but deliberate").

86. *See* James Madison, *Vices of the Political System of the United States (1787)*, reprinted in 9 THE PAPERS OF JAMES MADISON 351–52 (Robert A. Rutland & William M.E. Rachal eds., 1975). *See also* ALLAN NEVINS, THE AMERICAN STATES DURING AND AFTER THE REVOLUTION 1775–1789, at 273–74, 309–403, 404–05, 525–26, 570–72 (1969); James W. Thompson, *Anti-Loyalist Legislation During the American Revolution*, 3 ILL. L. REV. 81 (1908).

87. *See, e.g.,* 1 FARRAND's RECORDS, *supra* note 22, at 512 (quoting Gouverneur Morris). *See also* Barton H. Thompson, Jr., *The History of the Judicial Impairment Doctrine and Its Lessons for the Contract Clause*, 44 STAN. L. REV. 1373, 1380 (1992) ("Fears that mutable state laws were leading to economic instability and commercial disintegration were a major impetus to the adoption of the new federal Constitution.").

88. Brenner M. Fissell, *The Dual Standard of Review in Contracts Clause Jurisprudence*, 101 GEO. L.J. 1089, 1091 (2013).

89. *See* MARVIN MYERS, THE MIND OF THE FOUNDER: SOURCES OF THE POLITICAL THOUGHT OF JAMES MADISON, at xxxv (Marvin Meyers ed., rev. ed. 1981). As Madison later wrote to Jefferson:

> A Constitutional negative on the laws of the States seems equally necessary to secure individuals against encroachments on their rights. The mutability of the laws of the States is found to be a serious evil. The injustice of them has been so frequent and so flagrant as to alarm the most steadfast friends of Republicanism. I am persuaded I do not err in saying that the evils issuing from these sources contributed more to that uneasiness which produced the Convention, and prepared the public mind for a general reform, than those which accrued to our national character and interest from the inadequacy of the Confederation to its immediate objects.

> Letter from James Madison to Thomas Jefferson (Oct. 24, 1787), in 1 THE REPUBLIC OF LETTERS: THE CORRESPONDENCE BETWEEN JEFFERSON AND MADISON 1776–1826, at 500 (James Morton Smith ed., 1995).

90. Charles F. Hobson, *The Negative on State Laws: James Madison, the Constitution, and the Crisis of Republican Government*, 36 WM. & MARY Q. 215, 216 (1979).

91. McConnell, *supra* note 80, at 278.

92. Creating ratifying conventions, rather than simply relying on state legislatures, delegate Rufus King (Massachusetts) reasoned, was preferable because "[t]he Legislatures . . . being to lose power, will be most likely to raise objections." 1 FARRAND's RECORDS, *supra* note 22, at 123.

93. Publius Valerius, known also as "friend of the people," was a founder of the Roman Republic. ALBERT FURTWANGLER, THE AUTHORITY OF PUBLIUS: A READING OF THE FEDERALIST PAPERS 51 (1984). The *nom de guerre* was chosen because Hamilton and Madison attended the constitutional convention and did not want to reveal their actual identities. ERIC BARENDT, ANONYMOUS SPEECH: LITERATURE, LAW AND POLITICS 54 (2016). Also, in the months preceding publication of their essays, Anti-Federalists had assumed Roman monikers such as Cato and Brutus. FURTWANGLER, *supra*, at 48–49.

94. THE FEDERALIST, NO. 44, at 282 (James Madison) (Clinton Rossiter ed., 1961).

95. *Id.* at 282–83.

96. *Id.* at 282.

97. *See generally* PAULINE MAIER, RATIFICATION: THE PEOPLE DEBATE THE CONSTITUTION 1787–1788 (2011).

98. WOOD, *supra* note 6, at 271–73.

99. 3 FARRAND'S RECORDS, *supra* note 22, at 290.

100. *See, e.g.*, MAIER, *supra* note 97, at 284–85 (noting sentiment expressed during the Virginia ratifying convention).

101. For a discussion of the general reasons Federalists opposed inclusion of a bill of rights, see Paul Finkelman, *James Madison and the Bill of Rights: A Reluctant Paternity*, 1990 SUP. CT. REV. 301, 309–13 (1990). *See also Letter from James Madison to Thomas Jefferson* (Oct. 17, 1788), in 5 THE WRITINGS OF JAMES MADISON 1787–1790, at 271–75 (Gaillard Hunt ed., 1904); THE FEDERALIST NO. 84 (Alexander Hamilton).

102. *See* Finkelman, *supra* note 101, at 309–13.

103. *Id.* at 311–312. James Madison asserted that "[a bill of rights] would disparage those rights which were not placed in that enumeration; and it might follow, by implication, that those rights which were not singled out, were intended to be assigned into the hands of the General Government, and were consequently insecure." 1 ANNALS OF CONGRESS, *supra* note 85, at 455.

104. *See* Finkelman, *supra* note 101, at 309–13.

105. THE FEDERALIST NO. 84, at 511–12 (Alexander Hamilton). Hamilton added that "a minute detail of particular rights is certainly far less applicable to a Constitution like that under consideration, which is merely intended to regulate the general political interests of the nation, than to a constitution which has the regulation of every species of personal and private concerns." *Id.* at 513.

106. Gregory E. Maggs, *A Concise Guide to the Records of the State Ratifying Conventions as a Source of the Original Meaning of the U.S. Constitution*, 2009 U. ILL. L. REV. 457, 487–95 [hereinafter *Concise Guide-State*].

107. *Id.* at 481.

108. *See* THE DEBATES IN THE SEVERAL STATE CONVENTIONS, ON THE ADOPTION OF THE FEDERAL CONSTITUTION, AS RECOMMENDED BY THE GENERAL CONVENTION AT PHILADELPHIA, IN 1787 (J. Elliot ed., 1827–1830) [hereinafter ELLIOT'S DEBATES], available at https://memory.loc.gov/ammem/amlaw/lwed.html. Like Madison's *Notes*, the reliability of Elliot's *Debates* has been questioned. For example, James Hutson, chief of the Library of Congress Manuscripts Division, wrote that

> Elliot was not a scholar. Rather, he was a Washington political journalist turned editor, whose press was for sale to the highest bidder. John Quincy Adams, who

cancelled a government printing contract held by Elliot because he suspected price gouging, described him as 'an Englishman, having no character of his own—penurious and venal—metal to receive any stamp.' It appears that in the 1830s, Elliot was promoting the political fortunes of John C. Calhoun, although he had opposed the South Carolinian earlier. Some scholars believe that one of Elliot's purposes in preparing his Debates was to advance Calhoun's cause.

Hutson, *supra* note 28, at 15 (footnotes and citations omitted).

109. Maggs, *Concise Guide-State, supra* note 106, at 469.
110. 2 ELLIOT'S DEBATES, *supra* note 108, at 486.
111. 2 DOCUMENTARY HISTORY OF THE RATIFICATION OF THE U.S. CONSTITUTION (John P. Kaminski et al. eds., 1976–2007) 417 [hereinafter DOCUMENTARY HISTORY], available at http://www.wisconsinhistory.org/ratification/.
112. Maggs, *Concise Guide-State, supra* note 106, at 468.
113. VII DOCUMENTARY HISTORY, *supra* note 111, at 1816.
114. MASSACHUSETTS CENTINEL (Nov. 28, 1787), reprinted in Crosskey, *supra* note 5, at 544.
115. Maggs, *Concise Guide-State, supra* note 106, at 477.
116. 3 ELLIOT'S DEBATES, *supra* note 108, at 478.
117. *Id.* at 425.
118. *Id.* at 473. In a 1954 article, Irving Brant maintained that Madison's barely audible voice was due to the fact that he was quite sick at the time. Irving Brant, *Mr. Crosskey and Mr. Madison*, 54 COLUM. L. REV. 443, 448 (1954).
119. 3 ELLIOT'S DEBATES, *supra* note 108, at 477.
120. Oliver P. Field, *Ex Post Facto in the Constitution*, 20 MICH. L. REV. 315, 323 (1921).
121. 3 ELLIOT'S DEBATES, *supra* note 108, at 477.
122. *Id.* at 477–78.
123. *Id.* at 472–73.
124. *Id.*
125. *Id.* at 479.
126. *Id. See also id.* ("Whatever may be the professional meaning, [] the general meaning of *ex post facto* law is an act having a retrospective operation. This construction is agreeable to its primary etymology. Will it not be the duty of the federal court to say that such laws are prohibited?").
127. *Id.* at 472.
128. *Id.* at 473–76.
129. *Id.* at 140.
130. Maggs, *Concise Guide-State, supra* note 106, at 468.
131. Crosskey, *supra* note 5, at 552.
132. 4 ELLIOT'S DEBATES, *supra* note 108, at 184.
133. *Id.* at 185. Fellow Federalist Stephen Cabarrus similarly stated that

I contend that the clause which prohibits the states from emitting bills of credit will not affect our present paper money. The clause has no retrospective view. The Constitution declares, in the most positive terms, that *no ex post facto* law shall be passed by the general government. Were this clause to operate retrospectively, it would clearly be *ex post facto*, and repugnant to the express provision of the Constitution.

Id. at 184.

134. James Iredell, *Observations on George Mason's Objections to the Federal Constitution by Marcus, in* PAMPHLETS ON THE CONSTITUTION OF THE UNITED STATES 368 (Paul L. Ford ed., 1888).

135. 2 ELLIOT'S DEBATES, *supra* note 108, at 407.

136. 1 ELLIOT'S DEBATES, *supra* note 108, at 328; MAIER, *supra* note 97, at 396–98.

137. *See, e.g., Letters from a Countryman,* Jan. 17, 1788, contained in 6 THE COMPLETE ANTI-FEDERALIST, at 86 (Herbert J. Storing ed., 1981) (expressing concern that the prohibition would preclude collection of public debt from wealthy individuals); *Letter of Centinel to the People of Pennsylvania, Feb. 23, 1788, in* 2 THE COMPLETE ANTI-FEDERALIST, at 198 (Herbert J. Storing ed., 1981) (same).

138. Maggs, *Concise Guide-State, supra* note 106, at 468.

139. *Id.*

140. AMAR, *supra* note 75, at 7.

141. Rhode Island, sometimes referred to as "Rogue Island," had a rather notorious history for its prodigal issuance of paper money to address its economic problems, much of which resulted from its war debt, and the burdensome interest rates imposed by speculators. Eventually, deflation came into play, which affected private debtors as well. The legislature thereafter forced creditors to accept the paper money, including a law specifying that those who refused would be tried without juries and denied appeals. The legislature also refused to allow out-of-state debtors to use the devalued money to pay off Rhode Island creditors, which violated the "privileges and immunities" provision in the Articles of Confederation (and later the Constitution itself). At the same time, Rhode Island was concerned that the provision in Article I, section 10 denying states the right to print paper money would "throw the state into financial chaos." MAIER, *supra* note 97, at 224.

142. *See id.* at 457–59 (noting that North Carolina and Rhode Island in fact awaited amendments before ratifying in 1789 and 1790, respectively). Ratification in Massachusetts only came after state convention delegates Samuel Adams and John Hancock agreed to ratification on the condition that the convention also propose amendments, which it did (concerning grand jury indictment and reserving power to states not expressly given the federal government, which were later included in the Bill of Rights). RICHARD BEEMAN, PLAIN, HONEST MEN: THE MAKING OF THE AMERICAN CONSTITUTION 389–90 (2010). Later, promises of amendments also proved influential in the ratification secured in Virginia and New York. MAIER, *supra* note 97, at 431.

143. AMAR, *supra* note 75, at 318–19.

144. Madison himself faced a stiff congressional election challenge from James Monroe, in a gerrymandered district tilting Anti-Federalist, and defeated Monroe after pledging that he would introduce constitutional amendments constituting a bill of rights at the First Congress. RICHARD E. LABUNSKI, JAMES MADISON AND THE STRUGGLE FOR THE BILL OF RIGHTS 159, 174 (2006).

145. Massachusetts delegate Eldridge Gerry moved the convention to form a committee to devise a bill of rights, and George Mason of Virginia seconded the motion. However, the convention was near its end and the proposal was rejected. 2 FARRAND'S RECORDS, *supra* note 22, at 588.

146. AMAR, *supra* note 75, at 6–7.

147. LEVY, *supra* note 28, at 43.

148. Fletcher v. Peck, 10 U.S. (6 Cranch) 87, 137–38 (1810) (Marshall, C.J.). *See also* Cummings v. Missouri, 71 U.S. (4 Wall.) 277, 322 (1867) (noting that "[i]t was against the excited action of the States . . . that the framers of the Federal Constitution intended to guard").

149. *See* WOOD, *supra* note 6, at 134–63.

150. *See* ROSSITER, *supra* note 23, at 46 ("By the middle of the 1780s the unrest in every state had impelled all but the steadiest men in power to act impetuously. . . . Despite the energetic efforts of the gentry and its political allies, the control of most legislatures fell at one time or another into the hands of a small-farmer class that was chiefly interested in paying off old scores and new debts as speedily as possible."). *See also* ROBERT F. WILLIAMS, THE LAW OF THE AMERICAN STATE CONSTITUTIONS 66–67 (2009) (noting widespread concern among framers over democratic excesses of state legislatures, allowed by state constitutions, especially that of Pennsylvania).

151. WOOD, *supra* note 6, at 404. During the Constitutional Convention, delegate Elbridge Gerry (Massachusetts) complained that "[t]he evils we experience flow from the excess of democracy." 1 FARRAND'S RECORDS, *supra* note 22, at 48. *See also* MCDONALD, *supra* note 29, at 143–79 (describing legislative enactments during the Framing Era).

152. Alexander Hamilton, Letter from Phocion (1784), reprinted in CLINTON ROSSITER, ALEXANDER HAMILTON AND THE CONSTITUTION 132 (1964). *See also* James Iredell, *Observations on George Mason's Objections to the Federal Constitution, in* PAMPHLETS ON THE CONSTITUTION OF THE UNITED STATES, *supra* note 134, at 368 (noting an Ex Post Facto Clause prevented the exercise of "tyranny [that] would be intolerable to bear").

153. THE FEDERALIST, No. 84, 95, at 511 (Alexander Hamilton).

154. *Id.*, No. 44, at 282 (James Madison).

155. State v. Letalien, 985 A.2d 4, 13 (Maine 2009).

Chapter 2

1. *See generally* RON CHERNOW, ALEXANDER HAMILTON (2004).

2. THE FEDERALIST No. 78, at 466 (Alexander Hamilton) (Clinton Rossiter ed., 1961).

3. *Id.*

4. *Id.* at 466.

5. *Id.* at 467.

6. *Id.*

7. 1 PENNSYLVANIA AND THE FEDERAL CONSTITUTION, 1787–1788, at 354 (John B. McMaster & Frederick D. Stone eds., 1970).

8. 1 ANNALS OF CONGRESS 457 (J. Gales ed., 1834) (remarks of James Madison) (June 8, 1789).

9. *See* Saikrishna B. Prakash & John C. Yoo, *The Origins of Judicial Review*, 70 U. CHI. L. REV. 887, 947–51 (2003); *see also* DAVID P. CURRIE, THE CONSTITUTION IN THE SUPREME COURT: THE FIRST HUNDRED YEARS 1789–1888, at 41–49 (1992) (discussing the central place of *Calder* in the court's early history); Edward B. Foley, *The Bicentennial of* Calder v. Bull: *In Defense of a Constitutional Middle Ground*, 59 OHIO ST. L.J. 1599 (1998).

10. Marbury v. Madison, 5 U.S. (1 Cranch) 137, 177 (1803).

11. As indicated in the text, the necessity for judicial review was evident to the framers, but scholars have long argued over whether the Constitution itself ordains judicial review and whether judicial review actually occurred in the Framing Era. *See, e.g.,* LARRY D. KRAMER, THE PEOPLE THEMSELVES: POPULAR CONSTITUTIONALISM AND JUDICIAL

REVIEW (2004). Today, of course, judicial review is a foundational part of the nation's constitutional order, and more recent scholarship has shown that judicial review occurred with regularity from the Revolutionary War through the Framing Era, resulting in the invalidation of multiple state and federal statutes. *See* William M. Treanor, *Judicial Review Before* Marbury, 58 STAN. L. REV. 455 (2005).

12. 3 U.S. (Dallas) 386 (1798).

13. *Calder* is also remembered for the extended discussion in several of the justices' opinions regarding the role of natural law. Justice Chase suggested that a court might resort to supra-constitutional, natural-law principles as a basis for declaring a state law to be void. Justice Iredell firmly rejected this suggestion because "ideas of natural justice are regulated by no fixed standard: the ablest and the purest men have differed upon the subject." *Calder*, 3 U.S. at 399 (Iredell, J.).

14. *Id.* at 395 (Paterson, J.).

15. *Id.* at 386 (Chase, J.).

16. *Id.* at 396 (Paterson, J.).

17. 8 DOCUMENTARY HISTORY OF THE SUPREME COURT OF THE UNITED STATES, 1789–1800, at 92–93 (Maeva Marcus et al. eds., 1985–2007) [hereinafter DHSC]. Professor Marcus speculates that a reason for the continuances might be that "the parties or the Court wished to have a full bench to hear such an important case. In February 1797, Chief Justice Ellsworth was absent. He returned in August, but then James Wilson did not appear." *Id.* at 93 n.30.

18. Chief Justice Oliver Ellsworth and Justice James Wilson did not participate. Ellsworth's absence was apparently due to illness. 1 DHSC, *supra* note 17, at 298 n.288. Wilson appears to have been on the run from creditors, having fled Philadelphia, then the court's home, by the time of the eventual *Calder* oral argument. Wilson had taken refuge at the home of his colleague Justice James Iredell in Edenton, North Carolina, where he died two weeks after *Calder* was decided in August 1798. John Mikhail, *James Wilson, Early American Land Companies, and the Original Meaning of "Ex Post Law,"* 17 GEO. J. L. & PUB. POL'Y 79, 80 (2019).

19. Such opinions were a common convention until the time of the Marshall Court (1801–1835). John P. Kelsh, *The Opinion Delivery Practices of the United States Supreme Court 1790–1945,* 77 WASH. U. L. Q. 137, 140 (1999).

20. *Calder*, 3 U.S. at 398 (Iredell, J.); *id.* at 396 (Paterson, J.); *id.* at 400–01 (Cushing., J.). Justice Chase's opinion is more ambiguous on the matter. At one point, apparently speaking of ex post facto laws more generally, he wrote that "[a]n act of the legislature (for I cannot call it a law), contrary to the great first principles of the social compact, cannot be considered a rightful exercise of the legislative authority." *Id.* at 388 (Chase, J.). Although not clear, the foregoing appears to reflect the common view of the time that ex post facto laws were inherently unlawful and therefore void *ab initio*. At several points, when describing the challenged action of the Connecticut legislature, he uses the phrase "resolution (or law)," which suggests that he perhaps distinguished the two undertakings.

21. *Id.* at 398 (Iredell, J.).

22. *See Calder*, 3 U.S. at 390–92 (Chase, J.); *id.* at 396 (Paterson, J.); *id.* at 399–400 (Iredell, J.).

23. *Id.* at 400 (Cushing, J.). The Cushing concurrence in its entirety read: "The case appears to me to be clear of all difficulty, taken either way. If the act is a judicial act, it is not touched by the Federal Constitution: and, if it is a legislative act, it is maintained and justified by the ancient and uniform practice of the state of Connecticut." *Id.* at 400–01.

24. *Id.* at 389 (Chase, J.). *See also id.* (citations omitted) ("These acts were legislative judgments . . . Sometimes they respected the crime, by declaring acts to be treason, which were not treason, when committed, at other times, they violated the rules of evidence (to supply a deficiency of legal proof) by admitting one witness, when the existing law required two; by receiving evidence without oath; or the oath of the wife against the husband; or other testimony, which the courts of justice would not admit; at other times they inflicted punishments, where the party was not, by law, liable to any punishment; and in other cases, they inflicted greater punishment, than the law annexed to the offence.").

25. *Id.* (Chase, J.).

26. *Id.* at 388.

27. *Id.*

28. *Id.* at 390.

29. *Id.*

30. *Id.*

31. *Id.*

32. *Id.*

33. *Id.*

34. *Id.*

35. *Id.* at 397 (Paterson, J.).

36. *Id.* at 399–400 (Iredell, J.).

37. *Id.* at 400–01 (Cushing, J.).

38. *Id.* at 390 (Chase, J.).

39. *Id.* at 391. *See also id.* (stating that only criminal laws that "create, or aggravate, the crime; or increase the punishment, or change the rules of evidence, for the purpose of conviction" are prohibited).

40. *Id.* at 389 (Chase, J.).

41. *Id.* at 396 (Paterson, J.).

42. *Id.* at 399–400 (Iredell, J.).

43. *See Calder*, 3 U.S. at 396 (Paterson, J.) (stating that the judicial nature of the challenged act "militates against the plaintiffs in error [because] their counsel has contended for reversal of the judgment, on the ground, that the awarding of a new trial was the effect of a legislative act, and that it is unconstitutional, because an ex post facto law."); *id.* at 398 (Iredell, J.) (stating that the legislature's exercise of review "in the present instance . . . is an exercise of judicial not of legislative authority"); *id.* at 400 (Iredell, J.) (concluding that the challenge lacked merit because "1st. if the act of the Legislature of Connecticut was a judicial act, it is not within the words of the Constitution; and 2nd. even if it was a legislative act, it is not within the meaning of the prohibition."); *id.* at 400 (Cushing, J.) (noting that exercises of judicial authority are not "touched by the federal constitution").

44. With regard to the four categories specified by Justice Chase, Justice Ruth Bader Ginsburg, joined by three justices, noted in 2000 that "Justice Chase's [four-category] formulation was dictum, of course, because *Calder* involved a civil statute and the Court held that the statute was not ex post facto for that reason alone." Carmell v. Texas, 529 U.S. 513, 567 (2000) (Ginsburg, J., dissenting, joined by Rehnquist, C.J., and O'Connor & Kennedy, J.J.).

45. 27 U.S. (2 Pet.) 380 (1829).

46. 25 U.S. (12 Wheat.) 213, 286 (1827).

47. *Satterlee*, 27 U.S. at 416 (Johnson, J.).

48. Justice Johnson wrote that "all the judges who sat on the case of *Calder v. Bull*, concurred in the opinion" that the Connecticut legislature was exercising judicial, not legislative, authority. *Id.* at 416 n.a. (Johnson, J.). Johnson added:

> I then have a right to deny the construction intimated by three of the judges . . . is entitled to the weight of an adjudication. Nor is it immaterial, to observe, that an adjudication upon a fundamental law, ought never to be irrevocably settled by a decision that is not necessary and explicit.

   Id.
49. *Id.*
50. *Id.*
51. *Id.* For a contrarian view of why Blackstone in particular does not warrant his oracular status, *see* Martin Jordan Minot, Note, *The Irrelevance of Blackstone: Rethinking the Eighteenth Century Importance of the Commentaries*, 104 Va. L. Rev. 1359 (2018).
52. *Satterlee*, 27 U.S. at 416 (Johnson, J.).
53. *Id.*
54. *Id.* As noted in Chapter 1, at the time of the Philadelphia Convention in summer 1787, five of the eleven state constitutions contained ex post facto prohibitions of some kind. Although four made references to criminal laws, one state constitution—that of New Hampshire—did not, providing that "[r]etrospective laws are highly injurious, oppressive, and unjust. No such laws, therefore, should be made, either for the decision of civil causes, or the punishment of offenses." N.H. Const. Pt. 1, Art. 23 (adopted June 2, 1784, revising the original Constitution of 1776). Arguably, to the extent that state constitutions explicitly referenced criminal laws in their prohibitions, the absence of a similar limit in Article I is indicative of an intent to have a broader focus. Steve Selinger, *The Case Against Civil Ex Post Facto Laws*, 15 Cato J. 191, 197 (1995).

   Professor Gregory Maggs notes that a common reference resource on state constitutions was published in 1782 and was likely consulted by the framers. Notably, however, the resource was published two years before New Hampshire adopted its 1784 Constitution, with its unrestricted ex post facto prohibition. Gregory E. Maggs, *A Guide to the Index for Finding Evidence of the Original Meaning of the U.S. Constitution in Early State Constitutions and Declarations of Rights*, 98 N.C. L. Rev. 779, 784 (2020).
55. *Satterlee*, 27 U.S. at 416 n.a. (Johnson, J.).
56. *Id.*
57. Willis P. Whichard, Justice James Iredell 132 (2000). *See also* 4 The Debates in the Several State Conventions on the Adoption of the Federal Constitution, 185 (Jonathan Elliot ed., 1836) [hereinafter Elliot's Debates] (quoting James Iredell in the North Carolina Convention: "There is nothing in the Constitution which affects our present paper money. It prohibits, for the future, the emitting of any, but it does not interfere with the paper money now actually in circulation in several states. There is an express clause which protects it. It provides that there shall be no *ex post facto* law.").
58. James Iredell, *Marcus I*, Norfolk & Portsmouth J., Feb. 20, 1788, *in* 16 The Documentary History of the Ratification of the Constitution 164 (John P. Kaminski et al. eds., 1986).
59. James Iredell, *Observations on George Mason's Objections to the Federal Constitution, in* Pamphlets on the Constitution of the United States 336 (Paul L. Ford ed., 1888).

60. 3 THE RECORDS OF THE FEDERAL CONSTITUTION OF 1787, at 73, 589 (Max Farrand ed., 1937) [hereinafter FARRAND'S RECORDS] (noting that Paterson attended until July 23, 1787, and returned to sign the document on September 17). Interestingly, in *Calder*, Paterson stated that he "had an ardent desire to have extended the provision in the Constitution to retrospective laws in general. There is neither policy nor safety in such laws, and there-fore I have always had a strong aversion against them . . . But on full consideration I am convinced that ex post facto laws must be limited in the manner already expressed. . . ." *Calder*, 3 U.S. at 397 (Paterson, J.). According to one commentator, Paterson's reference to wanting to clarify broader coverage of the clause related to Paterson having missed the opportunity to do so at the convention on September 14, when he was absent and Mason sought to reopen consideration of the Clause. JULES GOEBEL, JR., 1 THE OLIVER WENDELL HOLMES DEVISE: HISTORY OF THE SUPREME COURT OF THE UNITED STATES 783 & n.71 (1971). Another possibility is that Paterson's reference concerned the view he expressed in the jury charge in *Van Horne's Lessee v. Dorrance*, noted in the text. 1 DHSC, *supra* note 17, at 98 n.56. More recently Professor Maeva Marcus speculated that "after hearing argument in *Calder* and probably consulting with his brethren, Paterson changed his mind." Maeva Marcus, *The Effect (or Non-Effect) of Founders on the Supreme Court Bench*, 80 GEO. WASH. L. REV. 1794, 1805 (2012).

   Justice Iredell left us with a similarly cryptic reference. *Calder* was argued before the Supreme Court in February 1798 and ultimately decided in August of that year. Iredell, in a June 1798 opinion when riding circuit in North Carolina, wrote that "(a) majority of the judges appeared to be convinced" of the "technical()" meaning of ex post facto, that is, that it was criminal-centric, but that "upon the doubt of one the case was not decided." Minge v. Gilmour, 17 F. Cas. 440, 443 (C.C.D.N.C. 1798) (No. 9,631) (Iredell, J.). Professor Marcus reasons that the minority justice could have dissented and speculates that the "one" referenced might have been Chief Justice Oliver Ellsworth, who was from Connecticut and had attended the Philadelphia Convention. Marcus, *supra*, at 1807. Ellsworth, who as noted did not attend the oral argument due to illness, and did not write an opinion in *Calder*, was present for the Philadelphia Convention's initial ex post facto discussion on August 22, stating that "ex post facto laws were void of themselves. It cannot, then, be nec-essary to prohibit them." He left sometime during the next week, missing the subsequent discussions and votes on sections 9 and 10. 3 FARRAND'S RECORDS, *supra*, at 587. A late September 1787 letter Ellsworth and fellow Convention delegate Roger Sherman sent to Connecticut Governor Samuel Huntington, which transmitted a copy of the Constitution and urged ratification, suggested Ellsworth's broader view, stating:

   > The restraint on the legislatures of the several states respecting emitting bills of credit, making any thing but money a tender in payment of debts, or impairing the obligation of contracts by ex post facto laws, was thought necessary as a security to commerce, in which the interest of foreigners as well as the citizens of different states may be affected.

   13 DHSC, *supra* note 17, at 471. The letter was first published in a New Haven newspaper in late October 1787, and subsequently reprinted in almost two dozen other newspapers. *Id.* at 470.

61. *See, e.g.*, Stuart v. Laird, 5 U.S. (1 Cranch) 299 (1803) (Paterson, J.) (discussing the practice of "circuit riding").

62. 2 U.S. (Dallas) 304 (1795).

63. William W. Crosskey, *The True Meaning of the Constitutional Prohibition of Ex Post Facto Laws*, 14 U. CHI. L. REV. 539, 557–58 (1947) [hereinafter Crosskey, *True Meaning*].

64. 10 U.S. 6 (Cranch) 87 (1810).

65. *Id.* at 138 (emphasis added).

66. JOSEPH STORY, COMMENTARIES ON THE CONSTITUTION 219–20 (5th ed. 1891) (1833).

67. *Id. See also* Stoddart v. Smith, 5 Binn. 355, 370 (Pa. 1812) (Brackenridge, J.) ("I take notice of the language of the Court of the United States, as confining ex post facto to a criminal case. It is an idea purely American, and not the worse for that, but it is incorrect. Ex post facto law, ex jure post facto, translated 'ex post facto law,' embraces civil contracts as well as criminal acts. The pœna and the action, ex jure post facto, or arising on an act done or a contract made before the law passed, are both embraced by this term. Our constitutions use the phrase ex post facto law, or law impairing contracts. They mean no more than to specify under the idea of impairing contracts, a kind of ex post facto law, which was embraced under the general term ex post facto.").

68. Society for the Propagation of the Gospel v. Wheeler, 22 Fed Cas. 756 (C. C. N. H. 1814) (Story, J.).

69. *See* Thomas Jefferson, Letter to Isaac McPherson, Aug. 13, 1813, 8 THE WRITINGS OF THOMAS JEFFERSON 326–27 (1903) ("Every man should be protected in his lawful acts, and be certain that no ex post facto law shall punish or endamage him for them. . . . (T)hey are equally unjust in civil as in criminal cases, and the omission of a caution which would have been right, does not justify the doing of what is wrong.").

70. See Oliver P. Field, *Ex Post Facto in the Constitution*, 20 MICH. L. REV. 315, 321–22 (1922) (noting that the convention debates contain "not a single mention of the practice of the British Parliament to which Justice Chase referred").

71. Selinger, *supra* note 54, at 191, 196.

72. Brainerd T. DeWitt, *Are Our Legal-Tender Laws Ex Post Facto?*, 15 POLITICAL SCI. Q. 96 (1900).

73. *See, e.g.,* Jane H. Aiken, *Ex Post Facto in the Civil Context: Unbridled Punishment*, 81 KY. L.J. 323 (1992); Crosskey, *True Meaning, supra* note 63; Field, *supra* note 70; John Mikhail, *supra* note 18; Caleb Nelson, *Originalism and Interpretive Conventions*, 70 U. CHI. L. REV. 519 (2003); Laura Ricciardi & Michael B.W. Sinclair, *Retroactive Civil Legislation*, 27 U. TOL. L. REV. 301 (1996); Selinger, *supra* note 54; Elmer Smead, *The Rule Against Retroactive Legislation: A Basic Principle of Jurisprudence*, 20 MIN. L. REV. 775 (1936); Evan C. Zoldan, *The Civil Ex Post Facto Clause*, 2015 WISC. L. REV. 727. According to Leonard Levy, *Calder*'s narrow view of the ex post facto prohibition "was more innovative than it was an accurate reflection of the opinions of the Framers and ratifiers. . . . [T]he history of the framing and ratification of the ex post facto clauses simply do not bear out the opinions in *Calder v. Bull*. The Court in that case reinvented the law on the subject." LEONARD W. LEVY, ORIGINAL INTENT AND THE FRAMER'S CONSTITUTION 74 (1988). *See also id.* at 65–74 (providing extensive critique and rebuttal of *Calder*'s narrow criminal-centric view).

74. 2 FARRAND'S RECORDS, *supra* note 60, at 440.

75. Field, *supra* note 70, at 319.

76. *Id.* at 320.

77. *Id.* at 324–25.

78. Mikhail, *supra* note 18, at 82.

79. *Id.* at 86 n.41.

80. Zoldan, *supra* note 73, at 768–71.
81. Crosskey, *True Meaning, supra* note 63.
82. William W. Crosskey, Politics and the Constitution in the History of the United States (1953) (Volumes I, II).
83. William W. Crosskey, *The Ex-Post-Facto and the Contracts Clauses in the Federal Constitution: A Note on the Editorial Ingenuity of James Madison*, 35 U. Chi. L. Rev. 248 (1968) [hereinafter Crosskey, *Editorial Ingenuity*]. In the article, Crosskey wrote:

> We have only Madison's word for it that Dickinson made the remarks in question; and that he did, in fact, do so, does not, inherently seem, very probable…Madison's story, obviously, is lacking in inherent credibility; and that means it is highly unlikely Dickinson made the remarks at the Convention, on August 29th, which Madison's notes record.

Id. at 251.
84. *Id.* at 250.
85. *See, e.g.*, Carpenter v. Pennsylvania, 58 U.S. (17 How.) 456, 463 (1854).
86. *See, e.g.*, Charles Warren, The Making of the Constitution 501–03, 553–57 (1928).
87. Crosskey, *Editorial Ingenuity, supra* note 83, at 252–54.
88. Mikhail, *supra* note 18, at 89.
89. *See, e.g.*, James H. Hutson, *The Creation of the Constitution: The Integrity of the Documentary Record*, 65 Tex. L. Rev. 2, 25 (1986); Gregory E. Maggs, *A Concise Guide to the Records of the Federal Constitutional Convention of 1787 as a Source of the Original Meaning of the U.S. Constitution*, 80 Geo. Wash. L. Rev. 1707, 1742 (2012).
90. *See* Mary S. Bilder, Madison's Hand: Revising the Constitutional Convention 141 (2015) (characterizing Madison's notes during the period as "particularly unreliable"). In a more recent work Professor Bilder states that

> beginning with August 22, Madison's notes present a significant problem. Madison served on multiple committees in late August, and also became sick. Whatever rough notes he took during the proceedings after that date were not written up during the summer of 1787. Instead, the section of Madison's notes from August 22 to the end of the convention was likely written two years later, in the winter and spring of 1789–90, when Madison knew that Thomas Jefferson finally would return to the United States from France [Madison promised that he would show his notes to Jefferson].

Mary S. Bilder, *Madison's Notes Don't Mean What Everyone Says They Mean*, The Atlantic, Dec. 22, 2019. It is worth noting that Madison, for his part, did not believe that his *Notes* regarding the Philadelphia Convention should definitively figure in the interpretation of the Constitution, as he regarded the Convention as only a drafting committee. Jack N. Rakove, Original Meanings: Politics and Ideas in the Making of the Constitution 362–65 (1996). Madison maintained that the best evidence of constitutional meaning could be found in records of the state ratifying conventions:

> [W]hatever veneration might be entertained for the body of men who formed our Constitution, the sense of that body could never be regarded as the oracular guide in expounding the Constitution. As the instrument came from them it was nothing more than the draft of a plan, nothing but a dead letter, until life and validity were breathed into it by the voice of the people, speaking through the several State Conventions. If we were to look, therefore, for the meaning of the instrument beyond the face of the instrument, we must look for it, not in the General Convention, which proposed, but in the State Conventions, which accepted and ratified the Constitution.

4 ANNALS OF CONGRESS 776 (1796), available at http://memory.loc.gov/cgi-bin/amp age?collId=llac&fileName=005/llac005.db&recNum=384.

91. *See, e.g.,* Mikhail, *supra* note 18, at 87–89.

92. SUPPLEMENT TO MAX FARRAND'S RECORDS OF THE FEDERAL CONVENTION OF 1787, at xxiii (James H. Hutson ed., 1987) (stating that "[t]here is no visual evidence to support these charges; an examination of the relevant manuscript pages of Madison's notes reveals no significant alteration of the text" and that a review of the paper used preclude conclusion that Madison "at a later date using a fresh supply of paper and substituted the newly composed sheets for the ones he had prepared earlier").

93. Wilson, according to Iredell's biographer, died in August 1798 in Edenton, and his financial exigency was such that he could not then be buried in Philadelphia, but rather was buried in Edenton, with his remains moved north to a cemetery only in 1906. WHICHARD, *supra* note 57, at 268–69.

94. Crosskey, *True Meaning, supra* note 63, at 560, 563. The persuasiveness of Crosskey's theory, but not his broader contention that *Calder* was wrong in its criminal-centric holding, is somewhat belied by the fact that when the bankruptcy bill was debated in Congress, its proponents failed to note *Calder's* narrow view. As Professor Leonard Levy more recently observed:

> *Calder* had the effect of clearing the way for a congressional bankruptcy act that had a retroactive operation. Despite *Calder*, congressional opponents of the bankruptcy act, which was purely civil in nature, described it as a prohibited ex post facto law, and when the opposition mustered a majority to repeal the act in 1803, only three years after its passage, those who sought vainly to save it insisted that it was not an ex post facto law. No one in the debates of 1799–1800 or 1803 stated that ex post facto laws did not apply to civil matters; and no one cited *Calder*.

LEVY, *supra* note 73, at 69.

95. Mikhail, *supra* note 18, at 86 n.41.

96. *See id.* at 146 (stating that "Crosskey may have gone too far in attacking Madison and questioning his honesty and integrity. Nonetheless, . . . it seems likely that he was on to something"); *id.* at 144 (concluding that historical sources and context examined "tend to make Madison's account of what occurred in Philadelphia with respect to the ex post facto clauses even less credible than it already appears").

97. Professor Mikhail notes that Justices James Wilson, William Paterson, and Oliver Ellsworth were all at the Philadelphia Convention but that only Wilson was present when both ex post facto provisions were discussed. Mikhail, *supra* note 18, at 81. Ellsworth was only present for the initial, August 22 debate, concerning the prohibition on Congress and Paterson departed Philadelphia sometime before August 21, returning to sign the final document in September. *Id.* at 81 n.5.

98. *Id.* at 146. That same year, Wilson also delivered a Memorial to Virginia and Congress making clear his belief that ex post facto laws could be civil or criminal in nature. *Id.* at 107–14, 139.

99. *Id.* at 145–46. Professor Mikhail notes that added embarrassment likely accrued to Chase (who was also a shareholder of the real estate venture) and Paterson (based on Wilson's use of his *Dorrance* opinion). *Id.*

100. *Id.* at 116.

101. *Id.* at 146.

102. *Calder*, 3 U.S. at 395 (Chase, J.).
103. For a contrary view, seeing the convention records as supportive of *Calder*'s narrow reading, *see* Robert G. Natelson, *Statutory Retroactivity: The Founders' View*, 39 IDAHO L. REV. 489, 517–18 (2002). Professor Natelson argues that although a broad view might have dominated "earlier in the adoption process," persistent concern that extending coverage to civil laws would encompass curative laws with salutary effect, vigorously raised by Anti-Federalists such as George Mason, pushed Federalists like Madison to a criminal-centric view. According to Natelson:

> Such a sweeping prohibition of retrospective laws proved to be too broad to be acceptable to most participants, who believed that curative laws were sometimes desirable. So to obtain approval at the national convention and in the ratification process, most federalists represented that the Ex Post Facto Clauses were purely criminal in nature. Based on previous history, this was not an unreasonable interpretation, and it apparently served as part of the basis of the ratification bargain.

Id. at 523 (footnotes omitted). *See also* Douglas Kmiec & John McGinnis, *The Contract Clause: A Return to the Original Understanding*, 14 HASTINGS CONST. L. Q. 525, 531 n.29 (1987) (similarly arguing that *Calder* was correct in limiting the ex post facto prohibition to criminal laws). Professor David Currie, in his classic work on the opinions of the early Supreme Court, written before much of the modern revisionist Framing Era scholarship was published, adopted a middle ground. *See* DAVID P. CURRIE, THE CONSTITUTION IN THE SUPREME COURT: THE FIRST HUNDRED YEARS 1789–1888 44 (1985) ("What this split of opinion [in Framing Era records] seems to indicate is that ... there was no clear answer to what the Framers meant by ex post facto laws.").

104. Field, *supra* note 70, at 320.
105. RICHARD WOODDESON, A SYSTEMATICAL VIEW OF THE LAWS OF ENGLAND 641 (1792).
106. *Calder*, 3 U.S. at 391 (emphasis added).

Chapter 3

1. 10 U.S. (6 Cranch) 87 (1810).
2. *Id.* at 131.
3. *See* JEAN EDWARD SMITH, JOHN MARSHALL: DEFINER OF A NATION 389 (1996) (footnotes omitted):

> The taint attached to the sale ignited a firestorm across Georgia. Rival politicians fanned the flames, and in the election that took place on 1796, the old legislature was swept out of office. The incoming assembly, as its first order of business, passed an act rescinding the grant. The lands that had been sold were declared to be "the sole property of the State," and all documents relating to the original transaction were ordered expunged from the records. These and the official copy of the 1795 act were burned on an elaborate public ceremony on the statehouse square, the fire supplied from heaven by means of a magnifying class that concentrated the sun's rays into a flame.

4. *Fletcher*, 10 U.S. at 127.
5. Fletcher was represented by Luther Martin, a Maryland delegate to the Philadelphia Convention, who it has been noted, "once was so intoxicated that Marshall took the unprecedented Action of adjourning temporarily so that [Martin] could recover." SMITH,

supra note 3, at 390. Peck, for his part, had two lawyers, Robert Goodloe Harper and Joseph Story, the latter a constitutional law luminary of the time and later a US Supreme Court Justice. *Id.*

6. *See* U.S. Const. art. I, § 10, cl. 1 ("No State shall . . . pass any . . . Law impairing the Obligation of Contracts.").

7. *Fletcher*, 10 U.S. at 137–38.

8. *Id.*

9. *Id.* at 138–39.

10. *Id.* at 138.

11. *Id.*

12. *Id.*

13. *See id.* at 138–39:

> This rescinding act would have the effect of an ex post facto law. It forfeits the estate of Fletcher for a crime not committed by himself, but by those from whom he purchased. This cannot be effected [sic] in the form of an ex post facto law, or bill of attainder; why, then, is it allowable in the form of a law annulling the original grant?

14. *Id.*

15. *See id.* at 128:

> The question, whether a law, be void for its repugnancy to the constitution, is at all times a question of much delicacy, which ought seldom, if ever, to be decided in the affirmative, in a doubtful case. The Court, when compelled by duty to render such a judgment, would be unworthy of its station if it were unmindful of the solemn obligations which that situation imposes.

16. In *Calder*, as noted in Chapter 2, the Connecticut "resolution or law" challenged arguably was a judicial, not legislative act, and thus not subject to the ex post facto prohibition.

17. 25 U.S. 213 (1827).

18. In addition to being argued by renowned orators, US Senators Daniel Webster and Henry Clay, *Ogden*'s claim to judicial fame is that it was the first time Chief Justice Marshall dissented in a constitutional law decision.

19. *See id.* at 266:

> There is nothing unjust or tyrannical in punishing offences prohibited by law, and committed in violation of that law. Nor can it be unjust, or oppressive, to declare by law, that contracts subsequently entered into, may be discharged in a way different from that which the parties have provided, but which they know, or may know, are liable, under certain circumstances, to be discharged in a manner contrary to the provisions of their contract.

20. *Id.*

21. *Id.*; *see also id.* at 330–31 (Trimble, J., concurring):

> [Those ratifying Article I section 10] must have understood, that these denunciations were just, as regarded bills of attainder, and ex post facto laws, because they were exercises of arbitrary power, perverting the justice and order of existing things by the reflex action of these laws. And would they not naturally and necessarily conclude, the denunciations were equally just as regarded laws passed to impair the obligation of existing contracts, for the same reason? . . . I cannot understand this language otherwise than as putting bills of attainder, ex post facto laws, and laws impairing the

obligation of contracts, all upon the same footing, and deprecating them all for the same cause. The language shows, clearly, that the whole clause was understood at the time of the adoption of the constitution to have been introduced into the instrument in the very same spirit, and for the very same purpose, namely, for the protection of personal security and of private rights.

22. *Id.* at 286 (Johnson, J., concurring).

23. *Id.* (emphasis in original) (citation omitted).

24. 27 U.S. 380 (1829).

25. *Satterlee*, 27 U.S. at 416 (Johnson, J., concurring).

26. *See id.* at 416 n.a.:

> Thus it appears, that all the judges who sat in the case of *Calder v. Bull*, concurred in the opinion, that the decision of the court of probate, and the lapse of the time given for an appeal to their court of errors, were not final upon the rights of the parties; that there still existed in the legislature, a controlling and revising power over the controversy; and that this was duly exercised in the reversal of the first decree of the court of probate . . . How, then, could the question, whether the phrase ex post facto was confined to criminal law, arise in this cause? [T]he law complained of was equally free from that characteristic; though the phrase be held to extend to laws of a civil character.
>
> I then have a right to deny that the construction intimated by three of the judges in the case of *Calder v. Bull*, is entitled to the weight of an adjudication.

27. *Id.* at 414–16.

28. *Id.* at 416 n.a.

29. *Id.*

30. 33 U.S. 88 (1834).

31. *Id.* at 110; *see also* Baltimore & S.R. Co. v. Nesbit, 51 U.S. 395, 401–02 (1850) (in rejecting a Contracts Clause challenge concerning a state law setting aside a determination in a land condemnation matter by a railroad, stating that the law "does not fall within any definition given of an ex post facto law, and is not therefore assailable on that account"); Thurlow v. Massachusetts, 46 U.S. 504, 504 n.1 (1847) (rejecting challenge to state law "if it lessens the value of liquor owned in the State previous to, and held at the time of its passage" because "such civil consequences do not make it retroact criminally, in such sense, or to bring it within the definition of an 'ex post facto' law."); Charles River Bridge v. Proprietors of Warren Bridge, 36 U.S. 420, 540 (1837) (denying a Contracts Clause challenge against a state law authorizing construction of a competing bridge, citing *Watson v. Mercer* and its statement for the criminal-centric focus of the Ex Post Facto Clause).

32. 58 U.S. (How.) 456 (1854).

33. *Id.* at 463.

34. Harold M. Hyman, *New Light on* Cohen v. Wright: *California's First Loyalty Oath Case*, 28 PACIFIC HIST. REV. 131, 131 (1959) (stating that "[b]y the end of 1863, the national Congress and more than a dozen loyal states enacted loyalty oath legislation. California was one of those states.").

35. Cummings v. Missouri, 71 U.S. (4 Wall.) 277, 279–80 (1867).

36. *Id.* at 281.

37. Donald Rau, Cummings v. Missouri: *Three Cheers for Father Cummings*, YEARBOOK: SUPREME CT. HIST. SOC., 20, 25 (1977).

38. *Id.* at 21–23, 25. Rau writes that "reaction to the test oath, among clergy in Missouri, ran the gamut from enthusiastic approval to cries of persecution . . . [The archbishop] saw the oath as an infringement of religious liberty and determined that it must be resisted at the outset." *Id.* at 22. Cummings "was an obscure priest, but two years ordained when arrested. When he died, some eight years later, he had returned to oblivion." *Id.* at 21.

39. *Id.* at 25.

40. DICTIONARY OF MISSOURI BIOGRAPHY 224 (Lawrence O. Christensen et al. eds., 1999).

41. Montgomery Blair, also a highly respected attorney of the time who earlier served in the Lincoln cabinet as postmaster general, served as co-counsel, and filed a brief, as did Reverdy Johnson, yet another esteemed member of the bar. Rau, *supra* note 37, at 316.

42. *Cummings*, 71 U.S. at 285.

43. *Id.*

44. *Id.* at 289.

45. *Id.* at 318–19.

46. *See* Peter G. Fish, *Secrecy and the Supreme Court: Judicial Indiscretion and Reconstruction Politics*, 8 WM. & MARY L. REV. 225 (1967). According to Fish, the first leak occurred in May 1866, many months before the actual issuance of the *Cummings* decision in January 1867, but before the crucial postwar Missouri election of 1866. *Id.* at 228, 231. Apparently, the offender was Justice Robert Grier, who "became, during his more than two decades on the bench, not only senile and obstinate, but also a major disseminator of 'inside' Supreme Court information." *Id.* at 233. For more on the early disclosure imbroglio, *see* CHARLES FAIRMAN, HISTORY OF THE SUPREME COURT OF THE UNITED STATES: RECONSTRUCTION AND REUNION, 1864–88, PART I, at 151–60 (1971). *See also* DAUN VAN EE, DAVID DUDLEY FIELD AND THE RECONSTRUCTION OF THE LAW 179–80 (1986) (noting that Democrats maintained that the loyalty oath test would be invalidated and urged voting without taking the oath).

47. Lincoln's relationship with David Dudley Field is thought to be a significant reason for Lincoln's consideration of his brother Stephen Field for the US Supreme Court. Lincoln is reported to have asked, "Does David want his brother to have it?" Upon hearing an affirmative answer Lincoln is said to have declared, "Then he shall have it." CARL SWISHER, STEPHEN J. FIELD: CRAFTSMAN OF THE LAW 116–17 (1963). When nominated, Field was chief justice of the California Supreme Court, and took his seat as the tenth justice on the US Supreme Court, an innovation by Congress in 1863 intended to provide greater geographic coverage of non-slave states, including California. Field wrote over five hundred opinions in his over thirty years on the Court (1863–1897), the longest serving justice at the time. *See* ROBERT FRIDLINGTON, THE RECONSTRUCTION COURT: 1864–1888 at 190 (1987).

48. Raised and legally trained in the east, Field made his way to California in the 1840s, becoming an alcade (a mayor with judicial powers) of a small gold rush town. He was considered a rather irascible individual, who during his California years carried a Bowie knife and pistol, and was involved in two challenges to duel (on both occasions withdrawn). FRIDLINGTON, *supra* note 47, at 189. Later in life, at seventy-three in 1889, amid a bitter ongoing quarrel with former Chief Justice of the California Supreme Court David Terry, Justice Field's bodyguard fatally shot Terry, allegedly because he thought that he was going to stab Field. The bodyguard, a deputy US Marshall named David Neagle, was apprehended, imprisoned, and later released upon issuance of a federal writ of habeas corpus. The matter eventually made its way to the US Supreme Court, with Justice Field recusing himself. *See*

Cunningham v. Neagle, 135 U.S. 1, 76 (1890) (holding that Neagle acted pursuant to federal law and therefore could not be held to account by California state courts).

49. Paul Kens, *Justice Stephen Field of California*, 33 J. Sup. Ct. Hist. 149, 156 (2008).

50. *Cummings*, 71 U.S. at 319.

51. See Paul Kens, Justice Stephen Field: Shaping Liberty from the Gold Rush to the Gilded Age 266–75 (1997).

52. Field reasoned that:

> [t]he oath could not, therefore, have been required as a means of ascertaining whether parties were qualified or not for their respective callings or the trusts with which they were charged. It was required in order to reach the person, not the calling. It was exacted, not from any notion that the several acts designated indicated unfitness for the callings, but because it was thought that the several acts deserved punishment, and that for many of them there was no way to inflict punishment except by depriving the parties, who had committed them, of some of the rights and privileges of the citizen.

Cummings, 71 U.S. at 320.

53. *Id.*

54. *Id.*

55. *Id.* at 320–21.

56. *Id.* at 321–22.

57. *Id.* at 322.

58. *Id.*

59. *Id.*

60. *Id.*

61. *Id.* (citation omitted).

62. *Id.* at 325.

63. *Id.* at 327.

64. *Id.* at 328.

65. *Id.*

66. *Id.* at 329.

67. *Id.* at 330.

68. 71 U.S. (4 Wall.) 333 (1867).

69. *Id.* at 377.

70. *Id.* at 380.

71. *Id.* at 377.

72. *Id.* at 393.

73. *Id.*

74. *Id.*

75. *Id.*

76. It is worth noting that other test oath cases later came before the court but went unresolved. One, *Ridley v. Sherbrook*, 3 Coldwell (43 Tenn.) 569 (1867), was a Tennessee Supreme Court case that in March 1867 upheld the oath requirement vis-à-vis losing the right to vote, distinguishing *Cummings* on the basis that it concerned the property right in a livelihood, which unlike the franchise could not be limited by a sovereignty. Two other cases came, like *Cummings*, from Missouri. *Blair v. Thompson & Ridgely*, 41 Mo. 63 (1867), also concerned voting, while the other, *State ex rel. Wingate v. Warren Woodson*, 41 Mo. 227 (1867),

concerned eligibility to hold office. In both cases, the Missouri Supreme Court upheld the prohibition, similarly distinguishing *Cummings*.

In March 1869, the three cases were argued before the US Supreme Court, which at the time had only eight justices (James Moore Wayne died in the summer 1867 and had not been replaced). On January 31, 1870, the court announced that one of the Missouri decisions, *Blair v. Thompson & Ridgley*, concerning voting, was affirmed by an equally divided court (4-4) without an opinion. The other Missouri case and the Tennessee case were dismissed (both Woodson and Ridley had died while the cases were pending). FAIRMAN, *supra* note 46, at 612–16; SWISHER, *supra* note 47, at 154 n.21. Technically, because the vote was a tie, the case lacks precedential value, serving only to leave intact the Missouri Supreme Court's rejection of the challenge. Fairman said of the cases that they "remained for two years in a deadlocked Court, until at last [they were] disposed of, inconclusively and inconspicuously. During all this time Democratic [newspaper] editors kept fussing at the Court for its delay." FAIRMAN, *supra* note 46, at 612. *See also id.* at 616 ("Affirmance of the judgment below by an equal division ended the litigation without leaving a trace in the United States Reports.").

77. Pierce v. Carskadon, 83 U.S. 234, 239 (1872). Justice Bradley, who was elevated to the court after *Cummings* and *Garland*, was the sole dissenter. *See id.* at 239–40 (Bradley, J., dissenting) (stating that he "dissented on the judgment, on the ground that the test oath in question was one which it was competent for the State to exact as a war measure in time of civil war.").

78. 97 U.S. 381 (1878).

79. *Id.* at 384–85.

80. *See* FRIDLINGTON, *supra* note 47, at 83 ("The dual decisions in the *Test Oath Cases* brought bitter criticism upon the Court and increased demands to limit the Court's appellate jurisdiction."). Agitation over *Cummings* and *Garland* was heightened because they were decided shortly after *Ex parte Milligan*, 71 U.S. 2 (1866), which held that the Lincoln administration lacked authority to try civilian Confederate sympathizers in federal military tribunals when civilian courts were functioning. Justice Field sided with the five-member majority (four justices concurred on separate grounds). *Cummings and Garland* were derided by Radical Republicans who likened the decisions to *Dred Scott v. Sandford*, the infamous 1857 decision by the court holding that enslaved African Americans were not entitled to the protections of the US Constitution. SWISHER, *supra* note 47 at 152–53. For more on the sectarian reaction to *Cummings* and *Garland*, see HAROLD HYMAN, ERA OF THE OATH: NORTHERN LOYALTY TESTS DURING THE CIVIL WAR AND RECONSTRUCTION 113–19 (1954).

Notably, President Lincoln drew a distinction between oaths testing past loyalty and those of future orientation: "On principle," he wrote in a February 1864 letter to his Secretary of War Edwin Stanton, "I dislike an oath which requires a man to swear he has not done wrong. It rejects the Christian principle of forgiveness on terms of repentance. I think it enough if a man does not wrong hereafter." IX COMPLETE WORKS OF ABRAHAM LINCOLN 3 (John G. Nicolay & John Hay eds., 1905).

81. Cummings v. Missouri, 71 U.S. (4 Wall.) 277, 329 (1867).

82. 76 U.S. 35 (1869).

83. *Id.* at 38.

Chapter 4

1. *See* Galvan v. Press, 347 U.S. 522, 531 n.4 (1954) (noting contrary views of Justice Johnson expressed in *Ogden v. Saunders* and *Satterlee* but citing *Calder* and stating "[i]t would be an unjustifiable reversal to overturn a view of the Constitution so deeply rooted and so consistently adhered to."); Lehman v. United States, 353 U.S. 685, 690 (1957) (Black, J., concurring) (expressing view that limiting the prohibition to criminal cases "confines the clause too narrowly"); Marcello v. Bonds, 349 U.S. 302, 319 (1955) (Douglas, J., dissenting) (noting that "[t]here is a school of thought that the Ex Post Facto Clause includes all retroactive legislation, civil as well as criminal.").

2. *See* Calder v. Bull, 3 (Dall.) U.S. 386, 390 (1798) (opinion of Chase, J.) ("I do not consider any law ex post facto . . . that mollifies the rigor of the criminal law; but only those that create, or aggravate, the crime, or increase the punishment, or change the rules of evidence, for the purpose of conviction.").

3. *Id.*

4. 97 U.S. 381 (1878).

5. *Id.* at 385.

6. 107 U.S. 221 (1883), *overruled by* Collins v. Youngblood, 497 U.S. 37 (1990).

7. *Id.* at 223–24.

8. *Id.* at 228.

9. *Id.* at 235.

10. *Id.* at 228.

11. *Id.* at 228–29 (emphasis in original) (quoting United States v. Hall, 26 F. Cas. 84, 86 (C.C. D. Pa. 1809)).

12. *Id.* at 229.

13. *Id.* at 231.

14. *Id.* at 232. The court elaborated:

    > in the former case [*Calder*] this court held that 'any law which alters the legal rules of evidence, and receives less or different testimony than the law requires at the time of the commission of the offense in order to convict the offender,' is an ex post facto law; and in the latter [*Cummings*], one of the reasons why the law was held to be ex post facto was that it changed the rule of evidence under which the party was punished. But it cannot be sustained without destroying the value of the constitutional provision that no law, however it may invade or modify the rights of a party charged with crime, is an ex post facto law within the constitutional provision, if it comes within either of these comprehensive branches of the law designated as 'pleading,' 'practice,' and 'evidence.'

    Id.

15. *Id.* at 232.

16. *Id.* at 235–36.

17. 110 U.S. 574 (1884).

18. *Id.* at 575.

19. *Id.* at 587.

20. *Id.*

21. *Id.* at 589–90.

22. Calder v. Bull, 3 U.S. (3 Dall.) 386, 389 (1798) (opinion of Chase, J.).

23. *Id.*

24. Hopt v. Utah, 110 U.S. 574, 589 (1884).

25. *Id.*

26. *Id.* at 590.

27. 170 U.S. 343 (1898), *overruled by* Collins v. Youngblood, 497 U.S. 37 (1990).

28. *Id.* at 351.

29. *Id.* at 352–53.

30. *Id.* at 352. It is worth noting that two years before, in *Gibson v. Mississippi*, 162 U.S. 565 (1896), Justice Harlan, writing for a unanimous court, rejected an ex post facto challenge against changes to the selection of grand and petit (trial) juries in the state of Mississippi. Even though it was alleged that the number of qualified African American jurors in the jurisdiction outnumbered whites 7,000 to 1,500, no African American had served for "a number of years." *Id.* at 584. Gibson, an African American, was convicted by an all-white jury of murdering a white landowner, and challenged retroactive changes to juror qualifications. The court held that the changes did not "affect[] in any degree the substantial rights of those who had committed crime prior to [their] going into effect." *Id.* at 589. The changes did not fall within any of the four *Calder* categories:

> The provisions in question related simply to procedure. They only prescribed remedies to be pursued in the administration of the law, making no change that could materially affect the rights of one accused of crime theretofore committed. The inhibition upon the passage of ex post facto laws does not give a criminal a right to be tried, in all respects, by the law in force when the crime charged was committed. The mode of trial is always under legislative control, subject only to the condition that the legislature may not, under the guise of establishing modes of procedure and prescribing remedies, violate the accepted principles that protect an accused person against ex post facto enactments.

Id. at 590. Justice Harlan's disinclination to fault the Mississippi jury selection stands in sharp contrast to his courageous, often extolled dissent from the court's infamous decision of the same year, *Plessy v. Ferguson*, 163 U.S. 537, 552 (1896), which upheld "separate but equal laws."

31. 171 U.S. 380 (1898).

32. *Id.* at 380–81.

33. *Id.* at 381.

34. *Id.* at 382.

35. *Id.* at 387–88.

36. *Id.*

37. *Id.* at 386.

38. *Id.* at 383 (quoting United States v. Hall, 2 Wash. C.C. 366, 373 (1809) and Kring v. Missouri, 107 U.S. 221 (1883)).

39. 269 U.S. 167 (1925).

40. *Id.* at 169.

41. *Id.*

42. *Id.* at 169–70. The genesis of defense as a category appears to date from statements made by the court in *Kring v. Missouri*, 107 U.S. 221, 229 (1882) and *Thompson v. Missouri*, 171 U.S. 380, 384 (1898), yet *Kring* was overruled in *Collins v. Youngblood* (1990). To the extent the "defense" category still enjoys recognition, it seemingly has been subsumed in *Calder* categories one and two.

43. *Beazell*, 269 U.S. at 169. In its next sentence, the court confusingly elaborated on its test, making reference to the second *Calder* category but yet again omitting the fourth:

> The constitutional prohibition and the judicial interpretation of [ex post facto] rest upon the notion that laws, whatever their form, which purport to make innocent acts criminal after the event, or to aggravate an offense, are harsh and oppressive, and that the criminal quality attributable to an act, either by the legal definition of the offense or by the nature or amount of the punishment imposed for its commission, should not be altered by legislative enactment, after the fact, to the disadvantage of the accused.

Id. at 170 (emphasis added).

44. *Id.*
45. *Id.*
46. *Id.*
47. *Id.* at 171.
48. *Id.* at 170 (citing Kring v. Missouri and Thompson v. Utah).
49. *Id.*
50. *Id.* (citation omitted).
51. 432 U.S. 282 (1977).
52. *Id.* at 288.
53. *Id.*
54. *Id.* at 289 n.5.
55. *Id.* at 287.
56. *Id.*
57. *Id.* at 293.
58. *Id.* at 292.
59. *Id.* at 293.
60. *Id.* at 293–94.
61. *Id.* at 294 (quoting Hopt v. Utah, 110 U.S. 574, 589–90 (1884)).
62. *Id.* The court elaborated in a footnote:

> For example, the jury's recommendation may have been affected by the fact that the members of the jury were not the final arbiters of life or death. They may have chosen leniency when they knew that that decision rested ultimately on the shoulders of the trial judge, but might not have followed the same course if their vote were final.

Id. at 294 n.7.

63. *Id.* at 295.
64. 497 U.S. 37 (1990).
65. *Id.* at 39.
66. *Id.* at 39–40.
67. *Id.* at 40.
68. *Id.* at 43.
69. *Id.* at 43 n.3 (citing Thompson v. Missouri, 171 U.S. 380, 386–87 (1898) and Hopt v. Utah, 110 U.S. 574, 588–90 (1884)).
70. *See id.* at 44 ("The new statute is a procedural change that allows reformation of improper verdicts. It does not alter the definition of the crime of aggravated sexual abuse, of which Youngblood was convicted, nor does it increase the punishment for which he is eligible as a result of that conviction.").

71. *Id.* at 45.

72. 107 U.S. 221 (1883).

73. 170 U.S. 343 (1898).

74. *Collins*, 497 U.S. at 45.

75. *Id.* at 47. While embracing its truncated version of the *Calder* categories, drawn from *Beazell*, and overruling *Kring* and *Thompson*, the *Collins* majority seemed untroubled by language in *Beazell* suggesting a broader view. *See Beazell*, 269 U.S. at 171 (asserting that the Ex Post Facto Clause "was intended to secure substantial personal rights against arbitrary and oppressive legislation").

76. *Collins*, 497 U.S. at 43 ("Legislatures may not retroactively alter the definition of crimes or increase the punishment for criminal acts."). *See also* Cal. Dep't of Corr. v. Morales, 514 U.S. 499, 510 n.7 (1995) ("The ex post facto standard we apply today is constant: It looks to whether a given legislative change has the prohibited effect of altering the definition of crimes or increasing punishments.").

77. *Collins*, 497 U.S. at 46.

78. 269 U.S. 167 (1925).

79. *Collins*, 497 U.S. at 43.

80. *See Beazell*, 269 U.S. at 169–70. The court elaborated as follows:

> It is settled, by decisions of this Court so well known that their citation may be dispensed with, that any statute which [1] punishes as a crime an act previously committed, which was innocent when done; [2] which makes more burdensome the punishment for a crime, after its commission, [3] which deprives one charged with crime of any defense available according to law at the time when the act was committed, is prohibited as ex post facto.

> *Id.*

81. Calder v. Bull, 3 U.S. (Dall.) 386, 391 (1798) (Chase, J.).

82. *Dobbert*, 432 U.S. at 293.

83. *Collins*, 497 U.S. at 45.

84. *Id.* at 46.

85. *Id.* at 43.

86. *Id.* at 46 (stating that "[s]ubtle ex post facto violations are no more permissible than overt ones").

87. *Id.* at 45.

88. 34 U.S. 160 (1890).

89. *Id.* at 171.

90. *Id.* at 172.

91. *Id.* The court, under similar facts, reached the same result in *In re Savage*, 134 U.S. 176 (1890).

92. 137 U.S. 483 (1890).

93. *Id.* at 491.

94. *Id.*

95. 196 U.S. 319 (1905).

96. *Id.* at 325.

97. *Id.* at 326.

98. *Id.*

99. 237 U.S. 180 (1915).

100. *Id.* at 185.

101. *Id. Compare* Shepherd v. People, 25 N.Y. 406 (1862) (deeming invalid legislative change from death to life imprisonment at hard labor, stating that the latter was of punishment of such different kind as to preclude the court from saying it was less severe). For a modern application of *Malloy*, in the context of a change in pharmaceuticals used in lethal injection, *see* Zink v. Lombardi, 783 F.3d 1089, 1107–08 (8th Cir. 2015) (construing Missouri law).

102. 301 U.S. 397 (1937).

103. *Id.* at 401.

104. 450 U.S. 24 (1981).

105. *Id.* at 33.

106. *Id.*

107. 482 U.S. 423 (1987).

108. *Id.* at 424 (quoting *Weaver*, 450 U.S. at 36).

109. Cummings v. Missouri, 71 U.S. 277, 319 (1867).

110. *Id.* at 320.

111. *Id.* at 322.

112. *Id.* at 320.

113. *Id.* at 322.

114. 170 U.S. 189 (1898).

115. *Id.* at 196. *See also id.* at 194 ("The physician is one whose relations to life and health are of the most intimate character. It is fitting, not merely that he should possess a knowledge of diseases and their remedies, but also that he should be one who may safely be trusted to apply those remedies.").

116. *Id.* at 198–99.

117. *Hawker*, 170 U.S. at 204 (Harlan, J., dissenting). *See also* Gabriel J. Chin, *Are Collateral Sanctions Premised on Conduct or Conviction: The Case of Abortion Doctors*, 30 FORDHAM URB. L.J. 1685, 1695–98 (2003) (noting that the language of the new statute did not mention character and conduct and arguing that it only embodied additional punishment for a past conviction).

118. *Id.* at 204–05 (Harlan, J., dissenting).

119. *Id.* at 205.

120. The resolution of the punishment question also determines whether other constitutional provisions are triggered, such as the prohibitions contained in the Fifth Amendment Double Jeopardy and Eighth Amendment Cruel and Unusual Punishment Clauses.

121. *See* Gabriel J. Chin, *The New Civil Death: Rethinking Punishment in the Era of Mass Incarceration*, 160 U. PA. L. REV. 1789, 1807 (2010) ("The modern law of collateral consequences seems to have begun with *Hawker v. New York*."); Chin, *Conduct or Conviction, supra* note 117, at 1687 ("*Hawker v. New York* is the seminal case for the idea that sanctions imposed exclusively on those convicted of crimes can nevertheless be 'civil.'").

122. 264 U.S. 32 (1924).

123. *See* Siegfried Hesse, *The Constitutional Status of the Lawfully Admitted Permanent Resident Alien: The Pre-1917 Cases*, 68 YALE L.J. 1578, 1585 (1959) (noting that "[t]he 1920 act, with which *Mahler* deals, was significant primarily because it was the first retroactive addition of grounds for expulsion not expressly related to a preexisting ground of exclusion.").

124. *Mahler*, 264 U.S. at 39.

125. *Id.*

126. *Id.*

127. *Id. Mahler* was not the first post-*Hawker* decision finding deportation non-punitive for ex post facto purposes. *See* Bugajewitz v. Adams, 228 U.S. 585 (1913) (upholding deportation of immigrant alien, an alleged prostitute, tersely concluding that the law was not ex post facto and stating that "determination by facts that might constitute a crime under local law is not a conviction of crime, nor is it a punishment; it is simply a refusal by the government to harbor persons who it does not want."); Johannessen v. United States, 225 U.S. 227 (1912) (deeming deportation non-punitive in a case of immigrant alien who previously secured citizenship by fraud, noting that deportation "simply deprives him of his ill-gotten privileges").

It is worth noting that James Madison was convinced that deportation qualified as punishment. When criticizing the president's power to deport noncitizens under the Alien and Sedition Acts, Madison stated in the congressional debate, on behalf of Virginia, that deportation was punishment regardless of whether Congress's motives were "preventive" or "penal." James Madison, *Report of the Committee to Whom Were Referred the Communications of Various States, Relative to the Resolutions of the Last General Assembly of This State, Concerning the Alien and Sedition Laws*, H.D. 1799–1800 Sess. (Va. 1800), *reprinted in* 4 JONATHAN ELLIOT, THE DEBATES IN THE SEVERAL STATE CONVENTIONS ON THE ADOPTION OF THE FEDERAL CONSTITUTION AS RECOMMENDED BY THE GENERAL CONVENTION AT PHILADELPHIA IN 1787, at 528 (2d ed. 1836), at 546, 554–55. Madison argued that deportation must be classified as a punishment because "if a banishment of this sort be not a punishment, and among the severest of punishments, it will be difficult to imagine a doom to which the name can be applied." *Id.*

128. 342 U.S. 580 (1952).

129. *Id.* at 594.

130. *Id.* at 595.

131. *See, e.g.,* Galvan v. Press, 347 U.S. 522, 530–31 (1954) (footnote omitted) (reaffirming, in case involving ex-Communist Party member, that deportation is not punitive, while stating that "since the intrinsic consequences of deportation are so close to punishment for crime, it might fairly be said also that the [E]x [P]ost [F]acto Clause, even though applicable only to punitive legislation, should be applied to deportation."); *see also id.* at 531 ("And whatever might have been said at an earlier date for applying the ex post facto Clause, it has been the unbroken rule of this Court that it has no application to deportation.").

132. *Harisiades*, 342 U.S. at 598 (Black, J., dissenting, joined by Douglas, J.).

133. *See id.* at 600 ("Banishment is punishment in the practical sense. It may deprive a man and his family of all that makes life worth while. Those who have their roots here have an important stake in this country. Their plans for themselves and their hopes for their children all depend on their right to stay. If they are uprooted and sent to lands no longer known to them, no longer hospitable, they become displaced, homeless people condemned to bitterness and despair.").

134. 353 U.S. 685 (1957).

135. *Id.* at 691 (Black, J., concurring).

136. 349 U.S. 302 (1955).

137. *Id.* at 320 (Douglas, J., dissenting) (citation omitted).

138. 341 U.S. 716 (1951).

139. *Id.* at 722–23.

140. *Id.* at 736 (Black, J., dissenting).

141. 356 U.S. 86 (1958).

142. *Id.* at 96.

143. *Id.* at 96 n.18.

144. *Id.*

145. *Id.*

146. *Id.*

147. *Id.* at 97.

148. *Id.* at 98.

149. *Id.* at 101. In a companion case to *Trop*, the court rejected a challenge to denationalization for the act of voting in a foreign election. Perez v. Brownell, 356 U.S. 44 (1958). Unlike in *Trop*, the court discerned no retributive purpose, reasoning that the sanction was a purely prospective exercise of congressional authority to regulate foreign affairs. *Id.* at 57–62.

150. 363 U.S. 144 (1960).

151. *Id.* at 160.

152. *Id.*

153. 363 U.S. 603 (1960).

154. *Id.* at 613.

155. *Id.* at 614.

156. *Id.* at 616 (quoting *Cummings*, 4 U.S. at 320).

157. *Id.*

158. *See id.* at 616 n.9 ("As prior decisions make clear, *compare Ex parte Garland, supra, with Hawker v. New York, supra,* the severity of a sanction is not determinative of its character as 'punishment.' ").

159. *Id.* at 617.

160. *Id.*

161. *Id.*

162. *Id.*

163. *Id.* at 619.

164. *Id.*

165. *Id.*

166. *See Nestor,* 363 U.S. at 628 (Black, J., dissenting) (stating that the decisions "represent positive precedents on highly important questions of individual liberty which should not be explained away with cobwebbery refinements. If the Court is going to overrule these cases in whole or in part, and adopt the views of previous dissenters, I believe it should be done clearly and forthrightly."); *id.* at 630 (Douglas, J., dissenting) (citing the *Cummings* rule that "[p]unishment . . . includes the 'deprivation or suspension of political or civil rights' "); *id.* at 635, 640 (Brennan, J., dissenting) ("The common sense of it is that he has been punished severely for his past conduct . . . Today's decision is to me a regretful retreat from *Lovett, Cummings,* and *Garland.*").

167. *Id.* at 622 (Black, J., dissenting).

168. *Id.* at 627.

169. *Id.* at 626–27 (citation omitted). Black concluded by saying:

> A basic constitutional infirmity of this Act, in my judgment, is that it is a part of a pattern of laws all of which violate the First Amendment out of fear that this country is in grave danger if it lets a handful of Communist fanatics or some other extremist group make their arguments and discuss their ideas. This fear, I think, is baseless. It reflects a lack of faith in the sturdy patriotism of our people and does not give to the world a true picture of our abiding strength. It is an unworthy fear in a country that has a Bill of Rights containing provisions for fair trials, freedom of speech, press and religion, and other specific safeguards designed to keep men free. I repeat once more that I think this Nation's greatest security lies, not in trusting to a momentary majority of this Court's view at any particular time of what is 'patently arbitrary,' but in wholehearted devotion to and observance of our constitutional freedoms.

> *Id.* at 628. The tone and content of Black's plea are strikingly similar to Justice Chase's assessment in *Calder v. Bull*, 3 U.S. (Dallas) 386 (1798), where when condemning ex post laws in England that figured in the ex post facto prohibition included in the Constitution, he wrote: "The ground for the exercise of such legislative power was this, that the safety of the kingdom depended on the death, or other punishment, of the offender: as if traitors, when discovered, could be so formidable, or the government so insecure!" *Id.* at 389 (Chase, J.).

170. *Nestor*, 363, U.S. at 637 n.3 (Brennan, J., dissenting).
171. *Id.* at 616.
172. *See* Ashwander v. Tennessee Valley Auth., 297 U.S. 288, 347 (1936) (Brandeis, J., concurring) ("The Court will not pass upon a constitutional question although properly presented by the record, if there is also present some other ground upon which the case may be disposed of.").
173. *Nestor*, 363 U.S. at 628 (Black, J., dissenting).
174. 372 U.S. 144 (1963).
175. *Id.* at 168.
176. *Id.* at 168–69.
177. *Id.* at 169.
178. *Id.*
179. *Id.*
180. *Id.* at 169 & 170 n.30.
181. Smith v. Doe, 538 U.S. 84, 97 (2003) (citations omitted). *See also Ward*, 448 U.S. at 250 (stating that factors are "neither exhaustive nor conclusive on the issue").
182. Fletcher v. Peck, 10 U.S. (6 Cranch) 87, 137 (1810) (Marshall, C.J.).
183. 2 U.S. (Dall.) 386, 388 (1798).
184. 432 U.S. 282 (1977).
185. *Id.* at 297.
186. In the case, the court held that a party could not challenge the constitutionality of a bankruptcy law if they did not raise the challenge in an earlier lawsuit, even if the law was deemed unconstitutional in the interim. *See id.* at 297–98 (citing Chicot County Drainage Dist. v. Baxter State Bank, 308 U.S. 371, 374 (1940)).
187. *Id.* at 298. *See also id.* at 297 ("Whether or not the old statute would, in the future, withstand constitutional attack, it clearly indicated Florida's view of the severity of murder and of the degree of punishment which the legislature wished to impose upon murderers").
188. *Id.* at 297.
189. *Id.*
190. *Id.* at 307 (Stevens, J., dissenting).

191. *Id.* at 308.

192. *Id.*

193. *Id.* at 307.

194. *Id.* at 308.

195. *Id.* at 309.

196. *Id.* at 311.

197. 450 U.S. 24 (1981). In the same Term as *Dobbert*, in *Marks v. United States*, 430 U.S. 188 (1977), a case addressing whether due process was violated by retroactive application of judicial interpretation of the standard regarding when material is obscene, the court alluded to the rationale stating "the principle on which the [Ex Post Facto] Clause is based—the notion that persons have a right to fair warning of that conduct which will give rise to criminal penalties—is fundamental to our concept of constitutional liberty." *Id.* at 191.

198. *Weaver*, 450 U.S. at 28–29.

199. *Id.* at 29.

200. *Id.* at 29 n.10.

201. 482 U.S. 423 (1987).

202. *Id.* at 430 (quoting *Weaver*, 450 U.S. at 30).

203. *Id.* at 431.

204. *Collins*, 497 U.S. at 43.

205. *Weaver*, 450 U.S. at 31.

206. A Pennsylvania case, *Commonwealth v. Rose*, 127 A.3d 794 (Pa. 2015), highlights the importance of how a court conceives of the "completed" requirement. In *Rose*, defendants brutally beat and raped a woman, resulting in her hospitalization in a vegetative state. Thereafter, defendant Rose was convicted of attempted murder and other offenses and sentenced. Fourteen years after the assault, the victim died, and Rose was convicted of third-degree murder, and sentenced under a law amended after the assault that doubled the maximum prison term for third-degree murder (compared to the law in effect when the assault occurred). The government argued that the murder was not complete until the victim died, which occurred after the statutory amendment. The *Rose* Court disagreed, concluding that "for purposes of evaluating whether a defendant's sentence violates the Ex Post Facto Clause, the date on which all of the elements of the statutory crime of third-degree murder are met, including the death of the victim, is not dispositive." *Id.* at 802–03. Based on the court's understanding of U.S. Supreme Court case law, the court reasoned that "the Ex Facto Clause was intended to prohibit the legislature from retroactively increasing the punishment not simply for completed crimes, but for an individual's prior criminal acts." *Id.* at 805.

207. At times, statutory law clarifies the issue. *See, e.g.*, State v. Solis, 378 P.3d 532 (Kan. 2016) (applying statute declaring that new criminal code was not applicable to crime for which "any of the essential elements" occurred before the new code's effective date).

208. 114 U.S. 15 (1885).

209. *See* L. Rex Sears, *Punishing the Saints for Their "Peculiar Institution": Congress on the Constitutional Dilemmas*, 2001 UTAH L. REV. 581, 608–14.

210. 114 U.S. 15, 43 (1885). *See also* United States v. Trans-Missouri Freight Ass'n, 166 U.S. 290 (1897) (concluding that action taken post-enactment was criminalized, not prior action).

211. 180 U.S. 311 (1901).

212. *Id.* at 312–13. The court reiterated its position on the question several decades later in *Gryger v. Burke*, 334 U.S. 728 (1948), stating that the enhanced penalty "is not to be viewed as either a new jeopardy or additional penalty for the earlier crimes. It is a stiffened penalty for the latest crime, which is considered to be an aggravated offense because a repetitive one." *Id.* at 732.

213. 267 U.S. 188 (1925).

214. *Id.* at 193.

215. *See, e.g.*, United States v. McKenzie, 922 F.2d 1323 (7th Cir. 1991).

216. J. Richard Broughton, *On Straddle Crimes and the Ex Post Facto Clauses*, 18 Geo. Mason L. Rev. 719, 720 (2011).

217. *Id.* The "straddle" concept also figures in penalty enhancement situations (concerning *Calder* categories two and three, as opposed to category one), addressed in Chapter 5.

218. *Id.* at 725.

219. *See, e.g.*, United States v. Manges, 110 F.3d 1162 (5th Cir. 1997).

220. Broughton, *supra* note 216, at 742.

221. Cal. Dep't of Corr. v. Morales, 514 U.S. 499, 510 n.7 (1995).

222. *Ex Parte Wall*, 107 U.S. 265, 302 (1883) (Field, J., dissenting).

223. *Id.* at 297.

224. *Weaver*, 450 U.S. at 28.

225. *Cf.* Warden v. Marrero, 417 U.S. 653, 663 (1974) (citation omitted) (stating in dictum that "a repealer of parole eligibility previously available to imprisoned offenders would clearly present the serious question under the ex post facto clause of Art. I, s 9, cl. 3, of the Constitution, of whether it imposed a 'greater or more severe punishment than was prescribed by law at the time of the . . . offense,'"). The list excludes *Kring v. Missouri* (1883) and *Thompson v. Utah* (1898), decisions granting relief to petitioners, which were later overruled by the court in *Collins v. Youngblood* (1990).

Chapter 5

1. *See generally* Wayne A. Logan, *Federal Habeas in the Information Age*, 85 Minn. L. Rev. 147, 161–67 (2000) (discussing rapid enactment of state and federal laws targeting sex offenders, including those allowing for involuntary confinement and registration and community notification); Jonathan Simon, *Megan's Law: Crime and Democracy in Late Modern America*, 25 Law & Soc. Inquiry 1111, 1139–42 (2000) (describing political and social forces inspiring registration and community notification laws).

2. Kristen Budd & Scott Desmond, *Sex Offenders and Sex Crime Recidivism: Investigating the Role of Sentence Length and Time Served*, 58 Intl. J. of Off. Therapy & Comp. Criminology 1481 (2014).

3. *See generally* Margaret Love, Jenny Roberts, and Wayne A. Logan, Collateral Consequences of Arrest and Conviction: Law, Policy and Practice (2021 ed.).

4. *See* Michael Tonry, *Rethinking Unthinkable Punishment Policies in America*, 46 UCLA L. Rev. 1751, 1752 (1999) (noting that "[w]e live in a repressive era when punishment policies that would be unthinkable in other times and places are not only commonplace but also are enthusiastically supported by public officials, policy intellectuals, and much of the general public").

5. *See* Katherine Beckett, *Political Preoccupation with Crime Leads, Not Follows, Public Opinion, in* PENAL REFORM IN OVERCROWDED TIMES 40 (Michael Tonry ed., 2001) (recognizing that "crime and punishment have taken a front-row seat in the theater of American political discourse"). *See also generally* KATHERINE BECKETT, MAKING CRIME PAY: LAW AND ORDER IN CONTEMPORARY AMERICAN POLITICS (1997); DAVID GARLAND, THE CULTURE OF CONTROL: CRIME AND SOCIAL ORDER IN CONTEMPORARY SOCIETY (2001); JONATHAN SIMON, GOVERNING THROUGH CRIME: CRIMINAL LAW AND THE RESHAPING OF AMERICAN GOVERNMENT 1965–2000 (2004); Harry A. Chernoff et al., *The Politics of Crime*, 33 HARV. J. ON LEGIS. 527 (1996).

6. *See* WAYNE A. LOGAN & MICHAEL O'HEAR, SENTENCING LAW, POLICY, AND PRACTICE at ch. 2 (2022). During the 1990s, US jurisdictions dispensed almost 16 million "person-years" of incarceration, roughly 4.5 million more years than if confinement rates would have remained unchanged after 1990. *See* HENRY RUTH & KEVIN R. REITZ, THE CHALLENGE OF CRIME: RETHINKING OUR RESPONSE 21 (2003). For an insightful examination of the factors contributing to this resort to punitive severity, *see* David Cole, *As Freedom Advances: The Paradox of Severity in American Criminal Justice*, 3 U. PA. J. CONST. L. 455 (2001).

7. *See generally* WAYNE A. LOGAN, KNOWLEDGE AS POWER: CRIMINAL REGISTRATION AND COMMUNITY NOTIFICATION LAWS IN AMERICA 85–90 (2009) [hereinafter Knowledge]. *See also, e.g.*, H.R. Rep. No. 104–555 at 2 (1996), reprinted in 1996 U.S.C.C.A.N. 980, 981 ("Perhaps no type of crime has received more attention in recent years than crimes against children involving sexual acts and violence"); Peter Davis, *The Sex Offender Next Door*, N.Y. TIMES MAG., July 28, 1996, at 20 (analogizing outcast-status of released sex offender to that of a leper); Mimi Hall, *A Furor Brews Over Release of Sex Offenders*, USA TODAY, Aug. 17, 1994, at A3 (describing nationwide public anger over sex crimes committed by recidivists and chronicling legislative efforts to address problem).

8. *See* LOGAN, KNOWLEDGE, *supra* note 7, at 49–108.

9. Eric S. Janus & Wayne A. Logan, *Substantive Due Process and the Involuntary Confinement of Sexually Violent Predators*, 35 CONN. L. REV. 319, 325 (2003).

10. *Id.* at 382.

11. *In re Hendricks*, 912 P.2d 129, 136–37 (Kan. 1996), *rev'd*, Kansas v. Hendricks, 521 U.S. 346 (1997).

12. 521 U.S. 346 (1997).

13. *See id.* at 361 (citing and quoting Allen v. Illinois, 478 U.S. 364 (1986)).

14. *Id.* .

15. *Id.* (quoting *Allen*, 478 U.S. at 369).

16. *Id.* (quoting United States v. Ward, 448 U.S. 242, 248–49 (1980)).

17. *Id.*

18. *Id.*

19. *Id.* at 361–62.

20. *Id.* at 362.

21. *Id.*

22. *Id.*

23. *Id.*

24. *Id.* at 350.

25. *Id.* at 363.

26. *Id.*

27. *Id.* at 350.
28. *Id.* at 364–65.
29. *Id.* at 366.
30. *Id.*
31. *Id.* at 367.
32. *Id.* at 371.
33. *Id.*
34. *Id.*
35. *Id.* at 372 (Kennedy, J., concurring).
36. *Id.* at 373 (Breyer, J., dissenting).
37. *Id.* at 381.
38. *Id.* at 383.
39. *Id.* at 385–86.
40. *Id.* at 387.
41. *Id.* at 387–88.
42. *Id.* at 395.
43. *Id.* at 396.
44. Earlier, in *Austin v. United States*, 509 U.S. 602 (1993), the court made clear that *Mendoza-Martinez* is inapposite when the claim before the court turns on whether "punishment" is being imposed—as opposed to whether a "criminal proceeding" is at issue (as in *Mendoza-Martinez*, regarding Fifth and Sixth Amendment procedural protections). *Id.* at 610 n.6. Although *Hendricks* indisputably posed a "punishment question," in particular whether the SVPA retroactively extended a sentence, Justice Thomas, as noted, mistakenly framed the question as being whether the SVPA established "criminal proceedings for constitutional purposes." *Hendricks*, 521 U.S. at 360–61.

    The court's move has not gone unnoticed by the lower courts. The Ninth Circuit, in a decision rejecting an ex post facto challenge against a retroactive sex offender registration and notification law, observed how *Hendricks* imported Double Jeopardy caselaw into its ex post facto analysis:

    > We are mindful that [*United States v.*] *Ursery* was a Double Jeopardy Clause case, and that it warned against lifting a test for punishment from one constitutional provision and applying it to another. In *Hendricks*, however, the Court used the same test for the Double Jeopardy and Ex Post Facto Clauses, leading us to conclude that the test for punishment is the same for both clauses.

    Russell v. Gregoire, 124 F.3d 1079, 1086 n.6 (9th Cir. 1997).
45. 71 U.S. 277 (1867).
46. *Id.* at 320 (emphasis added).
47. 363 U.S. 144 (1960).
48. *Id.* at 147. *See also, e.g.*, John F. Manning, *Textualism as a Nondelegation Doctrine*, 97 COLUM. L. REV. 673, 733 n.253 (1997) (recognizing that "[c]ourts have traditionally examined the events precipitating a statute's enactment to gain insight into its meaning").
49. *See* Stephen R. McAllister, *The Constitutionality of Kansas Laws Targeting Sex Offenders*, 36 WASHBURN L.J. 419, 427 (1997) (noting that sentence enhancements and the SVPA were enacted in "response to the Stephanie Schmidt case," involving a widely reported horrific rape and murder).
50. *Id.* at 434.

51. Brief for the American Psychiatric Ass'n as Amicus Curiae in Support of Leroy Hendricks at 13–14, Kansas v. Hendricks, 117 S. Ct. 2072 (1997) (Nos. 95–1649, 95–9075).

52. Brief of the American Civil Liberties Union et al. as Amici Curiae in Support of Respondent at 23, Kansas v. Hendricks, 117 S. Ct. 2072 (1997) (No. 95–1649).

53. *Id.*

54. Brief for the National Ass'n of Criminal Defense Lawyers and the Kansas Ass'n of Criminal Defense Lawyers as Amici Curiae in Support of Leroy Hendricks at 24, Kansas v. Hendricks, 117 S. Ct. 2072 (1997) (Nos. 95–1649, 95–9075).

55. *Id.*

56. *Id.*

57. *In re Hendricks*, 912 P.2d 129, 136 (Kan. 1996), *rev'd. sub nom.*, Kansas v. Hendricks, 521 U.S. 346 (1997).

58. *Id. See also Hendricks*, 521 U.S. at 386 (Breyer, J., dissenting) ("It is difficult to see why rational legislators who seek treatment would write the Act in this way—providing treatment years after the criminal act that indicated its necessity."). That Kansas felt "predators" to be unamenable to treatment before release, while still in prison, is evident from the Preamble of the SVPA itself: "The legislature further finds that the prognosis for rehabilitating sexually violent predators in a prison setting is poor . . ." Kan. Stat. Ann. § 59-29a01 (1994).

59. *See* McAllister, *supra* note 49, at 422–30 (noting that the state also adopted a registration and community notification law and substantially increased sentences for sex offender convictions).

60. Kelly A. McCaffrey, Comment, *The Civil Commitment of Sexually Violent Predators in Kansas: A Modern Law for Modern Times*, 42 KAN. L. REV. 887, 888 (1994). Bills proposing involuntary post-confinement commitment were proposed in the 1991 and 1992 Kansas legislative sessions, but were defeated both times in the House. The Schmidt murder and rape ignited new interest, resulting in the law's ultimate convincing margin of victory in 1994. *See id.* at 889.

61. *Id.*

62. *Hendricks*, 521 U.S. at 372 (Kennedy, J. concurring) (citing testimony of Schmidt Task Force Member Jim Blaufuss). The State of Washington's sexual predator law, which was the blueprint for that later enacted by Kansas, was borne of strikingly similar public outrage and fury, likewise stemming from a high-profile sexual assault. As in Kansas, the governor appointed a task force, and the task force's proposals steamrolled through the legislature (by a unanimous vote). *See* David Boerner, *Confronting Violence: In the Act and In the World*, 15 U. PUGET SOUND L. REV. 525, 575 (1992). Mr. Boerner, a task force member and chief drafter of the statute, commented: "I had no doubt that if the legislature was to extend the length of the sentences previously imposed, the courts would find the legislation unconstitutional. While the members of the Task Force could accept the legal judgment, they could not accept the result." *Id.* at 550. A similar history characterized the enactment of New Jersey's sexually violent predator law. *See* Claudine M. Leone, *New Jersey Assembly Bill 155, A Bill Allowing the Civil Commitment of Violent Sex Offenders After the Completion of a Criminal Sentence*, 18 SETON HALL LEGIS. J. 890 (1994).

63. Hendricks also brought double jeopardy, ex post facto, equal protection, and procedural due process claims but the Kansas Supreme Court resolved the matter on substantive due process grounds alone and did not address the other claims. *In re Hendricks*, 912 P.2d 129, 138 (Kan. 1996), *rev'd. sub nom.*, Kansas v. Hendricks, 521 U.S. 346 (1997).

64. *Id.* at 136.

65. Lindsey v. Washington, 301 U.S. 397, 400 (1937). Justice Breyer, dissenting, also challenged the *Hendricks* majority for this failure. *See Hendricks*, 521 U.S. at 383–84 (Breyer, J., dissenting). *Cf., e.g.*, Romer v. Evans, 517 U.S. 620, 626 (1996) (noting that in an equal protection challenge a state court provides "authoritative construction" of the state provision challenged).

66. Because retribution and revenge play a central role in the impulse to punish, logic would dictate that the effort to discern this purpose should be peculiarly sensitive to identifying vengeful sentiments expressed by a law's proponents. *See* JAMES F. STEPHEN, A GENERAL VIEW OF THE CRIMINAL LAW OF ENGLAND 99 (MacMillan, 1863) ("[T]he criminal law stands to the passion of revenge in much the same relation as marriage to the sexual appetite."). *See also* Joel Feinberg, *The Expressive Function of Punishment*, reprinted in THE PHILOSOPHY OF LAW 636 (4th ed. 1991) ("Punishment is a conventional device for the expression of attitudes of disapproval and reprobation, either on the part of the punishing authority or of those in whose name the punishment is imposed.").

67. 71 U.S. 277 (1867).

68. *Id.* at 322.

69. *Id.*

70. *Id.*

71. *Hendricks*, 521 U.S. at 381 (Breyer, J., dissenting).

72. *Id.* at 379 (citing state administrator's testimony).

73. *In re Hendricks*, 912 P.2d at 139 (Lockett, J., concurring).

74. Stephen J. Schulhofer, *Two Systems of Social Protection: Comments on the Civil-Criminal Distinction, with Particular Reference to Sexually Violent Predator Laws*, 7 J. CONTEMP. LEGAL ISS. 69, 78–79 (1996).

75. *Hendricks*, 521 U.S. at 396 (Breyer, J., dissenting).

76. *See, e.g.*, Smith v. Doe, 538 U.S. 84, 104 (2003).

77. 531 U.S. 250 (2001).

78. *Id.* at 263.

79. *Id.*

80. *Id.*

81. *Id.* at 267.

82. *Id.* at 263.

83. *Id.* at 269 (Scalia, J., concurring) (citations and footnote omitted).

84. *Id.* at 269 n.*

85. *Id.* at 267–68 (Scalia, J., concurring).

86. *Id.* at 272 (Thomas, J., concurring).

87. *Id.* at 276–77 (Stevens, J., dissenting).

88. *Id.*

89. *Id.* at 275.

90. Id. at 263.

91. LOGAN, KNOWLEDGE, *supra* note 7, at 20–48.

92. *Id.* at 49–84. The New Jersey legislature, embroiled in an election year, and under an emergency suspension of its rules that resulted in no hearings in the State House and limited hearings in the Senate, approved its law within a mere three months of the rape and murder of seven-year-old Megan Kanka by a convicted sex offender who lived nearby. *See* Symposium, *Critical Perspectives on Megan's Law: Protection vs. Privacy*, 13 N.Y.L.S. J. HUM. RTS. 1, 57 (1997). *See also* Robert Hanley, *Megan's Law Is Questioned*

as Injunction Is Extended, N.Y. TIMES, July 10, 1996, at B6 (recounting that legislators rushed bill through session with scant hearings in response to plea of Megan's parents and supporters); Bill Sanderson, *Glamour Politics Isn't the Name of the Game*, THE RECORD (New Jersey), Sept. 3, 1995, at O5 ("After a tearful testimonial from Megan Kanka's mother, the lawmakers ignored the few witnesses who raised questions.").

93. 538 U.S. 84 (2003).
94. *Id.* at 92 (citing Kansas v. Hendricks, 52 U.S. 346, 361 (1997)).
95. *Id.* (quoting United States v. Ward, 448 U.S. 242, 248–49 (1980)).
96. *Id.* (quoting *Ward*, 448 U.S. at 249).
97. *Id.* (citations omitted).
98. *Id.* at 93 (quoting *Hendricks*, 521 U.S. at 363).
99. *Id.* at 94.
100. *Id.*
101. *Id.* at 95.
102. *Id.* at 96.
103. 372 U.S. 144, 168–69 (1963).
104. *Smith*, 538 U.S. at 97.
105. *Id.* (citations omitted).
106. *Id.*
107. *Id.* at 98.
108. *Id.* at 99.
109. *Id.* at 100.
110. *Id.* at 101.
111. *Id.* at 102.
112. *Id.*
113. *Id.* (citation omitted).
114. *Id.* at 102–03.
115. *Id.* at 103.
116. *Id.*
117. *Id.* at 104.
118. *Id.* at 103 (quoting McKune v. Lile, 536 U.S. 24, 34 (2002)).
119. *Id.* at 105.
120. *Id.*
121. *Id.*
122. *Id.* at 105.
123. *Id.* at 106 (Thomas, J., concurring).
124. *Id.*
125. *Id.* at 107 (Souter, J., concurring).
126. *Id.*
127. *Id.* at 108.
128. *Id.*
129. *Id.* at 108–09.
130. *Id.* at 109.
131. *Id.*
132. *Id.* at 110.
133. *Id.*
134. *Id.* at 112 (Stevens, J., dissenting).

135. *Id.* at 113.

136. *Id.* at 114–15 (Ginsburg, J., dissenting).

137. *Id.* at 116.

138. *Id.*

139. *Id.* at 117.

140. *See, e.g.*, Clark v. Ryan, 836 F.3d 1013 (9th Cir. 2016) (rejecting challenge to Arizona SORN law); Shaw v. Patton, 823 F.3d 556 (10th Cir. 2016) (rejecting challenge to Oklahoma SORN law); Doe v. Cuomo, 755 F.3d 105, 111–12 (2d Cir. 2014) (rejecting challenge to federal SORN law); ACLU of Nev. v. Masto, 670 F.3d 1046 (9th Cir. 2012) (rejecting challenge to Nevada SORN law); State v. Aschbrenner, 926 N.W.2d 240 (Iowa 2019) (rejecting challenge to Iowa SORN law); Kammerer v. State, 322 P.3d 827 (Wyo. 2014) (rejecting challenge to Wyoming SORN law).

   One notable exception in the federal appellate courts is *Does #1-5 v. Snyder*, 834 F.3d 696 (6th Cir. 2016), *cert denied*, 138 S. Ct. 55 (2017), where the Sixth Circuit Court of Appeals deemed punitive Michigan's SORN law, which had the added important feature of significantly restricting where registrants could live. Also, as discussed in Chapter 6, several state supreme courts have resisted *Smith v. Doe* and invalidated state SORN laws on the basis of the U.S. or their own state constitutions' ex post facto provisions. For discussion of *Snyder* and the state decisions see Wayne A. Logan, *Challenging the Punitiveness of "New Generation" SORN Laws*, 21 New Crim. L. Rev. 426 (2018).

141. *See, e.g.*, Doe v. Miller, 405 F.3d 700, 718 (8th Cir. 2005) (relying on *Smith* in upholding Iowa residence exclusion law); *In re Justin B.*, 747 S.E.2d 774 (S.C. 2013) (relying on *Smith* in upholding lifetime electronic monitoring).

142. *Smith*, 538, U.S. at 113 (Stevens, J., dissenting).

143. 363 U.S. 603 (1960).

144. *See id.* at 637 n.3 (Brennan, J., joined by Warren, C.J., and Douglas, J., dissenting):

   > The Court, recognizing that *Cummings v. Missouri*, . . . and *Ex Parte Garland* . . . strongly favor the conclusion that s 202(n) was enacted with punitive intent, rejects the force of those precedents as drawing "heavily on the Court's first-hand acquaintance with the events and the mood of the then recent Civil War, and 'the fierce passions which that struggle aroused.'" This seems to me to say that the provision of s 202(n) which cuts off [social security] benefits from aliens deported for past Communist Party membership was not enacted in a similar atmosphere. Our judicial detachment from the realities of the national scene should not carry us so far. Our memory of the emotional climate stirred by the question of communism in the early 1950's cannot be so short.

   See also id. at 622 (Black, J., dissenting) ("The fact that the Court is sustaining this action indicates the extent to which people are willing to go these days to overlook violations of the Constitution perpetrated against anyone who has ever even innocently belonged to the Communist Party."); *id.* at 627 (noting "the general fashion of the day—that is, to punish in every way possible anyone who ever made the mistake of being a Communist in this country or who is supposed ever to have been associated with anyone who made that mistake").

145. *Smith*, 521 U.S. at 109 (Souter, J., concurring).

146. *See, e.g.*, Malloy v. South Carolina, 237 U.S. 180, 185 (1915) (finding no increase in punishment when death penalty law was amended to require death by electrocution rather than by hanging); Rooney v. North Dakota, 196 U.S. 319, 326 (1905) (finding no increase in

punishment when capital prisoners were subject to six to nine months in "close confinement" before execution, when original law required confinement in county jail for three to six months); *In re Medley*, 134 U.S. 160, 171 (1890) (invalidating law mandating solitary confinement for inmates awaiting execution because law imposed "additional punishment of the most important and painful character").

147. *See* Miller v. Florida, 482 U.S. 423, 435–36 (1987) (invalidating increase in prison term based on retroactive application of sentencing guidelines); Weaver v. Graham, 450 U.S. 24, 30 (1981) (invalidating retroactive cancellation of "good time" early release credits for inmates); Lindsey v. Washington, 301 U.S. 397, 401–02 (1937) (invalidating law that mandated a fifteen-year prison term, in lieu of prior law providing for a fifteen-year maximum, and made parole revocable at will). In *Lindsey*, the court held that it was irrelevant for ex post facto purposes that the sentence actually received by petitioners was permitted under both the new and old laws:

> It is true that petitioners might have been sentenced to fifteen years under the old statute. But the ex post facto clause looks to the standard of punishment prescribed by a statute, rather than to the sentence actually imposed. The Constitution forbids the application of any new punitive measure to a crime already consummated, to the detriment or material disadvantage of the wrongdoer. It is for this reason that an increase in the possible penalty is ex post facto, regardless of the length of the sentence actually imposed, since the measure of punishment prescribed by the later statute is more severe than that of the earlier.

Lindsey, 301 U.S. at 401 (citations omitted).

148. 514 U.S. 499 (1995).
149. *Id.* at 504.
150. *Id.* at 507.
151. *Id.* at 508 (quoting Miller v. Florida, 482 U.S. 423, 433 (1987)).
152. *Id.* at 509.
153. *Id.* at 506 n.3.
154. *Id.* at 509. The majority added that the Ex Post Facto Clause "does [not] require that the sentence be carried out under the identical legal regime that previously prevailed." *Id.* at 510 n.6.
155. *Id.* at 508.
156. *Id.* at 508–09.
157. *Id.* at 507.
158. *Id.* at 516 (Stevens, J., dissenting).
159. *Id.* at 522.
160. *Id.* at 526.
161. 519 U.S. 433 (1997).
162. *Id.* at 435.
163. Harold J. Krent, *Should* Bouie *Be Buoyed?: Judicial Retroactive Lawmaking and the Ex Post Facto Clause*, 3 ROGER WILLIAMS U. L. REV. 35, 35 (1997).
164. *Hendricks*, 519 U.S at 436.
165. *Id.* at 440.
166. *Id.* at 443.
167. *Id.* at 447. According to the court, "retroactive alteration of parole or early release provisions, like the retroactive application of provisions that govern initial sentencing, implicates the Ex Post Facto Clause because such credits are 'one determinant of

petitioner's prison term . . . and . . . [the petitioner's] effective sentence is altered once this determinant is changed.'" *Id.* at 445 (quoting Weaver v. Graham, 450 U.S. 24, 32 (1981)). *See also* Greenfield v. Scafati, 277 F. Supp. 644 (D. Mass. 1967), *aff'd per curiam*, 390 U.S. 713 (1968) (invalidating retrospective alteration of good-time credit system so that inmate violating parole would be barred from securing good-time credits upon return to prison).

168. *Id.* at 446 n.16, 447. The court, in a footnote, acknowledged the "sufficient risk" standard used in *Morales*. *Id.* at 443 n.14.

169. *Id.* at 442 (quoting *Weaver*, 450 U.S. at 33).

170. *Id.* at 450 (Thomas, J., concurring) (quoting *Morales*, 54 U.S. at 514).

171. *Id.*

172. *Id.*

173. 259 U.S. 244 (2000).

174. *Id.* at 251 (emphasis added). Notably, the court provided a general cite to *Morales* in support, despite the term being absent from the articulation of the test there (and in *Lynce*, for that matter).

175. *Id.* at 255.

176. *Id.*

177. *Id.* at 257.

178. 450 U.S. 24 (1981).

179. *Id.* at 33.

180. 51 U.S. 250 (2001).

181. *Garner*, 529 U.S. at 245.

182. *See, e.g.*, Gilman v. Brown, 814 F.3d 1007, 1016 (9th Cir. 2016) ("proving a significant risk of prolonged incarceration requires exacting evidence . . . [A] decrease is the frequency of parole hearings—without more—is not sufficient to prove a significant risk of lengthened incarceration.").

183. *See, e.g.*, Snodgrass v. Robinson, 512 F.3d 999, 1002 (8th Cir. 2008) (applying standard to change in commutation provision); Scott v. Baldwin, 225 F.3d 1020, 1022–23 (9th Cir. 2000) (applying standard to biennial review of dangerous offender review status).

184. Peugh v. United States, 569 U.S 530, 554 (2013) (using "sufficient" risk); *id.* at 550 (using "significant" risk). More recently, in restating the *Peugh* test in a case alleging that the federal sentencing guidelines were unconstitutionally vague, the court stated that its "ex post facto cases have focused on whether a change in law creates a 'significant risk' of a 'higher sentence.'" Beckles v. United States, 137 S. Ct. 886, 895 (2017) (quoting *Peugh*, 138 S. Ct. at 2018).

185. *Id.* at 255.

186. *See, e.g.*, Weaver v. Graham, 450 U.S. 24, 33 (1981) ("[Ex post facto] inquiry looks to the challenged provision, and not to . . . its effect on the particular individual."); Dobbert v. Florida, 432 U.S. 282, 294 (1977) (court looks at the new procedure in toto, rather than to any effect that it may have had on the defendant challenging it).

187. *See* Ronald F. Wright, *Three Strikes Legislation and Sentencing Commission Objectives*, 20 LAW & POL'Y 429, 430 (1998) (surveying legislative efforts nationwide in the mid-1990s to enact "three strikes laws").

188. 482 U.S. 423 (1987).

189. *Id.* at 432–33.

190. *Id.* at 435.

191. *See generally* KATE STITH & JOSÉ A. CABRANES, FEAR OF JUDGING (1998); *see also* Ilene H. Nagel, *Structuring Sentencing Discretion: The New Federal Sentencing Guidelines*, 80 J. CRIM. L. & CRIMINOLOGY 883, 883 (1990) ("The purpose of the [Sentencing Reform] Act was to attack the tripartite problems of disparity, dishonesty, and for some offenses, excessive leniency, all seemingly made worse by a system of near unfettered judicial discretion.").

192. 543 U.S. 220 (2005).

193. Freeman v. United States, 543 U.S. 522 (2011).

194. 569 U.S. 530 (2013).

195. *Peugh*, 569 U.S. at 543.

196. *Id.* at 544, 550.

197. *Id.* at 547.

198. *Id.* at 544 (citing THE FEDERALIST No. 44, p. 282 (C. Rossiter ed. 1961) (J. Madison)).

199. *Id.* (quoting Carmell v. Texas, 529 U.S. 533 (2000)).

200. *Id.* at 545.

201. *Id.*

202. Id. at 555 (Thomas, J., dissenting).

203. *Id.* at 552–55.

204. *Id.* at 558.

205. *Id.*

206. *Id.* (quoting *Calder*, 3 U.S. (Dall.) at 390).

207. *Id.* at 561 (Thomas, J., dissenting).

208. *Id.* at 560.

209. *Id.* at 559 fn.*.

210. *Id.* at 560.

211. *Id.* at 562–63.

212. *Id.* at 563 (Thomas, J., dissenting). *See also id.* at 563 ("The statutory range in effect at the time of petitioner's offense remained in effect at his sentencing. The Guidelines sentencing range is not the punishment affixed to the offense . . . Accordingly, sentencing petitioner under the amended Guidelines did not violate the Ex Post Facto Clause.").

213. *Id.* at 563 (Alito, J., dissenting).

214. *Id.*

215. *See Collins*, 497 U.S. at 54 (Stevens, J., concurring) (noting the "critical importance of evaluating the [rights of the defendant] by reference to the time of the offense").

216. 450 U.S. 24 (1981).

217. *Id.* at 31.

218. 180 U.S. 311 (1901).

219. *Id.* at 312–13.

220. 334 U.S. 728 (1948).

221. *Id.* at 732.

222. 267 U.S. 188 (1925).

223. *Id.* at 202.

224. Devon F. Ferris, Note, *Reconciling Ex Post Facto Analysis and Straddle Offenses: Alternative Approaches to Incomplete Crimes in* Commonwealth v. Rose, 54 DUQ. L. REV. 451 (2016).

225. *See, e.g.*, United States v. Brennan, 326 F.3d 176 (3d Cir. 2003).

226. U.S. Sentencing Commission, *Guidelines Manual* § 1B1.11(b)(3) (2015).

227. *Id.* § 1B1.11(b)(2).

228. *Id.* § 1B1.11(b)(1).
229. 736 F.3d 573, 598 (1st Cir. 2013).
230. *Id.* at 599.
231. 944 F.3d 352 (1st Cir. 2019).
232. *Id.* at 356.
233. *Id.* (citing United States v. Butler, 429 F.3d 140 (5th Cir. 2005)).
234. 3 U.S. 386 (1798).
235. Calder v. Bull, 3 U.S. (3 Dall.) 386, 390 (1798) (opinion of Chase, J.).
236. *Id.* at 391.
237. 529 U.S. 513 (2000).
238. *See* Akhil Reed Amar, *The Supreme Court, 1999 Term-—Foreword: The Document and the Doctrine*, 113 HARV. L. REV. 26, 96 (2000) (noting unprecedented nature of agreement among Justices Stevens, Souter, Thomas, Scalia, and Breyer). Although it cannot be said for certain, of course, the strong originalist tenor and content of Justice Stevens's opinion for the majority likely significantly contributed to garnering the votes of Justices Scalia and Thomas in particular. It also bears mention that ultimately, despite "winning" his case, Carmell remained subject to lifetime imprisonment as the result of other intact convictions, an outcome that perhaps affected the votes of Justices Thomas and Scalia, who otherwise do not often side with criminal defendants.
239. *Carmell*, 529 U.S. at 530.
240. *Id.* (citing *Calder*, 3 U.S. at 390).
241. *Id.* at 526-30.
242. *Id.* at 531.
243. *Id.* Stevens, in a footnote, added that:

> The Clause is, of course, also aimed at other concerns, "namely that legislative enactments give fair warning of their effect and permit individuals to rely on their meaning until explicitly changed," . . . and at reinforcing the separation of powers. . . . But those are not its only aims, and the absence of a reliance interest is not an argument in favor of abandoning the category itself. If it were, the same conclusion would follow for *Calder*'s third category (increases in punishment), as there are few, if any, reliance interests in planning future criminal activities based on the expectation of less severe repercussions.

> *Id.* at 531 n. 21 (quoting Miller v. Florida, 482 U.S. 423, 430 (1987), and citing Weaver v. Graham, 450 U.S. 24, 29 n.10 (1981)).

244. *Id.* at 532.
245. 519 U.S. 433, 440 (1997) (stating that "the Constitution places limits on the sovereign's ability to use its lawmaking power to modify bargains it has made with its subjects.").
246. *Carmell*, 529 U.S. at 532-33. According to Justice Stevens, "the pertinent rule altered in Fenwick's case went directly to the general issue of guilt, lowering the minimum quantum of evidence required to obtain a conviction. The Framers, quite clearly, viewed such maneuvers as grossly unfair, and adopted the Ex Post Facto Clause accordingly." *Id.* at 534.
247. *Id.* at 533. The court hastened to add, in a footnote, that not all changes in evidentiary law implicate the Ex Post Facto Clause:

> Ordinary rules of evidence, for example, do not violate the Clause. Rules of that nature are ordinarily evenhanded, in the sense that they may benefit either the State or the defendant in any given case. More crucially, such rules, by simply permitting evidence to be admitted at trial, do not at all subvert the presumption of innocence,

because they do not concern whether the admissible evidence is sufficient to overcome the presumption. Moreover, while the principle of unfairness helps explain and shape the Clause's scope, it is not a doctrine unto itself, invalidating laws under the Ex Post Facto Clause by its own force.

Id. at 533 n.23 (citation omitted).

248. *Id.* at 534–37.

249. *Carmell*, 529 U.S. at 538. "The better understanding of *Collins*," Justice Stevens contended, was "that it eliminated a doctrinal hitch" embodied in cases it overruled—*Kring v. Missouri* (1883) and *Thompson v. Utah* (1898)—"which purported to define the scope of the Clause along an axis distinguishing between laws involving 'substantial protections' and those that are merely 'procedural.'" *Id.* at 539.

250. *Id.*

251. *Id.* at 544.

252. *Id.* at 545. According to the court:

Under the law in effect at the time the acts were committed, the prosecution's case was legally insufficient . . . unless the state could produce both the victim's testimony and corroborative evidence. The amended law, however, changed the quantum of evidence necessary to sustain a conviction; under the new law, petitioner could be (and was) convicted on the victim's testimony alone, without any corroborating evidence.

Id. at 530.

253. *Id.* at 545.

254. *Id.* at 546.

255. *Id.* at 562 (Ginsburg, J., dissenting).

256. *Id.* at 566–67.

257. *Id.* at 567.

258. *Id.* at 566–70.

259. *Id.* at 567.

260. *Id.* at 568.

261. *Id.*

262. *Id.*

263. *Id.* at 573.

264. Despite *Carmell*'s formal re-recognition of the category, lower courts have continued to cite the truncated three-category list stated in *Beazell*. *See, e.g.*, United States v. Coleman, 675 F.3d 615, 619 (6th Cir. 2012); United States v. Rubenstein, 228 F. Supp. 3d 223, 230 (E.D.N.Y. 2017).

265. *Carmell*, 529 U.S. at 533 n.23.

266. 539 U.S. 607 (2003).

267. *Calder*, 3 U.S. (3 Dall.) at 390 (opinion of Chase, J.).

268. *Stogner*, 539 U.S. at 609–10.

269. *Id.* (quoting Calder v. Bull, 3 U.S. (3 Dall.) 386, 391 (1798), and Falter v. United States, 23 F.2d 420, 426 (2d Cir. 1928) (Hand, J.)).

270. *Id.* at 611 (quoting *Carmell*, 529 U.S. at 533).

271. *Id.*

272. *Id.*

273. *Id.* at 612–13 (quoting *Calder*, 3 U.S. at 389).

274. *Id.* at 613.

275. *Id.* at 613–14.

276. *Id.* at 615–16.

277. *Id.* at 616–21.

278. *Id.* at 621.

279. Id. at 631–32.

280. *Id.* at 632 (Kennedy, J., dissenting).

281. *Id.* at 640.

282. *Id.*

283. *Id.* at 641.

284. *Id.* at 653.

285. *Id.* at 633; *see also id.* at 653 (condemning the "Court's stretching of *Calder*'s second category").

286. Although not noted by the dissent, the Chase opinion in *Calder* also cited retroactive laws that "save time from the statute of limitations" as an example of a law that may be "proper or necessary, as the case may be." *Calder*, 3 U.S. (Dall.) at 391. Whether Chase had in mind extensions of *unexpired* statutes of limitation, which modern courts (including in *Stogner*) consider proper, remains unknown.

287. St. Regis Paper Co. v. United States, 368 U.S. 208, 229 (1961) (Black, J., dissenting).

288. *See* ADAM SAMPSON, ACTS OF ABUSE: SEX OFFENDERS AND THE CRIMINAL JUSTICE SYSTEM 124 (1994) (observing that the "vehemence of the hatred for sex offenders is unmatched by attitudes to any other offenders").

Chapter 6

1. Calder v. Bull, 3 U.S. (3 Dall.) 386, 390 (1798) (Chase, J.).

2. *Id.* at 391.

3. *Id.*

4. Dobbert v. Florida, 432 U.S. 282, 292 (1997) ("Our cases have not attempted to precisely delimit the scope of this Latin [ex post facto], but have instead given it substance by an accretion of case law.").

5. *See* California Dep't of Corr. v. Morales, 514 U.S. 499, 509 (1995) (citation omitted) (noting that the court has "declined to articulate a single 'formula'" for identifying when retroactive laws violate the clause).

6. 2 THE RECORDS OF THE FEDERAL CONVENTION OF 1787, at 376 (Max Farrand ed., 1911).

7. *Id.*

8. *Id.*

9. THE FEDERALIST PAPERS No. 44, at 282 (James Madison) (Clinton Rossiter ed., 1961) [hereinafter THE FEDERALIST]. Joseph Story, respected legal scholar and US Supreme Court justice, later echoed this same sentiment: "[r]etrospective laws . . . neither accord with sound legislation nor with the fundamental principles of the social compact." 2 JOSEPH STORY, COMMENTARIES ON THE CONSTITUTION OF THE UNITED STATES § 1398 (Melville M. Bigelow ed., 1994).

10. THE FEDERALIST No. 44, *supra* note 9, at 282–83 (James Madison).

11. *Id.*, No. 84, at 511 (Alexander Hamilton).

12. *Id.* at 511–12 (Alexander Hamilton). *See also* JOHN D. LEWIS, ANTI-FEDERALISTS VERSUS FEDERALISTS: SELECTED DOCUMENTS 50–51 (1967) (noting that although the authors of the *Federalist Papers* made most of their arguments on the basis of practical principles, their arguments in favor of the ex post facto clauses were based on natural law); *Observations on George Mason's Objections to the Federal Constitution*, 368, *in* PAMPHLETS ON THE CONSTITUTION OF THE UNITED STATES 333, 360–61 (Paul Leicester Ford ed., New York, Burt Franklin 1888) (James Iredell) (noting that the Ex Post Facto Clause prevents the exercise of "tyranny [that] would be intolerable to bear").

13. 3 U.S. (3 Dall.) 386 (1798).

14. *Id.* at 389 (Chase, J.).

15. *Id.* at 390.

16. 10 U.S. (6 Cranch) 87 (1810).

17. *Id.* at 137–38.

18. 25 U.S. 213 (1827).

19. *Id. See also id.* at 330–31 (Trimble, J., concurring) ("The language shows, clearly, that the whole clause was understood at the time of the adoption of the constitution to have been introduced into the instrument in the very same spirit, and for the very same purpose, namely, for the protection of personal security and of private rights.").

20. Weaver v. Graham, 450 U.S. 24, 29 (1981).

21. 529 U.S. 513 (2000).

22. *Id.* at 533.

23. *Id.*

24. 519 U.S. 433 (1997).

25. *Id.* at 440. *See also* Stogner v. California, 539 U.S. 607, 611 (2003) (emphasizing "fairness" concerns and the expectation that the government "play by its own rules," stating that "the Clause protects liberty by preventing governments from enacting statutes with 'manifestly unjust and oppressive' retroactive effects") (citing *Calder*, 3 U.S. (3 Dall.) at 391).

26. *Lynce*, 519 U.S. at 440.

27. *See* Landgraf v. USI Film Prods., 511 U.S. 244, 266 (1994) (acknowledging that a legislature's "responsivity to political pressures poses a risk that it may be tempted to use retroactive legislation as a means of retribution against unpopular groups or individuals"); Harold J. Krent, *The Puzzling Boundary Between Criminal and Civil Retroactive Lawmaking*, 84 GEO. L.J. 2143, 2171 (1996) (noting that "[p]rospectivity ensures that the legislature is at least willing to impose punishment on a larger group of people whose identities are unknown. The generality of the prospective provision helps prevent singling-out").

28. *See* Calif. Dep't of Corr. v Morales, 514 U.S. 499, 522 (1995) (Stevens, J., dissenting) ("The danger of legislative overreaching against which the Ex Post Facto Clause protects is particularly acute when the target of the legislation is a narrow group as unpopular (to put it mildly) as multiple murderers. There is obviously little legislative hay to be made in cultivating the multiple murderer vote.").

29. *See* RONALD D. ROTUNDA & JOHN E. NOVAK, TREATISE ON CONSTITUTIONAL LAW: SUBSTANCE AND PROCEDURE § 15.9, at 658 (3d ed. 1999) (noting that a "legislature can benefit or harm disfavored citizens more easily with retroactive laws than it can with prospective laws"); Charles B. Hochman, *The Supreme Court and the Constitutionality of Retroactive Legislation*, 73 HARV. L. REV. 692, 693 (1960) (a retroactive statute "may be passed with an exact knowledge of who will benefit from it"); Evan C. Zoldan, *Reviving Legislative Generality*, 98 MARQ. L. REV. 625, 654 (2014) (explaining that "[w]hen a

legislature enacts retroactive legislation, it acts with the knowledge of conduct that has already occurred" and that therefore "retroactive legislation permits the legislature to punish . . . an individual without naming him specifically but with knowledge of whom the legislation will . . . harm.").

30. As the Massachusetts Supreme Judicial Court long ago observed:

> The reason why [ex post facto] laws are so universally condemned is that they over-look the great object of all criminal law, which is, to hold up the fear and certainty of punishment as a counteracting motive, to the minds of persons tempted to crime, to prevent them from committing it. But a punishment prescribed after an act is done, cannot, of course, present any such motive. It is contrary to the fundamental principle of criminal justice, which is, that the person who violates a law deserves punishment, because he willfully breaks a law, which, in theory, he knows or may know to exist. But he cannot know of the existence of a law which does not, in fact, exist at the time, but is enacted afterwards.

Jacquins v. Commonwealth, 63 Mass. (9 Cush.) 279, 281 (1852).

31. *See* Eastern Enterprises v. Apfel, 524 U.S. 498, 848 (1988) (Kennedy, J., concurring) (citation omitted) (noting that the court's "cases reflect our recognition that retroactive law-making is a particular concern for the courts because of the legislative 'tempt[ation] to use retroactive legislation as a means of retribution against unpopular groups or individuals' ").

32. Sveen v. Melin, 138 S. Ct. 1815, 1826 (2018) (Gorsuch, J., dissenting). *See also* Evenwel v. Abbott, 578 U.S. 54, 85 (2016) (Thomas, J., concurring) (noting the "Framers' concerns about placing unchecked power in political majorities" and that they "sought to check majority rule to promote the common good and mitigate threats to fundamental rights").

33. Adrian Vermeule, *Veil of Ignorance Rules in Constitutional Law*, 111 YALE L.J. 399 (2001) (drawing on the work of JOHN RAWLS, A THEORY OF JUSTICE 118–23 (rev. ed. 1999)).

34. *Id.* at 408.

35. 450 U.S. 24 (1981).

36. *Id.* at 29 n.10. *See also* Stogner v. California, 539 U.S. 607, 611 (2003) (citation omitted) (stating that the clause guards against "allowing legislatures to pick and choose when to act retroactively," which "risks both 'arbitrary and potentially vindictive legislation,' and erosion of the separation of powers.").

37. United States v. Lovett, 328 U.S. 303, 315 (1946); *see also* Nixon v. Adm'r of Gen. Servs., 433 U.S. 425, 468 (1976) (holding that legislatures cannot "determine[] guilt and inflict [] punishment upon an identifiable individual without provision of the protections of a judicial trial").

38. *See* United States v. Brown, 381 U.S. 437, 442 (1965) (the BOAC is intended to serve as a "general safeguard against legislative exercise of the judicial function, or more simply—trial by legislature.").

39. *See* Rachel E. Barkow, *Separation of Powers and the Criminal Law*, 58 STAN. L. REV. 989, 994–45 (2006).

40. 432 U.S. 282, 298 (1977).

41. *See, e.g.*, Weaver v. Graham, 450 U.S. 24, 28 (1981) ("the Framers sought to assure that legislative Acts give fair warning of their effect and permit individuals to rely on their meaning until explicitly changed.").

42. Lynce v. Mathis, 519 U.S. 433, 440 (1997).

43. *But see* McBoyle v. United States, 283 U.S. 25, 27 (1931) (Holmes, J.) ("[I]t is not likely that a criminal will carefully consider the text of the law before he murders or steals. . . .").

44. *See generally* Anthony N. Doob & Cheryl M. Webster, *Sentence Severity and Crime: Accepting the Null Hypothesis*, 30 Crime & Just. 143 (2003).

45. 529 U.S. 513 (2000).

46. *Id.* at 533. Moreover, "the absence of a reliance interest is not an argument in favor of abandoning the [fourth category] category itself. If it were, the same conclusion would follow for *Calder's* third category (increases in punishment), as there are few if any reliance interests in planning future criminal activities based on the expectation of less severe repercussions." *Id.* at 531 n.21.

47. 482 U.S. 423 (1987).

48. *Id.* at 431.

49. Payne v. Tennessee, 501 U.S. 808, 867 (1991) (Stevens, J., dissenting) (citing Northern Securities Co. v. United States, 193 U.S. 197, 400–01 (1904) (Holmes, J., dissenting)).

50. Fletcher v. Peck, 10 U.S. (6 Cranch) 87, 138 (1810).

51. Jacobellis v. Ohio, 378 U.S. 184, 197 (1964) (Stewart, J., concurring).

52. *See generally* Kenneth Mann, *Punitive Civil Sanctions: The Middleground Between Criminal and Civil Law*, 101 Yale L.J. 1795, 1849–52 (1992).

53. 71 U.S. 277 (1867).

54. *Id.* at 320.

55. *Id.* at 322.

56. *Id.* at 329.

57. Kring v. Missouri, 107 U.S. 221, 229 (1883), *rev'd*, Collins v. Youngblood, 497 U.S. 37 (1990).

58. 363 U.S. 603 (1960).

59. *Id.* at 617. The court added that if legislative history is considered there must be "unmistakable evidence of punitive intent." *Id.* at 619.

60. 372 U.S. 144 (1963).

61. *Id.* at 169.

62. *Id.* at 169.

63. 448 U.S. 242 (1980).

64. *Id.* at 248.

65. *Ward*, 448 U.S. at 248.

66. *Smith*, 538 U.S. 92.

67. *Id.* at 93.

68. *Id.* at 92.

69. Kennedy v. Mendoza-Martinez, 373 U.S. 144, 168–69 (1963).

70. *Id.* at 209.

71. Kansas v. Hendricks, 521 U.S. 346, 361 (1997).

72. *Id.*

73. *See* Riley v. New Jersey State Parole Bd., 98 A.3d 544, 554 n.7 (N.J. 2014) (noting that "[i]n *Hendricks*, the Supreme Court did not strictly adhere to the *Mendoza-Martinez* framework").

74. 538 U.S. 84 (2003).

75. It is worth noting that although the court variously refers to "intent," "purpose," "objective," and "motive," the terms arguably have different meanings. *See, e.g.*, Sheffield Dev. Co. v. City of Troy, 298 N.W.2d 23, 25 (Mich. Ct. App. 1980) ("[motive] may be defined as the impelling force of reason which induces action and precedes it. . . . [Intent] signifies the . . . meaning of the enactment, the purpose it seeks to accomplish, (and) its construction."). *But see* Elena Kagan, *Private Speech, Public Purpose: The Role of Governmental*

Motive in First Amendment Doctrine, 63 U. CHI. L. REV. 413, 426 n.40 (1996) (noting tendency of the court to use various terms and rejecting distinctions between purpose, intent, motive, basis, and reason). A justification, however, can be fairly regarded as something quite different—the moral, political, or other basis for imposing what has already been classified as punishment.

76. 363 U.S. 603, 617 (1960).

77. *See, e.g.*, RONALD DWORKIN, LAW'S EMPIRE 317–33 (1986) (detailing the struggles of determining which legislators' intentions count, how these intentions combine, which mental states count as intentions, and how to deal with conflicting intentions); Joseph Landau, *Process Scrutiny: Motivational Inquiry and Constitutional Rights*, 119 COLUM. L. REV. 2147, 2156 (2019) ("Indeed, the presumption that one can know with certainty the internal attitudes, emotions and biases of a single person—let alone a multimember legislative body or administrative agency—appears dubious.").

78. 71 U.S. 277 (1867).

79. *Id.* at 329.

80. 97 U.S. 381 (1878).

81. *Id.* at 385. *Cf.* Breed v. Jones, 421 U.S. 519, 529–31 (1975) (holding that whether constitutional protections apply to juvenile proceedings cannot hinge on a civil label of sanctions).

82. Legislative packaging occurs in other constitutional contexts where criminal defendants—alone—are provided rights, which have fiscal impacts on governments and place obstacles in securing convictions, such as the right to counsel or a jury trial. Chief Justice Earl Warren recognized the naiveté of deferring to legislative labels, stating "[h]ow simple would be the tasks of constitutional adjudication and of law generally if specific problems could be solved by inspection of the labels pasted on them!" Trop v. Dulles, 356 U.S. 86, 94 (1958).

83. In Alaska, when the legislature was considering enactment of the SORN law ultimately challenged in *Smith v. Doe*, legislators were concerned that the law would violate the Ex Post Facto Clause and reasoned that they could avoid the constitutional infirmity by classifying the law as regulatory not penal. Reply Brief of Appellants at 3–4, Doe I v. Burton, No. 96-35873 (9th Cir. Feb. 12, 1997), 1997 WL 33574720.

84. Kansas v. Hendricks, 521 U.S. 346, 361 (1997).

85. The Ninth Circuit Court of Appeals, in rejecting a challenge to a sex offender registration and community notification law, cited *Hendricks* when it refused to consider the volatile legislative context in which the provision originated. According to the court, "[h]owever quickly a law was passed, and however heated the public sentiment around it, we look to the legislature's manifest intent—which is found in the text and structure of the law." Russell v. Gregoire, 124 F.3d 1079, 1087–88 (9th Cir. 1997), *cert. denied*, 523 U.S. 1007 (1998).

86. *Cummings*, 71 U.S. at 320 (emphasis added).

87. 363 U.S. 144 (1960).

88. *Id.* at 147. *See also* John F. Manning, *Textualism as a Nondelegation Doctrine*, 97 COLUM. L. REV. 673, 733 n.253 (1997) (recognizing that "[c]ourts have traditionally examined the events precipitating a statute's enactment to gain insight into its meaning").

89. *Smith*, 538 U.S. at 108 (Souter, J., concurring).

90. *Id.* at 93–94.

91. *See* Slaughter-House Cases, 83 U.S. 36, 62 (1873) (citation omitted) ("Upon [the police power] depends the security of social order, the life and health of the citizen" and the power "'extends to the protection of the lives, limbs, health, and comfort, and quiet of all persons, and the protection of all property within the State....'").

92. Christopher G. Tiedeman, A Treatise on the Limitations on Police Power in the United States Considered from Both a Civil and Criminal Standpoint 113 (1886).

93. *Id.* at 105, 114.

94. *Hendricks*, 521 U.S. at 379 (Breyer, J., dissenting).

95. United States v. Brown, 381 U.S. 437 (1965). *See also* James v. United States, 366 U.S. 213, 247 n.3 (1961) (Harlan, J., concurring in part and dissenting in part) (stating that "the policy of the prohibition against ex post facto legislation would seem to rest on the apprehension that the legislature in imposing penalties on past conduct . . . may be acting with a purpose not to prevent dangerous conduct generally but to impose by legislation a penalty against specific persons or classes of persons.").

96. *Brown*, 381 U.S. at 458.

97. *Smith*, 538 U.S. at 96.

98. *Hendricks*, 521 U.S. at 364–65.

99. *Id.* at 361.

100. The focus on "purpose" in the second step of the "intent-effects" test is odd. As the Ninth Circuit Court of Appeals has noted, "[t]he test is somewhat confusing, because the 'effects' prong includes an exploration into both the effects of the statute and its actual purpose. The legislature's purpose is, of course, necessarily considered in the examination conducted under the first prong (the intent prong) of the test." Doe I v. Otte, 259 F.3d 979, 995 n.5 (9th Cir. 2001), *rev'd on other grnds. Sub nom.* Smith v. Doe, 538 U.S. 84, 123 S. Ct. 1140, 155 L.Ed.2d 164 (2003).

101. Consideration of effects, moreover, is sensible because the impact of a sanction on an individual exists regardless of the legislature's motivation. Issachar Rosen-Zvi & Talia Fisher, *Overcoming Procedural Boundaries*, 94 Va. L. Rev. 79, 125 (2008).

102. 538 U.S. 84 (2003).

103. *Id.* at 97.

104. *See* Austin v. United States, 509 U.S. 602, 610 n.6 (1993) (stating that *Mendoza-Martinez* and United States v. Ward addressed "whether a nominally civil penalty should be reclassified as criminal and the [Fifth and Sixth Amendment] safeguards that attend a criminal prosecution should be required. . . . In addressing the separate question whether punishment is being imposed, the Court has not employed the tests articulated in *Mendoza-Martinez* and *Ward*."). In addition, although *Hendricks* indisputably posed a "punishment question," Justice Thomas mistakenly framed the question as being whether the SVPA established "criminal proceedings for constitutional purposes." *Hendricks*, 521 U.S. at 361.

105. *Smith*, 538 U.S. at 97 (citations omitted).

106. *See* Doe v. State, 189 P.3d 999, 1008 (Alaska 2008) ("The Supreme Court has not explained the relative weight to be afforded each factor . . . Determining whether a statute is punitive necessarily involves the weighing of relatively subjective factors."); Wallace v. State, 905 N.E.2d 371, 379 (Ind. 2015) (stating with respect to the *Mendoza-Martinez* factors that "[t]he Supreme Court has not explained the relative weight to be afforded each factor.").

107. *Smith*, 538 U.S. at 97 (quoting Hudson v. United States, 522 U.S. 93, 99 (1997)).

108. *Id.* (quoting United States v. Ward, 448 U.S. 242, 249 (1980)).

109. *Id.* at 102 (quoting *Ursery*, 518 U.S. at 290).

110. *See, e.g.*, Wallace v. State, 905 N.E.2d 371, 384 (Ind. 2009) (noting that a "number of courts" regard the seventh factor, regarding excessiveness, as most important in analysis); State v. Letalien, 985 A.3d 4, 24 (Maine 2009) (stating that "the first and second

factors, considered together, stand out as being most probative on the question of punitive effects"); Riley v. New Jersey Parole Bd., 98 A.3d 544, 557–58 (N.J. 2014) (stating that
"[t]he first two of the *Mendoza–Martinez* factors identified in *Smith* weigh most heavily in
our analysis.").

111. United States v. Harley, 315 Fed. Appx. 437, 41 n.3 (3d Cir. 2009).

112. State v. Trosclair, 89 So. 3d 340, 356 (La. 2012).

113. Joshua Kaiser, *We Know It When We See It: The Tenuous Line Between "Direct Punishment"
and "Collateral Consequences,"* 59 How. L.J. 341, 353 (2016) (footnotes omitted).

114. *See* William F. Shimko, Note, *Constitutional Law—The Supreme Court Still Hasn't Found
What It Should Be Looking For: A Test That Effectively and Consistently Defines Punishment
for Constitutional Protection Analysis,* Smith v. Doe, 123 S. Ct. 1140 (2003), 4 Wyo. L. Rev.
477, 508–13 (2004).

115. *Compare* Riley v. New Jersey Parole Bd., 98 A.3d 544 (N.J. 2014) (four justices finding requirement punitive, three justices disagreeing and dissenting) *with* State v. Bowditch, 700
S.E.2d 1 (N.C. 2010) (four justices finding requirement non-punitive, with three justices
disagreeing and dissenting). Similarly illustrative is the dissent of six judges from the
Sixth Circuit Court of Appeals' denial of the defendant's petition for rehearing en banc
regarding the retroactive application of GPS monitoring in *Doe v. Bredesen,* 507 F.3d 998
(6th Cir. 2007), *cert. denied,* 555 U.S. 921 (2008). *See* Doe v. Bredsen, 521 F.3d 680, 681 (6th
Cir. 2008) (Keith., J., dissenting from denial, joined by Martin, Daugherty, Moore, Cole,
and Clay, J.J.) (regarding use of GPS tracking device as among strategies that serve as "a
catalyst for public ridicule . . . a form of shaming, humiliation, and banishment, which
are well-recognized historical forms of punishment" and asserting that "[t]he majority,
in upholding the Surveillance Act, deliberately turned a blind eye to the obvious effects of
forcing [the defendant] to wear such a large box on his person").

116. *See, e.g.,* United States v. Gelais, 952 F.2d 90, 97 (5th Cir. 1992).

117. *Hendricks,* 521 U.S. at 363.

118. *See, e.g.,* Belleau v. Wall, 811 F.3d 929, 937–38 (7th Cir. 2016); State v. Bowditch, 700 S.E.2d,
10–11, 12 (N.C. 2010).

119. *See, e.g.,* People v. Mosley, 344 P.3d 788, 802 (Cal. 2015).

120. *Smith,* 538 U.S. at 100.

121. *Id.* at 101.

122. *Id.* at 104.

123. 497 U.S. 37 (1990).

124. *Id.* at 52.

125. *See* Doe v. Attorney Gen., 686 N.E.2d 1007, 1016 (Mass. 1997) (Fried, J., concurring)
(referring to registration as a "continuing, intrusive, and humiliating regulation of the
person himself").

126. *See* Kelly Socia, *The Ancillary Consequences of SORN, in* Sex Offender Registration
and Community Notification Laws: An Empirical Evaluation, at 78 (Wayne
A. Logan & J.J. Prescott eds., 2021).

127. This phrase is borrowed from Stanley Cohen, Visions of Social Control: Crime,
Punishment and Classification 71 (1985).

128. *See* Jeremy Bentham, The Panopticon Writings (Miran Bozovic ed., Vers.
1995) (1791).

129. Reg Whitaker, The End of Privacy: How Total Surveillance Is Becoming a
Reality 35 (1999) ("The Inspector sees without being seen. His presence, which is also an

absence, is in his gaze alone. Of course, the omnipresence of the Inspector is nothing more than an architectural artifice, really just an elaborate conjuring trick.").

130. MICHEL FOUCAULT, DISCIPLINE AND PUNISH 201 (Alan Sheridan trans., 1979).

131. *See id.* (noting that use of virtual disciplinary control "render[s] its actual exercise unnecessary"). *See also* Does # 1–5 v. Snyder, 834 F.3d 696, 703 (6th Cir. 2016) (stating with respect to Michigan SORN law, complemented by a law prohibiting where registrants can live, that "surely something is not 'minor and indirect' just because no one is actually being lugged off in cold irons bound. Indeed, those irons are always in the background since failure to comply with these restrictions carries with it the threat of serious punishment, including imprisonment."), *cert. denied,* 138 S. Ct. 55 (2017).

132. *See generally* DAVID GARLAND, THE CULTURE OF CONTROL: CRIME AND SOCIAL ORDER IN CONTEMPORARY SOCIETY (2001).

133. *Smith,* 538 U.S. at 97.

134. *Id.*

135. *See* Wayne A. Logan, *The Importance of Purpose in Probation Decision Making,* 7 BUFF. CRIM. L. REV. 171, 174–76 (2003).

136. Lee v. State, 895 So. 2d 1038, 1043 (Ala. Crim. App. 2004) (posing question as whether residence exclusion law "historically been regarded in Alabama's history as a punishment").

137. *See* Sanders v. Allison Engine Co., Inc., 703 F.3d 930, 945 n.13 (6th Cir. 2012) ("Our review of cases . . . suggests that the analysis under this factor is often conducted at a fairly high level of generality, suggesting that the historical view of monetary penalties generally is appropriately considered. . . .").

138. *Smith,* 538 U.S. at 97 (citation omitted).

139. *Id.*

140. *Id.* at 98.

141. *Id.*

142. *Id.* at 99. The problematic nature of the governmental disavowal of responsibility brings to mind Professor James Whitman's recognition about use of "shame" sanctions more generally. *See* James W. Whitman, *What Is Wrong with Inflicting Shame Sanctions?,* 107 YALE L.J. 1055, 1059 (1998) (noting that that lack of accountability entails "an improper partnership between the state and the crowd."); *see also id.* at 1088 ("Once the state stirs up public opprobrium against an offender, it cannot really control the way the public treats the offender . . . When our government dangles a sex offender or a drunk before the public, it has vanishingly little control over how the public treats the person.").

143. *Smith,* 538 U.S. at 99.

144. *Id.* at 99.

145. *Id.* at 109 (Souter, J., concurring).

146. Doe v. State, 111 A.3d 1077, 1097 (N.H. 2015).

147. *Id. See also* United States Dep't of Justice v. Reporters' Comm. For Freedom of the Press, 489 U.S. 749, 763 (1989) (noting with respect to a criminal "rap sheet" that "[p]lainly there is a vast difference between the public records that might be found after a diligent search of courthouse files, county archives, and local police stations throughout the country and a computerized summary located in a single clearinghouse of information."); *id.* at 763, 770 (dismissing government's "cramped notion of personal privacy" and stating that "the fact that an event is not wholly private does not mean that an individual has no interest in limiting disclosure or dissemination of the information."); Doe v. State, 189 P.3d 999, 1011 (Alaska 2008) ("[t]here is a significant distinction between retaining public paper

records of a conviction in state file drawers and posting the same information on a state-sponsored website; this posting has not merely improved public access but has broadly disseminated the registrant's information, some of which is not in the written public record of the conviction.").

148. Seth F. Kreimer, *Sunlight, Secrets, and Scarlet Letters: The Tension Between Privacy and Disclosure in Constitutional Law*, 140 U. Pa. L. Rev. 1, 7 (1991) (footnote omitted). *See also* Joint Anti-Fascist Refugee Committee v. McGrath, 341 U.S. 123, 175 (1951) (Douglas, J., concurring) (stating with regard to government's classification of organizations as communist or subversive, that rather than constituting mere dissemination of a public record, was "a determination of status.").

149. Malcolm Feeley & Jonathan Simon, *The New Penology: Notes on the Emerging Strategy of Corrections and Its Implications*, 30 Criminology 449 (1992). Today an enormous literature exists on the dominant role of risk management and prevention played in social control methodology. *See, e.g.*, Andrew Ashworth & Lucia Zedner, Preventive Justice (2014); Bill Hebenton & Toby Seddon, *From Dangerous to Precaution: Managing Sexual and Violent Offenders in an Insecure and Uncertain Age*, 49 Brit. J. Criminology 343 (2009); Sandra G. Mayson, *Collateral Consequences and the Preventive State*, 91 Notre Dame L. Rev. 301 (2015). For an insightful overview of the social, economic, and political forces driving this shift, *see* John Pratt & Michelle Miao, *Risk, Populism, and Criminal Law*, 22 New Crim. L. Rev. 391 (2019).

150. Jennifer C. Daskal, *Pre-Crime Restraints: The Explosion of Targeted, Noncustodial Prevention*, 99 Cornell L. Rev. 327 (2014).

151. 573 U.S. 373 (2014).

152. *Id.* at 393. The court added: "Modern cell phones, as a category, implicate privacy concerns far beyond those implicated by the search of a cigarette pack, a wallet, or a purse. A conclusion that inspecting the contents of an arrestee's pockets works no substantial additional intrusion on privacy beyond the arrest itself may make sense as applied to physical items, but any extension of that reasoning to digital data has to rest on its own bottom." *Id.*

153. *Hendricks*, 521 U.S. at 362.

154. *Smith*, 538 U.S. at 105.

155. *Id.*

156. *Id.*

157. *Id.*

158. *Smith*, 538 U.S. at 109 (Souter, J., concurring).

159. *Id.* at 116 (Ginsburg, J., dissenting).

160. *Id.* at 112 (Stevens, J., dissenting) (emphasis in original).

161. 905 N.E.2d 371 (2009).

162. *Id.* at 381.

163. *Id.* at 382.

164. *See, e.g.*, State v. Letalien, 985 A.2d 4 (Maine 2009); Doe v. State, 111 A.3d 1077 (N.H. 2015); Starkey v. Okla. Dep't of Corrections, 305 P.3d 1004 (Ok. 2013). *But see* Comm. v. Muniz, 164 A.3d 1189, 1214 & 1216 (Pa. 2017) (applying federal ex post facto provision and adopting approach taken in *Smith*).

165. *See, e.g.*, Comm. v. Cory, 911 N.E.2d 187, 195 (Mass. 2009) (regarding wearing of GPS device).

166. Simmons v. Galvin, 575 F.3d 24, 45 (1st Cir. 2009) (quoting United States v. Ursery, 518 U.S. 267, 291 (1996)).

167. *Mendoza-Martinez*, 372 U.S. at 168.

168. Hudson v. United States, 522 U.S. 93, 105 (1995) (citation omitted). *See also* Sanders v. Allison Engine Co., 703 F.3d 930, 946 (6th Cir. 2012) (stating in case rejecting ex post facto claim against change to federal False Claims Act that "a deterrent purpose may serve both civil and criminal goals, and the mere presence of a deterrent purpose is not enough to render sanctions criminal").

169. For several of the earliest and best discussions of the issue, *see* Mary M. Cheh, *Constitutional Limits on Using Civil Remedies to Achieve Criminal Law Objectives: Understanding and Transcending the Criminal-Civil Law Distinction*, 42 HASTINGS L.J. 1325 (1991); John C. Coffee, Jr., *Paradigms Lost: The Blurring of the Criminal and Civil Law Models—And What Can Be Done About It*, 101 YALE L.J. 1875 (1992); Kenneth Mann, *Punitive Civil Sanctions: The Middleground Between Criminal and Civil Law*, 101 YALE L.J. 1795 (1992).

170. *Smith*, 538 U.S. at 102.

171. *Id.*

172. *See* Henry M. Hart, Jr., *The Aims of the Criminal Law*, 23 L. & CONTEMP. PROBS. 401, 404 (1958) ("What distinguishes a criminal from a civil sanction . . . is the judgement of community condemnation which accompanies and justifies its imposition.").

173. *Smith*, 538 U.S. at 115 (Ginsburg, J., dissenting).

174. *See, e.g.,* United States v. Brown, 381 U.S. 437, 458 (1965) ("Punishment serves several purposes[:] retributive, rehabilitative, deterrent—and preventive.").

175. *Hendricks*, 521 U.S. at 365–66.

176. 381 U.S. 437 (1965).

177. *Id.* at 458.

178. Alice Ristroph, *State Intentions and the Law of Punishment*, 98 J. CRIM. L. & CRIMINOLOGY 1353, 1373 (2008).

179. *See Hendricks*, 521 U.S. at 367 ("Even if we accept [the conclusion of the Kansas Supreme Court] . . . that the provision of treatment was not the Kansas Legislature's 'overriding' or 'primary' purpose in passing the Act, this does not rule out the possibility that an ancillary purpose of the Act was to provide treatment, and it does not require us to conclude that the Act is punitive.").

180. In a case decided one year before *Smith*, but not since repudiated, the U.S. Seventh Circuit Court of Appeals reasoned that a law's purpose must be "solely" punitive, stating that "a law is not an *ex post facto* law if it does not aim to serve solely punitive goals." O'Grady v. Vill. of Libertyville, 304 F.3d 719, 723 (7th Cir. 2002).

181. *Smith*, 538 U.S. at 102 (quoting United States v. Ursery, 518 U.S. 267, 290 (1996)).

182. 518 U.S. 267 (1996).

183. *Compare, e.g.,* Does 1–7 v. Abbottt, 945 F.3d 307, 314 314 (5th Cir. 2019) (using "a") *with* United States v. Under Seal, 709 F.3d 257, 265 (4th Cir. 2013) (using "the").

184. *Smith*, 538 U.S. at 105 (emphasis added).

185. *See* Trump v. Hawaii, 138 S. Ct. 2392, 2402 (2018) (defining the rational basis inquiry as "whether the . . . policy is plausibly related to the Government's stated objective"); City of New Orleans v. Dukes, 427 U.S. 297, 303 (1976) (requiring only that "the classification challenged be rationally related to a legitimate state interest").

186. *See* Doe v. State, 189 P.3d 999, 1018 (Alaska 2008) ("We recognize that several of the [*Mendoza-Martinez*] factors seem closely related, and that discussion of one may overlap discussion of another.").

187. As the Ohio Court of Appeals recently put it, when rejecting an ex post facto claim based on the federal (not Ohio) Constitution, "[t]he analysis of a law's effect is inherently subjective and whether a law's effects are remedial or penal is a 'matter of degree.'" State v. Galloway, 50 N.E.3d 1001, 1007 (Ohio Ct. App. 2015) (citation omitted).

188. Kennedy v. Mendoza-Martinez, 373 U.S. 144, 169 (1963).

189. Issachar Rosen-Zvi & Talia Fisher, *Overcoming Procedural Boundaries*, 94 Va. L. Rev. 79, 126 (2008).

190. 531 U.S. 250 (2001).

191. *Id.* at 263.

192. As the Massachusetts Supreme Judicial Court has recognized, *Seling* "rejected the argument that a statute can be declared punitive 'as applied' to a particular person when the highest State court has already definitively construed the statute as civil." In re Dutil, 768 N.E.2d 1055, 1065 (Mass. 2002). *See also* Arthur v. United States, 253 A.3d 134, 141 (D.C. Ct. App. 2021) (citing *Dutil* and noting the same). One important ramification of conceiving of *Seling* in this way is that a law experiencing change in its "necessary operation," as the *Smith* Court put it, such as by amendment, could possibly be challenged anew on an as-applied basis.

193. *Seling*, 531 U.S. at 269 (Scalia, J., concurring) (citations and footnote omitted).

194. *Id.* at 269 n.*

195. *Id.* at 267–68 (Scalia, J., concurring).

196. *Id.* at 270–74 (Thomas, J., concurring).

197. *Smith*, 538 U.S. at 106 (Thomas, J., concurring).

198. 982 F.3d 784, 791 (9th Cir. 2020).

199. *Id.* at 791 (construing Idaho registration and community notification law). The court added that "courts must evaluate a law's positive effect based on a variety of factors such as the terms of the statute, the obligation it imposes, and the practical and foreseeable consequences of the obligations in relation to the statue on its face." *Id.*

200. 985 A.2d 4, 17 (Maine 2009).

201. *See, e.g.*, Doe v. Biang, 494 F. Supp. 2d 880, 887 n.7 (N.D. Ill. 2006) (stating that *Seling* "held that a plaintiff cannot mount an as-applied ex post facto challenge"); People v. Tucker, 879 N.W.2d 906, 911 n.4 (Mich. Ct. App. 2015) (*Seling* established that "ex post facto challenges cannot be brought on an as-applied basis"). A more recent decision, from a federal trial court in Alabama, highlights the confusion at times inspired by *Seling*. In *McGuire v. Strange*, 83 F. Supp. 3d 1231 (M.D. Ala. 2015), the court stated that "[a]s-applied challenges in ex post facto cases are directly barred by *Seling*." *Id.* at 1250 n.17. Turning to its assessment of the effects of the law challenged, as required by *Mendoza-Martinez*, the court disregarded "idiosyncratic effects" on individuals, considering effects "only to the extent that they explain or describe general effects flowing from the face or necessary operation of the statutory scheme." *Id.* at 1250–51.

202. *See, e.g.*, Garner v. Jones, 529 U.S. 244, 255 (2000) (stating in a challenge to a retroactive change in parole procedure that a challenger "must show that as applied to his own sentence[,] the [change in] law created a significant risk of increasing his punishment").

203. *See Smith*, 538 U.S. at 91 (stating that litigants sought to "declare the [law] void as to them under the Ex Post Facto Clause").

204. *Id.* at 99–100.

205. *Id.* at 91.

206. 834 F.3d 696 (6th Cir. 2016).

207. *Id.* at 698 (citation omitted).

208. *See, e.g.,* Does # 6, # 5 v. Miami-Dade Cty., 974 F.3d 1333, 1339 (11th Cir. 2020) (construing Florida county's residence exclusion law and considering the "personal experiences" of petitioners relevant in facial and as-applied challenges); *see also, e.g.,* Shaw v. Patton, 823 F.3d 556 (10th Cir. 2016) (construing Oklahoma SORN law); Doe v. Rausch, 382 F. Supp. 3d 783 (E.D. Tenn. 2019) (construing Tennessee SORN law); Valenti v. Hartford City, Ind., 225 F. Supp. 3d 770 (N.D. Ind. 2016) (construing local sex offender residence restriction law); State v. Davidson, 495 P.3d 9 (Kan. 2021) (construing Kansas SORN law). *Cf.* Doe v. State, 111 A.3d 1077 (N.H. 2015) (construing SORN law under state constitution). *See also* Andrew C. Adams, *One-Book, Two Sentences: Ex Post Facto Considerations of the One-Book Rule After* United States v. Kumar, 39 Am. J. Crim. L. 231, 244 (2012) (stating that "[i]n almost every paradigmatic ex post facto case, the challenge will be advanced as an 'as applied' constitutional challenge. . . ."). *See also, e.g.,* Doe v. State, 189 P.3d 999 (Ak. 2008) (as-applied challenge to Alaska SORN law under Alaska Constitution).

209. Sabri v. United States, 541 U.S. 600, 609 (2004).

210. United States v. Mitchell, 652 F.3d 387, 405 (3d Cir. 2011).

211. Wash. State Grange v. Wash. State Republican Party, 552 U.S. 442, 450 (2008).

212. City of Los Angeles v. Patel, 576 U.S. 409, 415 (2015).

213. Riley v. N.J. State Parole Bd., 98 A.3d 544, 557 (N.J. 2014).

214. *See* Socia, *supra* note 126. In a recent death penalty case involving an Eighth Amendment challenge to the use of lethal injection, the court spoke to the uncertainty in distinguishing facial versus applied categorization: "Suppose an inmate claims that the State's lethal injection protocol violates the Eighth Amendment when used to execute anyone with a very common but not quite universal health condition. Should such a claim be regarded as facial or as-applied?" Bucklew v. Precythe, 139 S. Ct. 1112, 1128 (2019).

215. *Hendricks,* 521 U.S. at 361. In *Flemming v. Nestor,* 363 U.S. 603 (1960), which first invoked the "clearest proof" standard of proof (see Chapter 4), the court used language suggesting an even more demanding standard: there must be *"unmistakable evidence* of punitive intent." *Id.* at 619 (emphasis added). It is unclear whether the latter remains a requirement as the language appears in neither *Smith v. Doe* nor *Kansas v. Hendricks.*

216. 522 U.S. 93 (1997).

217. *Id.* at 114 (Souter, J., concurring).

218. *Smith,* 538 U.S. at 107 (Souter, J., concurring).

219. *Id.* at 115 (Ginsburg, J., dissenting).

220. *See, e.g.,* Comm. v. Cory, 911 N.E.2d 187, 194 (Mass. 2009).

221. *See, e.g., id.* at 198–99 (Ireland, J., dissenting, joined by Spina and Cowin, J.J.).

222. The *Nestor* Court itself acknowledged this point. *See Nestor,* 363 U.S. at 617 ("[T]he presumption of constitutionality with which this enactment, like any other, comes to us forbids us lightly to choose that reading of the statute's setting which will invalidate it over that which will save it."). *See also E.B. v. Verniero,* 119 F.3d 1007, 1128 (3d Cir. 1997) ("I warn against placing too much emphasis on the meaning of 'clearest proof.' As [*Nestor*] and its progeny make patent, the standard is intended as a kind of warning to the federal courts to give legislatures the benefit of the doubt. It is thus consistent with familiar canons of statutory interpretation and constitutional adjudication stating that legislatures are rational bodies that intend to function within their powers to enact lawful measures.").

223. *Cf.* United States v. Davis, 139 S. Ct. 2319, 2333 (2019) (noting that application of the avoidance canon, which obliges that an ambiguous statute be interpreted whenever

possible to avoid finding the statute unconstitutional, and vagueness doctrine, are "at war with one another").

224. California Dep't of Corr. v. Morales, 514 U.S. 499, 522 (1995) (Stevens, J., dissenting).

225. *Smith*, 538 U.S. at 109 (Souter, J., concurring).

226. *See* Michelle A. Cubellis et al., *Sex Offender Stigma: An Exploration of Vigilantism Against Sex Offenders*, 40 DEVIANT BEHAV. 225 (2019).

227. *See* John Harrison, *The Constitutional Origins and Implications of Judicial Review*, 84 VA. L. REV. 333, 341 (1998) ("Affirmative limitations qualify the authority otherwise granted to the legislature, with the result that even properly enacted ex post facto laws are invalid and legally ineffective, to be treated by the courts as legal nullities.").

228. As of this writing, there appears to be disagreement in some courts regarding whether the "clearest proof" requirement applies in a motion to dismiss an ex post facto challenge (filed by a defendant in a civil case challenging the constitutionality of a law—as opposed to a challenge by a defendant in a criminal case). According to one panel of the Ninth Circuit Court of Appeals, a litigant need only "plausibly allege" that a law is punitive in effect. Does v. Wasden, 982 F.3d 784, 791 (9th Cir. 2020). *See also* Prynne v. Settle, 848 Fed. App'x 93, 100, 101 (4th Cir. 2021) (stating same and cautioning that "we do not intend to imply how the [*Mendoza-Martinez*] factors should be weighed at a later stage of the litigation"). *But see Does*, 982 F.3d at 798 (Vandyke, J., concurring and dissenting in part) (emphasis in original) (asserting that the "majority misunderstands the pleading requirement . . . Like other heightened legal thresholds, the 'clearest proof' standard is best understood as referring to a *presumption* that makes it harder for plaintiffs to win their challenge. As such, the 'clearest proof' standard is relevant at the motion to dismiss stage . . . [A] court is obligated to evaluate whether the plaintiffs' allegations—if true— would meet the heightened requirement."). Whether the view of the Fourth and Ninth Circuits becomes the prevailing view in ex post facto civil rights cases warrants continued attention. So too does the possibility that the view will migrate to criminal cases involving direct appeals and habeas corpus petitions (the latter technically a civil action).

229. *See* ART. I, § 10 ("No State shall . . . pass any Bill of Attainder, ex post facto Law, or Law impairing the Obligation of Contracts, or grant any Title of Nobility."). As discussed in Chapter 1, the framers elected to not impose a similar limit regarding contracts on Congress.

230. *See, e.g.*, Arizona v. Evans, 514 U.S. 1, 8 (1995) ("State courts . . . are not merely free to— they are bound to—interpret the United States Constitution.").

231. *See* Mullaney v. Wilbur, 421 U.S. 684, 691 (1975) ("[S]tate courts are the ultimate expositors of state law.").

232. A survey of state constitutions in existence as of 1868, when the Fourteenth Amendment was ratified, found that twenty-nine of thirty-seven constitutions (over three-quarters) contained an ex post facto prohibition. Steven G. Calabresi & Sarah E. Agudo, *Individual Rights Under State Constitutions When the Fourteenth Amendment Was Ratified in 1868: What Rights Are Deeply Rooted in American History and Tradition?*, 87 TEX. L. REV. 7, 68 (2008). Provisions were found in 87 percent of state constitutions in Southern states, 83 percent of Midwestern-Western states, and only 60 percent of Northeastern states. *Id.* Notably, only twenty-two of the state constitutions prohibited bills of attainder (compared to twenty-nine containing ex post facto prohibitions). *Id.* at 69.

233. Some states have constitutional prohibitions of "retroactive" or "retrospective" laws. *See, e.g.*, Doe v. Phillips, 194 S.W.3d 833 (Mo. 2006) (deeming invalid state SORN law based on

Missouri Constitution art. I, § 13 providing that "no . . . law . . . retrospective in its opera-tion . . . can be enacted," because it retroactively imposed new burdens); State v. Williams, 952 N.E.2d 1108 (Ohio 2011) (deeming invalid state SORN law based on Section 28, Article II of the Ohio Constitution providing that "[t]he general assembly shall have no power to pass retroactive laws," which bars retroactive new burdens and duties, and finding the law "punitive"). For similar state provisions, *see, e.g.*, Tenn. Const. Art. I, § 20 ("no retrospective law . . . shall be made"); Colo. Const. art. II, § 11 (no laws "retrospective in . . . operation"); N.H. Const. part I, Art. 23 ("Retrospective laws are highly injurious, oppressive, and unjust. No such laws . . . should be made, either for the decision of civil causes, or the punishment of offenses"). A complete listing of state ex post and retroactive/retrospective provisions is provided in Appendix B.

234. *See* Lawrence Friedman, *The Constitutional Value of Dialogue and the New Judicial Federalism*, 28 HASTINGS CONST. L.Q. 93, 102 (2000) ("Under the lockstep approach, the state constitutional analysis begins and ends with consideration of the U.S. Supreme Court's interpretation of the textual provision at issue.").

235. A large literature exists on state court authority to interpret state constitutional provisions more broadly than facially similar federal provisions. One commentator has spoken of why a state ex post facto provision could warrant broader prohibitory scope:

> unlike most of the guarantees of the Federal Bill of Rights, which were found to apply to the states through selective incorporation into the Fourteenth Amendment only within the past thirty years or so, the Ex Post Facto Clause of the United States Constitution has always bound the states. Thus the insertion of an ex post facto clause in any subsequent state constitution would be redundant and would serve no purpose unless it was intended, in at least some circumstances, to impose broader restraints on the legislature than what was already federally mandated. Furthermore, many state ex post facto clauses have been placed in state declarations of rights, rather than the state constitution. This placement differs from the location of the two ex post facto clauses found in Article I of the Federal Constitution, dealing with the legislative branch. Such placement implies that these state clauses are not merely limitations on legislative power, but rather affirmative grants of individual protec-tion. Hence, a less deferential standard of judicial review may be in order because courts are more inclined to strike down legislation when individual rights are at stake than if the question is solely whether the lawmakers exceeded their authority.

Marshall J. Tinkle, *Forward into the Past: State Constitutions and Retroactive Laws*, 65 TEMPLE L. REV. 1253, 1257–58 (1992) (footnotes omitted).

236. *See, e.g.*, Doe v. State, 189 P.3d 999 (Alaska 2008); Wallace v. Indiana, 905 N.E.2d 371 (Ind. 2009); Commonwealth v. Baker, 295 S.W.3d 437 (Ky. 2009); State v. Letalien, 985 A.2d 4 (Maine 2009); Doe v. Dept. of Pub. Safety and Corr. Servs., 62 A.3d 123 (Md. 2010); Doe v. State, 111 A.3d 1077 (N.H. 2015); Starkey v. Okla. Dep't of Corr., 305 P.3d 1004 (Okla. 20130; Commonwealth v. Muniz, 164 A.3d 1189 (Pa. 2017).

237. 189 P.3d 999 (Alaska 2008).

238. *Id.* at 1019 n.160.

239. *See id.* at 1007 ("the results of the federal opinions do not control our independent anal-ysis, when in interpreting the Alaska Constitution, we look for guidance to either the fed-eral precedent or the analytical framework applied by federal courts. Our adoption of the analytical approach approved by the federal courts likewise does not mean that we are bound by how the Supreme Court applied that approach in *Smith*.").

240. *Id.* at 1018. The court stated in a footnote that use of the "clearest proof" standard was inapt: "[i]mposing a heightened presumption requiring 'clearest proof' of punitive intent could threaten rights protected by the Alaska Constitution and might be inconsistent with the responsibilities of this court." *Id.* at 1008 n.62. In lieu of a "clearest proof" standard, the court "accord[s] the challenged statute a presumption of constitutionality." *Id.*

241. *See, e.g.,* Gonzalez v. State, 980 N.E.2d 312 (Ind. 2013); Starkey v. Okla. Dept. of Corrections, 305 P.3d 1004 (Okla. 2013).

242. Doe v. State, 111 A.3d 1077, 1090 (N.H. 2015) (citation omitted). *See also* Wallace v. State, 905 N.E.2d 371, 378 (Ind. 2009) (applying *Smith* regime and finding state law punitive, while noting "we often rely on federal authority to inform our analysis, even though the outcome may be different").

243. *Doe,* 111 A.3d at 1094 (citations omitted).

244. *Starkey,* 305 P.3d at 1030.

245. State v. Letalien, 985 A.2d 4 (Maine 2009).

246. Comm. v. Muniz, 164 A.3d 1189 (Pa. 2017).

247. Legislative changes to a law deemed punitive can result in a later court, in the same jurisdiction, rejecting an ex post facto challenge because the changes undid the previously identified punitive character of the law. *See, e.g.,* Doe I v. Williams, 61 A.3d 718 (Maine 2013).

248. *See, e.g.,* Wallace v. State, 905 N.E.2d 371 (Ind. 2009).

249. *Smith,* 538 U.S. at 97.

250. *See* Kennedy v. Mendoza-Martinez, 372 U.S. 144, 168 (1963) (noting that the task "has been extremely difficult and elusive of solution").

251. *See Morales,* 514 U.S. at 509 ("[W]e have long held that the question of what legislative adjustments 'will be held to be of sufficient moment to transgress the constitutional prohibition' must be a matter of degree.") (emphasis added) (citation omitted).

252. *See* DAVID GARLAND, PUNISHMENT AND MODERN SOCIETY: A STUDY IN SOCIAL THEORY 16–17 (1990) ("'[P]unishment' is in fact a complex set of interlinked processes and institutions rather than a uniform object or events . . . It is not susceptible to a logical or formulaic definition . . ."); *see also* NICOLA LACEY, STATE PUNISHMENT: POLITICAL PRINCIPLES AND COMMUNITY VALUES 4–15 (1988) (discussing difficulties with defining "punishment").

253. United States v. Brown, 381 U.S. 437, 442 (1965). *See also, e.g.,* Dufresne v. Baer, 744 F.2d 1543, 1546 (11th Cir. 1984) ("When subjecting a law to ex post facto scrutiny, courts should bear in mind the related aims of the ex post facto clause . . .").

254. *Smith,* 538 U.S. at 97 (citations omitted).

255. *See, e.g.,* United States v. Ursery, 518 U.S. 267, 287 (1996) (Fifth Amendment Double Jeopardy challenge against civil in rem forfeiture procedure); Austin v. United States, 509 U.S. 602, 610 (1993) (Eighth Amendment Excessive Fines Clause challenge to in rem civil forfeiture proceedings). *See also, e.g.,* Fushek v. State, 183 P.3d 536 (Ariz. 2008) (stating that that the *Mendoza-Martinez* test should not be used to determine whether a sanction is sufficiently severe to trigger the right to a jury trial under the Sixth Amendment).

256. Bryant Smith, *Retroactive Laws and Vested Rights II,* 6 TEXAS L. REV. 409, 419 (1928) (citations omitted) ("Ex post facto laws and bills of attainder, twin sisters of legislative oppression . . . were so vivid in the political background the framers of the constitution and so obnoxious to their ideals of justice as to call for an express constitutional prohibition."). *See also* United States v. Lovettt, 328 U.S. 303, 323 (1946) (Frankfurter, J., concurring)

("Frequently, a bill of attainder was [] doubly objectionable because of its ex post facto features. This is the historic explanation for uniting the two mischiefs in one clause—'No Bill of Attainder or ex post facto law shall be passed.'").

257. Nixon v. Adm'r of Gen. Serv., 433 U.S. 425, 468 (1977).

258. 529 U.S. 513 (2000).

259. *Id.* at 536. *See also* City of Richmond v. J.A. Croson Co., 488 U.S. 469, 513 (1989) (Stevens, J., concurring) ("the constitutional prohibitions against the enactment of ex post facto laws and bills of attainder reflect a valid concern about the use of the political process to punish or characterize past conduct of private citizens."); Nixon v. Adm'r of Gen. Servs., 433 U.S. 425, 469 n.30 (1977) (citation omitted) ("The linking of bills of attainder and ex post facto laws is explained by the fact that a legislative denunciation and condemnation of an individual often acted to impose retroactive punishment.").

260. 71 U.S. 277 (1867).

261. 71 U.S. 333 (1867).

262. *See* Foretich v. United States, 351 F.3d 1198, 1218 (D.C. Cir. 2003) (stating that "the principal touchstone of a bill of attainder is punishment").

263. *Cummings*, 71 U.S. at 329.

264. *Id.* at 325.

265. 381 U.S. 437 (1965).

266. Notably, only the dissent, not the majority, referenced *Mendoza-Martinez*. *See Brown*, 381 U.S. at 462 (White, J., dissenting, joined by Clark, Harlan, and Stewart, J.J.) (referring to *Mendoza-Martinez* as a "meticulous multifold analysis").

267. *Id.* at 442.

268. *Id.*

269. *Id.* at 448 (quoting Cummings v. Missouri, 71 U.S. 277, 320 (1867)).

270. Id. at 458.

271. *Id.*

272. 433 U.S. 425 (1977).

273. *Id.* at 469.

274. *Id.* at 476.

275. 468 U.S. 841 (1984).

276. *Id.* at 852 (citations omitted).

277. *Id.* at 856.

278. *See* Ogden v. Saunders, 25 U.S. (12 Wheat.) 212, 286 (1827) ("By classing bills of attainder, ex post facto laws, and laws impairing the obligation of contracts together, the general intent becomes very apparent; it is a general provision against arbitrary and tyrannical legislation over existing rights, whether of person or property."). *See also* Nixon v. Adm'r of Gen. Servs., 433 U.S. 425, 480 (1977) (the BOAC embodies "the fear that the legislature, in seeking to pander to an inflamed popular constituency, will find it expedient openly to assume the mantle of judge—or, worse still, lynch mob.").

279. Cummings v. Missouri, 71 U.S. 277, 320 (1867).

280. *See* 2 JOSEPH STORY, CONSTITUTION § 1398 (5th ed. 1891) ("Retrospective laws are, indeed, generally unjust; and, has been forcibly said, neither accord with sound legislation nor with fundamental principles of the social compact."). For discussion of the framers' major concern over retroactive laws, manifest in the Ex Post Facto Clause, the Contracts Clause, and other parts of the original Constitution, which the author refers to as central to the "constitutional bargain" allowing for its adoption, *see* Robert G. Natelson, *Statutory*

Retroactivity: The Founders' View, 39 IDAHO L. REV. 489 (2003). *See also generally* Elmer E. Smead, *The Rule Against Retroactive Legislation: A Basic Principle of Jurisprudence*, 20 MINN. L. REV. 775 (1936); Bryant Smith, *Retroactive Laws and Vested Rights*, 6 TEX. L. REV. 409 (1928); Edward S. Stimson, *Retroactive Application of Law-A Problem in Constitutional Law*, 38 MICH. L. REV. (1939).

281. Vartelas v. Holder, 566 U.S. 257, 266 (2012).

282. *MPIC*, 468 U.S. at 846–47 (stating that there are three requirements for a bill of attainder: (1) specification of the affected person(s), (2) punishment, and (3) lack of a judicial trial).

283. 529 U.S. 694 (2000).

284. *Id.* at 701.

285. 566 U.S. 257 (2012).

286. *Id.* at 266 (quoting Society for Propagation of Gospel v. Wheeler, 22 F. Cas. 756, 767 (No. 13,156) (CCNH 1814) (Story, J.)).

287. 527 U.S. 343 (1999).

288. *Id.* at 357–58 (citation omitted).

289. Cummings v. Missouri, 71 U.S. 277, 320 (1867).

290. *Id.* at 322. *See also* NORMAN J. SINGER, 2A SUTHERLAND ON STATUTORY CONSTRUCTION § 48.03, at 315 (5th ed. 1992) (citations omitted) (noting that "[i]t is established practice in American legal processes to consider relevant information concerning the historical background of an enactment. . . . extrinsic aids may show the circumstances under which the statute was passed, the mischief at which it was aimed and the object it was supposed to achieve.").

291. 328 U.S. 303 (1946).

292. Nixon v. Adm'r of Gen. Servs., 433 U.S. 425, 480 (1977) (quoting United States v. Lovett, 328 U.S. 303, 312 (1946)).

293. *Id.*

294. United States v. Fisher, 6 U.S. (2 Cranch) 358, 386 (1805).

295. *Nixon*, 433 U.S. at 475.

296. *Cummings*, 71 U.S. at 320.

297. Vartelas v. Holder, 566 U.S. 257, 266 (2012) (citation omitted). In *Vartelas*, the court, citing the Ex Post Facto Clause as among the constitutional provisions embodying the "presumption against retroactivity," concluded that a federal law limiting the travel of a lawful permanent resident, based on a conviction from years before the law's effective date, imposed a new "disability" and therefore should not be applied retroactively. *Id.* at 267–68.

298. *See* Doe v. State, 189 P.3d 999, 1008 n.62 (Alaska 2008) (stating same). *See also* Wallace v. State, 905 N.E.2d 371, 378 n.7 (Ind. 2009) (concluding in state constitution ex post facto challenge that "our standard of review for challenges to the constitutionality of a statute has never included a clearest proof element. Instead, a statute is presumed constitutional, and the party challenging its constitutionality has the burden of overcoming the presumption by a contrary showing.").

299. *See* U.S. Const. art. I, § 10, cl. 1 ("No State shall . . . pass any . . . Law impairing the Obligation of Contracts . . .").

300. Of the connected nature of the three prohibitions Justice Trimble said in *Ogden v. Saunders*, 25 U.S. (Wheat.) 213 (1827):

[Those ratifying Article I § 10] must have understood, that these denunciations were just, as regarded bills of attainder, and ex post facto laws, because they were exercises of arbitrary power, perverting the justice and order of existing things by the reflex action of these laws. And would they not naturally and necessarily conclude, the denunciations were equally just as regarded laws passed to impair the obligation of existing contracts, for the same reason? . . . I cannot understand this language otherwise than as putting bills of attainder, ex post facto laws, and laws impairing the obligation of contracts, all upon the same footing, and deprecating them all for the same cause. The language shows, clearly, that the whole clause was understood at the time of the adoption of the constitution to have been introduced into the instrument in the very same spirit, and for the very same purpose, namely, for the protection of personal security and of private rights.

Id. at 330 (Trimble, J., concurring). *See also* Douglas W. Kmiec & John O. McGinnis, *The Contract Clause: A Return to the Original Understanding*, 14 HASTINGS CONST. L.Q. 525, 527–28 (1987) (citations omitted) ("The prohibitions against bills of attainder, and ex post facto laws, and takings of property without just compensation, are all derived from strands of the concept of the rule of law: laws must be general, prospective, and relatively stable. The Contract Clause, like the Ex Post Facto Clause, is particularly concerned with the requirement of prospectivity.").

301. *See* Kmiec & McGinnis, *supra* note 300, at 530–33; *see also* Ogden v. Saunders, 25 U.S. (12 Wheat.) 213, 355 (1827) (noting that "the mischief had become so great, so alarming, as not only to impair commercial intercourse, and threaten the existence of credit, but to sap the morals of the people, and destroy the sanctity of private faith. To guard against the continuance of the evil was an object of deep interest with all the truly wise, as well as the virtuous, of this great community, and was one of the important benefits expected from a reform of the government."); Fletcher v. Peck, 6 U.S. (Cranch) 87, 137–38 (1810) (Marshall, C.J.) (explaining that the Contracts Clause came from the framers' desire to "shield themselves and their property from the effects of those sudden and strong passions to which men are exposed").

302. THE FEDERALIST NO. 44, *supra* note 9, at 282 (James Madison) (deeming them "contrary to the first principles of the social compact, and to every piece of sound legislation").

303. *See Fletcher*, 10 U.S. at 137–38 (Marshall, C.J.) (considering them a "bill of rights for the people of each state"); *id.* at 138 (stating that the three prohibitions are intended to restrain legislative power over the "lives and fortunes of individuals"). *See also Ogden*, 25 U.S. at 330–31 (Trimble, J.) (reasoning that the "language shows, clearly, that the whole clause was understood at the time of the adoption of the constitution to have been introduced into the instrument in the very same spirit, and for the very same purpose, namely, for the protection of personal security and of private rights").

304. *Fletcher*, 10 U.S. at 87 (stating "[a] party to a contract cannot pronounce its own deed invalid, although that party be a sovereign state.").

305. A key turning point, scholars agree, was the court's decision in *Home Building & Loan Association v. Blaisdell*, 290 U.S. 398 (1934), which upheld the right of a state to impose a moratorium on mortgage foreclosures during the Great Depression. *See generally* Thomas Halper, *The Living Constitution and the (Almost) Dead Contracts Clause*, 9 BRIT. J. AM. LEGAL STUD. 387 (2020); Kmiec & McGinnis, *supra* note 300. *See also* James W. Ely, Jr., *Whatever Happened to the Contract Clause?*, 4 CHARLESTON L. REV. 371, 371 (2010)

(noting that "during the nineteenth century the Contract Clause was the most litigated provision in the Constitution and was the chief restriction on state authority").

306. Sveen v. Melin, 138 S. Ct. 1815, 1821–22 (2018) (citations omitted).

307. *Id.* at 1822 (citation omitted). *See also* Emergency Reserves Group. Inc. Kansas Power & Light Co., 459 U.S. 400, 411–13, 425 (1983).

308. *Energy Reserves Group, Inc.*, 459 U.S. at 412–13 (quoting U.S. Trust Co. of New York v. New Jersey, 431 U.S. 1, 23 (1977)).

309. In its landmark decision *U.S. Trust Company of New York*, the court suggested that rational basis might be the standard of review. *See* U.S. Trust Co. of New York v. New Jersey, 431 U.S. 1, 22–23 (1977) ("[a]s is customary in reviewing economic and social regulation,... courts properly defer to legislative judgment as to the necessity and reasonableness of a particular measure."). However, the court later indicated a preference for a somewhat more rigorous standard. *See* Pension Benefit Guaranty Corp. v. R.A. Gray & Co., 467 U.S. 717, 733 (1984) ("to the extent that recent decisions of the Court have addressed the issue, we have contrasted the limitations imposed on States by the Contracts Clause with the less searching standards imposed on economic legislation by the Due Process Clauses."). *See also* Amer. Express Travel Related Servs., Inc. v. Sidamon-Eristoff, 669 F.3d 359, 369 (3d Cir. 2012) (Contracts Clause review is "more exacting" than rational-basis review, considering "appropriate" and "reasonable" tailoring). "The degree of deference differs depending on the severity of the impairment and on the State's self-interest." Elliott v. Bd. of School Trustees of Madison Consol. Schools, 876 F.3d 926, 937 (7th Cir. 2017).

310. *See U.S. Trust Co. of New York*, 431 U.S. at 25–26 (stating that "complete deference to a legislative assessment of reasonableness and necessity is not appropriate because the State's self-interest is at stake"). *See also id.* ("A governmental entity can always find a use for extra money, especially when taxes do not have to be raised. If a State could reduce its financial obligations whenever it wanted to spend the money for what it regarded as an important public purpose, the Contract Clause would provide no protection at all."). Furthermore, the extent of the impairment is "a relevant factor in determining its reasonableness." *Id.* at 27.

311. *See Energy Reserves Group, Inc.*, 459 U.S. at 411 ("[i]f the state regulation constitutes a substantial impairment, the State, in justification, must have a significant and legitimate public purpose behind the regulation[.]"); *U.S. Trust Company of New York*, 431 U.S. at 31 ("In the instant case the State has failed to demonstrate that repeal of the 1962 covenant was similarly necessary."). It is worth noting that the current paramount concern over contracts in which the state is a party deviates from the primary historical concern motivating adoption of the Contracts Clause, which was the enactment of state laws allowing private debtors to escape obligations from private debtors. *See* Kmiec & McGinnis, *supra* note 300. In significant part, the shift can be explained by the practical reality, starting especially in the New Deal Era and continuing thereafter, of governments increasingly contracting with private parties to fulfill their mounting obligations to provide public goods and services.

312. *See* Sullivan v. Nassau Cty. Interim Finance Auth., 959 F.3d 54, 66 (2d Cir. 2019) (taking no position on the question but noting that two of three federal circuit courts of appeal have placed the burden on the government). *See also* Andrews v. Lombardi, 231 A.3d 1108, 1123 (R.I. 2020) (applying state and federal Contracts Clauses and imposing burden on the government to produce credible evidence in support of reasonable and necessary requirements). The Eighth Circuit Court of Appeals, in challenges to laws only involving

private parties, imposes on the state "the burden of proof in showing a significant and legitimate public purpose underlying" the challenged law. Equip. Mfrs. Inst. v. Janklow, 300 F.3d 842, 859 (8th Cir. 2002).

313. *See, e.g., Sullivan*, 959 F.3d at 65–66; Southern Calif. Gas Co. v. City of Santa Ana, 336 F.3d 885, 894 (9th Cir. 2003). Ultimately, for impairment to be reasonable and necessary under less deferential scrutiny, it must be shown that the state did not (1) "consider impairing the . . . contracts on par with other policy alternatives," (2) "impose a drastic impairment when an evident and more moderate course would serve its purpose equally well," or (3) act unreasonably "in light of the surrounding circumstances." *U.S. Trust Co. of New York*, 431 U.S. at 30–31.

314. Carmell v. Texas, 529 U.S. 513, 533 (2000).

315. *Id.* at 546. *See also* Lynce v. Mathis, 519 U.S. 433, 440 (1997) ("the Constitution places limits on the sovereign's ability to use its lawmaking power to modify bargains it has made with its subjects.").

316. *See* LAWRENCE H. TRIBE, AMERICAN CONSTITUTIONAL LAW 637 (2d ed. 1988) (noting that the Court "has not been systematically attentive to the purposes of the ex post facto ban . . .").

317. Cummings v. Missouri, 71 U.S. (4 Wall.) 277, 329 (1867).

318. With Contracts Clause cases, not surprisingly, the switch in the burden most often results in state laws being deemed unconstitutional. *See Energy Reserves Group, Inc.*, 459 U.S. at 412 n.14 ("In *United States Trust Co.*, the State was one of the contracting parties. When a State itself enters into a contract, it cannot simply walk away from its financial obligations. In almost every case, the Court has held a governmental unit to its contractual obligations when it enters financial or other markets."); Maze v. Bd. of Dirs. For Comm. Postsecondary Prepaid Educ. Prepaid Tuition, 559 S.W.3d 354, 372 (Ky. 2018) ("In almost every case where this situation has arisen, the Supreme Court has held that the governmental unit was bound to its contractual obligations.").

319. Richard H. Fallon, Jr., Foreword, *Implementing the Constitution*, 111 HARV. L. REV. 56, 61 (1997).

320. *See* Stogner v. California, 539 U.S. 607, 616 (2003). In post-Civil War congressional debates in 1867, several Radical Republican congressmen rejected a bill that would have revived time-barred prosecutions for treason against Confederacy President Jefferson Davis and "his coconspirators." They opposed the bill because it would be an "ex post facto law." *Id.* (quoting from *Congressional Globe* the comment of Representative Roscoe Conklin).

The foregoing scenario contrasts starkly with that in the 1990s when the New York Assembly was considering adoption of its SORN law. As federal Judge Dennis Chin wrote in one decision, despite having constitutional doubts, assembly members nonetheless were willing to "'take a chance regardless of what it may be, the Constitution,' because of their view that sex offenders did not deserve protection." Doe v. Pataki, 940 F. Supp. 603, 622 n.15 (S.D.N.Y. 1996), *rev'd*, 120 F.3d 1263 (2d Cir. 1997), *cert. denied*, 118 S. Ct. 1066 (1998). Judge Chin also noted that one bill sponsor acknowledged that an effort was made in drafting to "'assure' that the Act would be considered 'more regulatory than punitive.'" *Id.*

321. Paul Brest, *The Conscientious Legislator's Guide to Constitutional Interpretation*, 27 STAN. L. REV. 567, 601 (1975). *See also* Michael J. Perry, *The Constitution, the Courts and the Question of Minimalism*, 88 NW. U. L. REV. 84, 138 (1993) ("The principal reason for doubting that ordinary politics can generally do a good job of specifying constitutional indeterminacy is that for most members of the Congress, incumbency is a fundamental

value.”); Frederick Schauer, Ashwander *Revisited*, 1995 Sup. Ct. Rev. 71, 92–93 (1995) (concluding that “given that the American political system does not penalize legislators for voting for good (in the eyes of voters) policies that are determined by the courts to be unconstitutional, one would expect members of Congress to be anything but risk-averse”).

322. 51 U.S. 244 (1994).

323. *Id.* at 273.

324. Fletcher v. Peck, 10 U.S. (6 Cranch) 87, 138 (1810).

325. Kansas v. Hendricks, 521 U.S. 346, 396 (1997) (Breyer, J., dissenting).

Chapter 7

1. 378 U.S. 347 (1964).

2. 3 U.S. (Dall.) 386 (1798).

3. *Id.* at 390 (Chase, J.).

4. *Id.*

5. *Id.*

6. *Id.* at 391.

7. *Calder*, 3 U.S. at 397 (Paterson, J.).

8. *Id.* at 399 (Iredell, J.).

9. *Id.* at 400–01 (Cushing, J.).

10. *See, e.g.*, 2 Records of the Federal Convention of 1787, at 617 (Max Farrand ed., 1966) [hereinafter Farrand's Records] (citing view of Mason at Federal Convention). Mason's position regarding broader coverage persisted into the ratifying convention in Virginia. 3 The Debates in the Several State Conventions on the Adoption of the Federal Constitution, at 472–73, 479 (Jonathan Elliot ed., 1836) [hereinafter Elliot's Debates]

11. *See, e.g.*, Elliott's Debates, *supra* note 10, at 440, 448 (citing Madison's use of ex post facto to refer to law that would shorten the statute of limitations for certain civil actions).

12. *Letter from James Madison to Andrew Stevenson* (Mar. 25, 1826), in 3 Farrand's Records, *supra* note 10, at 473–74. *See also* 4 Annals of Cong. 776 (1796) (remarks of James Madison):

> [W]hatever veneration might be entertained for the body of men who formed our Constitution, the sense of that body could never be regarded as the oracular guide in expounding the Constitution. As the instrument came from them it was nothing more than the draft of a plan, nothing but a dead letter, until life and validity were breathed into it by the voice of the people, speaking through the several State Conventions. If we were to look, therefore, for the meaning of the instrument beyond the face of the instrument, we must look for it, not in the General Convention, which proposed, but in the State Conventions, which accepted and ratified the Constitution.

13. Evan C. Zoldan, *The Civil Ex Post Facto Clause*, 2015 Wis. L. Rev. 727, 746.

14. Convention of North Carolina, in 3 Elliot's Debates, *supra* note 10, at 185 (statement of Iredell).

15. 2 Elliot's Debates, *supra* note 10, at 407.

16. 27 U.S. (2 Pet.) 380 (1829).

17. *Id. See also* Stoddart v. Smith, 5 Binn. 355, 370 (Pa. 1812) (Brackenridge, J.) ("I take notice of the language of the Court of the United States, as confining ex post facto to a criminal case. It is an idea purely American, and not the worse for that, but it is incorrect. Ex post facto law, ex jure post facto, translated 'ex post facto law,' embraces civil contracts as well as criminal acts.").

18. 71 U.S. 277 (1867).

19. 71 U.S. 333 (1867).

20. 97 U.S. 381 (1878).

21. *See* Flemming v. Nestor, 363 U.S. 603, 626 (1960) (Black, J., dissenting) (stating that he did not "believ[e] that the particular label 'punishment' is of decisive importance"); Lehman v. United States, 353 U.S. 685, 690 (1957) (Black, J., concurring) (expressing view that limiting the prohibition to criminal cases "confines the clause too narrowly"); Marcello v. Bonds, 349 U.S. 302, 319 (1955) (Douglas, J., dissenting) (noting that "[t]here is a school of thought that the Ex Post Facto Clause includes all retroactive legislation, civil as well as criminal.").

22. 497 U.S. 37 (1990).

23. *Id.* at 41.

24. Leonard W. Levy, Original Intent and the Framer's Constitution 74 (1988). Why the justices in *Calder* adopted their narrow view remains uncertain. As noted in Chapter 2, none of the justices writing for the court participated in the drafting of the clause in summer 1787 Philadelphia (Justice Paterson was a delegate but was not present at that particular time), and records of the secret proceedings were not actually available until after *Calder* was decided (with publication of the *Official Journal* in 1819, and James Madison's *Notes* in 1840, after his death). To the extent the criminal-centric view is based on Madison's *Notes*, researchers have since cast doubt on their reliability more generally and Professor William Crosskey accused Madison of outright fabrication regarding his recollection of the debates concerning the clause. For further discussion of the possible motivations of the justices, see chapter 2.

25. *See, e.g.*, Bucklew v. Precythe, 139 S. Ct. 1112, 1122 (2019) (stating in a case challenging the use of lethal injection that the court "first examine[s] the original and historical understanding of the Eighth Amendment"). Initially, originalism was mainly driven by the goal of ascertaining the intent of the framers (i.e., "original intent"), but the method in time fell into disfavor. *See* Lawrence B. Solum, *Originalist Methodology*, 84 U. Chi. L. Rev. 269 (2017). Today, "original public meaning" is the dominant originalist interpretative method. *See* Richard H. Fallon, Jr., *The Many and Varied Roles of History in Constitutional Adjudication*, 90 Notre Dame L. Rev. 1753, 1762 (2015) ("Today, most originalists maintain that 'original public' meaning should furnish the touchstone of constitutional analysis.").

26. That is, if indeed a singular view of the framers can be divined. *See* Gregory Maggs, *A Concise Guide to the Records of the Federal Constitutional Convention of 1787 as a Source of the Original Meaning of the U.S. Constitution*, 80 Geo. Wash. L. Rev. 1707, 1732 (2012):

> It would be very convenient for us now if at the Convention [delegates] . . . had made succinct speeches defining each of the terms in the Constitution, giving examples of how they should apply in a variety of situations, and then asking for and receiving some indication that the majority of the other deputies concurred. But that did not happen often. The deputies very rarely explicitly defined terms or addressed ambiguities. And they did not take votes about the correctness of everything that was said.

27. RICHARD H. FALLON, JR., LAW AND LEGITIMACY IN THE SUPREME COURT 47 (2018).

28. Lawrence B. Solum, *Themes from Fallon on Constitutional Theory*, 18 GEO. J. L. & PUB. POL'Y 287, 295 (2020).

29. *Id.* at 295 n.25.

30. *Calder*, 3 U.S. at 391 (Chase, J.).

31. *Id.* at 397 (Paterson, J.).

32. *See, e.g.*, Laura Kelman, *Border Patrol: Reflections on the Turn to History in Legal Scholarship*, 66 FORDHAM L. REV. 87, 94–95 (1997) (citations omitted) (stating that the "Reagan Administration's originalism seemed an especially bad example of 'law office history'" historians have long gotten their kicks out of disparaging, 'inept and perverted' research aimed at adorning work with "the trappings of scholarship and seeming roots in the past. . . .'").

33. *See* Lawrence B. Solum, *Originalism and Constitutional Construction*, 82 FORDHAM L. REV. 453, 455–58 (2013) (discussing the interpretation/construction distinction with regard to originalism). *See also* Robert J. Delahunty & John Yoo, *Saving Originalism*, 113 MICH. L. REV. 1081, 1099 (2015) (stating that "construction seems to be unavoidable even after the interpretive questions posed by a constitutional text have been fully answered").

34. *See* Hillary Chutter-Ames, *From Language to Law: Interpretation and Construction in Early American Judicial Practice*, 114 Nw. U. L. REV. 149, 162–65 (2019).

35. Delahunty & Yoo, *supra* note 33, at 1098.

36. *See* Payne v. Tennessee, 501 U.S. 808, 827 (1991) (stating that stare decisis "promotes the evenhanded, predictable, and consistent development of legal principles, fosters reliance on judicial decisions, and contributes to the actual and perceived integrity of the judicial process.").

37. *See, e.g.*, Collins v. Youngblood, 497 U.S. 37, 41 n.2 (1990) (noting debate about accuracy of *Calder* but electing to adhere to view expressed by Justice Chase); Galvan v. Press, 347 U.S. 522, 743 n.4 (1954) (noting the "characteristically persuasive attack" of Justice Johnson but stating that the "Court, however, has undeviatingly enforced the contrary position, first expressed in *Calder* v. Bull . . . It would be an unjustifiable reversal to overturn a view of the Constitution so deeply rooted and so consistently adhered to."); Harisiades v. Shaughnessy, 342 U.S. 580, 594 (1952) (noting disputed historical record but refusing to reconsider the view because of its long duration).

38. *See* Burnet v. Coronado Oil & Gas Co., 285 U.S. 393, 406 (1932) (Brandeis, J., dissenting) (noting principle that "it is more important that the applicable rule of law be settled than that it be settled right"). *See also* RANDY KOZEL, SETTLED VERSUS RIGHT: A THEORY OF PRECEDENT (2017).

39. Arizona v. Rumsey, 467 U.S. 203, 212 (1984).

40. Gamble v. United States, 139 S. Ct. 1960, 1969 (2019) (citations omitted).

41. *Id.*

42. 347 U.S. 522 (1954).

43. *Id.* at 531 n.4.

44. *See* Jack M. Balkin, *The New Originalism and the Uses of History*, 82 FORDHAM L. REV. 641, 657 (2013) ("Nonoriginalists and living constitutionalists tend to agree that adoption history is very important."); Mitchell N. Berman, *Originalism Is Bunk*, 84 N.Y.U. L. REV. 1, 24–25 (2009) ("Not a single self-identifying non-originalist of whom I'm aware argues that original meaning has no bearing on proper judicial constitutional interpretation."); Peter J. Smith, *How Different Are Originalism and Non-Originalism*, 62 HASTINGS L.J.

707, 722 (2011) ("[M]ost non-originalists—or at least most scholars or judges who do not readily identify as originalists—believe that the original meaning is highly relevant and often dispositive.") (footnotes omitted); Amul R. Thapar & Joe Masterman, *Fidelity and Construction*, 129 YALE L.J. 774, 779 (2020) ("Today, scholars and judges of all stripes acknowledge the importance of original meaning. Fidelity to meaning requires finding and applying that meaning.").

45. *See* Henry Paul Monaghan, *Supremacy Clause Textualism*, 110 COLUM. L. REV. 731, 786 (2010) (noting that "many prominent originalists . . . would accept only those [] precedents that arose close in time to the founding"). Central to this view is "liquidation," a concept advanced by James Madison whereby, post-framing, the meaning of indeterminate text is clarified and thereafter relied upon. This clarification and reliance, some originalists argue, can "fix" the meaning of the text. Curtis A. Bradley & Neil S. Siegel, *Historical Gloss, Madisonian Liquidation, and the Originalism Debate*, 106 VA. L. REV. 1, 142–43 (2020). *See also* THE FEDERALIST PAPERS No. 37, at 229 (James Madison) (Clinton Rossiter ed., 1961) ("All new laws, though penned with the greatest technical skill and passed on the fullest and most mature deliberation, are considered as more or less obscure and equivocal, until their meaning be liquidated and ascertained by a series of particular discussions and adjudications.").

46. Michael Stokes Paulsen, *The Intrinsically Corrupting Influence of Precedent*, 22 CONST. COMMENT. 289, 289 (2005).

47. *See* Eastern Enters. v. Apfel, 524 U.S. 498, 539 (1998) (Thomas, J., concurring) (stating that "[i]n an appropriate case" that he "would be willing to reconsider *Calder* and its progeny to determine whether a retroactive civil law that passes muster under our current Takings Clause jurisprudence is nonetheless unconstitutional under the Ex Post Facto Clause.").

48. *Gamble*, 139 S. Ct. at 1984 (Thomas, J., concurring).

49. *Id.* at 1984–85. *See also id.* at 1985 ("In sum, my view of *stare decisis* requires adherence to decisions made by the People—that is, to the original understanding of the relevant legal text—which may not align with decisions made by the Court.").

50. Ramos v. Louisiana, 140 S. Ct. 1390, 1405 (2020) (Gorsuch, J.) (citation omitted).

51. *See* ANTONIN SCALIA, A MATTER OF INTERPRETATION: FEDERAL COURTS AND THE LAW 140 (1997) (emphasis in original) (describing *stare decisis* as "not *part of* [his] originalist philosophy" but rather a "pragmatic *exception* to it"). *See also* ROBERT H. BORK, THE TEMPTING OF AMERICA: THE POLITICAL SEDUCTION OF THE LAW 158 (1990) (stating that a decision "may be clearly incorrect but nevertheless have become so embedded in the life of the nation, so accepted by the society, so fundamental to the private and public expectations of individuals and institutions, that the result should not be changed now.").

52. *See* Bradley & Siegel, *supra* note 45, at 1, 8.

53. *See Payne*, 501 U.S. at 827. This is mainly due to the pragmatic reason that the other governmental branches cannot supersede the court's Constitution-based determinations. Agnostini v. Felton, 521 U.S. 203, 235 (1997).

54. Alleyne v. United States, 570 U.S. 99, 116 n.5 (2013).

55. *See, e.g.*, Ramos v. Louisiana, 140 S. Ct. 1390 (2020) (reversing on Sixth Amendment grounds prior plurality decision seemingly allowing for non-unanimous criminal juries); Knick v. Township of Scott, 139 S. Ct. 2162 (2019) (reversing Fifth Amendment Takings Clause precedent); Franchise Tax Bd. Of Cal. V. Hyatt, 139 S. Ct. 1485 (2019) (reversing precedent concerning state sovereign immunity in lawsuits); Johnson v. United States, 576 U.S. 591 (2015) (reversing on due process grounds prior decision regarding what

qualifies as a "violent felony" under federal law); Montejo v. Louisiana, 556 U.S. 778 (2009) (reversing prior Sixth Amendment decision barring police from reapproaching a criminal defendant in effort to secure confession).

56. *See Calder*, 3 U.S. at 396 (Paterson, J.) (stating that the judicial nature of the challenged act "militates against the plaintiffs in error [because] their counsel has contended for reversal of the judgment, on the ground, that the awarding of a new trial was the effect of a legislative act, and that it is unconstitutional, because an ex post facto law."); *id.* at 398 (Iredell, J.) (stating that the legislature's exercise of review "in the present instance . . . is an exercise of judicial not of legislative authority"); *id.* at 400 (Cushing, J.) (noting that exercises of judicial authority are not "touched by the federal constitution"). Justice William Johnson concluded thirty years after *Calder* that "all the judges who sat on the case of *Calder v. Bull*, concurred in the opinion" that the Connecticut legislature was exercising judicial, not legislative, authority. Satterlee v. Matthewson, 27 U.S. (2 Pet.) 380, 416 n.a. (1829) (Johnson, J.). Justice Johnson added:

> I then have a right to deny the construction intimated by three of the judges . . . is entitled to the weight of an adjudication. Nor is it immaterial, to observe, that an adjudication upon a fundamental law, ought never to be irrevocably settled by a decision that is not necessary and explicit.

Id.

57. Palmer v. Clarke, 408 F.3d 423, 432 (8th Cir. 2005).
58. *See* JACK M. BALKIN, LIVING ORIGINALISM 149–59 (2011).
59. The timing of convention votes concerning the ex post facto prohibitions contained in sections 9 and 10 of Article I, it should be observed, has a tantalizing possible ramification regarding the coverage of the respective prohibitions. Delegates approved the congressional prohibition (in section 9) one week before the state prohibition (in section 10), in floor debates free of any express contention that the prohibition was limited to retroactive criminal laws. Arguably, the later approval of the state prohibition, and the subsequent decision by the Committee on Style and Arrangement to include a prohibition on the impairment of contracts in the state—but not federal—provision, perhaps suggests that the delegates believed that an explicitly civil (i.e., contracts-related) prohibition was needed, because the state ex post facto prohibition only addressed criminal laws. Thus, an argument can be made that, as a technical matter, the congressional prohibition encompasses civil and criminal laws, whereas, if one believes that *Calder* got it right, the state ex post facto prohibition proscribes only criminal laws.
60. *See* Jack Balkin, *Translating the Constitution*, 118 MICH. L. REV. 997, 981 (2020) (recognizing that "[p]ublic meaning originalists are textualists who regard the meaning of the constitutional text as fixed at the time of adoption"); *see also* Leslie H. Southwick, *A Survivor's Perspective: Federal Judicial Selection from George Bush to Donald Trump*, 95 NOTRE DAME L. REV. 1847, 1914 (2020) (noting that recent conservative presidents often look for originalists and textualists when nominating federal judges).
61. "Original intent," an early incarnation of originalism, was popularized by President Reagan's Attorney General Edwin Meese III. *See* Edwin Meese III, *Speech Before the American Bar Ass'n*, July 9, 1985, at 47, *in* ORIGINALISM: A QUARTER-CENTURY OF DEBATE (Steven G. Calabresi ed., 2007). Before Meese, Robert Bork, a former Yale Law School professor and later federal judge and unsuccessful Supreme Court nominee, wrote an article often thought the most influential salvo fired in favor of modern originalism methodology. *See*

Delahunty & Yoo, *supra* note 33, at 1089 (stating same and citing Robert H. Bork, *Neutral Principles and Some First Amendment Problems*, 47 IND. L.J. 1 (1971)). Professor Raoul Berger also invoked the principle. RAOUL BERGER, GOVERNMENT BY THE JUDICIARY: THE TRANSFORMATION OF THE FOURTEENTH AMENDMENT 363 (1977) (defining "original intention" as "the meaning attached by the framers to the words they employed in the Constitution and its Amendments"). Stanford Law Professor Paul Brest is credited with coining the term "originalism." *See* Delahunty & Yoo, *supra* note 33, at 1095 n.68 (citing Paul Brest, *The Misconceived Quest for the Original Understanding*, 60 B.U. L. REV. 204, 212–15 (1980)).

62. *See, e.g.*, ROBERT BORK, THE TEMPTING OF AMERICA: THE POLITICAL SEDUCTION OF THE LAW 141 (1991) (asserting that "[constitutional] theory must, therefore, enable us to say what is the limit of the judge's legitimate authority.").

63. The expansion, it is worth noting, would align with the view of Justice Hugo Black, who was not only a staunch libertarian and proponent of a broad construction of the clause, but a progenitor of originalism. David A. Strauss, *Why Conservatives Shouldn't Be Originalists*, 31 HARV. J.L. & PUB. POL'Y 969, 975 (2005).

64. An alternative, which would seem a political nonstarter in the United States, would be to follow Germany's approach, where the penal code provides that "[t]he punishment and its collateral consequences are determined by the law which is in force at the time of the act." German Penal Code section 2(1-5), StGB. *See also* Lithuania Penal Code Art. 3(4).

65. *See, e.g.*, Tenn. Stat. § 40-39-201 (2019) (stating with respect to SORN law that the "policy of authorizing release of necessary and relevant information about offenders to members of the general public is a means of assuring public protection and shall not be construed as punitive"). Another technique is to situate a challenged law in a non-penal part of a statutory code. Although the Supreme Court in *Smith* insisted that such placement of little moment, *Hendricks* very clearly attached importance to location. *See* Kansas v. Hendricks, 521 U.S. 346, 361 (1997) ("[The State's] objective to create a civil proceeding is evidenced by its placement of the Act within the [State's] probate code, instead of the criminal code."). Location importance is also evidenced in decisions of lower courts. *See, e.g.*, *Simmons v. Gavin*, 575 F.3d 24, 44 (1st Cir. 2009) (attaching importance to the fact that constitutional amendment retroactively disenfranchising incarcerated felons, later made a statute, was codified in a voter qualification section, not the state's criminal code).

66. 27 U.S. (2 Pet.) 380 (1829).

67. *Id.* at 416 n.a. (Johnson, J., concurring).

68. *Id.* Similarly, Thomas Jefferson, a few years earlier, in 1813, acknowledged *Calder's* criminal-centric view but reasoned that retroactive laws "are equally unjust in civil as in criminal cases." Thomas Jefferson, Letter to Isaac McPherson, August 13, 1813, available at https://founders.archives.gov/documents/Jefferson/03-06-02-0322.

69. Sessions v. Dimaya, 138 S. Ct. 1204, 1229 (2018) (Gorsuch, J., concurring in part).

70. 2 RICHARD WOODDESON, A SYSTEMATICAL VIEW OF THE LAWS OF ENGLAND 641 (1792). *See also Calder*, 3 U.S. at 399 (Iredell, J.) (reasoning that "[i]t is only in criminal cases, indeed, in which danger to be guarded against, is greatly to be apprehended").

71. In the international context, it is worth noting, criminal focus is the norm. The major human rights treaties and, with only a few exceptions, national constitutions, prohibit only retroactive crime creation and sentence increases. KENNETH S. GALLANT, THE PRINCIPLE OF LEGALITY IN INTERNATIONAL AND COMPARATIVE CRIMINAL LAW 392–93 (2009). International ex post facto provisions are discussed in Chapter 8, and while assuredly

important, the fact that they are overwhelmingly criminal-centric in focus does not detract from the argument that the limit should be abandoned in the United States, which is unique for its crime control political pathologies and constitutional history. *See also id.* at 393 (footnote omitted) (noting that "[a]t some point, the issue may arise . . . given that the UN Security Council has begun imposing 'non-criminal' sanctions, such as requiring states to freeze assets and deny entry, upon individuals and other non-state entities.").

72. LON FULLER, THE MORALITY OF LAW 59 (2d ed. 1969).

73. William J. Stuntz, *The Pathological Politics of Criminal Law*, 100 MICH. L. REV. 505, 529–30 (2001).

74. As one commentator recently observed:

> voters and their elected representatives consistently choose severe policies without sufficient regard for the people who bear the costs of these policies. . . . [T]he problem is a kind of political process failure, explained by the fact that ordinary voters can imagine themselves victims of crime but do not expect to be on the receiving end of criminal sanctions.

Daniel Epps, *Checks and Balances in the Criminal Law*, 74 VAND. L. REV. 1, 61 (2021). *See also generally* KATHERINE BECKETT, MAKING CRIME PAY: LAW AND ORDER IN CONTEMPORARY AMERICAN POLITICS 14–27, 62–63 (1997) (discussing influence of popular media reports on criminal justice legislation); KATHLYN TAYLOR GAUBATZ, CRIME IN THE PUBLIC MIND 5–8 (1995). As David Garland has noted, "TV has changed the rules of political speech. The TV encounter—with its soundbite rapidity, its emotional intensity, and its mass audience—has tended to push politicians to be more populist, more emotive, more evidently in tune with public feelings." DAVID GARLAND, THE CULTURE OF CONTROL: CRIME AND SOCIAL ORDER IN CONTEMPORARY SOCIETY 7 (2001).

75. Harold J. Krent, *The Puzzling Boundary Between Criminal and Civil Retroactive Lawmaking*, 84 GEO. L.J. 2143, 2168–69 (1996). For more on the practical reasons for this legislative unconcern, *see* Donald A. Dripps, *Criminal Procedure, Footnote Four, and the Theory of Public Choice; or, Why Don't Legislatures Give a Damn About the Rights of the Accused?*, 44 SYRACUSE L. REV. 1079 (1993); Daniel Epps, *The Consequences of Error in Criminal Justice*, 128 HARV. L. REV. 1065, 1065, 1115–17 (2015).

76. Krent, *supra* note 75, at 2167.

77. *See generally* Akhil R. Amar, *Constitutional Redundancies and Clarifying Clauses*, 33 VAL. U. L. REV. 1 (1998).

78. Calder v. Bull 3 U.S. (3 Dall.) 396, 390 (1798) (Chase, J.).

79. *See* Landgraf v. USI Film Prods., 511 U.S. 244, 266 (1994).

80. Andrew F. Hessick, *Doctrinal Redundancies*, 67 ALA. L. REV. 635, 648–49 (2016) (citing and discussing the Free Exercise Clause of the First Amendment and the Equal Protection Clause of the Fourteenth Amendment).

81. Duane L. Ostler, *The Forgotten Constitutional Spotlight: How Viewing the Ban on Bill of Attainder as a Takings Protection Clarifies Constitutional Principles*, 42 U. TOL. L. REV. 395, 417 (2011) (citing and discussing the Fifth Amendment's "Takings Clause" and the Bill of Attainder Clause).

82. *See Landgraf*, 511 U.S. at 267–68 (noting benefits of retrospective civil laws, including responding to emergencies, correcting mistakes, curbing circumvention of new statutes in intervals immediately preceding their passage, and providing more comprehensive effect to new laws Congress considers salutary).

83. *Calder*, 3 U.S. at 393 (Chase, J.); *see also id.* at 400 (Iredell, J.) (cautioning that "[w]ithout the possession of this power the operations of Government would often be obstructed, and society itself would be endangered.").

84. *See, e.g.*, DANIEL E. TROY, RETROACTIVE LEGISLATION (1998); Daniel W. Bell, *In Defense of Retroactive Laws*, 78 TEX. L. REV. 258 (1999); Jeffrey O. Usman, *Constitutional Constraints on Retroactive Civil Legislation: The Hollow Promises of the Federal Constitution and Unrealized Potential of State Constitutions*, 14 NEV. L.J. 63 (2013).

85. According to one survey, as of 1868, when the Fourteenth Amendment to the US Constitution was ratified, four states prohibited retroactive criminal and civil laws, all of which were ratified after the *Calder* Court limited the federal ex post facto provision to criminal laws. Steven G. Calabresi & Sarah E. Agudo, *Individual Rights Under State Constitutions When the Fourteenth Amendment Was Ratified in 1868: What Rights Are Deeply Rooted in American History and Tradition?*, 87 TEX. L. REV. 7, 69 (2008).

86. Usman, *supra* note 84, at 85. New Hampshire's provision, which dates back to 1784, before the genesis of Article I of the US Constitution, provides that "[r]etrospective laws are highly injurious, oppressive, and unjust. No such laws, therefore, should be made, either for the decision of civil causes, or the punishment of offenses." N.H. Const. Art. 23.

87. Bielat v. Bielat, 721 N.E.2d 28, 33 (Ohio 2000).

88. *See* Usman, *supra* note 84, at 88.

89. *See* Joseph E. Blocher, *What State Constitutional Law Can Tell Us About the Federal Constitution*, 115 PENN. ST. L. REV. 1035 (2011); Joseph E. Blocher, *Reverse Incorporation of State Constitutional Law*, 84 S. CAL. L. REV. 323 (2011).

90. Calder v. Bull, 3 U.S. (3 Dall.) 386, 390 (1798) (Chase, J.).

91. Oliver P. Field, *Ex Post Facto in the Constitution*, 20 MICH. L. REV. 315, 321–22 (1922).

92. 529 U.S. 513 (2000).

93. 539 U.S. 607 (2003).

94. *Calder,* 3 U.S. (3 Dall.) at 390–91.

95. *See, e.g.*, *Carmell*, 529 U.S. at 538–39; Collins v. Youngblood, 497 U.S. 37, 46 (1990); Miller v. Florida, 482 U.S. 423, 429 (1987); *see also Stogner*, 539 U.S. at 634 (Kennedy, J., dissenting, joined by Rehnquist, C.J., and Scalia and Thomas, J.J.) ("Our precedents hold that the reach of the *Ex Post Facto* Clause is strictly limited to the precise formulation of the *Calder* categories."); *Ex parte Garland*, 71 U.S. (4 Wall.) 333, 391 (1866) (Miller, J., dissenting) ("[*Calder's*] exposition of the nature of ex post facto laws has never been denied...").

96. 497 U.S. 37 (1990).

97. *See id.* at 43 ("Legislatures may not retroactively alter the definition of crimes or increase the punishment for criminal acts.").

98. *Id.* at 46. *See also* Calif. Dep't of Corr. v. Morales, 514 U.S. 499, 510 n.7 (1995) ("The ex post facto standard we apply today is constant: It looks to whether a given legislative change has the prohibited effect of altering the definition of crimes or increasing punishments.").

99. 269 U.S. 167 (1925).

100. *Collins*, 497 U.S. at 43.

101. *See Beazell*, 269 U.S. at 169–70 ("It is settled, by decisions of this Court so well known that their citation may be dispensed with, that any statute which [1] punishes as a crime an act previously committed, which was innocent when done; [2] which makes more burdensome the punishment for a crime, after its commission, or [3] which deprives one charged with crime of any defense available according to law at the time when the act was

committed, is prohibited as ex post facto."). Lower courts have followed suit. *See, e.g.,* State v. Patton, 503 P.3d 1022, 1032 (Kan. 2022) (relying on *Beazell's* three category test).

102. *See* Neil Coleman McCabe & Cynthia Ann Bell, *Ex Post Facto Provisions of State Constitutions,* 4 Emerging Issues in St. Const. L. 133, 134 (1991) (stating that the *Calder* categories "have not stood the test of time. On closer analysis, the second and third categories appear to be the same idea expressed in different ways"); *see also* Wayne R. LaFave & Austin W. Scott, Criminal Law 97 n.3 (2d ed. 1986) (offering the same conclusion that the second and third *Calder* categories are duplicative).

103. *Calder,* 3 U.S. at 397 (Paterson, J.).

104. 569 U.S. 530 (2013).

105. *Id.* at 533 (emphasis added).

106. 127 A.3d 794 (Pa. 2015).

107. *Id.* at 806–08.

108. *See id.* at 810–11 (Stevens, J., dissenting); *see also id.* at 812 ("Appellee was not disadvantaged by the changes to the sentencing scheme for third-degree murder which became effective in 1995 because he could not have been subjected to prosecution and punishment on a criminal homicide charge until the victim's death. Stated another way, Appellee's punishment pursuant to [the new law] was not made more burdensome or retroactive since he could not have been charged with or convicted of third-degree murder prior [the victim's death].").

109. 450 U.S. 24 (1981).

110. *Id.* at 32 n.17.

111. For a critique of *Rose* and helpful discussion of straddle crimes more generally, *see* Devon F. Ferris, Note, *Reconciling Ex Post Facto Analysis and Straddle Offenses: Alternative Approaches to Incomplete Crimes in* Commonwealth v. Rose, 54 Duq. L. Rev. 451, 473 (2016).

112. As one justice put it in the *Carmell* oral argument, "the trick is in the classification." Transcript of Oral Argument, Carmell v. Texas, 529 U.S. 513 (2000), 1999 WL 1134651, at *18 (Nov. 30, 1999).

113. *Cummings,* 71 U.S. at 329. *See also* Weaver v. Graham 450 U.S. 24, 31 (1981) ("[I]t is the effect, not the form, of the law that determines whether it is ex post facto.").

114. Stogner v. California, 539 U.S. 607, 612 (2003).

115. Nixon v. Adm'r of Gen. Serv., 433 U.S. 425, 469 (1977).

116. United States v. Brown, 381 U.S. 437, 447 (1965)

117. *Nixon,* 433 U.S. at 475; *see also id.* (stating that "[t]he Court, therefore, often has looked beyond mere historical experience and has applied a functional test"). For more on the court's "functional" approach to attainder cases, *see* Thomas B. Griffith, Note, *Beyond Process: A Substantive Rationale for the Bill of Attainder Clause,* 70 Va. L. Rev. 475, 477–92 (1984).

118. Carmell v. Texas, 529 U.S. 513, 567 (2000) (Ginsburg, J., dissenting, joined by Rehnquist, C.J., O'Connor, and Kennedy, J.J.).

119. Palmer v. Clarke, 408 F.3d 423, 432 (8th Cir. 2005).

120. *See* Bd. of Educ. v. Dowell, 498 U.S. 237, 245–46 (1991) (stating that the court's doctrine should not be treated as part of the Constitution); South Carolina v. Gathers, 490 U.S. 805, 825 (1989) (Scalia, J., dissenting) (positing that judges are duty-bound to enforce the Constitution, "not the gloss which [the Court] may have put on it"), *overruled by* Payne v. Tennessee, 501 U.S. 808 (1991); Graves v. New York ex rel. O'Keefe, 306 U.S. 466, 491–92

(1939) (Frankfurter, J., concurring) ("[T]he ultimate touchstone of constitutionality is the Constitution itself and not what we have said about it.").

121. *See* Nicholas Q. Rosenkranz, *The Objects of the Constitution*, 63 STAN. L. REV. 1005, 1019–20 (2011) (noting that the Constitution provides that the power to pass bills and laws belongs to Congress, not the judicial or executive branch); *id.* at 1025 (applying similar reasoning in concluding that Article I, section 10 applies to state legislatures). *See also* Marks v. United States, 430 U.S. 188, 191 (1977) ("The Ex Post Facto Clause is a limitation upon the powers of the Legislature, and does not of its own force apply to the Judicial Branch of government"); *Calder* v. Bull, 3 U.S. (3 Dall.) 386, 389 (1798) ("The Constitution of the United States, article I, section 9, prohibits the Legislature of the Unites States from passing any ex post facto law.").

122. Rosenkranz, *supra* note 121, at 1020.

123. 3 U.S. (3 Dall.) 386 (1798).

124. The fact did not go unnoticed by the justices writing opinions in *Calder. See, e.g., Calder,* 3 U.S. at 398 (Iredell, J.) (concluding that the challenge lacked merit because "1st. if the act of the Legislature of Connecticut was a judicial act, it is not within the words of the Constitution; and 2nd. even if it was a legislative act, it is not within the meaning of the prohibition."). Justice William Johnson, in his "note" critiquing *Calder* in *Satterlee v. Matthewson* (1829), recognized this as well, asserting that *Calder* was not "entitled to the weight of an adjudication." 27 U.S. (2 Pet.) 380, 416 n.a. (1829) (Johnson, J., concurring).

Of note, for a time the court applied the Contracts Clause to judicial acts even though it is also directed at a "Law." *See* Barton H. Thompson, *The History of the Judicial Impairment "Doctrine" and its Lessons for the Contract Clause*, 44 STAN. L. REV. 1373 (1992) (discussing how federal courts in the mid-nineteenth century protected individuals from state judicial decisions impairing contractual rights, albeit not always expressly on Contract Clause grounds).

125. 378 U.S. 347 (1964).

126. *Id.* at 352–54.

127. Rosenkranz, *supra* note 121, at 1056 (emphasis in original).

128. *See id.* (stating that so long as the Republican Form of Government Clause is satisfied, states "may delegate legislative power as they see fit—to, for example, governors or city councils. Indeed, the people themselves may retain some state legislative power, to exercise through populr referenda.").

129. *Id.* at 1056–57.

130. 227 U.S. 150 (1913).

131. *Id.* at 162–63.

132. 71 U.S. 277 (1867).

133. 152 U.S. 377 (1894).

134. Fred O. Smith, Jr., *Due Process, Republicanism, and Direct Democracy*, 89 N.Y.U. L. REV. 582, 585 (2014). In California, "voters have the power to change criminal sentencing law at the ballot box. They can amend statutes and the state constitution." Gilman v. Brown, 814 F.3d 1007, 1009 (9th Cir. 2016).

135. *See* Steven A. Krieger, *Do "Tough on Crime" Politicians Win More Elections? An Empirical Analysis of California State Legislators 1992–2000*, 45 CREIGHTON L. REV. 131, 146–64 (2011).

136. *See* Wayne A. Logan, *The Shadow Criminal Law of Municipal Governance*, 62 OHIO ST. L.J. 1409 (2001).

137. Outside the sentencing guidelines context, the court has at times considered executive branch implementation. *See, e.g.,* Garner v. Jones, 529 U.S. 244 (2000). At other times, it has steadfastly resisted doing so. *See, e.g.,* Seling v. Young, 531 U.S. 250 (2001).

138. *See* KATE STITH & JOSÉ A. CABRANES, FEAR OF JUDGING: SENTENCING GUIDELINES IN THE FEDERAL COURTS (1998).

139. *See generally* Stephen Breyer, *The Federal Sentencing Guidelines and the Key Compromises Upon Which They Rest,* 17 HOFSTRA L. REV. 1 (1988); Ilene H. Nagel, *Structuring Sentencing Discretion: The New Federal Sentencing Guidelines,* 80 J. CRIM. L. & CRIMINOLOGY 883 (1990).

140. 28 USC § 994(p).

141. 488 U.S. 361 (1989).

142. *Id.* at 426 (Scalia, J., dissenting).

143. *Id.* at 412.

144. The concern in part gave rise to what is known as the "one book rule": that the sentencing court must use "either the Sentencing Guidelines Manual in effect at sentencing or the one in effect when the crime was committed." United States v. Bailey, 123 F.3d 1381, 1403 (11th Cir. 1997). *See also* U.S.S.G. § 1B1.11(b)(2)11 (codifying the one-book rule).

145. 482 U.S. 423 (1987).

146. *Id.* at 425–26.

147. *Id.* at 435.

148. *Id.* at 434 (citing Wallace v. Christensen, 802 F.2d 1539 (9th Cir. 1986)).

149. Daniel M. Levy, *Defending* Demaree: *The Ex Post Facto Clause's Lack of Control Over the Federal Sentencing Guidelines After* Booker, 77 FORDHAM L. REV. 2623, 2635 (2009).

150. 15 F.3d 1380 (7th Cir. 1994).

151. *Id.* at 1391–92 (Easterbrook, J., concurring) (citations omitted).

152. 534 U.S. 220 (2005).

153. *Id.* at 245 (Breyer, J., concurring).

154. 459 F.3d 791, 794–95 (7th Cir. 2006), *cert. denied,* 127 S. Ct. 3055 (2007), *abrogated by* Peugh v. United States, 569 U.S. 530 (2013).

155. *Id.* at 795.

156. 569 U.S. 530 (2013).

157. *Id.* at 545.

158. *Id.*

159. Garner v. Jones, 529 U.S. 244, 253–54 (2000).

160. *Miller,* 482 U.S. at 435. *See also, e.g.,* Fletcher v. Dist. of Columbia, 391 F.3d 250, 251 (D.C. Cir. 2004) (stating that *Garner* had "foreclosed our categorical distinction between a measure with the force of law and 'guidelines [that] are merely policy statements,'" holding that either can be the source of an ex post facto violation) (citation omitted); Himes v. Thompson, 336 F.3d 848, 854 (9th Cir. 2003) (holding that more onerous parole regulation violated the Ex Post Facto Clause and that the term "laws" includes "'every form in which the legislative power . . . is exerted,' including 'a regulation or order'").

161. *See* Beazell v. Ohio, 269 U.S. 167, 171 (1925) (stating that the clause was "not [intended] to limit legislative control of remedies and modes of procedure which do not affect matters of substance").

162. 432 U.S. 282 (1977).

163. 497 U.S. 37 (1990).

164. *Dobbert,* 432 U.S. at 293.

165. *Collins,* 497 U.S. 44.
166. *Id.* at 46.
167. 162 U.S. 565 (1896).
168. *Id.* at 590.
169. 79 U.S. 35 (1870).
170. 152 U.S. 377 (1894).
171. Hanna v. Plumer, 380 U.S. 460, 471 (1965) (quoting Guaranty Trust Co. v. York, 326 U.S. 99 (1945)).
172. 482 U.S. 423 (1987).
173. *Id.* at 433; *see also* Murphy v. Kentucky, 465 U.S. 1072, 1073 (1984) (White, J., dissenting from denial of certiorari) (noting "evident confusion" among courts in drawing distinction); Carper v. W. Va. Parole Bd., 509 S.E.2d 864, 868 (W. Va. 1998) ("Just what alterations of procedure will be held to be of sufficient moment to transgress the constitutional prohibition cannot be embraced within a formula or stated in a general proposition. The distinction is one of degree.") (citation omitted). This same line-drawing challenge has bedeviled federal courts for years in choice-of-law determinations when resolving claims based on diversity of citizenship, an expansive body of law benefiting from no greater degree of certainty. *See generally* PETER W. LOW & JOHN C. JEFFRIES, JR., FEDERAL COURTS AND THE LAW OF FEDERAL-STATE RELATIONS 547–87 (5th ed. 2004). Similar challenges are evidenced in habeas corpus jurisprudence, where courts struggle to determine whether a ruling announces a "substantive" change in law, requiring its retroactive application to cases on collateral review. *See generally* 2 RANDY HERTZ & JAMES S. LIEBMAN, FEDERAL HABEAS CORPUS PRACTICE AND PROCEDURE § 25.1, at 1030–32 (7th ed. 2015).
174. 529 U.S. 513 (2000).
175. *See, e.g.,* Widom v. Sate, 656 So. 2d 432 (Fla. 1995) (rejecting challenge to law retroactively allowing "victim impact evidence" in capital trials).
176. *Cummings,* 71 U.S. at 329. *See also* Weaver v. Graham 450 U.S. 24, 31 (1981) ("[I]t is the effect, not the form, of the law that determines whether it is ex post facto.").
177. See, for instance, the at once broad and circular definition offered by the *Collins* Court: procedural changes refer to "changes in the procedures by which a criminal case is adjudicated, as opposed to changes in the substantive law of crimes." Collins v. Youngblood, 497 U.S. 37, 45 (1990). In *Collins,* the court overruled two prior cases granting ex post facto relief involving what the court saw as procedural laws (*Kring v. Missouri* (1883) and *Thompson v. Utah* (1898)), yet left intact decisions containing language attaching importance to the onerous consequences of laws possibly classified as procedural. *See, e.g., Beazell,* 269 U.S. at 170 (stating that procedural laws affecting defendants in a "harsh and arbitrary manner" are ex post facto); Thompson v. Missouri, 171 U.S. 380, 383–84, 388 (1898) (noting that a procedural change can be invalid when it "alter[s] the situation of a party to his disadvantage" or "entrench[es] upon any of the essential rights belonging to one put on trial"). Similarly, language in several of the court's decisions more generally has attached significance to the disadvantages associated with challenged laws. *See, e.g.,* Miller v. Florida, 482 U.S. 423, 431, 433 (1987) (stating that the clause prohibits any law that "clearly disadvantages" or alters a "substantial right"); Lindsey v. Washington, 301 U.S. 397, 401 (1937) (stating that the Ex Post Facto Clause forbids criminal laws accruing "to the detriment or material disadvantage of the wrongdoer"); Malloy v. South Carolina 237 U.S. 180, 183 (1915) (finding that ex post facto laws infringe on "substantial personal rights"); Duncan v. Missouri, 152 U.S. 377, 382–83 (1894) (stating that ex post facto laws

deprive the person of "substantial protections with which the existing law surrounds the person accused of [the] crime").

178. United States v. Jones, 565 U.S. 400, 411 (2012) (emphasis in the original). *See also id.* at 406 (quoting Kyllo v. United States, 533 U.S. 27, 34 (2001) ("we must 'assure preservation of that degree of privacy against government that existed when the Fourth Amendment was adopted.'").

179. *See generally* ADAM J. HIRSCH, THE RISE OF THE PENITENTIARY: PRISONS AND PUNISHMENT IN EARLY AMERICA 23–68 (1992).

180. JONATHAN SIMON, GOVERNING THROUGH CRIME: HOW THE WAR ON CRIME TRANSFORMED AMERICAN DEMOCRACY AND CREATED A CULTURE OF FEAR 75 (2007). *See also generally* MARKUS DUBBER, VICTIMS IN THE WAR ON CRIME: THE USES AND ABUSES OF VICTIMS RIGHTS (2002).

181. *See* WAYNE A. LOGAN, KNOWLEDGE AS POWER: CRIMINAL REGISTRATION AND COMMUNITY NOTIFICATION LAWS IN AMERICA 94–95 (2009) (noting that all of the eighteen victims of sex crimes Congress chose to memorialize by name in its Adam Walsh Act (2006) "roll call" were white, and with one exception, children).

182. 142 Cong. Rec. E732 (daily ed. May 8, 1996) (statement of Rep. Martini).

183. LOGAN, KNOWLEDGE AS POWER, *supra* note 181, at 95.

184. 142 Cong. Rec. H10313 (daily ed. May 7, 1996) (statement of Rep. Cunningham). For additional examples of colorful language used, *see* Mona Lynch, *Pedophiles and Cyber-Predators as Contaminating Forces: The Language of Disgust, Pollution, and Boundary Invasions in Federal Debates on Sex Offender Legislation,* 27 LAW & SOC. INQUIRY 529 (2002).

185. An important byproduct of increasing criminalization has been that those convicted of crimes, felonies in particular, lose the right to vote, very often for their lifetimes. Here, too, race plays a major role, with African Americans disenfranchised in significant disproportion to their population percentages, serving to remove their voice from the political-electoral process. *See* Epps, *Checks and Balances in the Criminal Law, supra* note 74, at 63–64. As Professor Epps notes, "[i]f it is a problem that most voters cannot imagine themselves as potential criminals, excluding the people most able to see things from the perspective of the convict is particularly damaging. As criminal law sweeps in more and more people with felony convictions, the electorate charged with power over policy [grows] even smaller." *Id.* at 64. And, this is not all, because of what has been called "prison gerrymandering"—the policy whereby prison populations are included in counts of the jurisdictions where they are located—which affects state and federal political representation. This is important because prisons, especially since the building boom commencing in the 1980s, are frequently situated in rural areas that very often contain more conservative voters. *See* Faith Stachulski, Note, *Prison Gerrymandering: Locking Up Elections and Diluting Representational Equality,* 2019 U. ILL. L. REV. 401.

186. *See, e.g.,* LAWRENCE M. FRIEDMAN, CRIME AND PUNISHMENT IN AMERICAN HISTORY 77–82 (1993) (describing gradual creation of the penitentiary, beginning in last decade of the eighteenth century, and the first decades of the nineteenth century).

187. Marie Gottschalk, referencing the evolution in the meaning of a "life" sentence, provides some telling statistics of the punitive shift:

> In 1913, a "life" sentence in the federal system was officially defined as fifteen years. Many states had comparable limits on "life" sentences.

Until the 1970s, even in a hard-line state such as Louisiana, which today has the nation's highest incarceration rate, a life sentence typically meant ten years and six months . . . Almost overnight the situation changed, as lawmakers first raised the minimum number of years before a prisoner could be considered for clemency and then mandated that all life sentences meant [life without possibility of parole, LWOP]. In 1970, only 143 people were serving LWOP in Louisiana. By 2012, that number had mushroomed to about 4,600—or nearly 12 percent of the state's entire prison population. Between 1992 and 2008, the number of prisoners serving LWOP sentences nationwide increased by 300 percent.

MARIE GOTTSCHALK, CAUGHT: THE PRISON STATE AND THE LOCKDOWN OF AMERICAN POLITICS 170–71 (2016) (footnotes omitted).

188. National Research Council, *The Growth of Incarceration in the United States: Exploring Causes and Consequences* 33 (Jeremy Travis et al. eds., 2014).

189. The Sentencing Project, *Fact Sheet: Trends in U.S. Corrections*, https://www.sentencing project.org/wp-content/uploads/2021/07/Trends-in-US-Corrections.pdf (last visited July 19 2021).

190. Katherine Beckett & Lindsey Beach, *The Place of Punishment in Twenty-First Century America: Understanding the Persistence of Mass Incarceration*, 46 LAW & SOC. INQUIRY 1 (2021); Andrew D. Leipold, *Is Mass Incarceration Inevitable?*, 56 AM. CRIM. L. REV. 1579, 1592–97 (2019).

191. As Franklin Zimring has observed, "[t]he expansion of felony convictions and their re-lated disabilities now threatens tens of millions of Americans. The pathological excess of penal disabilities and overincarceration in the Untied States are fraternal if not iden-tical twins." FRANKLIN E. ZIMRING, THE INSIDIOUS MOMENTUM OF AMERICAN MASS INCARCERATION 181 (2020).

192. We live, as one scholar put it, in an "era of mass convictions, not (just) mass imprison-ment." Gabriel J. Chin, *The New Civil Death: Rethinking Punishment in the Era of Mass Conviction*, 160 U. PA. L. REV. 1789, 1803 (2012).

193. *See, e.g.*, Mueller v. Raemisch, 740 F.3d 1128 (7th Cir. 2014) (rejecting ex post facto chal-lenge to $100 annual fee associated with Wisconsin's registration law).

194. *See* Wayne A. Logan, *When Mercy Seasons Justice: Interstate Recognition of Ex-Offender Rights*, 49 U.C.-DAVIS L. REV. 1 (2016).

195. *See* Wayne A. Logan, *Informal Collateral Consequences*, 88 WASH. L. REV. 1103 (2013).

196. For additional discussion of collateral consequences more generally, *see* MARGARET COLGATE LOVE, JENNY ROBERTS, & WAYNE A. LOGAN, COLLATERAL CONSEQUENCES OF CRIMINAL CONVICTION: LAW, POLICY, AND PRACTICE (2021).

197. Chin, *supra* note 192, at 1793–98.

198. ABA STANDARDS FOR CRIMINAL JUSTICE: LEGAL STATUS OF PRISONERS, Stnd. 23-8.2 cmt. (1983).

199. *See* Kathleen Olivares et al., *The Collateral Consequences of a Felony Conviction: A National Study of State Legal Codes 10 Years later*, 60 FED. PROBATION, Sept. 1996, at 10 (surveying marked increase in collateral consequences enacted in states 1986–1996).

200. Office of Justice Programs, National Inventory of Collateral Consequences, Feb. 4, 2016, http://www.nij.gov/topics/courts/pages/collateral-consequences-inventory.aspx [https://perma.cc/DR3K-SZQS].

201. People v. Pieri, 199 N.E. 495, 499 (N.Y. 1936) (Cardozo, J.).

202. Similar abhorrence was expressed some twenty-five years before by the Supreme Court, in *Weems v. United States*, 217 U.S. 349 (1910). In *Weems*, which originated in the Philippines, then a US territory, the court addressed a challenge to "cadena temporal," a punishment involving a period of imprisonment wearing chains while performing hard labor, as well as subsequent suffering of "accessory penalties," "civil interdiction," "perpetual absolute disqualification," and "subjection to surveillance during life." The court regarded the punishment collectively as violative of the Eighth Amendment's prohibition of cruel and unusual punishment, attaching particular importance to the post-imprisonment penalties:

> Its minimum degree is confinement in a penal institution for twelve years and one day, a chain at the ankle and wrist of the offender, hard and painful labor . . . These parts of his penalty endure for the term of imprisonment. From other parts there is no intermission. His prison bars and chains are removed, it is true, after twelve years, but he goes from them to a perpetual limitation of his liberty. He is forever kept under the shadow of his crime, forever kept within voice and view of the criminal magistrate, not being able to change his domicil[e] without giving notice to the 'authority immediately in charge of his surveillance,' and without permission in writing. He may not seek, even in other scenes and among other people, to retrieve his fall from rectitude. Even that hope is taken from him and he is subject to tormenting regulations that, if not so tangible as iron bars and stone walls, oppress as much by their continuity, and deprive of essential liberty.

    Id. at 366.

203. Michelle Alexander, The New Jim Crow: Mass Incarceration in the Age of Color Blindness 41 (2012). As Alexander notes, because collateral consequences are based on convictions, like prison populations, they also disproportionately affect African Americans. *Id.* at 173–208.

204. 538 U.S. 84 (2003).

205. *Id.* at 99.

206. Rachel E. Barkow, Prisoners of Politics: Breaking the Cycle of Mass Incarceration 112–19 (2019).

207. Emily Bazelon, Charged: The New Movement to Transform American Prosecution and End Mass Incarceration (2019); John Pfaff, Locked In: The True Causes of Mass Incarceration and How to Achieve Real Reform 206 (2017).

208. Ronald F. Wright, *How Prosecutor Elections Fail Us*, 6 Ohio St. J. Crim. L. 581 (2009).

209. Stuntz, *supra* note 73, at 510.

210. 165 U.S. 526 (1897).

211. *Id.* at 528.

212. 500 U.S. 160 (1991).

213. 139 S. Ct. 2116 (2019).

214. For more on the modern-day power of executive agencies in formulating and applying criminal laws and justice policy, *see* F. Andrew Hessick & Carissa Hessick, *Nondelegation and Criminal Law*, 107 Va. L. Rev. 281 (2021); Wayne A. Logan, *The Adam Walsh Act and the Failed Promise of Administrative Federalism*, 78 Geo. Wash. L. Rev. 993, 1011 (2010).

215. *See generally* Kate Stith & Jose A. Cabranes, Fear of Judging: Sentencing Guidelines in the Federal Courts (1998).

216. *See id.* at 130–42.

217. *See* Ronald F. Wright, *Charging and Plea Bargaining as Forms of Sentencing Discretion, in* THE OXFORD HANDBOOK OF SENTENCING AND CORRECTIONS 247, 247–69 (Joan Petersilia & Kevin R. Reitz eds., 2012) (discussing the significant authority that prosecutors have over sentencing in jurisdictions operating under guidelines).

218. Gerald E. Lynch, *Our Administrative System of Criminal Justice*, 66 FORDHAM L. REV. 2117, 2120, 2127 (1998).

219. Rachel E. Barkow, *Recharging the Jury: The Criminal Jury's Constitutional Role in an Era of Mandatory Sentencing*, 152 U. PA. L. REV. 33, 59 (2003). *See also* Codispoti v. Pennsylvania, 418 U.S. 506, 515–16 (1974) ("The Sixth Amendment represents a deep commitment of the Nation to the right of jury trial in serious criminal cases as a defense against arbitrary law enforcement."). At common law, moreover, juries also played a role in actually "finding" the law, whereas today they play the more limited role of fact-finders, and are expected to apply the law as instructed by the court. Matthew P. Harrington, *The Law-Finding Function of the American Jury*, 1999 WISC. L. REV. 377 (1999).

220. *See* Boykin v. Alabama, 395 U.S. 238, 243 n.5 (1969). Worse yet, much of the plea bargaining process itself is obscured from public view, with no or very little judicial oversight or involvement. *See* Jenia I. Turner, *Transparency in Plea Bargaining*, 96 NOTRE DAME L. REV. 973 (2021).

221. Amy Coney Barrett, *Substantive Canons and Faithful Agency*, 90 B.U. L. Rev. 109, 112 (2010).

222. F. Andrew Hessick & Carissa B. Hessick, *Constraining Criminal Laws* (April 27, 2021). Minnesota Law Review, Vol. 106, No. 2022, Manuscript at 23, Forthcoming, UNC Legal Studies Research Paper, Available at SSRN: https://ssrn.com/abstract=3835127.

223. *Id.* at 36.

224. See William N. Eskridge, Jr., *All About Words: Early Understandings of the "Judicial Power" in Statutory Interpretation, 1776–1806*, 101 COLUM. L. REV. 990, 1057 (2001).

225. *See* Shon Hopwood, *Restoring the Historical Rule of Lenity as Canon*, 95 N.Y.U. L. Rev. 918, 931 (2020) (noting that "lenity plays almost no role in deciding cases of statutory ambiguity").

226. *See generally* Kiel Brennan-Marquez, *Extremely Broad Laws*, 61 ARIZ. L. REV. 641, 658–60 (2019).

227. *See* Weaver v. Graham 450 U.S. 24, 29 n.8 (1981) ("So much importance did the [Convention] attach to [the ex post facto prohibition], that it is found twice in the Constitution.").

Chapter 8

1. Matthew Lippman, *Nuremberg: Forty Years Later*, 7 CONN. J. INT'L L. 1, 2–3 (1991) [hereinafter *Forty Years Later*].

2. Commission on The Responsibility of The Authors of The War and on The Enforcement of Penalties, Mar. 29, 1919, reprinted in 14 AM. J. INTL L. 95 (1920).

3. Memorandum of Reservations Presented By The Representatives of The United States to the Report of the Commission on Responsibilities, Apr. 4, 1919, Annex II, reprinted in 14 AM. J. Int'l L. 127 (1920).

4. *Id.* at 147.

5. *Id.* at 134.
6. Treaty of Peace with Germany (Treaty of Versailles) Art. 227, June 28, 1919, 2 Bevans 43, 136.
7. HOWARD BALL, PROSECUTING WAR CRIMES AND GENOCIDE: THE TWENTIETH-CENTURY EXPERIENCE 22 (1999).
8. James W. Garner, *Punishment of Offenders Against Laws of War*, 14 AM. J. INT'L L. 70 (1920).
9. The pact has inspired a sizable literature, with the vast majority of commentators condemning it as ineffectual and of little practical importance. *See, e.g.,* Julie M. Bunck & Michael R. Fowler, *The Kellogg-Briand Pact: A Reappraisal*, 27 TUL. J. INT'L & COMP. L. 229 (2019).
10. Henry L. Stimson, *The Nuremberg Trial: Landmark in Law*, 25 FOREIGN AFFAIRS 179, 179 (Jan. 1947).
11. BRADLEY F. SMITH, THE ROAD TO NUREMBERG 63–64 (1981).
12. American Memorandum Presented at San Francisco, April 30, 1945, *reprinted in* REPORT OF ROBERT H. JACKSON, REPRESENTATIVE TO THE INTERNATIONAL CONFERENCE ON MILITARY TRIALS, at 34 (1945).
13. According to one commentator of the time:

> Had each of the Allies taken his [sic] own body of law into Germany, it would have had to be administered precisely as in the country of its origin. To enable Goering to be charged with Crimes Against Humanity, before a representative international court, for example, a statute would have had to been enacted in each country represented on the Bench, legally creating the offense ex post facto, that is to say retrospectively.

Trevor Heath, *Crime in Retrospect—Nuremberg*, 18 THE AUSTRALIAN QTLY. 77, 78 (Sept. 1946).
14. Lippman, *Forty Years Later, supra note* 1, at 23.
15. Matthew Lippman, *Genocide, in* INTERNATIONAL CRIMINAL LAW 589, 591 (M. Cherif Bassiouni ed., 1999).
16. Lippman, *Forty Years Later, supra* note 1, at 24.
17. Quincy Wright, *The Law of the Nuremberg Trial*, 41 AM. J. INT'L L. 38, 41 (1947).
18. 22 TRIAL OF THE MAJOR WAR CRIMINALS BEFORE THE INTERNATIONAL MILITARY TRIBUNAL 427 (1948) [hereinafter 22 TRIAL OF THE MAJOR WAR CRIMINALS]. *See also* Bernard M. Meltzer, *A Note on Some Aspects of the Nuremberg Debate*, 14 U. CH. L. REV. 455, 461 (1947) (recognizing that "[t]he Chapter . . . neither adopted a pre-existing definition nor formulated a new one. It stated that aggression was a war a crime but did not state what aggression was.").
19. Theodor Meron, *Reflections on the Prosecution of War Crimes by International Tribunals*, 100 AM. J. INT'L L. 551, 562 (2006).
20. *See* Wright, *supra* note 17, at 42–43 n.14 (citing dozens of articles published from 1943–1946 taking opposing views on whether criminalization of "aggressive war" was ex post facto).
21. Hans Kelsen, *Will the Judgment in the Nuremberg Trial Constitute a Precedent in Int'l Law?*, 1 INT'L L. Q. 153, 162 (1947).
22. *Id.* at 164–65.
23. George A. Finch, *The Nuremberg Trial and International Law*, 41 AM. J. INT'L L. 20, 28 (1947).
24. KENNETH S. GALLANT, THE PRINCIPLE OF LEGALITY IN INTERNATIONAL AND COMPARATIVE LAW 59–60 (2009).

25. Jerome Hall, *Nulla Poena Sine Lege*, 47 YALE L.J. 165, 175 n.43 (1937) (citing German Act of June 28, 1935).

26. GALLANT, *supra* note 24, at 60 (citation omitted).

27. Control Council Law Proclamation No. 3 (Oct. 20, 1945), 1946 Y.B. ON HUM. RTS. 117 (1946); *see also* Control Council No. 10.

28. Meltzer, *supra* note 18, at 457 n.10 (citation omitted). *See also id.* at 357 ("The strict and automatic application of the rule against retroactivity to an undeveloped legal system would, of course, have widened the gap between the developing moral sense of the community and its lagging institutions. It would have made society the prisoner of its own particularly limited legal history. It is a luxury which an immature legal system cannot afford. The moral in connection with our unfortunately primitive system of international law requires no extended elaboration."); Stimson, *supra* note 10, at 180 ("International law is not a body of authoritative codes or statutes; it is the gradual expression, case by case, of the moral judgments of the civilized world. As such, it corresponds precisely to the common law of Anglo-American tradition. We can understand the law of Nuremberg only if we see it what it is—a great new case in the book of international law, and not a formal enforcement of codified statutes.").

29. 22 TRIAL OF THE MAJOR WAR CRIMINALS, *supra* note 18, at 461.

30. *Id.* at 464.

31. *Id.* Later, the tribunal reasoned that:

> It is not essential that a crime be specifically defined and charged in accordance with a particular ordinance, statute, or treaty if it is made crime by international convention, recognized customs and usages of war, or the general principles of criminal justice common to civilized nations generally. If the acts were charged were in facts crimes under international law when committed, they cannot be said to be *ex post facto* acts or retroactive punishments.

United States v. List, 11 Trials of War Criminals Before the Nuremberg Military Tribunals Under Control Council Law No. 10, at 759, 1239 (1950).

32. 22 TRIAL OF THE MAJOR WAR CRIMINALS, *supra* note 18, at 465.

33. 2 ROBERT JACKSON, TRIAL OF THE MAJOR WAR CRIMINALS BEFORE THE INTERNATIONAL MILITARY TRIBUNAL 99 (1945).

34. Dina G. McIntyre, *The Nuremberg Trials*, 24 U. PITT. L. REV. 73, 115 (1962).

35. Sheldon Glueck, *The Nuremberg Trial and Aggressive War*, 59 HARV. L. REV. 396, 405–06 (1946).

36. Meron, *supra* note 19, at 576. *See also* Heath, *supra* note 13, at 79 ("Such crimes belong to what the Romans used to call '*jus genitum*,' or law of all peoples; they exist and always have existed as offences against a man's conscience, but it is rarely that they ever achieve a sanction, a fact due mainly to the operation of the principle of State sovereignty. The Allies could not prevent the commission of the crimes, but they are morally bound to avenge them."); Max Radin, *War Crimes and the Crimes of War*, 21 VA. Q. REV. 497, 508 (1945) ("Most of the acts which are unmistakably crimes, acts like murder, robbery, rape, were punished for centuries although the detailed determination of just what acts were punishable under these names was found merely in custom and tradition and not in a statute. In other words, those who killed and robbed were punished because ordinary common sense and a general standard of conduct made their acts wrongful and dangerous and the perpetrators were not

heard to say that they did not know the character of their acts because no law had specifically prohibited them.").

37. Meltzer, *supra* note 18, at 458.

38. *See* GALLANT, *supra* note 24, at 115 ("It is very difficult to sustain that aggressive war in breach of treaties was a customary international law crime for individuals before World War II. It is also difficult to find any other law criminalizing the bare planning and waging of aggressive war by individuals during the period leading up to the beginning of World War II. The tribunal overstates the legal purport of, for example, the Kellogg-Briand Pact for the renunciation of war as an instrument of national policy[.]").

39. *See generally* John Finnis, *The Classical Tradition 1* & John Finnis, *Natural Law: The Modern Tradition 61, in* THE OXFORD HANDBOOK OF JURISPRUDENCE & PHILOSOPHY OF LAW (Jules Coleman & Scott Shapiro eds., 2002). *See also* Hugo Grotius, *De Jure Belli Ac Pacis Libri Tres*, 2 THE CLASSICS OF INTERNATIONAL LAW 38 (Francis Kelsey trans., James Scott ed., 1925) (defining natural law as "the dictate of right reason which points out that a given act, because of its opposition to or conformity with man's rational nature, is either morally wrong or morally necessary, and accordingly forbidden or commanded by God, the author of nature.").

40. WILLIAM J. BOSCH, JUDGMENT ON NUREMBERG: AMERICAN ATTITUDES TOWARD THE MAJOR GERMAN WAR-CRIME TRIALS 41 (1970).

41. *Id.* at 42.

42. *Id.* at 43–44.

43. *Id.* at 44–45.

44. *Id.* at 45.

45. *Id.*

46. 22 TRIAL OF THE MAJOR WAR CRIMINALS, *supra* note 18, at 461–62.

47. GALLANT, *supra* note 24, at 68.

48. *See generally* TIM MAGA, JUDGMENT AT TOKYO: THE JAPANESE WAR CRIMES TRIALS (2001); Matthew Lippman, *The Other Nuremberg: American Prosecution of Nazi War Criminals in Occupied Germany*, 3 IND. INT'L & COMP. L. REV. 1 (1992).

49. Walter W. Ruch, *Taft Condemns Hanging for Nazis as Unjust Verdict*, N.Y. TIMES, Oct. 6, 1946, at 10 (quoting Senator Taft).

50. WILLIAM O. DOUGLAS, AN ALMANAC OF LIBERTY 96 (1954).

51. Charles E. Wyzanski, Jr., *Nuremberg—A Fair Trial?*, THE ATLANTIC MONTHLY, Apr. 1946, at 66–70.

52. *Id.*

53. That a comprehensive permanent record be made of the Nazis' atrocities was a major reason for a trial from the perspective of President Franklin Roosevelt in particular:

> He was determined that the question of Hitler's guilt—and the guile of his gangsters—must not be left open for future debate. The whole nauseating matter should be spread out on a permanent record under oath by witnesses and with all the written documents . . . In short, there must never be any question anywhere by anyone about who was responsible for the war and for the uncivilized war crimes.

SAMUEL L. ROSENMAN, WORKING WITH ROOSEVELT 542–43 (1952).

54. BOSCH, *supra* note 40, at 91–94, 113, 233. Although perhaps true of European law and lawyers, it is not accurate to say that non-retroactivity was absent from constitutions of

countries worldwide, as evidenced by a 1946 survey of United Nations members. *See* GALLANT, *supra* note 24, at 425–37.

55. BOSCH, *supra* note 40, at 140. Writing several years later, James Brand, an associate justice on the Supreme Court of Oregon, who served as chief justice on a subsequent International Military Tribunal (No. III), echoed the view that the ex post facto prohibition, as conceived under US law, was inapposite:

> The ex post facto rule cannot apply in the international field as it does under constitutional mandate in the domestic field. Even in the domestic field the prohibition of the rule does not apply to the decisions of common-law courts, though the question at issue be novel. International law is not the product of statute for the simple reason that there is as yet no world authority empowered to enact statutes of universal application. . . . It would be sheer absurdity to suggest that the ex post facto rule, as known to constitutional states, could be applied to a treaty, custom, or a common law decision of an international tribunal, or to the international acquiescence which follows the event.

James T. Brand, *Crimes Against Humanity and the Nuremberg Trials*, 28 OR. L. REV. 93, 115 (1949).

The Soviet Union, it is worth noting, did not adopt the ex post facto prohibition until 1960, and then with exceptions. GALLANT, *supra* note 24, at 64–66. The Soviet position at Nuremberg was that the defendants had been convicted by virtue of the Allies' Moscow and Yalta Declarations, and that the Allies were entitled to create law regardless of the content of international law, leaving only the question of punishment. *Id.* at 79–81. Also, their position was that any rule of law, such as the ex post facto principle, not found in the Charter, had no force in the tribunal. *Id.* at 96.

56. GALLANT, *supra* note 24, at 237 & 240.
57. *Id.* at 155–56. Fascist Italy, an Axis ally of Germany, did not renounce its statutory prohibition of retroactive laws. M. CHERIF BASSIOUNI, CRIMES AGAINST HUMANITY IN INTERNATIONAL CRIMINAL LAW 130–31 (2d ed. 1999) (citation omitted).
58. *See* GALLANT, *supra* note 24, at 139–55.
59. *Id.* at 155–56.
60. G.A. Res. 217 (III) A, Universal Declaration of Human Rights art. 11(2) (Dec. 10, 1948) [hereinafter U.N. Declaration].
61. GALLANT, *supra* note 24, at 158.
62. International Covenant on Civil and Political Rights art. 15(1) Dec. 16, 1966, T.I.A.S. 92–908, 999 U.N.T.S. 171 171 [hereinafter ICCPR].
63. Convention for the Protection of Human Rights and Fundamental Freedoms art. 7, Nov. 4, 1950, 213 U.N.T.S. 221 [hereinafter ECHR].
64. American Convention on Human Rights art. 9, Nov. 22, 1969, O.A.S.T.S. No. 36, 1144 U.N.T.S. 123 [hereinafter ACHR].

It bears mention that the ICCPR contains a qualification: "Nothing in this article shall prejudice the trial and punishment of any person for any act or omission which, at the time it was committed, was criminal according to the general principles of law recognized by the community of nations." *See* ICCPR, *supra* note 62, Art. 15(2). The same qualification appears in the ECHR. *See* ECHR, *supra* note 63, Art. 7(2). The ACHR does not contain the qualification. *See* ACHR, *supra*. The qualifying language itself suggests, however, that the law in question was in existence (in some context) at the time of the act. Also of note, the ICCPR contains a *lex mitior* provision, ensuring that "[i]f, subsequent to the commission of the offense, provision is made by law for the imposition of a lighter penalty, the offender shall benefit thereby." ICCPR, *supra* note 62. Some fifty nations provide for the doctrine in their constitutions and it appears in the statutory law of at least nineteen more. GALLANT, *supra* note 24, at 271–72.

65. *See* Rome Statute of the International Criminal Court art. 5(2), July 17, 1998, 2187 U.N.T.S. 90, Art. 22(1) (providing that a "person shall not be criminally responsible under this Statute unless the conduct in question constitutes, at the time it takes place, a crime within the jurisdiction of the Court.").

66. Convention on the Rights of the Child, Art. 40(2)(a), Nov. 20, 1989, 1577 U.N.T.S 3.

67. GALLANT, *supra* note 24, at 241.

68. *See id.* at 301 ("Since the end of World War II, non-retroactivity of crimes and punishments has changed from a rule recognized by fewer than one-third of national constitutions, to a rule contained in over three-fourths. Almost all other states recognize the rule by statute or as the result of undertaking international human rights treaty obligations.").

69. *Id.* at 302.

70. THEODOR MERON, WAR CRIMES LAW COMES OF AGE 244 (1998); *see also* GALLANT, *supra* note 24, at 8–9 (arguing that non-retroactivity of crimes and punishments is a rule of customary international law and also a general principle of law recognized by the community of nations).

71. GALLANT, *supra* note 24, at 243.

72. *Id.*

73. *Id.*

74. *Id.* at 241. Professor Gallant adds that Bhutan and Brunei, as well as the Vatican, prohibit retroactive crime creation regarding juveniles in particular, through observance of the international Convention on Rights of the Child. *Id.*

75. U.N. Declaration, *supra* note 60, at 11(2).

76. Canadian Charter of Rights and Freedoms, Part I of the Constitution Act, 1982, being Schedule B to the Canada Act, 1982, c 11 §11(g) (U.K.) [hereinafter Canadian Charter].

77. French Declaration of the Rights of Man and Citizen art. VIII. *See also, e.g.*, Algerian Const. (1989), Ch. IV, Art. 58 ("No one may be considered guilty except by virtue of law duly promulgated before the commission of the incriminating act.").

78. GALLANT, *supra* note 24, at 255.

79. Albania Const. (Oct. 21, 1998), Ch. II, Art. 29(i). *See also* A. J. Ikpang, *Assessing the Principle of Legality in Nigerian Criminal Jurisprudence*, 58 J. L. POL'Y & GLOBALIZATION 119 (2017).

80. Maldives Const. (2008), Ch. II, Art. 59; Yemen Const. (1991, as amended Feb. 20, 2001), Ch. IV, Art. 47(1). For discussion of the principle in Islamic law, in Iran and more generally, see Mohammad Ja'far Habibzadeh, *Nullum Crimen, Nulla Poena Sine Lege: With an Approach to the Iranian Legal System*, 2 INT'L J. PUNISHMENT & SENT. 33 (2006).

81. GALLANT, *supra* note 24, at 255.

82. Costa Rica Const. (Nov. 8, 1949), Art. 34.

83. *Id.* Art. 39.

84. Mozambique Const. (2004, as amended June 12, 2018), Tit. III, Art. 57(i).

85. Myanmar Const. (May 29, 2008), Ch. 1, Part II, Art. 43.

86. Venezuela Const. (1999), Art. 24.

87. Israel Penal Code, 5737-1977, SH 5737 Sec. 3(b).

88. GALLANT, *supra* note 24, at 257.

89. Philippines Const. (Feb. 2, 1987), Art. III, Ch. 22.

90. Micronesia Const. (1978, as amended 1990), Art. IV, Sec. 11.

91. Marshall Is. Const. (1979, as amended Apr. 17, 1995), Art. II(8)(1).

92. Liberia Const. (1986), Ch. III, Art. 21(a)(i).

93. Canadian Charter, *supra* note 76, Sec. 1 ("The Canadian Charter of Rights and Freedoms guarantees the rights and freedoms set out in it subject only to such reasonable limits prescribed by law as can be demonstrably justified in a free and democratic society"); Sec. 33(1) ("Parliament or the legislature of a province may expressly declare in an Act of Parliament or of the legislature, as the case may be, that the Act or a provision thereof shall operate notwithstanding a provision" included in [section 11, which prohibits retroactive crime creation]).

94. R v. Oakes, 1 SCR 103 (1986).

95. El Salvador Const. (1983, as amended 2014), Title II, Art. 21(i).

96. Fitrakis Eftichis, *Principle of Legality in Greek Criminal Law*, 67 Revue Hellenique de Droit International 1199, 1207 (2014). Also, contrary to the blanket prohibition, there exists an exception for "penal procedural laws," similar to the exception in the United States. *Id.* India courts likewise except what are deemed retroactive procedural laws from coverage. Rao Shiv Bahadur Singh & Another v. State of Vindhya Pradesh, AIR 1954 SC 322 (1953).

97. HMG v. Chandra Bijaya Shah and [O]thers, NLR 2046, p. 161 (discussed in Matrika Prasad Acharya, *Nepali Case Laws [sic] on Protection against Double Jeopardy, [E]x Post Facto Criminal Laws and Self-Incrimination*, 10 NJA L. J. 41, 53 (2016)).

98. Nepal Const. (Dec. 16, 1962, as amended 1966, 1975, and 1980), Art. 11(3). *See also* Pasang Dawa Tamang (Lopchan) v. HMO, NLR 2057, p. 188 (discussed in Acharya, *supra* note 97, at 56) (case involving this human trafficking where intervening change in law imposed "onus of proof" concerning which law applied to the defendant, deeming the procedural and therefore not subject to the ex post facto prohibition).

99. Napal Const., *supra* note 98, at Art. 17(1), (2)(a)(b).

100. Acharya, *supra* note 97, at 53 (summarizing decision). The current Constitution (effective 2015) does not provide for an exception. *See* https://www.constituteproject.org/constitution/Nepal_2015.pdf.

101. Michael Skold, Note, *The Reform Act's Supreme Court: A Missed Opportunity for Judicial Review in the United Kingdom?*, 39 Conn. L. Rev. 2149, 2162 (2007).

102. A.W. Brian Simpson, *Britain and the European Convention*, 3 Cornell Intl. L.J. 523 (2010).

103. *See* ECHR, *supra* note 63, Art. 7.

104. 13 J. Afr. L. 103, 113 (P.C.) (Jun. 30, 1969).

105. *Id.*

106. Simon Butt & David Hansell, *The Masykur Abdul Kahir Case: Indonesian Constitutional Court Decision*, 6 Asian L. 176, 185 (2004) (providing a translation and detailed analysis of the decision).

107. Indonesia Const. (1945), Art. 28I(1).

108. Butt & Hansell, *supra* note 106, at 187 (translating opinion into English).

109. *Id.* at 181.

110. Rome Statute of the International Criminal Court Arts. 22 & 23, July 17, 1998, 2187 U.N.T.S. 90.

111. Law on Specialist Chambers and Specialist Prosecutor's Office (No. 05/L-053), Art. 3(2)(e) (Kos.); U.N. Transitional Admin. in E. Timor, Regulation on the Establishment of

Panels with Exclusive Jurisdiction over Serious Criminal Offences, §3, U.N. Doc. No. UNTAET/REG 2000/15 (June 6, 2000); Agreement between the U.N. and the Royal Gov. of Cambodia Concerning the Prosecution under Cambodian Law of Crimes Committed During the Period of Democratic Kampuchea Art. 12(2), U.N.-Cambodia, Jun. 6, 2003, 2329 U.N.T.S. 117.

112. Statute of the Iraqi Special Tribunal Art. 17(a), December 10, 2003. *Cf.* Al Bahlul v. United States, 767 F.3d 1 (D.C. Cir. 2014) (en banc) (assuming that Ex Post Facto Clause applies to Military Commission trial of Guantánamo Bay detainee, holding that conviction for providing material support for terrorism and solicitation of others to commit war crimes violated Clause, but rejecting challenge to conspiracy to commit war crimes, based on lengthy review of military legal materials dating back to the Civil War).

113. Weinberger Weisz v. Uruguay, U.N. Human Rights Committee, Communication No. 28/1978, U.N. Doc. No. CCPR/C/OP/1 at 57 (1985).

114. A. R. S. v. Canada, U.N. Human Rights Committee, Communication No. 91/1981, U.N. Doc. CCPR/C/OP/1 at 29 (1984).

115. *Id.* at para. 5(3).

116. 2009-VI Eur. Ct. H.R. at 169 (2009).

117. 521 U.S. 346 (1997).

118. *M.*, 2009-VI Eur. Ct. H.R., at paras. 125–133.

119. *Id.* para. 120.

120. *Id.*

121. *Id.*

122. *Id.* paras. 125, 128.

123. *Id.* para. 127.

124. *Id.* para. 129.

125. *Id.* paras. 135, 137.

126. Benjamin F. Krolikowski, Brown v. Plata: *The Struggle to Harmonize Human Dignity with the Constitution*, 33 PACE L. REV. 1255, 1258 (2013).

127. G.A. Res. 217 (III) A, Universal Declaration of Human Rights (Dec. 10, 1948). Earlier, in 1919, the Constitution of Finland "guarantee[d] the inviolability of human dignity." AHARON BARAK, HUMAN DIGNITY: THE CONSTITUTIONAL VALUE AND CONSTITUTIONAL RIGHT 50 (2015). *See also* Christopher McCrudden, *Human Dignity and Judicial Interpretations of Human Rights*, 19 EURO. J. OF INT'L L. 655, 664 (2008) (noting dignity was also incorporated in the constitutions of Mexico (1917) and Weimar Germany (1919), and later in Portugal (1933), Ireland (1937) and Cuba (1940)). Professor Samuel Moyn maintains that dignity entered global constitutional history through Irish constitutional politics in 1937 and the ensuing transnational Catholic discourse on dignity during the interwar period. Samuel Moyn, *The Secret History of Constitutional Dignity*, 17 YALE HUM. RTS. & DEV. L.J. 39 (2014).

128. *See* Rex D. Glensy, *The Right to Dignity*, 43 COLUM. HUM. RTS. L. REV. 65, 105 (2011).

129. Charter of Fundamental Rights of the European Union tit. I, Art. 1, 2012 O.J. (C 326) 6, https://eur-lex.europa.eu/legal-content/EN/TXT/PDF/?uri=CELEX:12012P/TXT&qid=1560716037231&From=EN [https://perma.cc/XH66-LMG9].

130. *See generally* Luis Roberto Barroso, *Here, There, and Everywhere: Human Dignity in Contemporary Law and in the Transnational Discourse*, 35 B.C. INT'L & COMP. L. REV. 331 (2012).

131. India Const. prmbl.

132. S. Afr. Const., 1996, art. 10.

133. Barroso, *supra* note 130, at 341.

134. Michael D. Rosen, Dignity: Its History and Meaning 1–2 (2012).

135. Maxine D. Goodman, *Human Dignity in Supreme Court Constitutional Jurisprudence*, 84 Neb. L. Rev. 740, 753 (2006).

136. 323 U.S. 214 (1944).

137. *See id.* at 240 (Murphy, J., dissenting) (condemning the racial stereotyping behind the internment as "one of the cruelest of the rationales used by our enemies to destroy the dignity of the individual and to encourage and open the door to discriminatory actions against other minority groups in the passions of tomorrow").

138. 329 U.S. 173 (1946).

139. *Id.* at 175.

140. Goodman, *supra* note 135, at 755 (citing Brinegar v. United States, 338 U.S. 160, 180–81 (1949) (Jackson, J., dissenting); Skinner v. Oklahoma, 316 U.S. 535, 546 (1946) (Jackson, J., concurring)).

141. 338 U.S. 160 (1949).

142. *Id.* at 180–81 (Jackson, J., dissenting).

143. Leslie M. Henry, *The Jurisprudence of Dignity*, 160 U. Pa. L. Rev. 169, 178 (2011).

144. Judith Resnik & Julie Chi-hye Suk, *Adding Insult to Injury: Questioning the Role of Dignity in Conceptions of Sovereignty*, 55 Stan. L. Rev. 1921, 1941 (2003).

145. As Justice Clarence Thomas has noted, "the Constitution contains no 'dignity' Clause." Obergefell v. Hodges, 135 S. Ct. at 2639 (2015) (Thomas, J., dissenting).

146. Goodman, *supra* note 135, at 747 (quoting William A. Parent, *Constitutional Values and Human Dignity, in* The Constitution of Rights, Human Dignity and American Values 47 (Michael J. Meyer & William A. Parent eds., 1992)).

147. Noah B. Lindell, *The Dignity Canon*, 27 Cornell J.L. & Pub. Pol'y 415, 421 (2017).

148. 539 U.S. 558 (2003).

149. *Id.* at 575.

150. Kevin Barry, *The Death Penalty & The Dignity Clauses*, 102 Iowa L. Rev. 383, 394 (2017).

151. Trop v. Dulles, 356 U.S. 86 (1958) (plurality opinion).

152. Lindell, *supra* note 147, at 426–27.

153. For book-length treatments of the subject, *see, e.g.,* Aharon Barak, Human Dignity: The Constitutional Value and the Constitutional Right (2015); Erin Daly, Dignity Rights: Courts, Constitutions, and the Worth of the Human Person (2013); Michael Rosen, Dignity: Its History and Meaning (2012).

154. ABA House of Delegates, Resolution 113B (Aug. 12–13, 2019), https://www.amer icanbar.org/content/dam/aba/directories/policy/annual-2019/113b-annual-2019.pdf.

155. James Q. Whitman, Harsh Justice: Criminal Punishment and the Widening Divide between America and Europe (2003).

156. Jonathan Simon, *The Second Coming of Dignity*, 375, *in* The New Criminal Justice Thinking (Sharon Dolovich & Alexandra Natapoff eds., 2017).

157. Carol S. Steiker, *"To See a World in a Grain of Sand": Dignity and Indignity in American Criminal Justice, in* The Punitive Imagination: Law, Justice, and Responsibility 19, 21 (Austin Sarat ed., 2014).

158. *See* Rex D. Glensy, *The Right to Dignity*, 43 Colum. Hum. Rts. L. Rev. 65, 86 (2011) (stating that "it is the Kantian vision of dignity that seemingly animates [the Supreme Court Justices]" when they discuss dignity in constitutional decisions).

159. Christopher McCrudden, *Human Dignity and Judicial Interpretation of Human Rights*, 19 Eur. J. Int'l L. 655, 660 (2008).

160. Immanuel Kant, Groundwork of the Metaphysics of Morals 46-47 (Allen W. Wood ed., 2002).

161. Landgraf v. USI Film Prods., 511 U.S. 244, 266 (1994) (acknowledging that a legislature's "responsivity to political pressures poses a risk that it may be tempted to use retroactive legislation as a means of retribution against unpopular groups or individuals").

162. *See* Harold J. Krent, *The Puzzling Boundary Between Criminal and Civil Retroactive Lawmaking*, 84 Geo. L.J. 2143, 2171 (1996) (noting that "[p]rospectivity ensures that the legislature is at least willing to impose punishment on a larger group of people whose identities are unknown. The generality of the prospective provision helps prevent singling-out").

163. *See* Ronald D. Rotunda & John E. Novak, Treatise on Constitutional Law: Substance and Procedure § 15.9, at 658 (3d ed. 1999) (noting that a "legislature can benefit or harm disfavored citizens more easily with retroactive laws than it can with prospective laws"); Charles B. Hochman, *The Supreme Court and the Constitutionality of Retroactive Legislation*, 73 Harv. L. Rev. 692, 693 (1960) (a retroactive statute "may be passed with an exact knowledge of who will benefit from it"); Evan C. Zoldan, *Reviving Legislative Generality*, 98 Marq. L. Rev. 625, 654 (2014) (explaining that "[w]hen a legislature enacts retroactive legislation, it acts with the knowledge of conduct that has already occurred" and that therefore "retroactive legislation permits the legislature to punish . . . an individual without naming him specifically but with knowledge of whom the legislation will . . . harm.").

164. *See* Kant, *supra* note 160, at 54.

165. As the Massachusetts Supreme Judicial Court long ago observed:

> The reason why [ex post facto] laws are so universally condemned is, that they overlook the great object of all criminal law, which is, to hold up the fear and certainty of punishment as a counteracting motive, to the minds of persons tempted to crime, to prevent them from committing it. But a punishment prescribed after an act is done, cannot, of course, present any such motive. It is contrary to the fundamental principle of criminal justice, which is, that the person who violates a law deserves punishment, because he willfully breaks a law, which, in theory, he knows or may know to exist. But he cannot know of the existence of a law which does not, in fact, exist at the time, but is enacted afterwards.

Jacquins v. Commonwealth, 63 Mass. (9 Cush.) 279, 281 (1852).

166. Charles Sampford, Retrospectivity and the Rule of Law 77 (2006).

167. Lon Fuller, The Morality of Law 162 (1964).

168. 554 U.S. 164 (2008).

169. *Id.* at 186–87 (Scalia, J., dissenting).

170. 529 U.S. 513 (2000).

171. *Id.* at 533.

172. *Id.*

173. 519 U.S. 433 (1997).

174. *Id.* at 440.

175. *See* Maxine D. Goodman, *In the Holocaust's Shadow: Can German and American Constitutional Jurisprudence Find a "New Guarantee" of Human Dignity?*, 4 Brit. J. Am. Legal Stud. 303 (2015).

176. Grundgesetz [GG] [Basic Law] Art. 1(1), translation at https://www.gesetze-im-internet. de/englisch_gg/englisch_gg.html.

177. 30 BVerfGE 173 (1971), https://perma.cc/4SAP-ER7M.

178. Edward J. Eberle, *Human Dignity, Privacy, and Personality in German and American Constitutional Law*, 1997 UTAH L. REV. 963, 971 (1997).

179. 1 BvR 209/83 (1983), https://perma.cc/7UGY-PJUU.

180. *Id.* at Summary II.

181. 35 BVerfGE 202 (1973), https://perma.cc/YGF4-HCN6.

182. DONALD P. KOMMERS & RUSSELL A. MILLER, THE CONSTITUTIONAL JURISPRUDENCE OF THE FEDERAL REPUBLIC OF GERMANY 482 (3d ed. 2012) (translating into English).

183. 538 U.S. 84 (2003).

184. *Id.* at 98.

185. *Id.* at 99.

186. Transcript of Oral Argument at 29, *Smith v. Doe*, 538 U.S. 84 (2003) (No. 01-729), available at https://www.supremecourt.gov/oral_arguments/argument_transcripts/2002/01-729.pdf.

187. *See* Robert C. Post, *Data Privacy and Dignitary Privacy: Google Spain, the Right to Be Forgotten, and the Construction of the Public Sphere*, 67 DUKE L.J. 981 (2018).

188. *See* Judith Resnik & Julie Chi-hye Suk, *Adding Insult to Injury: Questioning the Role of Dignity in Conceptions of Sovereignty*, 55 STAN. L. REV. 1921, 1926 (2003) ("Dignity talk in the law of the United States is an example of how US law is influenced by the norms of other nations, by transnational experiences, and by international legal documents.").

189. Barry, *supra* note 150, at 387.

Index

For the benefit of digital users, indexed terms that span two pages (e.g., 52–53) may, on occasion, appear on only one of those pages.